# WHEN SCHOOLS CARE
Creative Use of Groups in Secondary Schools

# WHEN SCHOOLS CARE

## Creative Use of Groups in Secondary Schools

Counseling Groups

Communication Groups

Collaboration and Consultation
by Mental Health Professionals

Crisis Groups

Parent-Student Groups

*Edited by*
IRVING H. BERKOVITZ, M.D.

BRUNNER/MAZEL *Publishers* • New York

## DEDICATION

This collection of experiences is dedicated to the many hard-working school personnel and mental health professionals whose caring provided helpful groups to young people in schools, and also to the lucky young people who were helped to grow in these groups.

Copyright © 1975 by IRVING H. BERKOVITZ, M.D.

*Published by*
BRUNNER/MAZEL, INC.
19 Union Square West, New York, New York 10003

Library of Congress Cataloging in Publication Data
Main entry under title:

WHEN SCHOOLS CARE.

Includes bibliographies and index.
1. Group work in education. 2. Group guidance in education. 3. Group counseling. 4. Personnel service in secondary education. I. Berkovitz, Irving H., ed.
LB1032.W48          373.1'4'044          73-94006
ISBN 0-87630-186-3

MANUFACTURED IN THE UNITED STATES OF AMERICA

# Preface

How does a psychoanalyst come to be editing a book about groups in public schools? Let me explain.

By 1960, I had spent nine years of intensive training and office practice in the psychotherapeutic and psychoanalytic treatment of neurotic and psychotic adults and children. That same year the Los Angeles County Department of Mental Health opened its doors, with the goal of helping existing community agencies to promote positive mental health and reduce the flow of cases to treatment agencies. In favor of this goal, I became a part-time employee in the Department of Mental Health and began weekly visits to the Santa Monica Unified School District.

There I met and worked with Mrs. Rosalie Waltz, the chief psychologist. Kindly, gracious, and skilled, she is deeply interested in the well-being of children, especially in schools. She guided me in providing relevant information and other useful messages to the school personnel. She and her staff were also ready to reassure and soothe me when my bruised ego recoiled from occasional less than grateful receptivity. We all learned in the process, and for me it was truly an apprenticeship. Drs. Donald Schwartz, Clyde Miller, and other colleagues, who were also consultants to schools, helped as well to clear my perspective and improve techniques.

In 1964, thanks to this apprenticeship, I was able to accept the half-time position, senior psychiatric consultant for schools in the Department of Mental Health. Harry Brickman, M.D., the director, understood the crucial role of schools to the health of children. For 10 years he encouraged me and the hundreds of other Mental Health Department consultants in promoting an exchange of ideas with thousands of school personnel in Los Angeles County (Berkovitz and Thompson, 1973).

During these 10 years, the importance of group counseling in both elementary and secondary schools impressed me significantly. I collected descriptions of such experiences, and these were the start of this volume. I have seen counseling, both group and individual, as an opportunity to help young people resolve some of their turmoil while still in school. This early help probably diverted many from the mental health or the judicial-penal systems. This is not to say that I would wish or expect educators to become therapists. An effective educational experience is also therapeutic. However, I would be happy—as would many of my colleagues—if our troubled patients could have been helped earlier in life and not have to be in our offices or clinics as adults—or as children.

Educators cannot be responsible for remedying the troubles of all young people. Many of these troubles began in troubled families years before the children entered school. Even mental health professionals have difficulties helping some. Fortunately, however, young people have for years received important affective, as well as cognitive, help in schools. I hope that the kinds of groups described here can enlarge the available help.

### THE STRUCTURE OF THIS BOOK

*This volume is designed* to have some features of a *casebook*, where examples of counseling groups will be presented in depth, with a lesser proportion of theoretical consideration. Perhaps some of the examples will prove to be new and innovative. In addition, I feel that a double message not found in most volumes is offered. After an introductory section, the *first message* is presented in Part II. This message is a familiar one: the discussion of group counseling and other group approaches as practiced by school personnel.

The *second message,* presented in Part III, is less familiar, namely, the practice of mental health consultation and assistance to school personnel, especially as these relate to group counseling or other useful groups. This collaboration, increasingly prevalent in recent years, has provided the opportunity for sharing of knowledge and experience between educators and mental health professionals. These mental health professionals (psychiatrists, psychologists, social workers, public health nurses, rehabilitation counselors, and others) have usually been invited to enter the schools to share their knowledge and techniques with school personnel of all categories (Berkovitz and Thomson, 1973). A part of this sharing has been didactic, collaborative and/or demonstration projects in group counseling. These types of experience are described in the second section of this volume. It may seem that two books are involved, since each half could well stand alone. Yet each would be less by this separation. Each discipline overlaps and complements the other.

Part IV describes experiences in schools involving parents with students in groups. While this is not a prevalent practice, it has proved useful.

Some of the articles may seem to repeat similar ideas but in most cases do present different attitudes or approaches. Rather than resolve authors' disagreements, I felt it would prove useful for the reader to see the range of useful attitudes and practices. Descriptions of individual points are scattered through several chapters rather than concentrated. Usually, this helped to preserve a feeling of spontaneity and enthusiasm. The index will expedite location of the various references.

Just as it may require a variety of individually tailored groups to provide for the many individual needs of students, so it may take a variety of different volumes to meet the particular needs and receptivities of the school person or the mental health professional who is contemplating or wavering about trying group counseling or other group approaches in the school.

Therefore, as a psychoanalyst, I felt it important to edit a book about group counseling in schools. No matter what the labels may be, psychoanalyst or educator, people helping people is the goal.

IRVING H. BERKOVITZ, M.D.
*Editor*

## BIBLIOGRAPHY

BERKOVITZ, I. H. (1972). *Adolescents Grow in Groups.* New York: Brunner/Mazel.
BERKOVITZ, I. H., and THOMPSON, M. (1973). Mental health consultation and assistance to school personnel of Los Angeles County. *Gen. Bull.* 171. Downey, Calif.: Office of the Los Angeles County Supt. of Schools.

# Contents

## PART IV: GROUPS TO HELP PARENTS AND STUDENTS

## PART V: APPENDIX

# Contributors

IRVING H. BERKOVITZ, M.D. (Editor)*—Senior Psychiatric Consultant for Schools, Los Angeles County Dept. of Health Services-Mental Health Services; Associate Clinical Professor of Psychiatry, Medical School, University of California at Los Angeles; Member of Southern California Psychoanalytic Institute/Society.

DEBORAH K. AGUADO, M.S.*—Director, Community Consultation & Education, Cedars-Sinai Medical Center, Thalians Community Mental Health Center, Los Angeles, California.

ROMAN ANSHIN, M.D.—Coordinator, Child Psychiatry Fellows, Cedars-Sinai Medical Center, Thalians Community Mental Health Center, Los Angeles, California.

STANLEY ASADA, M.S.—Mental Health Consultant, Mental Health Section, Los Angeles Unified School District, Los Angeles, California.

WILMA AWERBUCH, M.A.—School Psychologist, Downey Unified School District, Downey, California.

MARILYN BATES, Ph.D.—Counseling/School Psychology, School of Education, California State University, Fullerton, California.

SAMUEL BLACK, M.D.—Consultant, Day Treatment Center, Cedars-Sinai Medical Center, Thalians Community Mental Health Center, Los Angeles, California.

MICHELLE E. BOFFA, Ph.D.—Counseling Specialist for Adults Program, Extension Division, University of California, Los Angeles, California.

ALVA CASHION, P.H.N.— School Nurse, El Camino Real High School, Los Angeles Unified School District, Los Angeles, California.

EVELYN COHEN, M.S.W.*—Director of Counseling, Airport-Marina Counseling Service, Los Angeles, California.

MAURICE DEIGH, Ph.D.*—Coordinator, Consultation & Training, South Bay Mental Health Service, Hawthorne, California.

VIVIANE G. DURELL, Ph.D.—School Psychologist, Montgomery County Public Schools, Rockville, Maryland.

MINA ELKIN, P.H.N.—School Nurse, Lincoln High School, Los Angeles Unified School District, Los Angeles, California.

ALICE EVANS, M.S.—Principal, Mayfield School, Pasadena, California.

DOROTHY FLACY, M.S.W.*—Social Worker, South Bay Mental Health Service, Hawthorne, California.

KATHRYN FRASER, M.A.—Counselor, Warren High School, Downey Unified School District, Downey, California.

ALEX GODA, M.S.W.*—Social Worker, South Bay Mental Health Service, Hawthorne, California.

GERALD HAINES, Ed.D.—Principal, Pioneer High School, Whittier Union High School District, Whittier, California.

EDITH HILL, A.C.S.W.*—Coordinator of Consultation, Santa Monica West Mental Health Service, Santa Monica, California.

STEVEN M. JACOBS, Ph.D.*—Clinical Psychologist, Alhambra, California.

JACK JINES, M.S.—Personnel Director, Whittier Union High School District, Whittier, California.

ALAN V. JOHNSON, M.A.—Assistant Principal-Instruction Edison High School, Huntington Beach Union High School District, Huntington Beach, California.

GERALD F. JONES, M.S.—Counselor, Beverly Hills High School, Beverly Hills Unified School District, Beverly Hills, California.

CELESTE KAPLAN, A.C.S.W.—Executive Director, Child, Youth, and Parent Counseling Agency (also known as Council of Jewish Women of Los Angeles, Inc.), Los Angeles, California.

WILLIAM LEONG, M.S.—Counselor, Washington High School, Los Angeles Unified School District, Los Angeles, California.

KATHRYN LEWIS, Ed.D.—Guidance Consultant, Torrance Unified School District, Torrance, California.

PHILLIP LEWIS, M.S.—Coordinator, Counseling & Psychological Services, Administrative Area K, Los Angeles Unified School District, Los Angeles, California.

CLARENCE A. MAHLER, Ph.D.—Department of Psychology, California State University, Chico, California.

ROGER MANDEL, LL.B.—Headmaster, Rexford School, Beverly Hills, California.

IDELL NATTERSON, M.S.W.—Home/School Coordinator, Beverly Hills High School, Beverly Hills Unified School District, Beverly Hills, California.

NORA NICOSIA, M.S.—Counselor, Hamilton High School, Los Angeles Unified School District, Los Angeles, California.

WILLIAM O'REAR, M.A.—Assistant Principal, El Camino Real High School, Los Angeles Unified School District, Los Angeles, California.

ROBERT H. OYLER, Ph.D.—Chief Psychologist, Duarte Unified School District, Duarte, California.

HARRY PANNOR, A.C.S.W.—Casework Director, Jewish Big Brothers, Los Angeles, California.

PAUL W. PRETZEL, Th.D.*—Psychologist, Arcadia, California.

DAVID RAPPOPORT, M.Ed.—Group Counselor and School Psychologist, Burroughs Junior High School, Los Angeles Unified School District, Los Angeles, California.

F. WILLARD ROBINSON, JR., Ed.D.—Principal, Beverly Hills High School, Beverly Hills Unified School District, Beverly Hills, California.

CONSUELO G. RODRIGUEZ, M.A.—School Counselor; Instructor, Hispanic Urban Center, Los Angeles, California.

URI RUEVENI, Ph.D.—Director, Community Psychology Unit, Eastern Pennsylvania Psychiatric Institute, Philadelphia, Pennsylvania.

JEREMY SARCHET, Ph.D.*—Consulting Psychologist, Whittier, California.

DAVID E. SCHARFF, M.D.—Assistant Clinical Professor of Psychiatry, George Washington University School of Medicine, Washington, D. C.

ELLIE SCHNITZER, A.C.S.W.—Caseworker, Vista Del Mar Child Care Service, Los Angeles, California.

ROBERT SCHWARTZ, M.D.*—Department of Mental Health, St. Thomas, Virgin Islands.

MERVILLE C. SHAW, Ph.D.—Department of Psychology, California State University, Chico, California.

PHILIP A. SMITH, Ph.D.—Department of Psychology, California State University, Northridge, California.

ZANWIL SPERBER, Ph.D.—Chief Psychologist, Section of Child & Family Psychiatry, Cedars-Sinai Medical Center, Los Angeles, California.

ALFREDO T. SUESCUM, M.D.—Psychoanalyst, Panama City, Panama.

MAX SUGAR, M.D.—Clinical Professor of Psychiatry, Louisiana State University, New Orleans, Louisiana.

MURIEL THOMSON, Ed.D.—Consultant, Research & Pupil Personnel Services, Office of Los Angeles County Superintendent of Schools, Downey, California.

MAURICE VANDERPOL, M.D.—Director, School Consultation & Training Program, McLean Hospital, Belmont, Massachusetts.

LILLIAN B. VOGEL, Ph.D.*—Clinical Psychologist, Los Angeles, California.

* Presently or formerly employed part or full time by Los Angeles County, Department of Health Services, Mental Health Services.

# Acknowledgments

Many in education and mental health services have helped over the years to bring this volume to reality. In addition to Mrs. Rosalie Waltz, formerly chief psychologist, Santa Monica Unified School District, and Harry Brickman, M.D., deputy director, Mental Health Services, Los Angeles County Department of Health Services, S. Mark Doran, M.D., began it all by first offering me the opportunity to consult in Santa Monica U.S.D. Several administrators after him facilitated the development of the present large program of consultation to school personnel: Al Torribio, M.S.W., Maurice Deigh, Ph.D., Carlo Weber, Ph.D., and Areta Crowell, Ph.D. I appreciate their confidence that this was a volume which deserved support.

Muriel Thomson, consultant in the Office of the Los Angeles County Superintendent of Schools, shared my belief in and enthusiasm for group counseling in schools and provided articles as well as constant counsel, reading of drafts, and editorial assistance. Jim Burt, counselor at Crenshaw High School, was kind enough to read and evaluate. Marjorie Croner provided editorial assistance in many parts of the book.

Michelle Boffa, as well as co-authoring a chapter, was generous enough to read, edit, and offer useful suggestions which improved the final product. My older son Glenn helped, as he did in my previous book. Mary Koll and my wife, Anne, each contributed ideas which helped fashion the title. Joan Zilbach Fried contributed suggestions about more concise chapter titles. 'Gene Stecyk, Jean Camak, Carol Dakers, and Ruth Marx gave unstinting and expert secretarial support. 'Gene gave editorial help as well. To each of these helpful people, I give deep thanks.

The late Martin Olavarri, Ph.D., occupies a special place in my appreciation for the help he might have been able to give to this volume. Group counseling in schools was a subject of deep interest and concern to him. His untimely death deprived us of a warm human being, as well as valuable contributions. In our too brief association he did bring to my attention the work of Shaw and Mahler for inclusion here in Chapter 43.

The following journals gave permission to use previously published articles: *International Journal of Group Psychotherapy* (Chapter 42), *Personnel and Guidance Journal* (Chapter 2), *Educational Technology* (Chapter 3), *Children Today* (Chapter 35), and *The Research and Pupil Personnel Services Newsletter,* Office of Los Angeles County Superintendent of Schools, Muriel Thomson, Editor (Chapters 12, 13, 15, 17, 19, 20, 21, and 40). The American Society for Adolescent Psychiatry and Basic Books, Inc., gave permission to reproduce with modification a chapter from Volume III, *Adolescent Psychiatry* (Chapter 38).

I thank my publisher, Bernie Mazel, for the warm encouragement and confidence in my efforts. Many others helped in ways which I may have failed to mention here. I thank these as well, and apologize for any omission.

# Part I

## INTRODUCTION

## CHAPTER 1

# Caring and the Relevance of Small Groups in Secondary Schools, but with a Caution

Irving H. Berkovitz, M.D.

PEOPLE IN SCHOOLS care about each other in many, many ways. Teachers care about pupils when they help them to learn and enjoy their ability to learn. Pupils care when they please their teachers or their parents by learning and helping both to feel useful and fulfilled. Principals and superintendents care when they provide a secure, helpful atmosphere in which teachers and pupils may learn and grow. Parents care when they help their children feel secure and when they support teachers and principals by being active in P.T.A.'s, community advisory councils, or other support groups. Society cares when it provides funds through legislatures or the Congress to finance better education.

Yet, with all these acts of caring, there are many children who do not effectively receive the benefit. At times the caring seems disproportionately distributed. Students who excel or grossly misperform appear to receive larger shares of the caring and concern than the middle group who may be quietly going along.

In recent years one form of caring has been the meeting of adult educators with groups of 4 to 12 students for the purpose of discussions focused on the feelings and behavior of those in the groups. In the secondary school years—grades 7 to 12, ages 12 to 18—these small groups have been of value for providing a tangible form of caring which may not have been provided in any of the other programs and activities of the school experience.

"Normal" adolescents emancipating from parental security find themselves alienated, rootless, and with a tenuous sense of identity or security. Peer group formation becomes especially important and moves in directions that may be either helpful or harmful. The strong personal attachments to parents now made difficult by sexual feelings are transferred to peers and even adults other than parents. Spontaneous peer groups or adult-sponsored groups offer opportunities for support and growth. Friendships in school, whether with peers or teachers, become more important and more emotionally charged than in previous years. Dreamy rumination and slavish peer or adult attachment are two of the extremes of the teens.

The '60s and '70s have often been termed the "Group Era." During these years a wide variety of adult groups deliberately assembled to provide help, change, or simply reassuring association. They may have met in indigenous or mental health settings. Free clinics, churches, community houses, and even commercial entrepreneurs have offered groups for the ill, the lonely, the bored, and the adventurous. While some of this movement may seem at times to approach faddism, the essence does meet and often satisfy important human needs in our increasingly depersonalized society. The need to experience other persons closely and in ways that are more than cursory, commercial, or polite is essential in humans.

Since this need is especially pressing in adolescents, the group movement has also recently entered the schools. The relevance of a group experience to adolescents in clinical or indigenous settings has received increasing attention in the mental health literature. Some indications have been described as follows:

> To support assistance and confrontation from peers; to provide a miniature real life situation for study and change of behavior; to stimulate new ways of dealing with situations and developing new skills of human relations; to stimulate new concepts of self and new models of identification; to feel less isolated; to provide a feeling of protection from the adult while undergoing changes; as a bind to therapy to help maintain continued self-examination; to allow the swings of rebellion or submission which will encourage independence and identification with the leader; to uncover relationship problems not evident in individual therapy (Berkovitz, 1974).

A sincere, honest, one-to-one relation, whether in schools or in a therapeutic context, is important as well. In addition, meditation or time alone with oneself is needed by everyone. However, when painful or embarrassing new knowledge about oneself is involved, teen-agers will often be able to accept it more easily from peers than from even admired adults.

A part of the value which schools provide is the bringing of young people together to learn from each other, as well as from the adults in the schools. However, for those young people who do not interact successfully with others, a complete education could provide an opportunity to learn how to correct this. Schools cannot become mental health centers offering the same forms of assistance as are offered by clinics. However, an effective educational experience can and will improve self-esteem in most students, helping them make mature sublimations and increase their understanding of themselves.

Some emotional problems do interfere with the students' ability to effectively receive and pay attention to the available educational or social process. These problems may need attention simultaneously with, or preceding, any possible effective involvement in the educational process. Special education classes, opportunity rooms, and guidance classes are an accepted way of giving attention to these needs. Group counseling, rap rooms, and other opportunities for student exchange are further instruments available to meet these needs. Various group programs in schools have tried to meet a variety of needs, including academic underachievement and behavioral emotional problems, exceptionalities in schools, etc. (see Chapter 4).

In any school, there are students who have found no one friend or group with whom to feel the important sense of closeness. Some lucky ones find a teacher, counselor, coach, or janitor to whom they can relate and feel some warmth, and from whom they receive support to be gratefully remembered even years later. Others find the probation officer, opportunity room teacher, or the dean of girls or boys after they get into trouble. These latter relationships may often represent for some a last desperate cry for help before entry into the legal or mental-illness systems.

Groups can provide support, new understanding, additional growth, or all three. Perhaps a variety of groups are needed to meet the manifold individual needs of the variety of individuals involved. The number of groups described in this volume attests to the varied ways of creating a common meeting ground between the interested, sensitive adult and receptive, needy young people. Ideally, some day each school principal's or counselor's office will have a roster of variously oriented and constituted groups available so that any troubled or lonely student can find a group which meets his or her particular growth needs. We hope that this volume will increase the varieties of caring groups available in the secondary schools.

## The Status of Current Counseling Services

The increase in availability of caring groups cannot be separated from the *problems in counseling services generally*. A recent study by the California

State Department of Education Task Force (1973) to study conflict and violence in California high schools evaluated existing school counseling services for individuals as well as groups. These findings are no doubt relevant outside California as well. Let me include the following lengthy excerpt from this report:

> The Task Force found that the counseling program as presently administered is generally inadequate on most campuses, a fact disturbing to counselors and students alike. Traditionally, the role of the counselor in the high school has ideally been one of student advocacy. When all other adult sectors of the school community are closed to the student, it should be the counselor to whom the student can turn and expect results. However, findings of the study indicate that the counseling function is in danger of complete collapse. With few exceptions, the schools visited experienced most of the following problems, which have hindered and stifled the counseling role:
>
> 1. Extremely high caseloads average 450 to 500 students per counselor.
> 2. Massive amounts of paperwork related to program scheduling and changes burden the counselors.
> 3. Minority counselors are underrepresented on counseling staffs.
> 4. Vocational and career education have grown to such a degree that in most instances the counselors are unable to meet the demands for counseling in these areas.
> 5. Increased and diverse college offerings and scholarships make specialization in these areas a time-and-a-half job.
> 6. Crisis counseling is done only as counselors can "squeeze" it in.
> 7. The need for counseling on the effects of drugs and alcohol is being met only in part.
> 8. Most counselors see the need for group counseling but cannot find the time to conduct such counseling systematically.
> 9. Little time is available for students to talk to their counselors and get advice.
>
> Students wanted most of all to see their counselors on campus and to be able to talk to them personally. They also hoped that counselors would be ready to listen and would be concerned with their problems.
> One of the most promising practices which the Task Force witnessed was the growing use of group counseling to "cool" troubled campuses. Successful programs were characterized by (1) the formal retraining of all counselors; (2) the appointment of a single coordinator of counseling activity; and (3) the provision of counseling to a majority of students on a weekly basis for the entire year. One inner city school which had experienced continual violence for several years prior to the initiation of group counseling believed that the success of the counseling program had been a major factor in reducing violence.

Many suggestions were made by persons in all groups interviewed as to how to make the counselor more effective, including the following:

1. Counseling specialists were deemed a necessity. There is a need for multilevel counseling; counselors who are trained to handle problems for individual students; counselors who are trained to help students seek appropriate careers; counselors who are informed regarding all facets of college preparation and scholarships; counselors who are specialists in handling problems related to drugs, crisis, and conflict.
2. Intensive counseling is necessary for the "hard-core" problem student and for those with severe problems not related to school.
3. District-level attention should be directed toward instituting counseling programs at levels below the senior high school level in order to develop preventative activities.
4. Adequate facilities for counseling must be provided. Separate administrative offices, areas for group counseling sessions, and privacy for the counselor and those counseled should be provided.
5. Counselors should have staggered workdays so that they are available before and after school to students and parents. Implementation of a schedule of regular home visitations should be instituted.
6. Bilingual and minority counselors must be included on the counseling staff.

Washington High School* in the Los Angeles Unified School District, for example, has an unusually effective counseling program. When given local prerogative, the staff made a clear choice to improve its counseling services to students. The staffing pattern was readjusted to increase the counseling staff. Next, the counseling staff re-evaluated its priorities to provide a group counseling program for all students. The school offered group counseling programs for "regular" and for "problem" students in addition to regular counseling services. All counselors directed at least one group, and one counselor coordinated all groups. Group sessions were also available for staff members.

The message in favor of improved and expanded counseling services in high schools is loud and clear! I would extend this to junior high schools as well. One hopes the present volume can assist in that direction in all secondary schools. Yet group counseling is not the only format where group interaction occurs that is essential, useful, and integral in schools. The classroom is a group, as are the faculty and its various subgroups. The P.T.A., community advisory councils, etc., are also groups. Some of these

---

* For fuller description see Chapter 10.

and their beneficial or detrimental influence on the lives of students and educators will be described as well. Another message here is that personnel of almost any category, with proper motivation, safeguards, and preparation, can conduct useful groups for young people.

### but with a caution!*

Yet with all this caring in groups, one must keep in mind a caution. It may be too easy to develop these groups as facilities for referring troubled students to an extra-classroom, "fix the troubled student" dumping ground and overlook other underlying trouble spots in the system itself. Part of some students' difficulties may be in the interaction between their needs and those of their teachers or counselors. The problem of all three, on the other hand, might lie in trying to fit human needs to a traditional classroom-school setting. The examples of continuation high schools, alternative schools, or school-within-a-school, i.e., units of 200 to 400, show the potential of a smaller, more flexible, more individualized setting. Many students (and teachers?) in these smaller settings improve in adjustment, health, maturation, and achievement.

Perhaps the large megalopolis high school is dangerous to human health! Group counseling, therefore, may be dealing with the symptomatic casualties of a more basic structural trouble. Such basics are harder to change, and casualties need attention, too. It is hoped that this volume will help to reinforce awareness of the need for attention to basic changes as well. Any administrator considering a group counseling program would do well first to assay the priorities and goals in his school in general, and how the counseling program aids or impedes these goals.

If, after this assay, the administrator and staff feel a group counseling program can be useful, it is hoped that this volume may help the school personnel (or mental health professional) to gather the courage, the knowledge, and the sensitivity to give some of the needed caring assistance to the future generations in our schools.

### BIBLIOGRAPHY

BERKOVITZ, I. H. (1974). Indications and contraindications for adolescent group psychotherapy. In M. Sugar (Ed.), *The Adolescent in Group and Family Therapy.* New York: Brunner/Mazel.

*A Report on Conflict and Violence in California's High Schools* (1973). Sacramento, Calif.: California State Dept. of Education.

---

* With thanks to stimulation by Don Muhich, M.D.

## CHAPTER 2

# Group Counseling

Clarence A. Mahler, Ph.D.

This article reviews the major concerns of group counseling
and differentiates among group guidance, group counseling,
and group therapy. It also evaluates the research status of
group counseling. Finally, the author presents implications
for the future of this research.

THE DEVELOPMENT OF GROUP COUNSELING has a short history of 30 to 40
years. It was slow in gaining acceptance. In the last 10 years, however, group
counseling has expanded rapidly in both school and nonschool settings. Its
location as a helping procedure between education on one hand and group
therapy on the other has been confusing. Perhaps the most supporting evidence for a legitimate place for group counseling has come from the broad
acceptance of encounter and sensitivity groups. This acceptance has been a
mixed blessing, since the weaknesses of sensitivity training are often focused
upon group counseling programs.

Two other areas that have contributed much to the growth of group counseling have been the steady development of group psychotherapy in the past
30 years and the rapid expansion of research in group dynamics. So while
there is still a lack of adequate theoretical views and definitive research,
there is increased sophistication in the design of programs and in the
research with groups.

*Concerns about the present status*

Many of the leaders in group counseling, myself included, have concerns
with the growth process of this area. It appears that our favorite child,

From *Personnel and Guidance Journal,* 49, 601-608, April 1971. Copyright
American Personnel and Guidance Association. Reprinted with permission.

group counseling, has attained the adolescent stage of development, with all the anxiety and confusion accompanying it.

One major concern is the too frequent, naive view that the mere placing of individuals in a group will be good for them. This view holds that anyone trained in individual counseling would be able to do group counseling. Further, individuals, particularly teachers, who have experienced the exhilaration and all too often temporary intimacy of encounter weekends, endeavor to apply the encounter experience to their subject matter area.

Perhaps the most naive example of misapplication I have ever known was a young sociology instructor who attended an encounter weekend in the summer. Then, in September, he began all four of his sociology courses with nonverbal methods. The students responded well, and they did feel the emotional forces, both personal and group, that emanate from closer personal contact with others. But the main problem, from my position, was that the young instructor had no idea how to move from the deeply satisfying mood of being personally involved to the broader goals of his classes. I am personally very concerned that emotional experiences, long neglected in our whole educational system, should not merely *replace* cognitive experiences. The cognitive side of man needs to be deeply integrated with his emotional nature. This integration is not, however, accomplished by superficial group experiences.

Another facet of the superficial view of group work is a belief that "groups" have an "innate" capacity to become groups without the leader's having a frame of reference or an adequate repertoire of techniques. Some of the recent research at Chico State College on the impact that the leader has on group functioning indicates that poor leaders do indeed leave college freshmen confused and lost, whereas skilled group counselors facilitate school progress as well as personal growth (Fox, 1970). I feel that a superficial approach to group counseling, both in group process and leader functioning, is worse than having no groups at all.

My second major area of concern relates to the position group counseling has in the school setting or in other agencies. We must guard against expecting it to make up for gross deficiencies in the way individuals are treated in an agency. Group counseling, like individual counseling, is of major value in an agency that deeply respects its members and wants to further their individual growth.

Group methods have been used effectively in a number of school districts to manage deep, conflicting issues, such as racial tensions. But the primary value of group counseling does not lie in the management of behavior. Thus, group counseling should be seen as complementing the basic goals of an agency. It is possible to delineate clearly where and how group counseling fits in the elementary school, the secondary school, the state employment office, the welfare office, the probation office, and juvenile hall. In fact, it is highly desirable that this process of integrating the potentiality of group counseling with the major purposes of a given agency be accomplished clearly before the program begins.

My third major concern is related to the frequent lack of a theoretical rationale for the group effort. Some counselors have very limited conceptual ideas of what counseling may accomplish. Gradually we are seeing that a theoretical point of view is essential for a counselor, whether working with individuals or groups.

Some group workers, particularly the encounter type, assume that learning derives from experience. These leaders often feel that catharsis and exhilarating responses will lead to changed behavior. Transfer-of-learning experiments have produced too much evidence that change of behavior is not easy enough to leave it to chance.

Some group counselor trainers have followed an Adlerian or behavioral view of counseling. In respect to theoretical rationale, behavioral counseling has had a clear awareness of its rationale and the procedures that may attain the desired change of behavior.

It has been my experience that many counselors and counselor trainers who claim to be eclectic are deficient in formulating their own theoretical views and integrating them with their counseling behavior. A sound conceptual frame of reference undergirding one's group efforts seems desirable and necessary before we even begin programs in group counseling.

### Group counseling defined

Counseling can be viewed as a process aimed at aiding individuals to understand better their own and other people's behavior. The process may be concerned with a problem, with life patterns, and/or with identity-seeking. Progress in counseling has been found to be closely related to the development of mutual respect, trust, and acceptance. Thus, it is important that, in aiding the client's growth and development, the counselor learns to be congruent, open, understanding, and accepting. In group as well as in individual counseling, it is important that the clients feel they are being understood, which means that the counselor and group members must learn to listen perceptively and with understanding. Clients may not be able to ex-

plain themselves clearly, but they know immediately when they feel understood by the leader and group members.

One definition of group counseling is:

> Group counseling is a dynamic, interpersonal process focusing on con-
> scious thought and behavior and involving the therapy functions of per-
> missiveness, orientation to reality, catharsis, and mutual trust, caring,
> understanding, acceptance, and support. The therapy functions are cre-
> ated and nurtured in a small group through the sharing of personal
> concerns with one's peers and the counselors. The group counselees are
> basically normal individuals with various concerns which are not debili-
> tating to the extent of requiring extensive personality change. The group
> counselees may utilize group interaction to increase understanding and
> acceptance of values and goals and to learn and/or unlearn certain atti-
> tudes and behaviors (Gazda, Duncan and Meadows, 1967, p. 306).

In group counseling the major concerns that individuals bring up center
on the socialization process. The main questions they ask are: How do I
maintain a close relationship with my family and yet establish my own
individuality? Who am I, anyway? How do people really see me? What are
my abilities and talents and where can I use them? Do men's and women's
world views differ?

With this background I have defined group counseling as:

> . . . the process of using group interaction to facilitate deeper self-under-
> standing and self-acceptance. There is a need for a climate of mutual
> respect and acceptance, so that individuals can loosen their defenses suf-
> ficiently to explore both the meaning of behavior and new ways of
> behaving. The concerns and problems encountered are centered in the
> developmental tasks of each member rather than on pathological blocks
> and distortions of reality (Mahler, 1969, p. 11).

### *Group counseling versus group guidance and group therapy*

Group counseling, group guidance, and group therapy can be clearly differentiated even though they overlap considerably.

*Group guidance* is primarily a class of education experience, mainly involved with giving out information. In schools, it is usually oriented toward
encouraging students to know what the adults think the participants should
know. Although the same topics discussed in group counseling may also be
discussed in group guidance, the major responsibility in guidance remains
with the teacher. In group counseling the focus is upon each member, not
the topic being discussed, and upon changing his or her behavior, not changing behavior in general.

*Group therapy* is more concerned with unconscious motivation. Because of the depth of the growth problems faced by the clients, it is not unusual for the process to last months and even years. It is aimed at the more disturbed individuals.

*Group counseling* is a social experience that deals with the developmental problems and attitudes of individuals in a secure setting. Sensitivity training and encounter groups can best be classified as variations of group counseling. While many encounter-sensitivity groups have structured experiences planned as part of the lesson, they clearly do not fit under group guidance.

How do these three approaches differ?* We can establish clear distinctions in *six major areas*—size of group, the way content is managed, the length of group life, the responsibilities of the leader, the severity of problems, and the competencies of the leader.

*Size*

On the basis of size, I prefer to divide group counseling into large group and small group counseling. A large group may be designated as one having from 10 to 20 members, a small group from 2 to 10 members. The group dynamics, the role of the leader, the selection of techniques, the responsibilities of members all vary considerably according to the size of the group.

Group guidance in a school or agency setting is usually of class size or larger. In a few cases the size of a group has been over 20 and has still attained the objectives sufficiently enough to be considered group counseling.

The size of groups from 2 to 10 fits both small group counseling and group therapy. Therefore, additional distinguishing features are needed to differentiate between small group counseling and group therapy.

In one NDEA (National Defense Education Act) Institute at New York University, we utilized size of group to help get group counseling into the high schools. There was a reluctance to have counseling groups of 7 or 8 students because that might be considered group therapy, and the school system was very definitely against group therapy there. So, groups of 15 members were established and thus could the program fit the desired goal—that group counseling must be a part of the education program.

*Management of content*

Considerable difference exists among the three approaches in ways that subject matter or content of discussion is dealt with. There is also variation

---

* Editor's note: See also Chapter 9, Figure 1.

within each area as to how content is managed; but, by and large, the differentiation is greater between areas than within areas.

In *group guidance* the topics of experiences are usually selected by the leader or are part of a regular program of instruction. For example, in a "How to Study" unit the content and procedures are often ready to use regardless of the particular class and the readiness of members for the topic. Secondly, the content is often handled in an "academic" manner. That is, the topic is talked about or the discussion is about the topic rather than the members of the class being responsible for establishing their own views on the topic or evaluating for themselves what the class experience means personally. The danger lies in the result that something is done to a class rather than the members themselves being involved meaningfully in the learning experience.

In *group counseling* the topic is derived from the immediate or stated concerns of the group members. Many of the same topics covered in a group guidance unit come up in group counseling. But the real issue is that the choice is up to the members: They select the topic or specific group they wish to participate in. Thus, from the counseling point of view each member selects the topic or area he or she wishes to work on. The prior selection of a topic is much less the issue than the way in which it is managed.

*Behavioral counseling,* as a form of group counseling, selects an area of concern and programs procedures to accomplish the specific goals. But there is a real concern for the personal involvement of the participants. In fact, even more than in "laissez faire" or "I hope we go somewhere" group counseling, there is an aim to change specific behavior of the participants.

In *group therapy* the content derives from the problems presented by the members. Regardless of the variation in leader role, from very nondirective and noninterpretative to confrontative and directive, the content grows out of the life experiences of the group members.

### Length of group life

In group guidance or orientation-type programs, the life of the group is determined mainly by organizational aspects. A semester or a three-week unit or other variations set the time limits. In group counseling there has been experimentation in setting a specified number of sessions for a group versus allowing a group to go as long as the members desire. The experience of behavioral counseling and Adlerian counseling programs in setting the number of sessions in advance holds on solid theoretical grounds. More research is needed to help practitioners in this important area. The goals set by group members will often suggest the length of time that might be appropriate.

In group therapy the most frequent pattern seems to be to allow groups to go on without limiting the number of sessions. At the present time it is not possible to prescribe so many sessions for a certain group or a specific problem area. The *main weakness,* particularly in doctoral dissertations, is expecting extensive behavioral change in too few sessions. For example, underachievement, regardless of whether at the elementary, high school, or college level, is not easily reversed by 5, 10, or 15 group sessions. Group participation is much more closely related to the socialization process than is individual counseling. Therefore the change process is more gradual, and often comes about by identification and modeling of group members and the leader. The best recommendation that can be made at present is to set a specific number of sessions when one starts a group. Then the leader can make provisions to have a second series of sessions with the same group members or to reconstitute the group with different members or new goals.

There is a strong tendency for all well-functioning groups to want to continue. In fact, the tendency for exclusiveness of groups within a larger program, such as school or church, can be partly controlled by the design of the group program, i.e., by the number of sessions and by mixing group members in subsequent time blocks.

### Responsibility of leader

In *group guidance,* the leaders are usually responsible for the structure and conduct of the session. Imparting information is often one of their major functions. Good discussion techniques and creative teaching methods can indeed make a meaningful group guidance program. The fact that many group guidance programs are poorly conducted, in the same manner that a subject matter class may be well or poorly taught, does not mean that group guidance is bad. A clear statement of goals for a total guidance program will go a long way in establishing the kind of guidance experiences most likely to help members. So, in group guidance the leader is seen as being mainly responsible for content and letting the personal meaning of the experiences be the member's responsibility.

In *group counseling* the role is largely reversed. A skilled group counselor can take almost any topic or concern and help the individual members work through their own personal meanings. Here again, it is not so much who selects the topic, member or leader, but how the topic is managed that differentiates group counseling from group guidance.

In group counseling and group therapy the basic responsibility of the leader is very similar. The difference between the two approaches lies more in the composition of the groups.

Group counselors learn that they should not deal with problems that will take extensive time to understand and solve. A student may, for instance, mention in a group counseling session that his parents have "grounded" him as a penalty for poor grades. The counselor may be aware of severe emotional problems in the family—for example, that deep neurotic conflicts and attachments of the son to his mother are helping to immobilize the youth and preventing him from doing better work. However, the counselor will recognize the need to guide the discussion toward those aspects of the problem which the students and members of the group are capable of handling. Thus, it is not that a counselor is unaware of deeper problems or afraid of deep disturbance, but more that he or she is realistic about what it takes to change behavior. One of the prime reasons for proposing group counseling programs is that group guidance efforts do not sufficiently change behavior; but, on the other hand, we should not expect group counseling to change deep-seated emotional problems.

*Severity of problems*

One of the main differences between members of group therapy and participants in group counseling lies in the severity of the presenting problem. Excessive acting out, deep emotional disturbance, and delinquency are considered to place the members in need of therapy (group and individual). In group counseling it is assumed that almost all members of the institution, such as a school or church, are potential members. The emphasis is more on factors of socialization than on deep emotional disturbance. Often a topic of concern can be proposed as the central reason for joining a group. For example, in a college dorm all students who feel lonely and unskilled in making friends might be invited to sign up for group counseling. A recent extensive study on the content of individual therapy sessions with young adult women indicated a primary focus upon the "outer" or interpersonal sphere of their lives and the least focus upon the "inner" or intrapersonal aspect (Howard, Orlinsky, & Hill, 1969). The specific topics discussed most frequently were heterosexual involvements, occupational concerns, and hopes or fears for the future.

There is some evidence that topics in group counseling are very similar. Such evidence suggests that rather than having jurisdictional disputes over who helps whom, we need to focus on how best to help individuals with the concerns they bring to counseling or therapy. This leads to the last area for differentiating among approaches.

*Competency of the leader*

Let us assume that leaders in all three approaches—group guidance, group counseling, and group therapy—are competent. What, then, is the difference in competency suggested? The difference lies in the depth of psychological understanding of individual behavior and group dynamics. What difference in competencies would we like to see in leaders discussing with young adults their heterosexual involvements, occupational concerns, and hopes or fears for the future? Not only should leaders be versed in individual dynamics of behavior but they also need a sound background in social psychology and group dynamics. So rather than highly different training, leaders need increasing depth of training in essentially the same areas.

In group guidance classes centered on family relations, it is desirable that the leaders be well versed in the theoretical and research literature on the topic. We need not expect that they would have the skills to translate theoretical knowledge into a new learning opportunity for group members. Theoretical and conceptual knowledge in depth is essential for all group leaders; where the leaders differ is in their skill in utilizing the knowledge for personal growth.

*Research on group counseling*

Group counseling programs have expanded rapidly in the last 10 years. However, the research and evaluative efforts, as in group psychotherapy, have lagged far behind. Gazda and Larsen (1968) conducted a comprehensive appraisal of group counseling research. Approximately 100 studies, dating from 1938 to 1968 and relating directly to group counseling, were reviewed. The main weaknesses found in the studies were: (a) theoretical orientations vague or poorly stated; (b) the nature of treatment process not clearly presented; (c) qualification of the group counselor not clearly identified; (d) because outcome variables too global to be tied down to ways treatment may affect them, specific goals needed that can be stated in precise, measurable terms; (e) tendency not to have specific outcome goals for each group member; (f) many evaluation instruments unsuitable for evaluating outcome variables (grade point average, as the most popular means of evaluating the outcome of group counseling, indicates a low degree of sophistication; tests of function much closer to awareness of actual performance in interpersonal relations would be much better); (g) difficulty in obtaining adequate control groups.

The past research efforts in group counseling have had generally inconclusive results. In describing the present state of evaluative efforts, it is notable that one of the most promising trends is to indicate specific measurable outcome objectives. Behavioral counseling research has been particularly helpful in showing that if one focuses upon one or two precise behaviors, it is possible to ascertain much more clearly the treatment effects. The practices of using global adjustments as an outcome variable will continue to decrease. We need to explore a wider variety of significant behaviors than were studied in early work on behavioral counseling. The trend to study deeper and more significant problems is evident.

The future of research on methods, processes, and outcomes will undoubtedly be greatly influenced by the outstanding work of Carkhuff (1969). Carkhuff not only tackles the whole process of counseling and counseling outcomes, but he also derives a method of training to go along with the theoretical basis and procedures for those who want to be helpers. He has submitted a much-needed challenge to all trainers of professionals to validate their training methods in terms of change in client behavior. Carkhuff feels that it may be more feasible to train lay personnel to help than to make real helpers out of group leaders. The benefits of these present trends will hold not only for group therapy and encounter groups but for group guidance as well. Since we will be concerned with changing behavior, there will be experiments on ways in which behavior might be changed in large group (i.e., class size) instruction.

*Group therapy research* has had much the same weaknesses as group counseling. The research in encounter groups has been even less sophisticated. From now on, however, it can be expected that all helping efforts will have improved statements of theoretical assumptions, treatment efforts, and specific outcomes. The exuberant and somewhat irresponsible adolescent period of group counseling (all of group work, for that matter) seems to be approaching a more responsible, adult position. I hope that we can better contain the "bandwagon" rush to implement group work in every possible helping agency. In schools, employment agencies, probation offices, welfare services, and church settings we must strengthen our in-service efforts to train group leaders more adequately.*

---

* Editor's note:—and to this end we have assembled this present volume.

# BIBLIOGRAPHY

CARKHUFF, R. R. (1969). *Helping and Human Relations.* Vols. I and II. New York: Holt, Rinehart, and Winston.

CARKHUFF, R. R. and BERENSON, B. G. (1967). *Beyond Counseling and Therapy.* New York: Holt, Rinehart, and Winston.

Fox, W. T. (1970). "The relationship between group counselor functioning and the counseling group's perception of the campus environment." Unpublished master's thesis. Chico State University, Calif.

GAZDA, G. M., DUNCAN, J. A., and MEADOWS, M. E. (1967). Group counseling and group procedures—Report of a survey. *Counselor Ed. and Supervision,* 6, 305-310.

GAZDA, G. M., and LARSEN, M. J. (1968). A comprehensive appraisal of group and multiple counseling. *J. of Res. and Devel. in Ed.,* 1, 57-132.

HOWARD, K. I., ORLINSKY, D. E., and HILL, J. A. (1969). Content of dialogue in psychotherapy. *J. of Counseling Psychol.,* 16, 396-404.

MAHLER, C. A. (1969). *Group Counseling in the Schools.* Boston: Houghton Mifflin.

OHLSEN, M. M. (1970). *Group Counseling.* New York: Holt, Rinehart, and Winston.

## CHAPTER 3

# Minimal Necessary Conditions in Schools for Effecting Group Counseling

### Clarence A. Mahler, Ph.D.

THE RAPID EXPANSION IN POPULARITY of group counseling and sensitivity groups gives rise to a grave concern on the part of many counselor trainers. This concern is in the extreme difficulties met by counselor trainers and school pupil personnel directors in establishing and expanding programs of group counseling in the public school setting. An analysis of the factors contributing to this problem and the necessary minimal conditions for effective group counseling in schools are discussed below.

What are the major obstacles that have impeded the development of comprehensive group counseling programs in the schools? The obstacles can be summarized under six areas: community resistance, administrative resistance, teacher resistance, student resistance, counselor resistance, and lack of clearly developed programs.

*Community resistance*

Group counseling programs, like sex education in the schools, hit close to conflicting values of parents and community leaders. The freedom of students to discuss personally relevant material is still a threat to parents, administrators, teachers—and even to students and counselors. In California the John Birch Society has been as concerned about sensitivity groups as it has been about sex education.

Inherent in parent resistance, as well as teacher and administrator resistance, has been the lack of agreement that the affective side of man should

Reprinted with permission and slight changes from *Educational Technology*, 13, 21-33, February, 1973.

have a significant place in the educational process. While some counselor trainers, this one included, blend the cognitive and affective into the group process, there is no denying that one of the main values of group counseling lies in the stress on the affective side of the person.

*Administrative resistance*

The organization of public schools, both elementary and secondary, in which the development of new curricular programs resides largely in the school principal, makes the introduction and expansion of new programs, such as a group counseling program, extremely difficult. Each individual high school must select and establish new programs such as group counseling. Seldom does a school district have an organizational pattern that facilitates expanding new programs. Many large school districts seem to stay stuck in the pilot study phase of implementing new curricular or guidance programs. In contrast, the author was able to provide extensive group counselor training, over a three-year period, to over 200 state employment counselors throughout California.

The present widespread criticism of school leadership is not conducive to strengthening administrators to support new, creative, and innovative programs in curriculum revision, let alone group counseling.

*Teacher resistance*

Teacher resistance seems to stem from a lack of clear understanding that the freedom to talk about anything which concerns a group member does not mean the group leader is encouraging and condoning criticism of teachers and parents. A second area of real concern on the part of teachers has been in school settings where scheduling patterns make it necessary to take group members from a class.

*Student resistance*

By and large, students in present-day elementary and secondary schools are very eager for the opportunities provided by group counseling programs. However, some resistance can be expected from two sources: when shyness make participation very difficult and when the group counseling program is perceived by the students as being Establishment oriented. If the counselors are seen as part of the adminstrative hierarchy, then participation in a group may be perceived as a more subtle way of manipulating the student toward adult-imposed values.

### Counselor resistance

Of all the resistances to initiating group counseling programs, the *most prominent and widespread* is counselor resistance. In one high school district, a creative superintendent tried to push counselors in three high schools into establishing a group counseling program. When he left, after four years of intensive in-service training, the counselors went back to their clerical and crisis intervention duties. It must be admitted that for many counselors trained five or more years ago very little group counseling training was then available. But even where districts have been willing to provide in-service training in group work, many counselors are reluctant to risk entering into the realm of group counseling. With many graduates of training programs being much better trained in group work and eager to institute groups, it can be expected that this area of resistance will diminish gradually.

### Lack of clearly developed programs

Counselor trainers and directors of pupil personnel services must accept responsibility for a decided weakness in establishing integrated guidance programs and in developing ways of getting the new programs into each school. Groups in a school setting must clearly fit the school program and have a continuity built in. Only a few program leaders have established a program of guidance efforts that show clearly where and when group counseling is indicated. The greatly improved quality of training in group work now throughout the country will lead to counselor discouragement and apathy unless pupil personnel program developers begin to establish coordinated programs.

### Minimal necessary conditions

The resistances and difficulties of providing a group counseling program in the school setting have been stated. Let us now review the minimal necessary conditions that are needed for an effective group counseling program.

*First: A designed program.* An effective group counseling program needs both a theoretical framework and an organizational plan. Counseling, let alone group counseling, has been greatly hindered by inadequate theoretical foundations to build helping techniques and procedures.

The slow growth of learning theory has handicapped educational practitioners in both teaching procedures and counseling procedures. Fortunately, recent developments in behavior modification have shown that procedures used in helping students can be based on theoretically sound ground. Furthermore, it has been demonstrated that theoretical assumptions can lead to specific counseling strategies for a wide array of client problems. The fear among some counselors that behavior modification efforts were based on too narrow a realm of behaviors needing change has been countered effectively by Thoresen's development of a humanistic behavioral position (Thoresen, 1970).

So, it is necessary that each district desiring to install a group counseling program specify the goals of the program. These goals must fit closely the overall instructional goals of the school district.

For example, a district might specify the following goals for its group counseling program: (1) to assist academic underachievers; (2) to assist students who have ineffective social skills; (3) to train all students in more efficient decision-making skills; (4) to assist students with excessive fears and anxieties; (5) to help students to explore life style and career possibilities; (6) to reduce interpersonal hostilities in our school. With a prepared list of goals and objectives the counselors are ready to explain their efforts to the school board, parents, administrators, and teachers.*

The development of goals for the total program then permits the counselor to prepare procedures for helping students, parents, and teachers to identify individual needs and select experiences that aim to alleviate the problem or provide for growth in specific skills.

With the development of goals for the group counseling programs and for the individual student, attention must be given to organizational aspects within the school setting. It is clear from the list of six possible objectives for a group counseling program that a wide variety of group experiences would be indicated. The time needed to help students with various problems and concerns will vary widely. Underachievers often take more than a school year of group work for change in actual achievement, whereas other problem areas, such as poor study skills, could take a much smaller number of experiences to gain a stated goal. The school schedule needs to provide time for group counseling experiences and preferably not from regular classes. One solution, when a group counseling goal involves a total class, is to have counselors divide the class on a once-a-week basis for a period of weeks.

Group counselors should not be allowed to define their programs by size of group. With the curriculum development of many personal development units, such as the decision-making units of the Palo Alto School District in

---

* Editor's note: Input from students would be useful, too.

California, we can expect counselors to return to even class-size groups to carry out program objectives.

*Second: Administrative support.* Assuming the first minimal necessary condition for establishing a strong group counseling program is met, one is faced next with the necessity of strong administrative support. Numerous administrators would need only the first condition to be carried out to insure their strong backing of a new program. However, in those schools where the principal is more of a status quo, don't-rock-the-boat type of person, it is virtually impossible for a strong group counseling program to get established. Problems, misunderstandings, misperceptions, and conflict of values cannot all be resolved ahead of time. A program needs a chance to get started and a design for gaining broad acceptance as it develops. Strong administrative support is a basic necessity.

*Third: Counselors willing to work.* The final necessary condition for establishing a new program is the quality of the counselors. There is accumulating research evidence to show that training in individual counseling does not prepare one adequately to be a group counselor. In fact, in one study by Conger (1970), the findings indicated that poor group leaders left their group members worse off in academic performance than a control group not receiving any counseling. The strong group counselor, however, did influence the attainment of increased academic performance.

Without an intensive in-service training program in group work, it is not fair to insist that all counselors must do group work.

It is very important that the in-service training be a practicum type experience, with audiotape or videotape reviews of the counselors working with their own groups.

*Summary*

In summary, to institute a new group counseling program for a school district the following minimal necessary conditions are needed: (1) A theoretical framework and organizational design must clearly focus on change in behavior—it must enable participants and interested observers to know what is happening; (2) Strong administrative support is necessary to get innovative school programs established. Such programs cannot be mandated or authorized, however; the program can grow only with creative leadership; (3) Counselors who are willing to *risk* are needed to begin the new group counseling program. It is not possible to hide what one does in a group. Thus, it takes courage to go ahead and begin a new program. Not all *individual* counselors can be expected to become good *group* counselors. With these necessary conditions met, a school district is ready to begin a group counseling program.

## BIBLIOGRAPHY

CONGER, V. (1970). 'The differential effects of high and low functioning group counselors upon the academic performance of students in an educational opportunity program." M.A. thesis, Chico State University, Calif.

MAHLER, C. A. (1969). *Group Counseling in the Schools*. Boston: Houghton Mifflin.

THORESEN, C. E. (1970). "On developing personally competent individuals." Paper presented at American Psychological Association Convention, Miami Beach.

## CHAPTER 4

# Indications for Use of Groups in Secondary Schools and Review of Literature

Irving H. Berkovitz, M.D.

IN THE SCHOOL SETTING it is necessary to distinguish between group guidance, group counseling, and group therapy. Mahler has given one construct in Chapter 2. Other authors (Glanz & Hayes, 1968) state that group counseling proposes to resolve personal and emotional problems, whereas group guidance is more directly concerned with acquiring information, gaining orientation to new problems, planning and implementing student activities, and collecting data for occupational and educational decisions. These authors feel that guidance connotes a positive and preventive view, while counseling and therapy connote a concern with the correction or removal of a present handicap or illness.

My own feeling is that group counseling can come close to resembling group therapy as adapted to teenagers. This is so, for example, when the group composition is of drug abusers or moderately delinquent youngsters and the counselor has had specific training in conducting this type of group. Usually, however, the counseling focus in schools will be on school-related problems and only briefly on causal factors such as family or childhood problems. If the counselor has received training and has the sanction of the school district, the school counseling group may more often approach a group therapy type of experience with the limitations of the school calendar year and usually a shorter session time of 40 to 50 minutes.

Despite these differences, group counseling is widely used in both public schools and colleges. In public schools there has been a wide variety of goals and purposes in the groups involved. Some have been: (1) to raise

26

the grade point average (G.P.A.) or change patterns of underachievement; (2) to reduce feelings of alienation; (3) to reduce drug abuse behavior; (4) to improve motivation for college; (5) to reduce behavior disorder; (6) to help exceptionalities, e.g., stutterers, the educable mentally retarded, the deaf, etc.; (7) to improve sex education classes. This group of goals is not intended to be all-inclusive.

Many school personnel borrow elements from clinical techniques. As described in Part II of this volume, school personnel occasionally receive consultation or supervision from clinical mental health personnel. Community mental health includes the attempt to help children in schools to avoid needing clinical facilities. With help in the normal setting, more youngsters can be spared entry into the patient role. There is an extensive body of literature on various group approaches in the schools. I shall touch on only a few of these articles, concentrating especially on those pertaining to students in the secondary schools.

While the initial focus of the groups to be described may have been school-related behavior, it frequently occurred that the focus broadened to include other aspects of the young person's personality and behavior. Some school counselors, from fear of getting into areas of psychopathology beyond their training or knowledge, limited the scope of the group discussion. Here the risk was of too little effective involvement. Yet youngsters not seriously disturbed got some help from even this seemingly superficial procedure when the counselor was somewhat sensitive.

The counseling orientation of school counselors and school psychologists varies widely. Some have had training experiences in an espoused orientation ranging from psychoanalytic to role playing, to Gestalt, to eclectic, etc. One orientation of special interest to school counselors is that described by Carkhuff and Berenson (1967). Briefly, in this orientation, "Trainees develop facility in offering prescribed levels of accurate empathy, positive regard, and genuineness within their counseling relationships." * One criticism of papers presented in this area is that inadequate descriptions of techniques actually used made it difficult to compare and replicate results (Gurman, 1969).

### Academic underachievement

A prime indication, as would be expected in the school setting, was the problem of academic underachievement. A wide and often disparate variety

---

* See Chapter 2.

of individuals were grouped under this label, thus rendering results hard to compare. Some authors were more precise in their criteria for selection and definition of underachievement. "Offering a treatment, e.g., 'group counseling,' to a mixed group is highly likely to produce no average gain, since gains by some subjects are canceled by losses of others" (Island, 1969). Benson and Blochner (1967) selected a group of *tenth grade* underachieving boys with negative feelings and attitudes toward school. The 28 boys who agreed to participate were randomly assigned to experimental and control groups. After 18 weeks of group counseling, thoroughly described but difficult to replicate, the experimental group showed G.P.A. improvement that was significantly greater on the average than the controls.

> Improved G.P.A. is a commonly found short-term gain in many underachievement investigations. Long-range results need greater attention, but unfortunately few long-range follow-ups have been published (Island, 1969).

Goodstein (1967) found that *initial gain in G.P.A. was completely negated five years later*. In fact, higher proportions of control subjects graduated than did counseled subjects. Dickenson and Truax (1966), in examining pre- and post-treatment results, counted the number of subjects who *moved from probation to nonprobation in status*. Such data may be more important than determining whether significant increases in average G.P.A. occurred. Laxer et al. (1966) described a project in which 13 volunteer counselors worked with 260 underachievers in *grades 4 to 11*. Counseled and controlled subjects were paired on the bases of achievement, school grades, age, and sex. Counseling was extended for 600 hours. This group reported that "After treatment the counseled group did not differ from the control group on any of the battery tests, nor on school marks."

However, many *other papers do report improvement* after group counseling. Some included some follow-up, but not for the five-year period mentioned above. Gurman (1969) stated *more specific criteria* for group structure:

> Leader-structured groups appear to be the most effective group method for the counseling of underachievers. If this is so, and the evidence in this regard is not yet clear, it implies that insight, as it is defined by psychoanalytically oriented counselors and therapists, is not essential to the successful treatment of underachievers. This should be verified by comparing the effectiveness of cognitively directed, goal-directed, and problem solving groups with more purely interpersonal techniques, such as sensitivity training groups.

Bates (1968) compared traditional interaction (*weekly meetings*) and accelerated interaction (*two-day continuous session* during school hours).

> The G.P.A.'s of accelerated and controls deteriorated, while the students in the traditional group sustained the G.P.A. and also projected themselves into more occupations and facilitated the individuation process.

Finney and Van Dalsem (1969) reported that 69 *gifted, underachieving high school sophomores* were given four semesters of weekly group counseling. He compared this with a control group of 85. He found no difference of improvement in the G.P.A., but the counseled students were rated by teachers as being less resistive and more cooperative in the classroom and less frequently absent from class.

Ofman (1964) compared five groups of 60 students. Results indicated that the groups were comparable in ability and differed only in initial G.P.A. As a function of counseling, the experimental group's G.P.A. became comparable to the baseline group's and significantly higher than the control and dropout group's G.P.A. The wait group did not improve until after counseling. G.P.A. of the control and dropout groups did not improve at all. This investigator concluded that the group counseling procedure described was *effective in improving scholastic behavior*.

Roth et al. (1967) reported that 174 selected failing students were provided group counseling as a condition of their remaining in school. Fifty-two male subjects were randomly selected for study, as were 52 probationary, noncounseled males, who were used as a comparison group. The results indicated that the counseled group increased their G.P.A. significantly and that these changes held over time. The G.P.A. of the comparison group did not increase significantly.

Freeman (1969) reported on a four-year demonstration project involving 110 bright *eleventh grade academic underachievers*. "A focused group discussion seminar was introduced into the curriculum as an elective subject for eligible pupils." This discussion was

> operationally defined as small group problem solving based upon the common factors of pupil underachievement and willingness to participate. . . . From the outset the thrust of the demonstration project was aimed not at improvement in grades per se, but rather at a change in pupil attitudes about self-worth and satisfactions to be derived from personally meaningful productivity and creativity.

Each course was limited to an enrollment of 12 pupils and consisted of once-weekly, regular 50-minute classroom sessions for the duration of one semester.

> Over the four years more eligible pupils volunteered for the course than could be accommodated. This made control groups possible. Although course grades were never established as a criterion of success, those pupils who participated obtained higher grades and had a higher percentage of post-secondary school admissions than those in the control groups.

In this regard Clements (1966) reported that experience in small group counseling, as studied in a control group and an experimental group of college-bound high school seniors, was followed by *significantly lower levels of anxiety* in the experimental group.

Small group counseling has been reported with various *minority groups* in the schools. Gilliland (1968) worked with a group of 30 *Black students,* using pre- and post-tests on random experimental and control groups. He reported:

> After one year of group counseling, experimental groups showed significant gains in vocabulary, reading, English usage, occupational aspiration, and vocational maturity. . . . Upon request of experimental students, multiracial counseling groups were later initiated, including interested white and Negro students not previously involved.

Klitgaard (1969) reported on a group of 20 *ninth grade Mexican-American students* of college potential in a minority high school in a low socioeconomic area. This group met with him for a lunch-time conference daily during the freshman year, twice per week in the sophomore year, and occasionally during the junior and senior years. Topics of discussion ranged far and wide, although the primary focus was on why education was important, how to get into college, and special problems of the Mexican-American students. The group was very informal and developed excellent rapport. Of the 35, 30 entered college and did well; seven received scholarships.

Various investigators introduced innovative arrangements in working with various groups of students. Vriend (1969) made use of the concept that peer approval is a major aspect of the adolescent subculture, and that the peer *influence model* has been utilized to influence school achievement positively. He demonstrated that:

> Achieving disadvantaged students can be trained as peer leaders to serve as models for fellow students and to help them to develop attitudes and behaviors that improve school performance.

He felt, however, that:

> The group did not replace the need for individual counseling for some students with special problems. The experience, however, did encourage many students to seek individual assistance from teachers and counselors.

Several investigators involved *components of the youngster's family* in the counseling effort. Perkins and Wicas (1971) reported an interesting consequence when working *only with mothers.*

> This study investigated the use of counseling with small groups of bright, underachieving ninth grade boys and/or their mothers. One hundred twenty boys and 60 mothers comprised the total sample. Five male public school counselors were trying to offer minimal levels of accurate empathy, regard, and genuineness within a group counseling context. Post-treatment results revealed significant increases in G.P.A.'s and self-acceptance. Additionally, when counselors worked with mothers, with or without students, the effect on underachievers was equal to or greater than when counselors worked only with underachievers.

Durell (1969) (see Chapter 42) conducted a *group in a junior high school* consisting of four families, each of whom had a problem pupil of at least average intelligence. Eleven sessions of 1½ hours each were held. The chief counselor provided a liaison between the school and the group; a psychologist was the group leader, and the assistant to the supervisor of guidance functioned as an observer. The boys' academic performance and behavior had substantially improved after the 11 weeks. The group leader's role was very different from that of the traditional group therapist, who does not generally interact with the other social systems to which the group members belong. *Intensive work with school personnel was also needed,* since the pupils were involved in negative interactions with the school staff. This experience, more than any of the previous, demonstrated a mixture of clinical and school-based therapeutic approaches.

### Alienation in students

A second indication in the school setting for group techniques, in addition to the various features associated with underachievement, was the problem of the student exhibiting signs and behavior of alienation. In one study in a *junior high school* (Talmadge et al., 1969) alienation was described as follows:

> . . . not accepting the mores and values of the school system. The trait of alienation was determined by an apathetic attitude towards school

as well as a history of disciplinary infractions and poor cooperation. Other indices of the trait included limited motivation, a lack of academic drive, and the expressed desire to drop out of school when legally possible.

Those who appeared "emotionally disturbed rather than alienated were excluded." Of 125 boys, 10 were thus excluded. A treatment and control group of 13 boys each was selected. Testing at the end of the school year suggested:

> 1) an overall, more positive adjustment in the sphere of personality, 2) significantly less alienation for the treatment group, and 3) marked increases in school achievement. Over and above the effect of the program on the students, the research had a favorable impact on the orientation of the administration and faculty.

Another study involved 180 juniors in *three lower-middle-class suburban high schools*. They had scored one standard deviation above the mean, indicating a high degree of alienation on a scale of alienation developed by Dean (1961). The study was organized as follows:

> In each school the counselor conducted two model reinforcement groups, two verbal reinforcement groups, one placebo group, and a control group, which received no counseling. In the model reinforcement and verbal reinforcement groups, the goal of the counselor was to keep the discussion focused on the students' feelings of alienation and to give positive verbal reinforcement to statements made by the students which suggested positive attitudes toward their position in the social structure. The specific aim was to get the students to consider positive steps that they might take to eliminate their alienation from the society. Often this involved consideration of means by which they could bring about changes in the status quo of society rather than focusing entirely on their need to change themselves. . . . All of the groups except for the control group met for six sessions of 40 minutes each.
>
> An earlier investigation had demonstrated that the behavioral counseling did reduce students' feelings of alienation. The results of this six-month follow-up demonstrated that not only were the covert feelings changed, but that six months later the overt behavior of those in the two behavioral treatments were rated as more appropriate than the behaviors of students who participated in either placebo counseling or who received no counseling (Warner, 1971).

## Behavior problems

Another indication for group methods in schools was the occurrence of behavior problems. In one group described (Schaeffer and Von Nessen, 1967), the school psychologist set up certain *role playing situations* and helped the girls with the analysis of these. In the meantime, the girls' counselor took part in role playing of previous situations in which girls got into trouble. This was used to develop techniques through which the girls could learn to cope with problem areas such as *learning to turn aside aggression* without feeling loss of face.

The behavior change of the girls outside of group sessions was dramatic. No girl was again referred for discipline; all improved scholastically and in their context with the larger social group in the school.

This improvement was maintained several months later. Laxer et al. (1967) reported that:

Three groups of junior high school conduct problem students received approximately 600 minutes of counseling over an eight-week period. Several personality and academic measures were observed before and after counseling. A comparison of the counseled and the noncounseled (control) groups revealed no significant differences for any of the variables.

### Stutterers

Laeder and Francis (1968) reported:

A workshop program was instituted to provide group therapy for stutterers in isolated, rural high schools. The workshop sessions were held once or twice during the school year. Opportunities for problem sharing and group discussion were given in each session.

The workshops proved to be of great value and continued for seven years.

### The deaf student

Sarlin and Altshuler (1968) detailed the first year of an attempt at preventive group psychotherapy with deaf adolescents in a school setting.

The therapist had consistently to be alert to maturational lags and experiential naivete, and he had to computize (sic) abstract concepts so that interpretations could be made meaningful. While interest in sexual behavior was high, knowledge of reproductive functions was limited, and the responsibilities and reasons for rules governing sexual behavior were difficult to bring to the fore. Repetition and a great deal of work were required to increase the depth of awareness in the group from rules memorized by rote to a more mature grasp of concepts. The group resembled a more delinquent population, yet with a scattering of high ideals and an absence of generalized rebelliousness. Defiance, when encountered, commonly had to do with simple wilfullness—the youngsters wanted to do what they wanted to do—rather than motivated rebellion against authority.

## Educable mentally retarded adolescents

Group counseling has been useful in school classes for educable mentally retarded adolescents (i.e., IQ 53-77). Some authors have felt that there was special value of group techniques for retardates, because group techniques partially eliminated the requirement for the retardates to formulate verbally their own concerns (Cotzin, 1948). Groups tended, through emphasis on social interaction, to attack those dimensions of personality structure that were most troublesome to retardates, for example, self-concept and interpersonal relations (Ringelheim & Polatsek, 1955; Stacey & De Martino, 1957).

Lodato et al. (1964) used group counseling with slow learners wherein some retardates were included. Mann et al. (1969) showed with *pre-adolescent, educable mentally retarded boys* that group counseling tended to develop greater improvement in self-concept, more reduction in anxiety, and better grades in deportment and the academic subjects of reading and arithmetic than in those retarded boys who did not receive the counseling. He felt that age and IQ were not found to be significant factors in the counseled group.

Humes (1971) described a *specialized method,* "a problem-oriented tactic using ambiguous pictures as stimuli," for discussion with educable retardates aged 13 to 16 with IQ's of 53 to 77. The use of the stimulus cards "appeared to bridge the gap between the unstructured and structured periods" of discussion. Socialization and interpersonal relationships seemed at a higher level after counseling, evidenced by

> talking to each other rather than to the counselors. The verbal participation and degree of problem involvement reached by the counseled groups indicated that the IQ labeling process, so often used with finality in dealing with retardates, failed to take into consideration the broad spectrum of abilities and resources demonstrated by the group members during the sessions.

Humes et al. (1969) met with groups formed from a *junior high school class of retardates* one hour per week for 12 weeks. They failed to find statistical significance for "several self-concept dependent variables." However, adjustment, as seen by teacher ratings on the behavior scale, did improve, as well as scores on standardized personality inventory. They concluded that: (1) modification of self-concept in educable adolescent retardates may need "a long-term approach, inasmuch as self-concept represents a deeper personality characteristic"; and (2) the nature of the construct is difficult to measure directly with assessment instruments.

### Drug-abusing students

Many secondary schools have established rap rooms, rap groups, and group counseling to help students whose drug use got them into trouble at school. In some schools police are called to remove and counsel the "stoned" student. In other schools the student is referred to or required to attend a group or other program. Anderson (1971) told of one such weekly group of 10 to 20 students in a *junior high school*. In the meetings a no-preach and no-praise approach was used in discussing drugs, with the students setting up their own rules with these two exceptions: (a) there must be no violence during the group meeting, and (b) everything discussed must be kept highly confidential. At the end of the school year, 3 of 10 regular members had stopped using drugs. A second group, consisting of 9 eighth graders, began meetings. At the end of the year, 6 of the 9 had reduced drug usage considerably. This group also went on field trips to drug treatment centers. Some later decided to teach sixth graders about drug use and abuse.*

### Sex education

Nash (1968) described the experience of a social worker from outside the school attending the sex education class in a *junior high school* to conduct group discussion. "The role of the social worker was that of a catalyst for change in the direction of group process. . . . The outside resource person should be blended into the existing group by the leader." Three hundred eighty students indicated in answer to a questionnaire that 78 percent liked the "group classes," and 53 percent reported that they had been helped to do better school work and to get along better with other people. Fifty-eight percent reported they had learned to better understand themselves.

While some reports in the literature offer occasional disagreement, the overall impression seems to indicate value and improvement of target behavior in many instances. The target behavior often needs more precise

---

* Refer to Chapters 32 and 40.

description and attention. Other chapters in this volume will offer additional examples of beneficial changes resulting from group procedures in schools.

## BIBLIOGRAPHY

ANDERSON, S. (1971). Group counseling in drug awareness. *School Counselor,* 19, 123-125.
BATES, M. (1968). A test of group counseling. *Pers. and Guid. J.,* 46, 749-753.
BENSON, R. L. and BLOCHNER, D. H. (1967). Evaluation of developmental counseling with groups of low achievers in a high school setting. *School Counselor,* 14, 215-220.
CARKHUFF, R. R. and BERENSON, B. G. (1967). *Beyond Counseling and Therapy.* New York: Holt, Rinehart, and Winston.
CLEMENTS, B. E. (1966). Transitional adolescents, anxiety, and group counseling. *Pers. and Guid. J.,* 45:1, 67-71.
COTZIN, M. (1948). Group psychotherapy with mentally defective problem boys. *Am. J. Mental Defic.,* 53, 268-283.
DICKENSON, W. A. and TRUAX, C. B. (1966). Group counseling with college underachievers. *Pers. and Guid. J.,* 45:3, 243-247.
DEAN, D. G. (1961). Alienation: Its meaning and measurement. *Am. Sociol. Rev.,* 26, 753-758.
DUNCAN, J. A. (1966). The effects of short-term group counseling on selected characteristics of culturally deprived ninth grade students. *Dissertation Abstracts,* 27, 387-A.
DURELL, V. G. (1969). Adolescents in multiple family group therapy in a school setting. *Int. J. Gr. Psychother.,* 19, 44-52.
FINNEY, B. C. and VAN DALSEM, E. (1969). Group counseling for gifted underachieving high school students. *J. of Counseling Psychol.,* 16, 87-94.
FREEMAN, W. J. (1969). Focused group discussion as an aid to bright high school underachievers. *Am. J. Orthopsych.,* 39, 302-303.
GILLILAND, B. E. (1968). Small group counseling with Negro adolescents in a public high school. *J. of Counseling Psychol.,* 15, 147-152.
GLANZ, E. C. and HAYES, R. W. (1968). *Groups in Guidance* (second edition). Boston: Allyn and Bacon.
GLASS, S. D. (1969). *Practical Handbook of Group Counseling.* Baltimore: B.C.S. Publishing Co.
GOODSTEIN, L. D. (1967). Group counseling with male underachieving college volunteers. *Pers. and Guid. J.,* 45:5, 469-476.
GURMAN, A. S. (1969). Group counseling with underachievers: A review and evaluation of methodology. *Int. J. Gr. Psychother.,* 14, 463-473.
HUMES, C. W., JR., ADAMCZYK, J. S., and MYCO, R. W. (1969). A school study of group counseling with educable retarded adolescents. *Am. J. Mental Defic.,* 74, 191-195.
HUMES, C. W., JR. (1971). A novel group approach to school counseling of educable retardates. *Training Sch. Bull.,* 67, 164-171.
ISLAND, D. D. (1969). Counseling students with special problems. *Rev. of Ed. Res.,* 39, 239-250.
KLITGAARD, G. C. (1969). A gap is bridged. *J. of Secondary Ed.,* 44, 55-57.
LAEDER, R. and FRANCIS, W. C. (1968). Stuttering workshops: Group therapy in a rural high school setting. *J. of Speech and Hearing Disorders,* 33:1, 38-41.

LAXER, R. M., KENNEDY, D. R., QUARTER, J. J., and ISNOR, C. (1966). Counseling small groups of underachievers in secondary schools: An experimental study. *Ontario J. of Ed. Res.*, 9:1, 49-57.

LAXER, R. M., QUARTER, J. J., ISNOR, C., and KENNEDY, D. R. (1967). Counseling small groups of behavior problem students in junior high schools. *J. of Counseling Psychol.*, 14:5, 454-457.

LODATO, F., SOKOLOFF, M., and SCHWARTZ, L. (1964). Group counseling as a method of modifying attitudes in slow learners. *School Counselor*, 12, 27-29.

MAHLER, C. A. (1969). *Group Counseling in the Schools.* Boston: Houghton Mifflin Co.

MANN, P. H., BEABER, J. D., and JACOBSON, M. D. (1969). The effect of group counseling on educable mentally retarded boys' self-concepts. *Exceptional Children*, 35, 359-366.

NASH, K. B. (1968). Group guidance and counseling programs: A vehicle for the introduction of sex education for adolescents in the public school. *J. of Sch. Health*, 38, 577-583.

OFMAN, W. (1964). Evaluation of a group counseling procedure. *J. of Counseling Psychol.*, 11, 152-158.

PERKINS, J. A. and WICAS, E. A. (1971). Group counseling bright underachievers and their mothers. *J. of Counseling Psychol.*, 18, 273-278.

RINGELHEIM, D. and POLATSEK, I. (1955). Group therapy with a male defective group. *Am. J. Mental Defic.*, 60, 157-162.

ROTH, R. M., MAUKSCH, H. O., and PEISER, K. (1967). The nonachievement syndrome, group therapy, and achievement change. *Pers. and Guid. J.*, 46, 393-398.

SARLIN, M. B. and ALTSHULER, K. Z. (1968). Group psychotherapy with deaf adolescents in a school setting. *Int. J. Gr. Psychother.*, 18, 337-344.

SCHAEFFER, D. T. and VON NESSEN, R. W. (1967). An intervention technique for acting-out adolescent girls: Implications for bringing insight to school faculties regarding the disadvantaged. *Am. J. Orthopsychiat.*, 37, 376.

STACEY, C. and DEMARTINO, M. (Eds.) (1957). *Counseling and Psychotherapy with the Mentally Retarded.* Glencoe, Ill.: Free Press.

TALMADGE, M., HAYDEN, B. S., and KULLA, M. (1969). The alienated junior high school student: A research evaluation of a program. *Am. J. Orthopsychiat.*, 39, 299-300.

VRIEND, T. J. (1969). High-performing inner city adolescents assist low-performing peers in counseling groups. *Pers. and Guid. J.*, 47, 897-903.

WARNER, R. W., JR. (1971). Alienated students: Six months after receiving behavioral group counseling. *J. Consulting Psychol.*, 18, 426-430.

# Part II

## GROUP COUNSELING IN SCHOOLS AS CONDUCTED BY SCHOOL PERSONNEL

A.  General Articles
B.  The Role of Administrators in Group Discussion and Counseling with Students
C.  Special Techniques
D.  Brief Descriptions of Programs in Schools

## CHAPTER 5

# Overcoming: The First Step

David Rappoport, M.Ed.

A NATURAL FEAR tends to swarm inside me when I begin as a group leader for the very first time. It is natural because I am doing something for the first time, and the unknown provokes the uneasiness of not knowing what to expect. As a school counselor caught up in the momentum of the school day, I tend to try to solve as many problems as I encounter—and problems begin as early as seven in the morning. If you are counseling in a school that has a pupil ratio of over 400 pupils to each counselor, you don't allow yourself the luxury of thinking, of listening, of even standing or sitting off by yourself to get a feeling of what the day is like. For years I simply did things I believed were counseling. I programmed. I made phone calls. I talked to teachers. I responded to agency questionnaires. I saw counselees, but at times I wondered if I was counseling the students. Was I accomplishing something? Was the paper work slopped over my desk ever going to be cleaned up? I had to prepare the next bulletin.

When I began my first group at school, I simply started it out of desire to be with students. I had been given enough referrals from the teachers. I had interviewed each student. Now the battle was with myself. I had to begin. I placed an agenda inside my head and resolved that I would succeed in solving problems of academic failure, tardiness, and poor homework.

I know that during the first few meetings of the group I did a great deal of the talking. I began the problem solving, and I had answers for every problem. But the group was very patient with me. I began to learn how to listen to others as well as to myself. I developed confidence in the group members and came to realize that the group could develop its own structure, its own agenda, and its own goals. I slowly discovered that group needs vary, goals are flexible, and changes are hard to see.

41

As I changed my own attitudes, I noticed changes in group members. I stopped worrying about how successful I had to be. I discovered much more support among my colleagues than I had imagined. I moved from a structured table to a circle of chairs and from structured topics and discussions to feeling experiences. I discovered beautiful new horizons in people, because I discovered them in myself. I could accept criticism and not crumble. I also realistically examined my limitations. Being involved with group process enabled me to deal with my prejudices and made me more aware of the uniqueness of each individual. I feel I became more accepting of others. I discovered students listening to each other and to me.

School became an exciting place where students came to be with me, not because I summoned them, but because they felt acceptance and trusted me. They also allowed for failure on my part. Counseling in groups helped me develop a wider acceptance of counseling. I became a more involved person, a real person. I simply had to take the first step and had to try something new for myself. I shared my pitfalls with other counselors new to group process. We helped each other grow. The doors and windows of our minds opened wide. Fresh air flowed in, the fresh air of discovering people.

## CHAPTER 6

# Small Group Counseling in Secondary Schools

Phillip Lewis, M.S., and
Muriel Thomson, Ed.D.

COUNSELING IN SMALL GROUPS provides an ideal opportunity in the school setting for students to discuss their concerns, to air their feelings, and to learn to receive and give help. It is not offered in lieu of individual counseling as an economy measure in time, but as a technique which offers a unique way of helping students.

*Definition*

Group counseling is described by Warters (1960) as a group method designed to help individuals with problems. It is a planned process that includes identification with, analysis by, and support from, the group. Some of the properties attributed by her to this type of counseling include permissiveness, protection, and privileged communication. She also states that it is possible for positive changes in personality and behavior to take place in the group counseling situation more rapidly than in life in general.

The term "multiple counseling" is employed by Driver (1954) to imply that the counseling function is shared among the group members as well as the leaders. The relationship of the members to the group helps each client through support, reassurance, and frank discussions, since mutual aid is characteristic of group activity.

*Guidance committee*

A guidance committee should function in each school to assist in: (1) stating the objectives of the program in the school; (2) determining best methods of keeping the faculty informed of the program and of receiving needed information from them; (3) insuring appropriate use of counseling facilities; (4) selecting the pupils who will participate in the program; and (5) developing a program of continuous evaluation of the program in terms of the stated objectives.

The committee should have representatives of the administration, pupil personnel, and teaching staffs, and should plan to meet on an established schedule.*

*Administrative support*

Understanding of the small group counseling program and active support of it by the chief administrator in the school are imperative to its success.** Such support insures that all legal provisions will have been covered, that scheduling may be facilitated, that teachers will receive adequate in-service education and will be kept integrated on the total program, that encouragement will be provided when needed, that there will be a resource in the event of adjustment problems, that parents will be properly notified, and that students will be made to feel secure about this added pupil personnel service.

*Size of groups*

There is general agreement among authors and those who have worked with groups that size is best kept at close to 5 to 10 members. Some counselors have had success with as many as 15 or as few as 4. However, the counselor engaging in small group counseling with students will soon be able to tell the size of a group with which he or she personally feels most comfortable and effective. If a group is too large, some students may find difficulty in taking part, or the group may simply never become cohesive. If a group is too small, it may become uninteresting or convert into a social unit. In this case the social dynamics inhibit the freedom and security necessary for group counseling to take place. Too small a group is also adversely affected through the semester by absences or attrition.

Starting with 10 pupils in a group and arriving at the semester's end with from 5 to 8 of the original membership has been a common experience and has generally proved workable. This number is sufficient for good interaction and allows a group to be continuous. When a group is radically reduced for

---

* Editor's note: Include student representatives, too?
** See Chapter 3.

some unforeseen reason, it may be necessary to invite several new members. However, this is tantamount to beginning again.

## Composition of groups

Groups ordinarily include both boys and girls unless specific objectives exist for having an all-male or all-female group.* In regard to homogeneity or heterogeneity of problems, opinions vary. Driver (1954) urges homogeneity, but much of her work is based on groups where homogeneity is the rule, such as with probation officers and in institutions. A school setting offers a heterogeneity of problems and even in the event of a few students evidencing some common manifestation, close examination will reveal different etiologies of behavior.

A degree of balance of personality types of students in a group is desirable. If a group is made up entirely of shy persons, the group may not progress in free discussion. Conversely, a group in which all students are aggressive may produce meetings that will be too highly animated for desirable outcomes.

## Inviting the pupil to participate

Once identified, those students who are to be invited to join a group should be seen individually. At this time the leader may advise the individual of the nature of group work: that from this, one may come to learn more about oneself and about getting along with others. The prospective member needs to know that what is discussed will be kept confidential by both the pupil and the leader and that there will be complete freedom of discussion but no physical activity which would be disruptive to the group. *If a tape recorder* is to be used, the pupil should be told of this and that its purpose is to have the tape available to the leader and members for later use if they wish it.

If students indicate a wish to join a group, they should be asked to discuss it with their parents and to obtain their permission. It is sometimes advisable for the leader to discuss the project with the pupils' parents and possibly also obtain written consent.

## Mechanics of group arrangement

The *frequency and duration of meetings* are still matters of experimentation. In a secondary school, the class period is a natural unit of time, and

---

* See Chapter 34.

pupils become easily oriented to a 40- or 50-minute counseling session. For maximum attendance, it is suggested that the sessions be held during the school day. Since most schools operate on a schedule of five to seven periods a day, it is usually possible to arrange for sessions to be staggered so that absence is not unduly frequent for any one class.

Meeting once a week for one semester is adequate for many groups. However, some groups may be set up for short contact meetings of two or three sessions only to resolve a particular problem. Others may go on for two or more semesters. Also, students may request that a group be renewed after it has been terminated. Therefore, since the needs of groups vary, frequency and duration of the sessions must usually be determined by the counselor.

The *physical setting* in which the group meets is less important than the climate produced by the leader. Some schools are fortunate in having one or more conference rooms available, while in others a classroom may be used. The school doctor's office in many schools has proved to be convenient, since this is occupied at most one day a week by a school physician.

A good *seating arrangement* is to have the group around a large table. Otherwise, the chairs may be arranged conveniently in a circle. In any case, the members should be able to see each other, and there should be no authority implied by the seating arrangement, such as having the counselor sit at the head of the group or behind a desk.

### Individual counseling in addition to group participation

The members of the group may seek out the leader or may be invited to see the leader individually to discuss some of the topics which have arisen or problems they do not yet feel able to present openly. On the whole, group and individual sessions tend to augment each other.

### Initial sessions

Members of a newly formed group usually feel awkward in the situation. Through the first meetings they ordinarily will be cautious in exposing themselves to the leader and the other members and, consequently, will tend to sit, listen, and wait. Soon one of the more talkative members will offer an observation, or ask to review the reason for the sessions.

After a *"thawing out" period,* which may take from one to as many as four sessions, discussions are light and of a nature that makes it possible for pupils to protect themselves. In this situation, the members are using each other as allies and protectors but are testing the leader. The content of their discussion may involve bizarre stories and incidents and the use of profanity.

As rapport and trust become established, the *ventilation of feelings develops*. In a school setting this ventilation is generally directed toward teachers and vice-principals. The leader, by avoiding disapproval and showing interest in understanding the problems, allows the members to learn to feel more at ease with each other and the leader. At the same time, the leader is teaching the students, by example, how to reflect the *feeling* expressed in the speaker's words. Warters (1960) recommends that in the early sessions the counselor should respond frequently in this manner. Gradually, as the members of the group adopt the techniques of reflecting and examining expressed feeling, the counselor will need to respond less and less frequently.

### Later sessions

Many groups, depending upon their nature and the ability of the members to handle discussion, will be seriously discussing their personal problems and interacting with wisdom upon the problems of their peers by the fourth to eighth session.

In a group, according to Warters (1960), members are able to discern the defensive distortions of reality expressed by individuals, to challenge these distortions, and also to accept the challenging of their own distortions by the other members. In groups, she states, there appears to be a therapeutic compulsion to improve.

### Likeness of the group to the family

People learn their patterns of interaction with others in the family setting. If, as children, their relationship has been less than healthy and the adult models either weak or absent, the child will develop poor ways of relating to others. The small group counseling setting provides a family-like situation in which peers can encourage, support, criticize, and offer suggestions as siblings within a family. In the security of a trusted group each can experiment with new patterns of behavior and learn directly from the reactions of those around him/her.

### BIBLIOGRAPHY

BERNE, E. (1961). *Transactional Analysis in Psychotherapy.* New York: Grove Press.

CAPLAN, S. W. (1957) The effects of group counseling on junior high school boys' concepts of themselves in school. *J. of Counseling Psychol.*, 4:2.

DRIVER, H. I. (1954). *Multiple Counseling: A Small Group Discussion Method for Personal Growth.* Madison, Wis.: Monona Publications.

DRIVER, H. I., et al. (1958). *Counseling and Learning Through Small-group Discussion.* Madison, Wis.: Monona Publications.

HINCKLEY, R. G. and HERMANN, L. (1951). *Group Treatment in Psychotherapy.* Minneapolis: Univ. of Minnesota Press.

MORENO, J. L. (1959). Definitions of group psychotherapy. *Group Psychother.*, 12.

ROGERS, C. R. and DYMOND, R. F. (Eds.) (1954). *Psychotherapy and Personality Change.* Illinois: Univ. of Chicago Press.

SLAVSON, S. R. (1962). *The Practice of Group Therapy.* New York: International Universities Press.

WARTERS, J. (1960). *Group Guidance: Principles and Practices.* New York: McGraw-Hill Book Co.

CHAPTER 7

# Special Advantages of Group Counseling in the School Setting

Idell Natterson, M.S.W.

GROUP COUNSELING IN A SCHOOL SETTING offers unique advantages for enhancing students' growth that are not available in groups that meet in other community settings. When meetings are held in the familiar school environment, it is often more possible to reach students who have minimal or ambivalent motivation. But above all, the counselor has the advantage of almost immediate access to behavioral data from teachers and students. In addition, counselors are in the special position of being able to provide useful additional services, such as adjusting schedules, intervening with teachers, and providing individual as well as the group counseling.

The population of counseling groups in school settings usually differs from that of counseling groups in clinical settings. A segment of students who display few externally identifiable symptoms, are not in serious trouble with their parents or school—but who are aware of inner tension, unhappiness, and unrelatedness—will often more easily avail themselves of a school group. These students may feel that the inner difficulties they are experiencing do not require clinical assistance. Isolated, timid, lacking friends or peer group, they will not seek outside help, but, once their problems are identified and defined, will welcome an available school group.

Others who come to a school group are students who have been disappointed in attempts at therapy in outside facilities but are willing to try

I wish to thank the principal, F. W. Robinson; the superintendent, K. Peters; and the assistant superintendent, W. Jenkins, for encouragement and support in use of the group approach to counseling.

again in a different setting. Students who are fearful of a stigma associated with psychotherapy are also attracted to a school group counseling situation. Students from families with marginal incomes will hesitate to go to a clinic, but they are pleased to receive help when there is no question of financial obligation. Students with low esteem and low self-concept often appreciate a counseling group which gives respite from school groups and classes where orientation is based on success or failure. Associating with peers may be easier in a counseling group, where success or failure is not an issue, but maturity and growth are prized.

In public schools there is an assumption that students operate within the boundaries of normal behavior. Although some students have recognizable problems, most schools look upon these problems as manageable, with maturation and flexible educational approaches encouraging improvement and growth. Every public high school has some extremely troubled students making borderline adjustments, even some who transfer in and out of mental hospitals. Students who are ill are a part of every high school population, but they usually manage to meet the academic demands made on them by the school.

Mental health clinics and family agencies, on the other hand, focus on the treatment of people who are not normal, people whose lives are malfunctioning and disturbed. The ticket for admission is a problem—a child or family in crisis, panic, or disequilibrium. Health is not the assumption at a clinic. The act of entering a clinic is a self-definition of illness: an inability to cope and the need to turn to others.

Turning to others for help is an acceptable type of behavior in the school setting, a normal part of the educational experience. From the time youngsters first enter school, they have opportunities to ask people for help. They can turn to a teacher, teacher's aide, counselor, principal, or vice-principal. Entrance into high school brings them into contact with even more people who specialize in giving help, such as reading consultants, work experience coordinators, math tutors, etc. In the high school setting, which is mostly nonthreatening, it is easy for many to turn to people who are there to help with inner emotional conflicts. The students are not burdened by feeling they are "different" and require "therapy."

Another distinction is that the school counselors behave differently because of the difference of the setting. They assume that the school environment is healthy, and they work more with the healthy part of the student. While pathology is recognized, as it would be in a clinic, the language and perception in the school environment change the counselors' outlook to one of greater optimism. Since outcomes in counseling are frequently positive, an expectation of improvement often becomes a self-fulfilling prophecy.

For a counseling program to be effective, however, administrators and teachers need to be aware of the relatedness between mental health, psychological growth, and education. They must perceive mental health services as integral to the educational experience. Such an awareness exists at Beverly Hills High School, a four-year high school with a student body of 2,500, one of the outstanding secondary schools in the country.

Innovations and creative approaches are welcomed there by an enlightened administration, which not only is interested in the promotion of academic excellence, but also is aware that interpersonal and intrafamilial pressures on students can prevent achievement of educational goals. In addition to a highly trained and psychologically oriented counseling staff, there are both a school psychologist and a home-school coordinator (the author). The latter is an M.S.W. in psychiatric social work. The counselors, psychologist, and home-school coordinator work cooperatively in trying to alleviate social and psychological pressures that inhibit academic growth. They try to facilitate maturational experiences.

Referrals to the home-school coordinator come from students, the principal, counselors, teachers, parents, assistant principals, and secretaries and other employees. These referrals are made primarily for problems involving truancy and school avoidance. Such problems often are symptoms of underlying psychological and intrafamilial problems. Often associated with truancy are disruptive classroom behavior, disruptive general behavior, and conflicts with teachers, administration, or peers. Dormant problems, often identified for the first time, include ruptured communication at home, a potential for running away, and peer conflicts.

Referrals to the home-school coordinator are also made by the school or an individual student or family for consideration of transfer to "continuation school." This is an alternative school which meets off the campus and includes 50 students of normal or above normal intelligence, aged 16 to 18, who can no longer cope with the larger high school.

The home-school coordinator makes a diagnostic study by evaluating information from the student's family, counselor, and teachers, and the school psychologist. The coordinator then decides on a plan which will best serve the student's needs. The plan may have one or several parts, such as a change in school milieu (switching classes or teachers or transferring to continuation school); referral to a private therapist, clinic, or family agency for individual or group therapy; or, if private or community help cannot be arranged, a recommendation for individual or group counseling in the school itself.

Membership in a school counseling group offers students a way to find guidelines for acceptable behavior and a safe place to discuss issues and improve peer relations. A description of one of the groups led by the home-school coordinator will demonstrate other ways in which the students benefit.

*Group description*

The group had been meeting for 1½ years, once a week, except for vacations and holidays. Meetings were *two school periods long,* approximately 1¾ hours. Sessions were scheduled so that the same classes would not be missed more than once every few weeks. Members were responsible for keeping abreast of the current schedule, which was made up and distributed one month in advance.

The eight-member group originally had begun as an *all-girls'* group composed of *ninth through eleventh graders.* Membership remained relatively stable. Vacancies occurred when members graduated, transferred to continuation school, or dropped out because of dissatisfaction and disappointment with the group. Because the girls wanted to learn to be more comfortable in relating to boys, one year after the group began, at the girls' request, *boys were added* to fill openings.

During the first 1½ years, a total of 16 students were in the group. All were of average or above average intelligence, and two were "gifted." All but two attended school erratically and had problems with truancy. Because of excessive absences, several showed poor academic performance. Only 3 of the 16 were from homes having two parents. Divorce or suicide had created the single-parent homes. Two students lived with parents who made repeated suicidal attempts. Although some of the divorced parents had remarried, the student lived with the unmarried parent. The economic standard of living ranged from families on welfare to families of wealth. Several students held jobs to earn spending money, and all, regardless of their parents' economic status, were on the lookout for jobs.

A brief description of some of the members follows: *Gail's* poor school work and erratic attendance were related to her obsession with family pressures and with fear of a sexually provocative father. *Irene,* intimidated by a controlling, suicidal father, had repressed her anger, but through the support of the group risked expressing her rage and became freer as a person. *Terry* had a problem with drugs. She attempted to replace their use by developing better verbal communication. *Nancy,* a Caucasian girl, related only to boys who were Black and cut classes to meet them. *Ada* hated school, was chronically truant, and had no school friends. She had applied for continuation school, had been turned down and recommended to the group. Here she learned that people did care about her, and she was glad she had remained in the regular school program.

An *excerpt from an encounter* in one of the sessions illustrates how clarification and definition of interaction between group members enhanced daily functioning in school, improved family relationships, and stimulated insights in other members.

*Bernice*, ready to run away from home because of constant battling with her mother, had a history of intense fighting with parents, teachers, and peers. She blamed others, held them responsible for her unsatisfying interpersonal relationships, and felt she was the innocent victim. While she yearned for friends and was able to form new friendships easily, when people dropped her she was puzzled and dismayed. She had no awareness of the role she played in this rejection.

Bernice's participation in the group for the first few months was minimal. Listening to others, she sat slumped over with a pained, bored expression. When others spoke, she giggled, acted silly, whispered, or discourteously interrupted. When invited to participate more actively, she said that group communication was inappropriate for her. When members criticized her disruptive behavior, she became defensive and threatened to leave. Her pattern was to arrive late—sometimes by a whole period—barge in and self-righteously justify her lateness by claiming she had needed to attend the previous class. She said her grades were bad enough and she did not want to annoy her teachers, who were already critical of her group attendance.

I learned from her teachers that Bernice's grades were, indeed, caused by her absences from classes. In fact, she rarely showed up at all for certain classes! The teachers also reported the same provocative behavior and immaturity in the classroom, such as giggling when others made a serious effort. *School behavior paralleled group behavior:* peers and teachers were provoked.

One day, when Bernice arrived a full hour late, an important encounter was occurring between two members of the group. Bernice realized the encounter's importance; she found it interesting and wished to be included. And so Bernice loudly and intrusively asked what was going on.

My answer was that if she'd come on time she'd know. A reaction followed. Bernice cried and had hysterics. She had rightly observed my annoyance, but saw my confrontation as rejection. She defensively insisted that this time she had a good reason for being late: She'd been at home talking with her mother. Was I trying to interfere with her relationship with her mother? she asked provocatively. Didn't I feel it was just as important for her to be with her mother as to attend the group meeting? She accused us of picking on her and singling her out for attack and said she could not understand the reason. She had come to the group for help, and if this was our idea of help, she didn't need it.

I interpreted to her how she had invited the attack by repeatedly coming in late and disrupting others. I pointed out that this was a characteristic action on her part, resulting in the negative reaction of others to her. Bernice wanted to leave the group after this encounter, but she requested two individual sessions. In these, I encouraged her to return and work out her negative feelings before discontinuing. When she came back to the group, the members supported her staying—and she stayed. She began to participate more realistically, and she faced the part she had played in provoking others.

Bernice's outbursts provided the *stimulus for another member of the group to get in touch with his own angry feelings.* Doug was frightened to see rage and emotion expressed so openly. His low self-esteem and lack of friends had been of several years' duration. Lonely and isolated, an avid reader who avoided social relationships with both sexes, he would miss school for weeks at a time. He reacted to Bernice's outburst with depression and guilt. Although there had been only a minimal exchange between them, he felt he might have been responsible for her rage.

Feeling responsible for the unhappiness of others turned out to be his usual and typical pattern. If anger, rage, or disagreement were expressed, he felt responsible. On one occasion he even left the group because he believed he was the cause of hostile exchanges. I interpreted to him that he did not have the power to control others to this extent. He was unable to believe that the group had warm feelings for him. He warded off praise, expressions of friendship, and positive communication by either not hearing it, misunderstanding, or devaluing and diminishing the character of the sender.

Struck by the depth of Bernice's rage, he came to my office on the day following her outburst. Although he recognized Bernice's overreaction to my interpretation, he expressed guilt feelings that he had been responsible. He saw Bernice as a person similar to his mother, who also overreacted. He now revealed to me that his mother was ill and that for years she had blamed him for her illness. His burden of guilt was ever present. Connecting unhappiness in others to his presence had caused him to live a hermitlike existence with his books.

This group encounter and its interpretation, insight, and clarification *dif-*

*fered from what might have happened in a community group*. Many features overlap, but some distinctions exist. Because the group met at school, the home-school coordinator was able to observe the students in the halls and form a picture of their daily functioning with peers. From talks with counselors and teachers, the coordinator was able to learn about both of the above students and their characteristic ways of behaving. Teachers tend to be relatively objective. They are in daily contact with students. Their reactions and observations provide invaluable clues in diagnosis and therapy. Thus, school group leaders gain a broad picture of current habits and patterns of functioning, enabling them more readily to recognize these characteristics when they occur in the group.

In a community agency, where the objective information about the adolescent comes from the parent, there is conscious or unconscious censoring and distortion. Telephone or letter communications between an outside therapist and the school are often inadequate. The direct observation of daily functioning at school can give a clearer picture of students' behavior.

Another distinct feature of a school group is that members frequently point out how they perceive the other members in classes, halls, cafeterias, and other areas. Students are interested in finding out how they come across to others and are frequently surprised to learn they are regarded as friendly, standoffish, or stuck-up. Thus, an invaluable feedback mechanism is provided for the student who does not know how he appears to others.

A *negative aspect of school groups* must be mentioned. As in all groups, students—particularly in the opening meeting—are fearful of disclosure to others. They guard their secrets carefully. Confidentiality and guarding against its breach is a factor that must be dealt with constantly. There is a great temptation to go out and "spill the beans." Community groups from which the youngsters leave and go their separate ways might not have this particular problem.

The advantages of group counseling in a school setting far outweigh the disadvantages. The home-school coordinator often locates troubled students and, through the use of group structure and counseling, gives them opportunities to grow and mature in a context of peer relationships. School groups reach and help a segment of students who may never find their way to community agencies and clinics.

# CHAPTER 8

# Themes in Group Counseling with Adolescents

## Marilyn Bates, Ph.D.

SINCE THE UNEXPECTED CONFRONTATION is the expected encounter in group counseling, even seasoned group counselors approach each session with an edge of anxiety, knowing they need all the professional skill they can muster to deal with the complex nuances of the group's dynamics. Inexperienced group counselors may approach their first session naively confident that their individual counseling skills will carry them through the complexities of the group process, but it requires only a few grueling sessions to raise their panic level to the red button stage. Unfortunately, there are no panic buttons in the group counseling room. There is only a small group of students putting trust in the professional skills of the group counselor.

It was in an effort to improve their professional skills that *one group of counselors critiqued tapes* of their group counseling sessions recorded over a period of a year in a seminar at the University of Southern California under the guidance of Dr. Jane Warters. A facet of professional competency which grew out of the seminar was an awareness that a group counselor could anticipate *certain patterns of content* in the group process. The element of the unexpected will never be removed from human dynamics, of course, but it was found through listening to many taped recordings that there was a reservoir of themes which arose in the counseling content of group after group. It is hoped that a delineation of these recurring elements will be of help to other counselors as they work with groups. The themes have been somewhat facetiously entitled: "My Vices," "Outwitting the Adults," "Problem Parents," "My Brother, the Brat," "My Public Image," "Nobody Loves Me," and "Let's Change the Rules." Other themes emerge occasionally, such as fear of mental illness, concern over academic ability, dating problems, and fascination for the macabre and death, but these did not appear consistently. The seven major themes which are developed here seem to account for much of the group counseling content when the counselees are adolescents. Obviously, all identifying data have been omitted from the extracts of recordings which are presented as illustrative material, necessarily out of context.

## My Vices*

Generally speaking, no particular sequence of themes was noted, but the "My Vices" theme tended to appear early in the sessions and then, once worked over, was given little further attention by the counselees. While at times this verbal "muscle flexing" consisted of efforts to top each other's tales, often severely taxing the counselor's credulity, usually a serious discussion of values evolved. In the nonjudgmental atmosphere of the group counseling situation, the students were able to turn to an examination of the reason for their "vices," analyzing with each other possible consequences, working through rationalizations to the true reasons for their behavior. The following example is fairly typical of the kind of discussion which can be expected in a group counseling situation:

*Mavis:* If you're going to smoke and your parents don't let you, you're just going to smoke behind their backs anyway.

*Counselor:* You feel it's better to tell them and be honest than sneak behind their backs.

*Jean:* I do. I mean, I can see how your parents wouldn't want you to smoke around their friends, but I think it's better to smoke in front of them than behind their backs.

*Counselor:* Implying that if a son or daughter smoked in front of their friends, parents might be embarrassed?

*Jean:* Yeah.

*Bill:* My parents don't feel that way. I asked my dad whether he wanted me to smoke in front of him or behind his back, and he said he didn't want me to smoke at all!

*Gary:* Does your dad smoke?

---

* Editor's note: This paper was written prior to the marijuana, narcotic, and pill era of adolescent experimentation. References to use and abuse of these substances would appear more often in group discussions occurring currently.

*Bill:* Yeah, but they try to tell me it's a bad habit. "I'd sure like to get off it, Son. You'd better not start." But they keep right on smoking.

*Counselor:* I hear you questioning whether it's all right for parents to smoke and not let their kids smoke.

*Bill:* No, I don't think it is. If they don't want you to smoke, then they should set the example and not do it. If they don't want you to drink and run around, then they shouldn't drink and run around, 'cause you usually go by what your own parents set before you.

*Counselor:* That there should be one standard for all ages?

*Mavis:* I disagree with that! I think you should do as you're told by your parents. When you're young, you're not old enough to do all the things you can do when you're grown up.

*Jean:* I agree with you, Mavis. Part of the enjoyment of smoking is the sneaking around. When my mom told me I could smoke, I didn't enjoy it any more and I stopped.

*Counselor:* Part of the fun was the feeling of getting away with something. . . .

As the students elaborate on their "vices," comments on drinking frequently follow a discussion of smoking. Ordinarily the drinking problem is not developed as thoroughly, although it patterns into the same general attitudes:

*Mary:* The only reason kids drink is to think they're big.

*Joe:* Yeah, you can't have it, so that's why you do it.

The groups usually capsulate the "My Vices" theme into a conclusion that the main attraction involved is the lure of forbidden fruits, yet seldom do they suggest seriously that teen-agers be allowed more freedom in these areas.

### Outwitting the Adults

In group counseling, the getting-away-with-it idea occurs over and over in many guises. Indeed, the pervasive theme, "Outwitting the Adults," seemed to occur in one form or another in almost every session. Outwitting the adults is an activity which apparently occupies a great deal of a teen-ager's time and energy and consequently is a ubiquitous topic in group counseling. The adults may be teachers, parents, juvenile authorities—the "who" was not so important as the process of playing the game. Interestingly enough, the "Outwitting the Adults" game is not taken particularly seriously, and the teen-ager seems to expect to be on the losing side as often as not, taking wins or losses quite philosophically:

> *Cliff:* This dope sitting here cried his way out of a ticket for speeding. I'm not kidding. He told the cops such a big sob story about how he'd try to do better and didn't mean to be going so fast, and the cop believed him and let him off. He really put on an act!
>
> *Joe:* Well, I'm proud of it. The dumb cop believed me, so I must have made it good. And I didn't have to pay, did I?
>
> ———
>
> *June:* In the cafeteria we had the most fun. When the teacher wasn't looking, we would flip peas on our spoons over onto the other kids, and then when the teacher would look around, we would look innocent-like, like something was hitting us. Boy, did we ever fool that teacher.
>
> *Roger:* Yeah, and then you got caught and got in trouble.
>
> *June:* Sure, but we had fun first.
>
> ———
>
> *John:* When we needed eggs for an egg fight, we would go from house to house and pretend to be on a scavenger hunt, and tell the people we needed two things, a green tomato and a rotten egg. So they would say, "All we have is a good egg," and we would say, "Okay," and that way we'd get enough eggs for our egg fight. Almost everyone gave us eggs.

It is the "Outwitting the Adults" and "My Vices" themes which place the greater pressure on any "teacher trace" which may remain in the counselor. The urge to make "tut-tut" noises may be hard to resist, but if the counselor steadfastly reflects and clarifies, he can almost be sure that group members will themselves present society's views of right and wrong. For example, after a group had griped at length about how the juvenile authorities picked on teen-agers, a rather silent member spoke up:

> *Judy:* Now I want a chance to talk. You guys have a pretty dim view of life. You really do. Jill, you asked for trouble in the stupid way you snuck out of the show.
>
> *Jill:* (downcast voice) Yeah, I suppose so.
>
> *Judy:* And Dave, the way you ran from the cops—common sense would tell you . . . Me, I've gotten busted at so many parties. I've got a record bigger than Abraham Lincoln's right arm (laughter). I mean it. But common sense tells you a kid, a teen-ager don't go out in public

with beer. You show a cop a little bit of respect and he'll show you respect. You get smart with a cop and he's going to get smart right back.

*Maria:* Yeah, half the kids who get in trouble are just asking for it. If they wouldn't talk to the cops like they do, they wouldn't get in half the trouble they're in. Sneaking isn't the right thing.

At times, as a member verbalizes his actions and reactions, the awareness of individual responsibility appears through a student's own self-analysis, rather than another group member's reaction:

*Bob:* I guess I just don't have a conscience. I didn't take into consideration of how my mother would feel when I ran away. I didn't think of calling her and telling her I was okay. I guess I just thought about myself 'cause I guess maybe I'm selfish or something.

## Problem Parents

The theme of students' relationship with their parents has appeared in tape analysis almost as frequently as "Outwitting the Adults," but the latter is usually a maneuvering, manipulative sort of game, which is not taken too seriously. The parental relationship theme usually appears with overtones of pathos and involves the adolescent struggle for identity. It also involves deep feelings and often deep pain. Groups return to the "Problem Parents" theme over and over throughout the course of the group counseling sessions.

*Avis:* You might not show it, basically right out. But deep down you may think you despise your parents and might tell everybody you hate them, but deep down you actually know you really love your parents. Kids under 18 have to have someone over them, and they actually are afraid of losing that, but they don't really know it.

*Counselor:* Afraid of losing the security of having someone responsible for you.

*Avis:* Yeah. Everybody wants to be wanted. If you do something wrong and your parents put you on restriction, it proves they love you.

*Jim:* But parents will love you no matter what you do.

*Greg:* You might not lose their love, but you lose their respect and then you lose your freedom.

The students seem almost desperate at times as they explore the parent-child relationship, but the process of talking about their feelings and problems in the safety of the group counseling situation seems to lessen tensions, even though the problem is insoluble for the time being:

> *Bill:* Parents seem to be afraid to let you go out on your own. They don't want to lose their little baby. My mother's afraid I'll move out. I'm just her little boy. I work, pay my own bills, my car, all my clothes, but I'm still supposed to rely on her.
>
> *Counselor:* She wants you to lean on her a bit.
>
> *Bill:* Yeah, she just won't let go. She just can't realize I'm big enough that maybe I can support myself now. Sure, I don't pay for my food or the bed I sleep in yet, but . . .

Two subcategories of the "Problem Parents" relationship theme appear consistently. The first is an irritated resentment with being told what to do. Since the teen-agers feel that they are old enough to do what is expected without constant reminders (the unfortunate fact that this is not usually true is beside the point), they find the parental prompting which earlier was taken in good grace now an intolerable "nagging."

> *Greg:* I have an hour after I get home from school before I go to work, and the minute I walk in that house I get nagged at—nothing but complaints. I get woke up in the morning with, "Your room's a mess." "Get up, you're going to be late for school." But never anything else, never anything good.
>
> *Counselor:* You feel like you just can't do anything right.
>
> *Greg:* You can't. No matter what you try to do, it's always wrong.

The second subcategory concerns parental relationship within the framework of peer relationships, usually centering around resentment over not being able to make plans with friends because parents reserve the right to make last-minute changes:

> *Ruth:* If your parents make plans and they want to do something and the dishes aren't done, they say, "Oh, let them wait until tomorrow." But if the kids make plans, the dishes have to be done *right now*, no matter what! Because the kids have to grow up to be RESPONSIBLE PEOPLE.
>
> *Nancy:* So when we get older we do the same thing—we're not responsible. We let the dishes wait, just like our parents do.
>
> *Counselor:* One rule for parents and another for kids.

*Jean:* Yeah, but our parents must have had the same trouble we have when they were kids with parents.

*Counselor:* It's kind of a circle, then, that goes on and on . . .

*Nancy:* Yeah, but I'm going to change it. I don't want my kids to go through what I have. I want them to be self-reliant, but not to the point where they have no affection for their family.

Sometimes amateur psychiatry gets into the act:

*Jim:* I'll get ready and my mother knows I have a date and want to leave, but she keeps thinking up little things I have to do first—and she does this just to irritate me.

*Lila:* No, it's not to irritate you. It's just to keep you so you won't go out and leave. She wants you to stay with her. She's jealous of your girl friend.

### My Brother, the Brat

The examination of the "Problem Parent" often involves a discussion of sibling rivalry, sometimes long and bitterly developed. The "My Brother, the Brat" theme does not seem to involve as deep a feeling as does the parental relationship theme. This theme, however, is usually developed with many expressions of hostility:

*Joan:* And that's another thing. I get $3 a week for lunch, and I have to go without lunch and save my money for clothes. My little brother has lots saved up, but when *he* wants clothes, he gets all he wants.

*Jean:* Maybe because he's younger.

*Joan:* No, it's because he gets straight *A*'s in school.

*Jean:* Well, that does it. That makes them proud of him. He's a model kid. He's the one who will get the car and everything else.

*Joan:* Yeah, anything my little brother wants, he gets.

Since the group process presents an opportunity for members to interact— and learn how to interact—in the "substitute family" group, the "My Brother, the Brat" theme may occur as heated interchange between group members:

*Ronda:* Shut up! You think you know everything and you don't. You can't smoke on a school campus.

*Eric: I* think I know everything!

*Ronda:* You just said, "When you're 18 they can't do nothing," and you're so positive, so sure, and you're wrong. So don't blab out like that.

Or the theme may be reflected in a student's value system:

*Joe:* It's all right to pick on little kids 'cause when you were little everybody picked on you.

Or it may be expressed as resentment against a silent member:

*Martin:* Why doesn't she ever talk? She just sits there the whole time.

*Counselor:* Mattie's silence bothers you.

*Martin:* Yeah, she never says a thing. She just sits there and looks at you.

*Mattie:* I like to just listen. It makes me nervous to talk.

*Martin:* Yeah, but it makes me nervous when you don't. I want to know what you're thinking.

The group will find that one of the values of the group process lies in the opportunity it presents for members to learn social relationships within the small, controlled environment of the group situation. And time spent on practicing these skills is time well spent, whether it takes the form of venting hostilities caused by sibling rivalry as in the "My Brother, the Brat" theme or the form of seeking a clarification of self-concepts.

## My Public Image

The adolescents' struggle to clarify a value system which parallels and permeates their developmental task of seeking to discover "Who Am I?" seldom emerges as a clear-cut theme, but will thread in and out of the sessions as the students examine the behavior of both adults and young people. This theme has been labeled "My Public Image." The intense pre-occupation with self, particularly the physical self, of the teen-ager, makes this topic a very sensitive one for both boys and girls. At times it takes the form of trying to determine the "proper" way to behave in public:

*Sue:* I don't think either girls or boys should fight. It doesn't prove anything.

*Counselor:* The boys have been saying that boys should fight, but this is not acceptable behavior for girls.

*Pam:* But if someone walks up to you and calls you a filthy name you have to defend yourself.

*Counselor:* That somehow the name rubbed off on you and you had to fight to get rid of it.

*Pam:* That's right.

*Steve:* It would be better for a girl to ignore it. If you fight you're on the same level as the person who called you a name.

*Sue:* When someone calls you a name, they're putting themselves so low for even trying to start a fight.

*Counselor:* In other words, why sink to their level?

*Sue:* Yeah, that's it.

The varying standards of different age groups seem well understood and accepted (with resignation, albeit) as part of the struggle for a suitable "Public Image."

*Vince:* Yeah, my mom tells me not to invite my friends over when she has company. My friends aren't bad, they just look bad. They have a jerky appearance.

*Counselor:* Your mother doesn't approve of the way they look.

*Vince:* If she's going to have company, she tells me, "Tell your friends to stay away today." They're just guys from the pool hall.

*Counselor:* You seem to resent this.

*Vince:* No, they look like jerks, and I don't want her to be embarrassed. I think she's right about their dress.

*Marvin:* Well, I mind it. If my parents don't like my friends, they don't have to like me.

In line with the frankness of a real family situation, group members often pass candid comments about the appearance of group members, and the "My Public Image" theme gets very personal at times:

*Terry:* You mean you paid $6 to have your hair styled?

*John:* Yeah, I had it styled a week ago, and look at it. It looks so much better.

*Bob:* And if you'd comb it right, it'd look even more better.

*Terry:* (to counselor) What do you think about boys' getting their hair styled?

*Counselor:* The thing that matters most is what do *you* think?

*Terry:* I think it's a waste.

*John:* Just 'cause you're a surfer.

*Terry:* Yeah, man, everybody's going back toward women. I don't like it.

*Counselor:* I hear you saying you think it's sissified.

*Terry:* I sure do.

*John:* It isn't sissified. It keeps your hair in place. They have hair spray for men now.

*Counselor:* It's all a matter of getting used to?

*Bob:* What about perfume? Women had perfume first, and men wear perfume now.

Besides a discussion of personal appearance, the "My Public Image" theme may delve into personality characteristics:

*Rick:* I think you're a leech. You borrow money and don't pay it back and make a big joke out of everything. You invite yourself everywhere.

*Rob:* What do you mean, leech? You're talking about yourself when you said that about me.

*Counselor:* You seem to feel, Rick, that since you share money when you have it, you kind of expect others to do the same.

*Rick:* Sure. If I borrow a dime, I don't expect to pay it back, but a dollar is different.

*Rob:* Well, I think that's being a leech!

The degree to which the "My Public Image" theme contributes to a change or clarification of self-concept is difficult to assess. Silent members may be gaining as much as the more vocal members. As much development may take place between sessions as during sessions. Of this we can be certain: The "Public Image" theme constitutes an important content of group counseling.

*Nobody Loves Me*

An elaboration of attitudes toward school in general is, of course, a frequent topic in discussions, but as a group progresses and feelings are revealed, a common reaction which can be identified is the student's feeling of helplessness, of being an insignificant cipher in a world which belongs to the adults. The "Nobody Loves Me" theme usually develops after groups have been together for some time and members have learned to feel comfortable with each other—and with the counselor.

> *Richard:* Some teachers get a first impression of you and they keep that all the time, and actually you're not that way. Sometimes you're judged by the way you dress, or the way you look. A kid can walk in the first day and they'll look at you and you can just see them say, "You and I aren't going to get along!" They sort of seem to have a grudge against you like they knew you all your life.
>
> *Counselor:* Are you saying they jump to conclusions because of your hair or your dress. . . .
>
> *Richard:* That's about it, about it.
>
> *Counselor:* You seem to feel there's no solution.
>
> *Richard:* Well, parents take the part of the teacher before they take the part of the student, so you haven't anyone who will help you.
>
> *Brenda:* I don't see why grown-ups have the right to jump to conclusions about kids. And I don't see why they think they have the right to tell you how horrible you look and how horrible you are, and we have to stand there in front of the whole class and take it or we get in more trouble.
>
> *Richard:* Yeah, just be criticized and not say a word!
>
> *Brenda:* We ought to have the right to speak—even to adults—in the right way, of course.
>
> *Counselor:* You're saying, then, that you are expected to respect adults, and they should treat you with the same respect and courtesy.
>
> *Sandra:* Yeah, just because you're young doesn't mean you're inferior. Adults think they're better than us; we're only students, just little grades in a book.
>
> *Brenda:* Well, some teachers do care. They don't all feel that way. If you do the right thing, and you do your work, you don't have trouble.
>
> *Counselor:* Sort of the idea that people bring their troubles on themselves?

*Let's Change the Rules*

As feelings about school and being a student are explored, usually groups will spend time devising "better" ways of doing things and seem to enjoy the game of "Let's Change the Rules." Some groups perform this as a purely academic exercise, knowing full well that existing conditions are not likely to be changed. And at other times a press for action may develop. Individual members may require the counselor's subtle support as they advance highly impractical suggestions, which are met by the well-expressed derision of the group. The "Let's Change the Rules" theme may also hold a trap for unwary counselors as the groups try to maneuver them into defending and justifying school rules. Or they may seek to make the group counselor their "front" person with the administration, rather than submit their suggestions themselves:

*Tom:* Suspension is stupid. That's what a lot of people want. Just a vacation, so they can go home and goof off. They don't want to go to school anyway.

*Carla:* Yeah, when I got suspended my mother was mad at me for one day. Then she let me go to the beach and stuff the rest of the time. She didn't care.

*Jerry:* Yeah, detention doesn't help, either. Everybody turns around and does the same thing over.

*Counselor:* What do you suggest?

*Jerry:* Well, pick up papers—or something.

---

*Ronald:* I don't see why we don't have open campus. Other schools do. This makes us feel like we're in jail. Colleges don't make their students stay inside a fence, like prisoners.

---

*Bill:* I don't see why we can't have a smoking room. Other schools do. Why can't the counselors do something about it?

At times the "Let's Change the Rules" theme can be the springboard for sensible action, but again, counselors must be alert that they are not drawn into a commitment for action, but that the initiative is left in the hands of the students:

*Carl:* Well, I think that's one thing the school needs, a car club. We had one last year and the year before we had one, too, but this year it was discontinued, and it was closed to only mostly the auto shop, and the school just didn't get behind it at all. They never put our name in the bulletin or anything and, well, that's really a boss thing for a school to have is a car club. You'd be surprised how a car club—that's almost like a continuation school for high school dropouts. It's really the socializing part of it. A car club is really the thing, you know. It speaks well for your school, just as a good football team speaks well of your school.

*Dick:* It doesn't speak well of your school if half the guys in it are ding bats and. . . .

*Carl:* Man, you're not going to fool around with anyone who gets tickets; in fact, that's the biggest rule.

*Counselor:* You'd like to see the car club started up again.

*Carl:* Yeah, I think we should do something.

Frequently, as the "Let's Change the Rules" theme progresses, group members verbalize a preference for law and order:

*Tod:* I don't like teachers that let kids do anything they want.

*Rodney:* Yeah. I like a teacher that can control the class, make them be quiet when they want to, but who is real cool, you know, laughs every once in a while because—I don't think a teacher should just go in there and go right by the book, day after day.

## In conclusion

The process of group counseling is a fascinating one and one which makes great demands on the counselor, both inexperienced and experienced. It is hoped that this teasing out of themes from the many tape recordings of one group of counselors will contribute to the professional skills of other group counselors. The light titling of the themes, "My Vices," "Outwitting the Adults," "Problem Parents," "My Brother, the Brat," "My Public Image," "Nobody Loves Me," and "Let's Change the Rules," is not intended to imply that the group counseling process is to be taken lightly. The world of the adolescent is a very real world, and the rules are for keeps. Your role of trusted counselor, which permits you to enter this world, carries with it the responsibility to understand and to accept. If you dare judge or moralize, the masks will be assumed, and politely but firmly the doors to this world will be closed. If you can enter into this world reflecting, clarifying, summarizing, in the group but not of the group, functioning as a counselor and not a member, then through the group process the counselees can clarify their value system as they struggle with their search for identity. You, as counselor, may even do a little of the same.

# CHAPTER 9

# Small-Group Work in an Affluent High School

## Robert H. Oyler, Ph.D.

SUCH CONSTRUCTS AS "CODE OF SILENCE" and "generation gap" provoke a variety of responses in caretaking adults. The writer has made a persistent attempt to generate some "sound" in the "silence" or to be *exactly* "30 years old" during those "gap" years in which youth less than 30 and adults over 30 mistrust each other. This attempt included immediate but discreet reinforcement and attention to self-referred or to walk-in counselees from our high school. It also included multiple counseling as well as consultation with self-selected parents. Because much is said about counseling that frightens counselors, I wanted to say something about group work as it really was for us.

A *predominantly self-referred group* of ninth to eleventh grade girls commenced regular weekly meetings at midyear. Two girls' groups met one hour per week during those class periods which were most feasible or were least committed for academic or for employment purposes. Typically, *ten girls* participated in each counseling group on a voluntary basis throughout the balance of the semester. Six (from both original groups) asked to continue meeting through July and during the following school year.

Four anonymous responses to "Who are you?" were made in writing by each group member during early meetings. These were read aloud anonymously and discussed early in those groups to *help clarify "Why are we here, really?"* Many of these self-perceptions indicated: (a) confused identity; (b) disgust with own variability, hypocrisy, and self-consciousness; (c) guilt; (d) concern over dependency on parents and peer group; (e) hesitancy to trust and to confide: (f) wanting to be wanted and loved; (g) social and philosophical concern; (h) uncertainty regarding future; (i) difficulty communicating within the family; and (j) pursuit of individuality. Typical staff descriptions of the group included: "has family problems," "uses narcotics," "hippie," "delinquent," "poor self-image," "capable, but not achieving."

Counselees were permitted to smoke during group sessions. *Limits were few and simple*—no breach of confidentiality, no physical harm to other members, care of the meeting room, one person talking at a time, and setting length of sessions.

Verbal and nonverbal interaction seemed to deal with a variety of recurrent themes*: disturbing conversations and events in families; mixed feelings about continued use of narcotics (to "put down" or not "put down," or both); "My damn parents"; "My own 'damn-bivalence' "; racial prejudice; materialism; sexuality; popularity and self-worth; studies; relations with selected school staff; delight and dismay in intimate friendship with both sexes; runaway and suicide; "My poor, unhappy, pathetic parents"; "Am I pregnant?"; how to express or handle anger; guilt, deceit and lying; true womanhood, maturation; freedom; "Is college for me or not?"; counselors; Vietnam; personal depression; "Am I letting my parents or myself down?"; death; helpful books and teachers.

Other than sincere liking for the counselees and an attempt to be personally honest and authentic, the psychologist consciously employed *some technical strategies*: (a) trying to put group members' feelings into his words and guess what is wrong; (b) providing labels or concepts for common human experiences or behaviors (e.g., rationalization, ambivalence, projection, and disillusionment); (c) describing, facilitating, and regulating interaction between members; (d) supporting members, particularly during crisis (often in individual counseling at hours other than group sessions), or being a person who makes the group member feel someone *does* care; (e) providing leading questions and general information; (f) offering alternative explanations for consideration; (g) answering questions in an honest and humane way; (h) helping generate "sets" of solutions; and (i) listening carefully for a long time and clarifying verbalizations.

These behaviors seemed to counteract self-doubt and to meet deep human needs arising from within students whose affluent homes provided primarily for bodily and material needs. Student contacts, affectional ties, and communication with fathers were typically poor or nonexistent. Mothers were

---

* See Chapter 8.

more available but were often not respected or were irritants to group members. The youngsters did not feel that they were popular or well socialized with their age mates. "Triangles" (all combinations and permutations of both sexes) were rampant. The group seemed to provide peer acceptance during jealousies, clashes, and periods of real inadequacy or failure.

In Leo Goldman's terms (see Figure 1), the group functioned at content-process interaction levels 8 and 9 most of the time (Goldman, 1962).

*Supporting adjuncts* to the group work beyond the individual counseling previously mentioned included: (a) meeting parents of almost 50 percent of group members (usually more than once) in an effort at mutual interpretation of needs and behavior (requested by student, or approved by student if parent initiated the conference request); (b) conferences with counselors, teachers, and dean of women; (c) referral, with member's consent and knowledge, for medical assistance, family counseling, foster placement, etc.; (d) employment, placement; (e) cross-age teaching or teacher aide work with primary age children; (f) alteration of courses and academic demands; (g) continuation school placement; (h) leader's availability by telephone 24 hours per day; and (i) his having a red beard.

It must be emphasized that *confidentiality was maintained* in the conferences mentioned above as requested by the group member. She gave prior permission to the leader to respond to or initiate such conferences; certain topics were "out of conference bounds" according to the member's maturity and wishes. The leader gave judicious but complete recapitulations to the member or answered her questions honestly afterward. One major value of group participation was absolute privacy to the girls.

*Evaluation of counseling end points* or personal growth has been informal or subjective. Earlier groups were formally evaluated with pre- and post-Q sorts, parent and teacher questionnaires, studies of grade point averages, etc. The points in the following "ledger" seem representative and valid:

*Negative events*

1. Three members acted out more and were detained by police; one is currently in juvenile hall pending placement. The other two are on probation and attend continuation school. Narcotics and theft were the complaints.

2. In two families, problems arose between parents, and separation resulted.

3. Two other parents have been painfully self-conscious about their daughter's need for the group counseling.

4. Three students did not participate verbally or overtly more than once, though they regularly attended. (One-to-one counseling before group participation is needed by some.)

5. Some staff objected formally to the group's smoking privilege, but this privilege was probably the major motive for three girls' attendance in the group.

6. Some girls became highly dependent on each other and on the leader; a weaning process is necessary.

7. Occasionally, two or three girls seemed to be vying or competing to have the most dramatic or serious problem to put before the group.

8. No dramatic, statistically significant rise in grade point average can be demonstrated the same school year for the groups, as groups (individuals showed improvement, however).

9. The school psychologist got fewer pupils tested and placed in special education classes.

## Positive results

1. Voluntary group attendance held up in over 90 percent of members.

2. Four of six members requested continuation through summer (one month vacation) and returned in September.

3. Five parents have reported improvement. Two parents spontaneously reported depression on the days the group met, which may or may not have meant benefit. No comment came from the majority of parents. One parent called to sample the leader's philosophy and style and then expressed relief and approval that "you aren't a Freudian psychoanalyst."

4. Spontaneous verbalized feedback from students took the form of exchange of crisis-inspired poetry; a fatherless one's calling the leader "Daddy"; "I couldn't hack it without the group" from a girl with three suicide attempts; "I'd have dropped out of school long ago except for the Monday group"; "I've been trying to put down narcotics . . . I've put down for six weeks now"; "My second semester grades are the best I've ever made; they blew my parents' mind"; "It's so bitchin' to be giving instead of getting"; "We've had beautiful conversations. Yeah, we're loaded; we been smokin' people."

5. Significant *nonverbal behaviors* from several members were: (a) repeated incidents of spontaneous help and moral support between members in leader's absence; (b) smiles and enthusiasm regarding reopening of school in September and first-day hugs for the leader; (c) flowers for the leader's hospitalized wife; (d) some patience or suspended retorts with parents;

spontaneous chores or assistance around the house; some empathy for parents; (e) a few changes in sexual practices, dating behavior, and choice of companions.

6. *Staff comment* came mostly from counselors and the dean of women, who observed that students are happier, more articulate, staying in class more, and seem to have more self-identity.

There are *many implications to the multiple counseling* as it happened and to these statements which attempt to describe it. In closing, I'd like to emphasize several points:

Growing students in affluent communities still have psycho-bio-social concerns which can preempt their intellectual awareness or can close them to school learning.

Contrary to common professional belief, conflicted adolescents will refer themselves to adult counselors they perceive as liking them (caring), as trustworthy, and as open to listening to new ideas or to the unconventional.

Sensitive, fatherless, uncertain girls of above-average intelligence in an affluent community particularly need male adult and peer support during developmental crises or depressions. (The same phenomenon has been observed with motherless junior high school boys in this district who need female counselors.)

School policies should describe different dispositions and procedures in cases of self-referred versus detected narcotics use.

Such group counseling is essentially combatting dissatisfaction with self and requires good referral resources in the community (especially medical and family counseling).

Adults attempting such a counseling project should expect to spend a lot of time and energy on it, with many interruptions to office routine. They will need what Hinckley and Hermann (1951) call "prudent management of personal feelings." This prudence is constantly tested; without control a leader can become insensitive, "just one of the group," or too involved.

Before group counseling is undertaken, *leaders will need to prethink their ethical position and procedures* on questions of students' withholding information from their parents; in-school cheating and "cutting"; teen-age drinking and promiscuity; various behaviors with narcotics (e.g., sale versus use, addictive and nonaddictive); runaways; and suicide. Group members test leaders for articulateness and authenticity in such behaviors.

FIGURE 1

Interaction of Content and Process in Group Guidance,
Group Counseling, and Group Therapy

| | PROCESS | | |
|---|---|---|---|
| CONTENT | *Level I*<br>Leader plans topics<br>Lecture and recitation<br>Facts and skills emphasized<br>Units in regular classes | *Level II*<br>Leader and group members collaborate in planning topics<br>Discussions, projects, panels, visits<br>Attitudes and opinions emphasized<br>Separate guidance groups meet on schedule | *Level III*<br>Topics originate with group members<br>Free discussion, role playing<br>Feelings and needs emphasized<br>Groups organized as needed, meet as needed |
| *Type A*<br>Usual school subject matter: mathematics, English, etc. | 1 | 4 | 7 |
| *Type B*<br>School-related topics: the world of work, choosing a college, how to study, etc. | 2 | 5 | 8 |
| *Type C*<br>Non-school topics: dating behavior, parent-child relations, handling frustrations, etc. | 3 | 6 | 9 |

Explanation of Figure 1 (from: Leo Goldman, Ph.D. Group Guidance: Content and Process. *Personnel and Guidance Journal*, Feb. 1962, pp. 518-522):

The thesis here is that for a group activity to move from the teaching of a school subject to a guidance activity requires changes both of content and process. Referring to Figure 1, the movement is diagonally from upper left to lower right. In cell 1 would be found the kind of classroom that is probably typical at the college level and that decreases in frequency of occurrence as one moves backward through secondary and elementary schools. At the other extreme, in cell 9, is the kind of activity that is usually referred to as group therapy. Somewhere around cell 5 is what the writer would call group guidance; in cells 6 and 8 are the activities that he would identify with the label group counseling or multiple counseling. Others prefer to define these terms differently and would therefore place them differently among the cells.

In the writer's observations, group guidance and group counseling have in many instances gone awry in schools because they have been cell 2 and 3 kinds of operations. . . . The group leaders have usually been classroom teachers, many of them without any special training in guidance, who spend only a fraction of their time in this so-called guidance activity, be it in a homeroom, a unit of an academic subject, or a once-a-week "guidance" or "occupations" class. It should not surprise us, then, that they use much the same approach in their guidance activities as in the classroom: assigning readings in textbooks, asking pupils to recite in the class, doing much explaining, advising, and exhorting, and even giving grades at the end of a unit or course. Imagine, a grade in "Guidance!"

Even well-trained guidance counselors often find it difficult to depart from Level I in their group guidance work. They too have had their group leadership experience as teachers in subject-matter classrooms. Unfortunately, they receive little preparation for group guidance activities in most counselor education programs; supervised practice in group guidance or group counseling is almost unheard of. It is understandable, then, that even professional, full-time counselors find it difficult to shift to Level II and III approaches.

What seems to happen in many schools, then, is that "group guidance" becomes merely another academic subject. Yet counselors, teachers, and administrators sometimes expect Level II or III outcomes, such as more realistic planning, changes of attitude, and even changes of observed behavior. When these outcomes are not obtained, too often "group guidance" is denounced as the culprit.

*Teaching at Levels II and III.* To complete the analysis of Figure 1, we should note that not all teachers use Level I methods exclusively. There are English teachers who use a novel or play to help pupils to understand their own motivations and problems. There are home economics teachers who use a variety of methods to sharpen and develop children's understandings of the roles of various family members. There are social studies teachers who stimulate youngsters to explore opinions, attitudes, and prejudices regarding political and economic matters. One might say that all these teachers are performing guidance kinds of functions. The writer would prefer to regard these rather as a variety of teaching—an excellent variety indeed. The term Guidance, with a capital G, might better be reserved for those activities which are guidance both in content and process.

The purpose here is not to segregate teaching from guidance but simply to maintain a meaningful distinction between the *major* functions of teachers and of guidance specialists in today's schools. Admittedly, the distinction is not perfect, since good teachers sometimes operate at Levels II and III, and good guidance workers sometimes operate at Level I. When one compares the work of teachers as a whole with that of guidance workers as a whole, however, the distinction has validity and serves a useful purpose.

## BIBLIOGRAPHY

GOLDMAN, L. (1962). Group guidance: Content and process. *Pers. and Guid. J.,* 40, 518-522.

HINCKLEY, R. G. and HERMANN, L. (1951). *Group Treatment in Psychotherapy.* Minneapolis: Univ. of Minnesota Press.

CHAPTER 10

# A Total Commitment
# Group Counseling Program
# in an Inner City High School

William Leong, M.S.

THE GROUP COUNSELING PROGRAM at Washington High School is a full-time service offered to students by the school counseling staff and represents a sizable part of a total guidance system, which includes also full-time career counseling and full-time college counseling. Like these other components, group counseling is a program which is not merely sandwiched between more traditional program offerings; nor is it a fashionable filler used to occupy openings and spaces in the curriculum as they become available. Rather, it represents a commitment on the part of the administration and the counseling staff to offer total counseling services for students and additional supportive services to teachers.

The program is allocated the *services of a full-time counselor,* who has *no* additional guidance assignment, and the use of physical facilities adequate to implement the system.

Being a part of the total school guidance system enables the group counseling component to draw on the resources and strengths of the entire counseling staff. During the year 1973, with strong support from the administration, the head counselor, and the counseling staff itself, the group counseling component expanded to the point where every counselor was personally conducting at least one group per week. Some had more than one. The head counselor herself conducted three. At one stage during the year, *24 groups were being conducted each and every week* at Washington.

This diversity has in itself become a source of strength, as the counselors bring to the program distinctive skills and personalities, thereby broadening

77

the program's capability to meet a wider range of individual student needs. The counselors in the program are white, Black, Asian, female, male, supportive, questioning, demanding, motherly, avuncular, empathetic, skeptical, reflective, directive, and confrontative. In formal and informal post-sessions, counselors share with and learn from each other.

Students enter the program through a *variety* of referrals: *Teachers* refer those students who they feel could benefit from a group counseling experience; *vice principals* refer those who they judge would gain more from counseling than from punitive measures; the *registrar* refers those students who, for whatever reason, have established or are beginning to establish sporadic attendance patterns; the *counselors* themselves are often privy to the personal anxieties and struggles of many of their regular counselees; *parents* often request the group counseling experience be made available to their children; and, so frequently that it is no longer a surprise, however gratifying, *students* themselves will ask to be placed in a group. Recently, a group of nine students presented themselves to a counselor and asked to be taken on as an instant, preformed group, having heard about the program from their friends.

## Procedures

Once a group begins, it always meets on the same day of the week, but during rotating periods. A group which will meet every Monday, for example, might meet during period one the first week, then period two the following Monday, and so forth. Thus a student would not miss the same class any more than once every four or five weeks. Occasionally, a group may need to continue longer than the allotted hour, but generally all groups are urged to limit their sessions to one class period. By so doing students avoid the risk of missing an inordinate amount of classroom instruction and also learn that the hour for group counseling is a valuable one not to be squandered. Frequently, groups will wander aimlessly during a session until the realization that their allotted hour is drawing to a close forces them to focus on more urgent and shared concerns. In addition, the counselors are spared the task of writing excessive tardy and absence excuses, a considerable task with as many as four or five groups being conducted each day.

One of the administrative problems in implementing a group counseling program of this magnitude is devising *a method by which students are called together to attend a session* with minimum confusion and disruption. The traditional method has been to send out office summonses at the beginning of each school day, informing students of the period their groups will be meeting. The disadvantages of this method are: the time taken to write more than 200 summonses each week; the need for student messengers to deliver them; excessive use of already scarce office supplies and paper; and frequent classroom interruptions, which understandably alienate teachers. Advantages are: increased probability of full group attendance and establishment of a system which can account more strictly for a student's absence from and return to class, an especially important consideration in schools where class cutting is a major problem.

An alternative method is to give each student a *group counseling membership card,* on which a complete schedule of the group's meeting dates and times for the entire school year is printed. The great advantage of this, of course, is that it eliminates all of the unfavorable conditions of the summons system, while giving the students the opportunity to exercise freedom of choice and making them assume the responsibility for their attendance. Unfortunately, these words often are more stirring as a sentiment than they are valid as an observation, for the schedule system has its own pitfalls. Students abuse the membership card by attempting to use it to cover unauthorized absences, and this inevitably leads to teachers' refusal to accept the card as proof that the student is attending a group counseling session. Students often lose their schedules or require a great deal of time to develop the habit of consulting schedules regularly enough to attend every meeting. The printing of the cards is costly, as well.

We have experimented with both methods, and neither has proved totally satisfactory for all groups. Some groups develop cohesiveness and group maturity rapidly, find their needs being met, and require only a schedule to bring themselves together for subsequent meetings, often with much impatience and anticipation. Other groups, struggling painfully, frustratingly, and sometimes indifferently (as paradoxical as that may sound) for a group identity, need constant affirmation of their continued existence as well as constant reminders of their next meeting.

## Group size and process

The groups at Washington High School have ranged in *size from 5 to 18* members. We have found it difficult if not impossible to describe or define optimum effectiveness in terms merely of group size. There are simply too many variables: interpersonal dynamics, collective and individual expectations of a group, verbal facility of a group, and the attitude of the counselor. Some counselors like the intimacy of a small group; others enjoy the tension and challenge of a large one. We have generally found that adding a member or two to a struggling group often has a salutary effect, while losing members through illnesses, transfers, dropouts, etc., can weaken the bond among those remaining, leading eventually to weakened attendance. This is especially so if the lost member had been a strong presence in the group. For this and other reasons, we have found it best to *bring each individual in a group to a participating and contributing role as soon as possible,* rather than allow the group to depend upon one or two forceful members for movement.

Our counselors generally feel that five is the minimum number required to make the activity worthwhile and to justify the expenditure of their time. Occasionally, however, during test days in the classroom, assembly periods, flu epidemics, or difficult days, only a few students, or sometimes only a single student, will appear for group counseling. What then? Those counselors who could successfully resist the pressures of their clerical duties and the temptation to dismiss the student in order to return to the office found that the one-to-one situation presented an unparalleled opportunity for counseling.

Too often in the leader's office the atmosphere is not conducive to good counseling. Distractions take the forms of lack of privacy, too many phone calls or interruptions, piles of work in front of the counselor, students waiting outside the door, and sometimes simply lack of mental and emotional preparation on the part of counselor or student. On the other hand, in the group counseling room the very atmosphere sharpens the counselor's concept and expectation of self and quickens the counselee's willingness to enter into the give and take of the meeting. Some leaders claim they always experience tightness in the stomach when entering the group counseling room. In this sense, group counseling, even though it is put aside for that particular period, can yet lead to a more rewarding kind of individual counseling.

The group counseling program at Washington has *no set guidelines regarding group makeup.* Over the years the program has included the educable mentally retarded, the academically gifted, gang members, Sunday school gospel singers, athletes, unwed mothers, addicts, pushers, Black Muslims, Bank of America award winners, and the wondrous average student—all gloriously and randomly mixed together in group counseling. We have not had a homogeneous group, possibly because definition is difficult.

In response to suggestions and requests, we formally analyze, quantify, measure, diagnose, and codify the group counseling program in order to systematize its goals, functions, and results. Requests have come from *local graduate schools* for candidates to sit in and observe. Our policy regarding this has been evolved over a long period of time and is certainly not inflexible. We welcome others to join us with the realization that if others have something to gain from us, then ultimately the profession of counseling as a whole, as well as all young people who cross paths with it, may benefit. We require only that those who sit in with us do so as full-fledged participants, not as clinical observers or researchers. If the group counseling program has benefitted any student of Washington High School at all, it has done so only because its *counselors have related to our students as human beings,* not as problems to be dealt with and certainly not as clinical specimens to be studied, juggled, and manipulated.

### Group members

"But what happens in these groups?" is a question frequently asked. A complete answer to this question is usually not forthcoming, not attempted, and indeed may not be possible. No matter what the answer, neither the questioner nor the answerer is usually satisfied, and such will probably be the case here. Nevertheless, the following may help shade in the picture for those who wish to know about goals, functions, and results:

*Goldie* was fat, and she felt nobody liked her. In the beginning, even her group was somewhat repulsed by her grossness and her unkempt appearance. Furthermore, during her first semester in group, she made little attempt to establish real contact with others. She kept her feelings and thoughts to herself, listened to others, but offered and shared little. The group as a whole struggled in their relationships with Goldie, but with little improvement. By the second semester her attendance in group had become sporadic. One day a student remarked about her absence and the group discussed it. Finally, someone offered to seek Goldie out and invite her to attend more regularly.

She attended the next meeting, and the group greeted her, "Hi, Goldie, how you been?" and "Hey, where you been hiding?" This was something they had not done before with any feeling. The remainder of the session was spent in a group attempt at drawing Goldie out a little more. Her attendance thereafter improved, and by the third semester it became obvious that the other students were no longer responding to the physical appearance, but to the person within. Sometime during this semester she started wearing her hair in a natural and seemed quite pleased with it.

*Peter* had recently arrived in the United States. He was visibly apprehensive at finding himself in an inner city Black school. He tried to make friends but found it beyond his social skills; the more he tried, the more awkward he became, and the more he was ridiculed. During his first semester he was victimized by extortion so often that he eventually left all his money at home. He was constantly inquiring about transferring to another school. It took a long time to talk him into joining group counseling. After he joined, it took even longer for him to share his troubles with the group.

When he finally learned to trust the group and reveal his anxieties, the others earnestly tried to help: "Don't walk around like you're afraid of us, man. That is the *worst* thing you can do!" Some went out of their way to greet him in the hallway, though no one was strong or comfortable enough to be seen hanging around with him. Eventually, the group helped Peter develop enough feel of the nuance of social discourse at the school for him to make more contacts. In turn, he offered to tutor struggling math and science students. Instead of transferring to another school, he graduated from Washington with honors and was invited to a graduation party given by a member of his group. He did not attend because, as he told the hostess later, his father, never having been in group counseling, was afraid to let him attend.

Nothing could be done about *Cynthia's* problems: an alcoholic mother, runaway father, brothers and sisters who were drug addicts, gang members, thieves, and constantly in and out of trouble with the police. All she could do was tell us about it. All we could do was listen and offer whatever we could. She must have gleaned something from the sessions, because she came every week for two years, except for illness. She often came to school just to attend group and left immediately afterward.

*Denise*, 16, considered herself grown, and could not understand why her mother would not allow her to go out more often and stay later. Her situation began a spirited and animated discussion in group, with the boys giving their masculine points of view and the girls all offering Denise their sympathy and assurances that they shared her burden. When elements of trust between mother and daughter became a topic of discussion, one member pointed out to Denise that apparently she was demanding trust from her mother but did little to earn it. She protested until she was reminded that she had made the same charge against teachers at a previous meeting: "I want a teacher to come in and *earn my respect*. I don't give it to her just because she's a teacher." Denise still objected, but everyone realized that she was protesting too much.

The first time *Gerald* came to a group meeting, he swaggered in, displaying all the trademarks which identified him as a member of a certain gang:

wide-brim hat, earrings, and eye-fixing stare. Some of the other students were obviously apprehensive and kept their physical and social distance. The group exchanged autobiographical questions and answers as their initial icebreaker, but Gerald held back, asking no questions and answering only in grunts and monosyllables. He seemed to be studying everyone and everything, suspicious, not quite sure what this was all about and what was in it for him. Some of the others wondered the same thing. Afterwards, one of them asked the counselor, "What's *he* doing in here?" But Gerald came back for subsequent meetings regularly, always wearing his uniform, always swaggering and super cool.

Nothing significant happened throughout the first semester. It seemed as if everyone was holding back, afraid to make any sudden sounds or movements. Sometime during the second semester Gerald began greeting everyone when he came into the room, "How's it goin', Princess? What's happening, blood?" and taking over as group leader. It became apparent that he *liked* them, even though they could not bring themselves to believe it or to trust him. For the remainder of the semester Gerald worked the group, getting people to talk, asking questions, introducing minor topics, and enjoying himself immensely. Near the end, one of the girls asked him to remove his hat, not because it offended her but because she just wanted to see what he really looked like. He hesitated but then complied. The sides of his natural were indented and pushed in a variety of dips and depressions, and the sight brought hesitant laughter from everyone. Gerald smiled almost a shy, embarrassed, little boy smile, which encouraged everyone to laugh more freely and loudly, and then Gerald joined in the laughter. He was transferred to another school not long after this, but his group still speaks of him with some affection.

Lest one get the impression that counselors are always cognizant of significant happenings during the course of a group session or that dramatic breakthroughs are the norm, let the saga of *Lewis* put the entire matter into more realistic perspective. He was absolutely impossible. Playful, mischievous, constantly jiving around, talking loudly, and never serious about anything, Lewis controlled every group in which he participated. In a sense, he ruined every one of them. His presence in a group was the kiss of death for the counselor and set the tone for the entire group. No personality was strong enough to subordinate his. Nothing worked to stop his destructive antics—not threats or anger from the counselor, not appeals to his better nature, no amount of pleading or cajolery, no amount of feigned indifference.

It was impossible to ignore him or to carry on group work above or around him.

After almost two years of rampaging and running amok through the group counseling program, Lewis somehow graduated. At commencement, resplendent in Superfly suit and cape, a model of deportment, Lewis introduced his mother to the group counselor. The mother enthusiastically and sincerely thanked the counselor for the remarkable change she had seen in Lewis since he had been in the program.

Finally, a word about the Mary and Johnny Does, the so-called average kids who came to the sessions through the years and talked, listened, sympathized, offered advice, and left, seemingly never having offered any more of themselves than common courtesy and social compliance. Did group counseling do anything for them? It is as difficult to envision any process more capable than group counseling of doing something for its participants as it is to delineate what that "something" may be for each and every individual. Perhaps one of the many Mary Does said it best in the following exchange just before summer vacation:

*Counselor:* I'm not sure what you meant when you said that you were different here.

*Mary:* I mean that at home all it seems I do is argue. I argue with my mother about doing the dishes, I argue with my brothers about what program to watch and staying out of my room, and at school I *know* my teachers think I got a big mouth, the way I'm always carrying on. And even with my friends I know I get mean.

*Counselor:* And here?

*Mary:* I talk different.

*Counselor:* Different?

*Mary:* Better, I mean I talk better.

*Counselor: Which* Mary do you like better?

*Mary:* This one.

EDITOR'S POSTSCRIPT:

*This high school was singled out in "A Report on Conflict and Violence in California's High Schools"\* and described as follows:*

> *One inner city school which had experienced continual violence for several years prior to the initiation of group counseling believed that*

---

\* California State Department of Education, Sacramento, 1973, p. 16.

*the success of the counseling program had been a major factor in reducing violence. . . . When given local prerogative, the staff made a clear choice to improve its counseling services to students. The staffing pattern was readjusted to increase the counseling staff. Next, the counseling staff re-evaluated its priorities to provide a group counseling program for "regular" and for "problem" students in addition to regular counseling services. All counselors directed at least one group, and one counselor coordinated all groups. Group sessions were also available for staff members.*

## PART II: B. THE ROLE OF ADMINISTRATORS

## EDITOR'S NOTE

*Ideally, the school administrator should be familiar with and make use of counseling knowledge, techniques, and attitudes. Vice-principals or deans especially can use this knowledge. However, the modern school principal is also one of the most overloaded of school executive personnel. Many persons expect the principal to be all things to all people: counselor, father confessor, community worker, statistician, labor negotiator, educational specialist, etc. Needless to say, few can fulfill all of these expectations.*

*If one were to assign priorities, possibly counseling teachers and, at times, parents would be prime. Other personnel already counsel students. Is it conceivable that at times the principal (or superintendent) could be counseled by students? In the urban high school of 2,000 to 3,000 students it is not unusual that the principal gets isolated from meaningful contact with students. Conceivably this loneliness and isolation of the decision maker at the top might at times be relieved by a mutually rewarding contact with students.*

*There are other reasons in favor of this student-administrator contact. In the cases of administrators and other senior personnel, one of the hazards of getting older and wiser is becoming less tolerant and responsive to the age-appropriate experimentations and innovations of teen-agers. Informal open discussion without the barrier of official decorum might well reduce some of this communication gap. In the California Department of Education Report on Conflict and Violence in California High Schools (1973), productive examples of superintendents' conferring periodically with groups of 50 to 75 students are described. This is yet another step toward reducing the student-administrator barrier and administrator isolation. Chapters 12, 13, and 37 demonstrate the values of a person-to-person interaction versus an administrator-to-student interaction.*

*In one large urban high school the principal and three students did set up a unique mutual counseling situation which benefitted all four, and possibly the rest of the school as well. This experience (described in Chapter 11) was unplanned and fortuitous and progressed because of the special values to those involved. Whether one could have deliberately and intentionally de-*

86

*signed such an event is questionable. Yet there may be moments in the professional lives of other administrators when this kind of opportunity has presented or will present itself. Describing the experience here may encourage other administrators to see the advantage of similar opportunities. The degree of mutual personal self-exposure in the experience to be detailed is impressive and may seem undesirable to some. Yet the ultimate value of the experience speaks for itself.*

*The following account of this experience was obtained with the aid of a tape-recorded interview. Quotes of the principal and interviewer are used in the latter half.*

## CHAPTER 11

# A Principal Benefits from Weekly Meetings with a Selected Group of Students

### F. Willard Robinson, Jr., Ed.D.

IT STARTED WHEN I RECEIVED A CALL from a senior boy, who was very sensitive, a tremendous boy on our campus, and really outstanding. He said he wanted to come in and talk with me. This isn't unusual. I try to meet individually with parents, faculty members, and students. *It's amazing how many of them do come in.* Mainly, I listened and was very intrigued with some of the things that he had to say, that he was struggling with some very deep personal problems, some family matters, concern with others, dealing with his personal philosophy, and his personal goals and objectives. I didn't project too much but just listened to him. He asked if he could come back and spend some more time with me. I thought, "I don't mind spending time with you, because I really enjoy your sharing these things with me." I said, "You're well known on campus; I'm sure that there are others that might profit from this, and it might be helpful to me. I won't take the initiative for it, but if you want to go out and get one or two others together, I'll try to set up some time."

A day or two later he had two other boys, with whom I'd always had a "hello" relationship on campus. I never knew them as people. They came in, and we spent an hour-and-a-half a week together. We would schedule each time on a shifting basis. We didn't want the same time each week. Sometimes they would have to be out of class, and I didn't want to pull them out of the same class. For young people who had never had any background in group work, they amazed and intrigued me, because I didn't give them any direction. If one person would get up and philosophize about something,

88

another boy would quickly say, "I don't care two hoots about that. I want to know what you're feeling about it. I want to know where you are." They wouldn't let the subject veer to others. I was intrigued with what came naturally with these boys in really cutting through, being so open and honest, and then challenging another if he didn't talk about it.

I felt if they were going to come in, I wanted to be free to talk about some things, too. They were most helpful to me. It was a risky thing, because of some of the things I talked with them about. If we hadn't built a trust within the group, it would have boomeranged. I would talk about things I was struggling with. They wouldn't let me get away with talking about other people. I went into some very emotional kinds of things. For instance, if I were going into a meeting with the school staff, I wanted to examine not only my emotions but also my motives for approaching a certain problem in a particular way. Maybe I was confused in terms of my motives. Was it an ego thing that made me want to react in a certain way, or was this really in the best interest of the school? These matters to do with staff, sometimes on a district level, a high-powered kind of thing, required that I think them through and be sure of my own motives and feelings. The boys were very helpful to me in a number of these. For instance, I was concerned about meaningful communication between this office and the district office. My feeling was that we could never do much with the staff or with students until, at the leadership level, we could build a feeling of trust, openness, and honesty with one another.

We got into some very personal kinds of things, too. They had known my wife and admired her when she had attended a few activities on campus. They had observed our relationship and were intrigued because they had seen so many marital relationships deteriorate around them. On the surface it seemed that our relationship looked pretty good. The boys were very curious and asked me about this. As an example, I said communication hadn't always been easy between my wife and me. For years she expressed a feeling of insecurity. I came from a background of the culture of the old West, where the man was always strong and adequate. If he fulfilled his wife's needs he came on as a strong member of the household. When she tried to express feelings of inadequacy or insecurity, my reaction had been that this was a put-down to me. She has everything, and that's ridiculous. I just really closed her off in terms of meaningful communication. It was only at the point where I could say, "Man, I don't have it all put together," that I could share with her some of my needs in a very open way. This, in turn, began to free her as a person. All of a sudden I realized that to put on the strong play of having it all put together with anyone as close as a wife was the very thing that would break down communication in a relationship. As a couple we were working very successfully on this.

One of the boys said he could see problems in his own family and the insights gained from our discussion led to some very meaningful communication with his family that had never occurred before.

I talked of the dynamics of communication with the boys, and this involved exploration of my relationship with my wife. She is a very open person, and if she felt threatened she would attack. If I was threatened with attack, I retreated and closed up. If these two characteristics got together, not much went on in the way of communication. I told the youngsters in an open and honest way what we had gone through and of its fascination to me. Their families did not resent the ideas they took home. I have been invited to some of the homes on social occasions and have met some of the parents.

Group involvement is a brand new area for me, and I guess it could be a risky one. I'm not sure I would have done it when I was 35 years old, but I'm at retirement age, and I've already gone through so much in this district. I feel freer about some of these things now, I guess freer to be just myself and my own man!

In the group we had no agenda, but just the ever-present question, "Where are you now?" No one had to say, "Gee, I think you're doing this wrong." We made no judgments or evaluations. It was a chance in which we affirmed each other as individuals and accepted each other completely. They had some real personal problems. On the surface these particular boys, outstanding athletes, were squared away, but underneath they were struggling, too.

Q.* So, they're boys who wouldn't have come into any counseling. Did you get the impression that they had the same kind of relationship at home with their fathers?

A: Not necessarily . . . our relationship just grew naturally, a feeling of trust and love for one another. It was natural.

Q: Did you ever think of bringing anybody else along other than the initial three?

A: I suggested it, but they got to the point where they liked what was going on; they didn't want to. . . .

Q: It seems to me that one of the hardest things for a principal, especially

---

* This portion of the chapter was taken from the tape recording of the interview.

of a large high school, is not to become isolated. You're hearing about kids second hand all the time. You're getting the problem kids, and you could lose contact with the nonproblem kids, and kids as kids.

A: I don't have too much contact with the problem kids, because that's handled in other offices, but even this is changing. I do work, spend a lot of time with student leaders, talking. But there we're just talking, not getting into what is really bothering them. . . . It's on a task-oriented level. It is a problem, because I'm expected to get out reports and to answer phone calls on schedule. I'm expected to evaluate the staff. Frankly, a few things went by the board last year that weren't as high as other things on my priority scale . . . it's a matter of priorities. Should relationships come first, or should procedures come first? It really isn't an either/or proposition. That wasn't the only thing. I was meeting with teachers on an individual basis. I was meeting with many students on an individual basis. To me, that was the priority at the particular time.

Q: Have you done reading about groups?

A: Some. In the brief experiences that I had in sensitivity training and encounter groups, I thought there was a lot lacking. However, I did become aware of the depth of people's needs and their hurts because of that experience. I saw some tender personalities, it seemed to me, damaged through the process. I wanted to be involved more with freeing people. I knew I was a sensitive person, but I had difficulty in communicating this sensitivity to others. As I came into a new depth in my own spiritual life—and this was very involved—I experienced a freeing and acceptance of myself that moved my life into a completely new dimension.

Q: Can you explain this process?

A: The process involved an integration of relational theology and the techniques of modern psychology. It was helpful to struggle openly and acceptingly with others. There was support, affirmation, and trust as opposed to encounter. We need to get out of our protective shell, but it's like bringing forth a new chick. You hatch it with warmth and in a supportive environment. You don't break it out of its shell with a hammer.

Q: Did the group experience conflict or encounter?

A: It seemed to me that possibly you might call it that, but not until after a lot of trust and acceptance had been established.

Q: How was that trust established?

A: I guess it is a matter of empathy. Well, it's even more than that. Our group seemed to take on all the qualities of a "covenant" relationship. Accurate empathy, non-possessive warmth, and self-disclosure were ingredients.

Q: The experience was a learning process for you, too?

A: Oh, yes. As I was accepted for who I really was, I became less judgmental about myself and of others. I began to see people in a relationship of love, and this has become very, very real to me. Just listening, getting with them on an experiential level, not having to come up with the answers or advice—that's a very freeing thing.

I never talked about religion. The boys were going through struggles in this area, and they did talk. They were involved—questioning on a spiritual level—and they would talk about their kind of thing. They spoke of their struggles from the standpoint that they weren't really free in terms of their parents' background. Finally, one day, not in the group but after they had graduated, one of the boys came to me and said, "How come you never talk about where you are spiritually, because we know you had an experience . . . ?" I didn't want to evade the situation. I told him exactly where I was. It was brief but very special. I pointed out that I thought you don't communicate this through words, but rather by living a life style. I respected where they were. . . .

CHAPTER 12

# The Administrator as Group Counselor

## Alice Evans, M.S.

I WOULD LIKE TO ENCOURAGE the reader to *reexamine administrative roles* and the images that they project. Many times we misidentify roles and have to shake ourselves loose from preconceived ideas or habits. How many times have we heard that authority figures could not be effective counselors and, specifically, that these people should not be group leaders? We have been told that the counseling relationship is lost when the counselor becomes a "bad guy" and the authoritarian role is rendered ineffectual by trying to be a counselor.

Experience has taught me that as a dean with disciplinarian responsibilities I have been more effective in bringing about behavior modification in students with whom I have worked in groups than in those whom I saw only individually.

*As a dean of girls*, it is my *primary responsibility* to be a *disciplinarian*. I am expected to try to keep the peace, as it were, in any matter relating to misbehavior in the classroom and/or on the campus. By the very nature of this job I am the "bad guy," and my image is a negative one. This image is one of restrictions, limits, "don'ts," punishments, and consequences.

Personally, being negative turns me off. Also, I have found that a person with a negative philosophy, which is expressed in "don'ts" and finger pointing, turns off teen-agers. I see any position which primarily serves punitive purposes as meeting resistance and rebellion. Such a position rarely merits cooperation or healthy change, and it never merits growth.

Reprinted with permission from *Research and Pupil Personnel Services Newsletter*, Office of Los Angeles County Superintendent of Schools, October, 1971.

*Basic principles for the administrator/counselor*

Some of the principles and personal beliefs which have guided my work are:

1. High school students are aware of what they are doing and know the general rules that exist in their school and society.

2. Students should be allowed to exercise their free will by making choices.

3. Students have the right to fail as well as to succeed.

4. Students want limits and push for them, and with these limits they feel secure in their experimentation.

5. Students who choose to break the rules and are caught have the right to take the responsibility for the consequences.

6. As a corollary to the above, students should be able to "buy" consequences as well as be expected to accept the results of their own actions.

*The right to consequences*

The principle that a student has a right to make choices and expect concomitant results is particularly important. If a student wishes to be suspended and the rules of the school state that students who smoke get suspended, a girl who smokes and gets caught has the right to be suspended.

There should be an automatic understanding that what a student chooses to do, fully aware of the consequences or rewards, is a vital part of a student's development and growth. This choice is one method of communication. I approach the consequences of misbehavior in almost computer-like fashion:

$$\text{INPUT} = \text{Misbehavior}$$
$$\text{OUTPUT} = \text{Consequence}$$

Specifically:

$$\text{INPUT} = \text{Student smokes}$$
$$\text{OUTPUT} = \text{Suspension}$$

I generally do not lecture to the student who has chosen the route of breaking a rule. I may or may not discuss with her the choice of actions and consequences. An aware, fully functioning student knows the rules, takes the chance, and, I think, appreciates the rapidity with which the occasion passes.

Actions taken by this kind of student to precipitate events do not usually have counseling implications as far as I am concerned. However, when the consequences of a choice surprise the student or in some way upset her, or if she is "buying" too many consequences, I believe I should become involved as a counselor. The input-output are fact; they happened. The acceptance or awareness or the handling of this and the next choice can be discussed. It is at this point that an invitation to join a group may be appropriate.

*Selection of group members*

Girls whom I believe it would be appropriate to invite into a group counseling situation include those who:

1. Are uneasy about the choices they are making.
2. May be unhappy about the way their life is developing.
3. Are unable to make friends.
4. Can get attention only in negative ways.
5. May be angry at me, their teachers, their parents, or themselves, or their circumstances.

When I see evidence of one or more of these problems, I suggest to the girl that she consider joining a group. In the group she will have a chance to work out her problems with other students who are working out theirs by talking about them in a group setting and expressing their feelings. I may say that I am worried about the choices she is making and that if she continues this way she probably will not be in a position to make *any* choices on our campus. This is a fact, not a threat, and I try to convey it by my attitude and my tone of voice.

Usually, I discuss group counseling with a girl during an individual conference or when talking with her and her parent(s). I state the existence of the group as one of the fringe benefits of attending this school. I make it clear that the group is available but is never assigned. In short, I try to tell her, "If you are unhappy about your choices and the consequences of your actions, group counseling may be for you. Try it if you like. If you like the choices you are making and are willing to accept the responsibility for your actions, then group counseling is not for you."

In addition to those who act out, there are those quiet ones with internal pressures just as great, who are unable to "tell you" by actions that they are troubled. Group counseling has been a means to help me reach these and other students more effectively than I could otherwise. By working with them in groups it is possible for the following to happen:

1. More students have the chance for help.
2. Students can help each other with their problems in a way that I cannot.
3. The students have available something positive in terms of me as an authority figure, and ultimately this can have a positive effect in making their choices.

### Trust as a facet of group counseling

My role as a group leader is based on mutual trust. I trust these students to help each other in ways that I cannot help them; to be honest; and by their presence to be willing to work on their own "thing." They trust me first by coming, but it is a tentative, testing trust. Their trust in me as an authority figure must be allowed to develop. I believe they ultimately transfer some of this trust to other authority figures.

What happens or is discussed in the group is *privileged communication*, and under no circumstances do I reveal what is said by the group members except under the provisions of the American Psychological Association code. As applied in the group, this means to the girls that:

1. Information discussed in the group is not acted upon by me unless the best interests of the girl or others require it. If it is necessary to take action, the situation is discussed first with the girl.
2. Parents are not informed of the content of group discussions; e.g., "I know your daughter is taking drugs."
3. The group is not used as a pipeline to the underground activities of the school.

This last is a touchy problem. There is an impression that I have a moral obligation to act on the information, but I do not believe this. If it were not for the groups I would not know the information. If I find out the same facts outside the group, I will take the action that is appropriate.

### The role of the administrator as a leader

My role as a facilitator in the group is to be myself, to be honest, to listen, and to clarify. It is much the same as the role of the student in that I am *for* them, although not one of them. Sometimes I become a participating member in that I bring up problems which have developed in school or in a class or personally among members of the group. They do not always respond to what I have introduced, but sometimes one will gain valuable insight from the discussion and the mirroring which is done by the others.

The group, in turn, bring up the problems which they have with me. This is especially true if I have had to suspend a girl who is a group member from school. The girl will usually ask for support from the group by saying, "It wasn't fair." The fact that 90 percent of the girls in the group have behavior problems and have been suspended makes the discussion lively, particularly when they bring up resentments left over from their own suspensions. It is axiomatic that dealing constructively with authority is a major task for girls in this type of group.

Dealing with their *feelings about me as an authority figure* is one of the critical phases of the groups. The outcome of these discussions is also critical to the growth of the group. The group will spend much of its time playing around with these feelings about me until they are resolved. When they have been, the group can grow and deal effectively with other problems concerning me as a leader.

In those groups where tension is not too high, the issue of my authority will be attacked and resolved relatively early, perhaps in one meeting. Ideally, the girl suspended assumes responsibility for her own actions, and I become no more than the computer. In this case our relationship is not affected. In other groups the process may not be so simple. The most angry girls are frequently the most disturbed at my efforts to get them to work through this authority thing.

Let me give an *example*. I intentionally placed into a second semester group a Caucasian girl, Leslie, who was not afraid to speak her mind and who was a fighter. This placement was to provide some reaction to a Mexican-American girl, Lucy, who got a "yes" from everyone; there was no challenge to anything she said. Lucy was a manipulator and fighter outside the group. I believe that most of the girls feared her. Both Lucy and Leslie had tremendous resentment toward authority, and with the two girls in the same group they joined forces to gain support from each other against me. The other members of the group were not strong enough to counter this opposition. Any of my reflections or interpretations were met with, "There you go again," or "No, that doesn't seem that way," etc.

I almost dreaded the group. I began to whip out all my tricks, none of which worked. Then one day the same routine began, and I had had it. I forgot all my tricks, and when they criticized a rather obvious observation, I got with my own feelings and said something to the effect that I felt frustrated and defeated in the group and that either I had valid opinions in the group or I didn't, but this was about all I could take. Lucy quietly said, "Let it all hang out, Mrs. E." That was the end of the struggle. Lucy and Leslie relaxed and could be honest. Basically, I hadn't been honest, and yet I had expected them to be. I was playing group leader, and I wasn't me.

*The fact that I wear two hats can be confusing.* One girl stated it this way: "You are so two-faced. No! You are two people. You are against us out there and sit on your big seat of judgment and are all business. In here, you are all social." We all wear many hats; so do the students. We are many-faced individuals; being responsible and aware while wearing each of the hats enables us to handle each situation to a good end, making wise and satisfying choices. The students come to realize that they, too, wear two hats—in the group and outside the group—and many find that their so-called "image" suffers by the very fact that they attend group meetings. Out there they are the rough-tough, name-calling kids with no problems; in the group they are concerned, growing youth, worrying through the things that they are unhappy about.

The girls develop a *relationship with the group as a body.* At times they use the group as the ultimate in "getting it out." Some girls tell all outside the group and get the other girls to help them bring it out in the group for solutions. Other girls tell me problems personally but cannot accept themselves enough to discuss their problems in the group. But here again, their goal is to be able to "get it out" in the group. Two examples:

(1) Cecilia was three months pregnant and unsure of the father. She was convinced that her mother would kick her out if she found out. The girl was terrified and considering suicide. Her friends in the group knew and were worried, so they laid the groundwork for her to talk about it in the group. Cecilia began talking around the issue, and an unknowing member asked her if she were "p.g." She said, "No," but began to cry, and with the help of the group, discussed her fears. The group elected me to take her home right then and help her tell her mother.

(2) Cindy came to me personally after being in group for several months. She was having an affair with a girl and felt certain she was a lesbian. After a year in group she never mentioned this; she continued to discuss it with me personally. Although she was inactive as far as that problem was concerned, she actively participated in discussions regarding others' problems, had a tremendous amount of empathy, and over the year said it was her most meaningful experience. She stated that for the first time in her life she began to like herself.

*Results in terms of school behavior*

As mentioned previously, effect is difficult to measure when the criterion for contact is misbehavior. This past year I began keeping records on the 120 students involved in the group counseling.* Because of the number of students involved, I used averages in comparing citizenship, grade point average, number of referrals, attendance in school, and group. Some of the students were in group for only a semester and some for an entire year. The four junior girls who remained in group for an entire year had a grade point average for their freshmen and sophomore years of 1.8.** At the end of the first semester of group the average was 1.5, and at the end of the year the G.P.A. was 2.4.

I am not convinced that any of these findings are necessarily good, insignificant, positive, or negative. I do believe the students who do have significant problems in making it in school will improve as they feel better about themselves through group work. Grades, citizenship, and attendance are only mentioned when they are seen by a specific individual as a specific problem.

*School performance is affected in other ways* not in the statistics, but directly related to the group work. One major help to teachers, as well as to the student herself, is that when a problem is brewing in the class, oftentimes the girl will make a self-referral concerning the problem before the teacher refers the student. The same procedure of parent-counselor-teacher conference can be followed, but it places the student in a responsible position, which enables an exploratory conference for reasonable solutions without anyone's being on the defensive. These self-referrals come from group work, I believe, because the student is allowed self-expression and respect from a group situation.

Some teachers feel the group is "a lot of nothing" and "a waste of time" —their time. The majority of teachers, however, have been supportive.

Many teachers have commented that they have taken an extra look at students who were getting help through group work. Many teachers have checked with me when unusual changes have occurred in certain students. Teachers have made suggestions on placement in groups. All of this has contributed substantially to the students' well-being.

---

* Ninety-eight girls and 22 Mexican-American boys were involved in group counseling with me. The first semester 5 groups of all girls and the second semester 7 girls' groups and 2 boys' groups consumed approximately 210 hours of my working days.
** Grade point average of 4.0=A.

*Highlights of the group events*

*Sylvia* was a freshman girl, giddy and very overweight, who was being expelled from several classes a week. She entered group during the first semester. At the end of that semester she had an average citizenship grade of 2.0* and a G.P.A. of 1.0. She failed English, and the teacher recommended she be placed in remedial English. She was very upset and brought the problem to the group. The members told her that she had refused to give a speech and didn't do her homework, so what could she expect? All the members agreed that she could probably do it if she tried, and perhaps she could be given another chance. I was elected by the group to speak to the teacher after Sylvia presented her case to the teacher alone. The teacher agreed to give her six weeks to prove herself. She remained in the class the entire semester, received a *C+* and gave a speech on drug abuse, a topic often discussed in the group. I was invited to hear the speech. Her G.P.A. at the end of the semester was 1.6, and her average citizenship grade improved to 1.4.

*Cynthia* would probably have been classified as a school phobic. Her problem was at home more than at school. She talked about the leniency of her mother and the fearfulness of her father. One day she came in furious at a teacher. As she was ranting on and on about this teacher, one of the group members noted a similarity between the way she described the teacher and the way she described her father. I suggested *role playing*. Cynthia was to play her father or the teacher, and Lucy played Cynthia. Cynthia was delighted at the opportunity to show how really awful her father was. Lucy portrayed Cynthia accurately, and Cynthia got the message. She said, "Do I really push him like that?"

*Jesse,* a senior boy, wasn't coming to school and had pretty well decided to forget about graduation. The group seemed distressed when he was absent one day. They discussed how stupid he was to throw away four years and decided to take the matter into their own hands. They asked to borrow the phone, and three other seniors told him, "We want you to graduate. . . . Hurry up, dress, and make it for the end of group." He was there in 30 minutes. He attended every day until the end of school, about three weeks. He was not permitted to graduate with his class because he had missed too many assignments, but he decided to go to summer school. He was the first of eight siblings in his family to graduate.

Another boy, *Robert,* had been making an issue all year about the length of his hair. He decided to be expelled rather than cut it. He came to the

---

* 1 = satisfactory; 2 = needs to improve; 3 = unsatisfactory.

group meeting and discussed his decision. No one in the group agreed with him that it was worth it. He argued vigorously and then came to school the next day with his hair shorter than I had seen it since the beginning of the year.

*Pam,* a tenth grader, had required a pre-enrollment conference because of four unsatisfactory grades in citizenship the previous year. She had a 1.5 G.P.A. for her ninth grade. When she came into group she stated she couldn't care less about her grades because no one else cared. At the end of the first semester she excitedly asked that the group have a special meeting after the grades were handed out. I said it could be a voluntary meeting, and I would be there. All eight members arrived. Pam had made all 1's in citizenship and a 2.4 G.P.A. I posted it on my bulletin board.

### As I see myself in the group

My roles are not confusing or conflicting. As a group leader I am in a position to accept, not to approve, behavior. As a dean of girls I accept the choices made by girls and am the conveyor of consequences. As the group work proceeds, I frequently see that the choices made outside this testing ground are less in need of consequences.

I consider myself a firm disciplinarian. I find my responsibilities in changing individual student behavior are most effectively met through the group process.

## CHAPTER 13

# An Administrator Team as Group Counselors to an Opportunity Class

---

Alice Evans, M.S.,
Alan V. Johnson, M.A., and
Muriel Thomson, Ed.D.

IN A UNIQUE EXPERIMENTAL PROJECT involving the use of group counseling sessions with an opportunity class, two high school deans, working as a team, have demonstrated the effectiveness of administrators in a counseling situation with children who have serious problems.

*The opportunity class*

In the fall semester of 1968 an opportunity class for 14- and 15-year-olds was established at San Gabriel High School to provide one additional opportunity for students with severe behavior difficulties, or for habitual truants, to work out some of their problems in the school setting in the hope that they would then be able to reenter the regular classroom program. The class has continued through the present time and is an integral part of the school system. It meets for the last three periods of the day, and one teacher is in charge throughout. Students are assigned for one semester at a time, and at the end of each semester their progress is evaluated and a decision is made about their return to the regular school program or reassignment to the opportunity class.

---

Reprinted with permission from *Research and Pupil Personnel Services Newsletter,* Office of Los Angeles County Superintendent of Schools, June 30, 1972.

102

*Early operation of the opportunity class*

During the first year of operation of the class, it seemed logical to assume that every effort had been made to help the students, and no more responsibility could be taken by the school than to give them the "opportunity." Their class teacher was now their sole resource. Since they were problem children, the level of expectation was less than for the regular students, and it was easy to forget them and computerize them out of concern: Either they made it or they didn't.

It became obvious that by the time students were entered in the opportunity class there were few instances in which they could gain recognition for positive behavior. The odds were against them because teacher patience had worn down, the deans' patience had worn down, and the frustration of their fellow students had increased. The only avenue to attention was misbehavior, and many decided that negative attention was better than none at all.

*A unique aid is offered*

As the primary disciplinarians on the campus, the deans knew the students' unique problems and were responsible for the placement of the students in the opportunity class. For this reason, they selected two means of offering help:

1. Instead of having the attendance of these students processed through the attendance office, which monitored the entire school, they processed it themselves and became directly responsible for home contact on absences.

2. The deans became co-counselors to the group in a one-hour-weekly series of sessions.

The goal was to increase the school success of the students and increase their rate of return to the regular school program. The dean of girls had had considerable experience in group counseling with students having serious problems, and the dean of boys had had no prior group counseling experience.

*The group counseling procedure*

The regular teacher left the classroom during the session, and the physical setting was altered by having the students arrange their chairs in a circle for the hour. Participation in the group was nonvoluntary in that the counseling situation replaced class time. However, it was voluntary in the sense that the students had the right to participate or to remain outside the circle and not become involved. In actual practice, no student ever elected to remain outside the circle.

The *rules established* with the group, from the beginning, included:

1. That no matter what was said or done during the group, the deans would take no administrative action on the basis of it, either during or after the group.

2. That all comments were confidential and were to be kept within the group.

3. That conversation should include only matters related to group members.

### The deans as group leaders

The deans served as co-counselors to the group with an evident, unique result. In addition to the usual relationship between counselors and counselees, the students came to perceive them in "mother" and "father" roles. In essence, they became parents in a firm, loving, and dependable way, and the *students became members of a "family."* The "brothers" and "sisters" worked together in the group and also began to help each other outside of it.

Both adults assumed the role of *good parents* by accident and as a result of the expectations of the members of the class. They became parents who did not overreact to crisis situations, who set limits on behavior, and who expected the children to assume the consequences of their acts. Most of all, these good parents *accepted* the children. This acceptance appeared to have been lacking in the homes of the students.

As their roles developed, the leaders became aware that *certain factors were extremely important to the students.*

1. On a level of mechanics of group operation, it was imperative that the leaders arrive at the group promptly, that they be consistent in their participation, and that they evidence a willingness to "shut off" the rest of the campus and devote the entire time to the group. The latter was particularly demonstrated by not accepting phone calls or responding to other campus needs, regardless of the emergency.

2. In terms of relating to the students, the primary consideration was to "hear" what they said, to recognize the feeling tone of what was expressed, and be able to reflect it back so that it could be looked at and dealt with. Added to that were the important courtesies of being nonjudgmental, respecting decisions made by the group members, and attending to requests.

3. In the less tangible realm, but probably of paramount value, were the

processes of making it possible for them to trust by being trustworthy, genuinely caring for them and about them, and being positive adult figures after whom the students could model themselves.

## Results

The table on page 106 indicates the movement of students in and out of the opportunity class in the seven semesters since its inception. The first four columns indicate the movement prior to the beginning of the group counseling experience. The last three columns are what has happened since the deans have worked with the group on a regular basis.

## Student performance since group counseling

The *rate of return to the regular school program* of students in the opportunity class has *doubled* in the year-and-a-half since the group counseling has been in process. Seven students each semester have been able to return, as contrasted to an average of 3.3 students a semester for the first two years of the program. Similarly, *placement in continuation school has increased,* with 6 students a semester going out to this form of education, as compared to an average of 4.5 students during the first two years. This increased rate of students leaving the regular campus and attending the continuation school was a significant and unexpected positive result. Fewer students remained static and therefore more students were able to make decisions regarding their lives.

It became apparent that "assuming responsibility for their own lives" was more involved than returning to regular school. In some cases accepting responsibility was a recognition that, in fact, they were not ready to handle a certain situation and that it was in their own best interest not to return to regular school but instead try an alternate type of schooling better suited to their needs. By the same token, some students chose to attend the opportunity class for a part of their day or requested that they remain in the opportunity class but be allowed to add one regular class to their program. An example of this was a unique plan figured out by one of the girls: She wanted a four-period day, alternating her class periods in regular school and in the opportunity class. She felt that in this way she could ease herself into the regular program and still have the security of the opportunity class. It worked for her.

| | PRIOR TO GROUP | | | | SINCE GROUP | | |
|---|---|---|---|---|---|---|---|
| | 1st Sem. 68-69 | 2nd Sem. 68-69 | 1st Sem. 69-70 | 2nd Sem. 69-70 | 1st Sem. 70-71 | 2nd Sem. 70-71 | 1st Sem. 71-72 |
| Number of students placed in Opportunity Class | 12 | 16 | 13 | 18 | 14 | 14 | 18 |
| Number remaining in Opportunity Class to next semester | 5 | 11 | 12 | 8 | 11 | 6 | 6 |
| Number "in and out" involvement in semester | 12 | 21 | 24 | 30 | 22 | 25 | 24 |
| Number checked out to other districts during semester | 1 | 3 | 2 | 3 | 3 | 1 | 2 |
| Number placed by court detention facilities or on home teaching | 1 | 1 | 2 | 3 | 0 | 3 | 0 |
| Number placed in continuation high school | 2 | 3 | 7 | 6 | 6 | 8 | 4 |
| Number returned to regular school | 2 | 1 | 3 | 7 | 2 | 9 | 9 |
| Percent returned to regular school | 17% | 6% | 12½% | 23% | 9% | 36% | 37½% |

*A. Observations and conclusions drawn from the group counseling*

Objectives of this group experience became:

1. To help each of the group members improve their concepts of self.

2. To help them return to regular school and/or make decisions regarding their educational lives so that they could function positively.

3. To help them assume responsibility for themselves and their education.

*B. Some of the changes apparent in the students*

1. There was evidence of an *increased ability to handle relationships* with peers and adults.

    a. *Tom* admitted he was strung out on pills. He responded to limits by promising the group he would stay clean for one month. His friends verified that he stayed within the limits he agreed to, including the Christmas vacation time, when apparently they saw him frequently at parties.

    b. *Carlos,* who was in the regular school program, was being transferred to the continuation high school because of nonattendance. His friends in the group asked the deans to give him a chance in the opportunity class. He was adopted into the family like a foster child, and the group promised to get him to school, which they did.

    c. *Mike* could not sit still for 10 minutes at a time in class. *Lydia* explained Mike's problem the way she saw it, and the deans showed respect for the opinions of students by accepting her conclusions and acting upon them. The insights of a 13-year-old girl, who had her own set of unique problems, in this case provided the clue the administrators were needing.

2. The *capacity to trust adults appeared to increase.* Although there is no way to measure the trust level of adults per se, at least the co-counselors were aware of marked differences in individual students between kinds of responses they made before the group sessions and after them.

3. The students seemed generally *more willing to accept responsibility for their own actions* and see themselves as they really were. Once these 14- and 15-year-olds trusted enough to express themselves and to identify with each other, their insights acted as powerful deterrents on each other's behavior. For example, when new members entered the group, they were asked why they had been transferred into the class. In many cases it was the first time in their high school experience that they had been asked to

look at their own behavior and acknowledge their responsibility for it. They seemed to realize that the group could not be "conned," and they did explain the specific reasons. Subsequently, they began to accept responsibility for their actions.

C. *Advantages of having deans as co-counselors of an*
   *opportunity class in this high school*

1. The students were familiar with the deans. A few of them blamed the deans for the fact that they were in the class, so it was possible for their hostility to be direct. In most instances, however, the deans were seen as having given many chances, and the students perceived them as helping agents.

2. Entering the group initially as authoritarian figures, the deans did not have to put up with the resistance other staff members had faced.

3. The deans were not seen as "shrinks."

4. The deans had already set limits, so the students did not need to test for them.

5. Discovering that the dean could be a caring, loving counselor or parent as well as an authoritarian helped increase the student's dimension of relating to authority figures.

6. Although the assumption that regular school was always the best solution was erroneous, the data appear to indicate that the success rate of returning to regular school could be improved through group counseling. Despite the fact that some were still "lost," the students seemed to leave the school knowing, or more importantly feeling, that they had not been cast away or rejected.

D. *Disadvantages of having the deans as counselors*
   *for the opportunity class*

1. The major problem is commitment of time. The involvement of the leaders cannot be spasmodic. Their *punctual and consistent attendance is imperative.*

2. The opportunity class teacher and the deans lose much of their control over the consequences of a student's behavior. The learning process of individual decision-making through the group appears to be more significant than any single decision by the deans.

*E. Special factors which have accompanied this project*

1. The necessity for preparing the teacher of the class for its effect on the student. The teacher needed to be prepared for changes in the student's behavior. If the process had not been clarified and the teacher's feelings considered, the teacher could, understandably, have felt undermined and in return undermine what was happening.

2. To the program formerly provided the opportunity class students, another dimension was added through the group counseling process.

3. For the first time a *follow-up group will be held for all those returning to regular school*. It has been found that those who did not have a follow-up seemed to fall back into old patterns of behavior. Thus, the commitment to these special students has to continue until they feel special enough to themselves to not have to be special to us.

In short, as school personnel, the deans' primary commitment has been to the students. When one becomes a "squeaky wheel," there is a responsibility to see that he gets "oiled." The oiling has been done through group counseling.

## PART II: C. SPECIAL TECHNIQUES

## EDITOR'S NOTE

*Diversity of student populations calls for diversity of counseling approaches. The following chapter illustrates one approach based on making initial contact with the students in their own segregated ethnic realm. Gradually, the thrust became more multi-ethnic. The counselor's own ethnic identification with the students was obviously vastly helpful, but perhaps not essential.*

## CHAPTER 14

# An Experience in Counseling Young Chicanas

Consuelo G. Rodriguez, M.A.

COUNSELING IN TODAY'S EDUCATION SYSTEM is not meeting the needs of many students. This is especially true for minorities such as Chicanos (Mexican-Americans), and particularly for the Chicanas (girls). One aspect of this is cited in the following quote:

> Guidance counselors in Mexican-American schools, for example, regularly steer students into "realistic" vocational programs, advice that just about locks young Chicanos into the poverty cycle. Overall, the insensitivity of Anglos—whether in government, in education, or simply on a person-to-person basis—has amounted to psychological oppression of incalculable dimensions. (*Newsweek*, p. 23, June 1970)

Counselors must give serious consideration to the fact that Chicanas have the highest dropout rate from high schools in comparison to their Black or white sisters (Sanchez, 1973).

> In the State of California the percentage of women 26 years and over who graduated from high school were as follows: 38.5% of the Chicana population; 51.8% of the Black population; 61.1% of the White population. The two major reasons for girls aged 16 to 21 dropping out of school were: (1) marriage, and (2) pregnancy. (Ramirez, 1967)

Better education opportunities and counseling with cultural awareness would have a tremendous effect on the outrageous percentage of Chicanas dropping out of school. Thus, we must look seriously at the kind of guidance and

---

I want to thank Esther Muños for her help and friendship. Also of assistance were Ms. Pat Conry and Mr. Pascual Martinez.

education provided or not provided the Chicana and her Indian, Black, and white counterpart!

Horton (1970) has summarized the relationship between counselors and their lower-class and middle-class clients in the following way:

> Evidence from several studies indicates that about one-half of the clients in personal counseling will terminate prematurely. It would obviously be economical of time and effort if premature terminators could be identified prior to initiation of counseling sessions. Efforts toward this goal have shown that middle class clients tend to remain and lower class clients tend to drop out of therapy . . . (pp. 98-99).

In most cases, young Chicana students, depending on the degree of acculturation, have had the reinforcement of a traditional culture and language that adds a unique dimension to the counseling situation. Thus Chicanas range from being totally assimilated individuals to being bilingual-bicultural individuals more immersed in their native culture. In whatever world they are living, the question of individual identity influences the manner in which they relate to society in general and their choice of life style. These diverse life styles must be considered, understood, and acknowledged before a counselor can enter into a successful counseling relationship (either individually or in a group) with Chicanas.

The high school Chicana experience is one in which she is confronted by the complexity of living in a white-controlled society with prevailing emphasis on white Anglo-Saxon male dominance. Yet the Chicana's white counterpart (the white Anglo-Saxon female) is in positions in which education, economics, material gains, basic rights, etc., are more accessible and feasible. In some instances the Chicana is attempting to relate to her white sisters' movement for liberation (feminism), but in too many instances she experiences rejection and competition from her white, liberal, freedom-seeking sisters. Another element with which she must cope is society's negative expectations of her as a female and as a member of the total Mexican-American community.

This process of oppression and racism is experienced in regard to total society, be they educators, politicians, waitresses, males or females, brothers or sisters. On the other hand, the Chicana is also a member of a cultural group which has strictly adhered to "traditional" female values and roles. For example, she has had to cope and adjust to the complexity of her own cultural mores (standard behavior), the tradition, and cultural peer group. Roles are manageable within the culture context, but when exposed to a society that often holds values of women in direct conflict with the parent culture, Chicanas experience many difficulties, such as in role adjustment, role identity, role definition, and role acceptance.

A traditional phenomenon of the white dominant male culture has been the placement of total responsibility for oppressive conditions on the minorities and the blaming of the victims for their deprived state of powerlessness and poverty! This area of concern and responsibility can be used effectively by the counselor in group counseling; however, it can also be used ineffectively if the counselor lacks sincere interest in or knowledge of the culture and the individual. One of the damaging practices, from the author's observation, has been that of the *counselor's using cultural stereotypes* to reinforce certain predicted behavioral patterns for the student. Whether this is done intentionally or unintentionally, the effect on the student has been the same. For example, note the contrast between saying, "I guess all of the girls in your family have been raised in the traditional Mexican role, are suppressed, and expected to be virgins," versus "How was your mother raised? Is she expected to act a certain way as a woman? Do you act and do certain things because it's expected of you? Do you think your mother's (or father's) behavior has had an effect on the way you behave? What kinds of things do you do that are different from the behavior of your parents, your brothers and sisters? What kinds of ways would you prefer to act? Do you do things differently from your mother?"

Rosenthal and Jacobson (1968) showed that in most cases if a teacher expects a student to fail, she will. As a result the student learns to see herself as incapable of handling academic work and sees her work, her world, and herself as irrelevant and even nonexistent. Other studies and research (Ramirez, 1967, and Purkey, 1970) have shown that the "self-fulfilling prophecy" is a conditioning process that truly occurs in our educational institutions, and programs Chicanas and other minorities for failure.

In a study done on the Mexican-American child, Rosenthal and Jacobson (1968) reported:

> The highest achievers in the upper grades looked more American to both groups of teachers. The study presented the possibility that if a Mexican child looked more American (that is, Anglo-Saxon) to a teacher, academic expectation for him might be like expectations for middle class children as compared to those for the Mexican child who looked more Mexican or lower class, with resultant differences in performance (p. 55).

Of significance in regard to the above statements is the crucial lack of experienced, well-trained teachers and counselors in dealing with Chicanos. This is particularly critical considering the conflict between the parent culture and the dominant culture as experienced individually or as a subgroup, and awareness on the part of the counselor is needed.

The *second counseling dimension* that can be of great service or disservice to the Chicana is that of the *counselor's attitude* toward her. The need for counselors who can relate positively to Chicanas is crucial to the reinforcement necessary in self-development. Cicirelli and Cicirelli (1970) state:

> The attitude of the counselor is particularly relevant in dealing with disadvantaged youth. Often suspicious and withdrawn, the disadvantaged youth seems to need special reassurance to let down his defenses and enter into a counseling relationship (p. 178).

*Third,* we need better trained counselors and well trained group counselors in the Chicana/Chicano experience who can relate to the Chicana's bicultural and bilingual world in a group process. One of the most decisive steps counselors can take, if they are to be effective and to understand the student, is to learn those skills which will enable them to accept the life style of the student, accept the student's perception of the world, and thus enter into her world of reality.

The following experience was especially impressive to the author and involved several of these points. A particular group of Chicanas had responded well to counseling assistance in the junior high school. When this group came into the high school there was no such counseling available. Instead, they felt lost and wandered the corridors during classes. Their educational progress was being neglected because the administration felt unable and/or unwilling to cope with the problem of providing a suitable program and insisting on class attendance. Instead, the girls were ignored by the staff, as if they were invisible. While this may have happened in some schools even with Caucasians, the minority factor probably was significant in this case.

Related literature reveals the following significant needs in relation to the effectiveness of counselor interaction with Chicana students and other minority groups:

(1) to be specifically aware of the historical and cultural influences of the Chicano;

(2) to be especially aware of behavior typical of youth growing in certain

environments and social settings (gangs, urban, rural, drug, etc.) owing to social pressures;

(3) to be able to distinguish between the effect of poverty and that of the Mexican-American culture;

(4) to become aware of the differences in students in terms of their background, rural or urban;

(5) to be aware of the effects of positive or negative acculturation and/or assimilation on productivity and emotional stability of the Chicana student, and the effect on the student of total assimilation into the parent culture;

(6) to investigate and sincerely analyze personal biases and stereotyping attitudes toward Mexican-Americans. If working with Chicanas in particular, the counselor should examine any negative attitudes or role expectations;

(7) to be aware of significant negative counselor attitudes toward guidance of Mexican-American students;

(8) to become familiar with the community in which one works and extend oneself into the homes of the students. The counselor should utilize other respected community resources.

The specifics given in the previous material relate to counselors working with Chicanas and Chicanos; however, much of the material is relevant to work with other minorities. Counselors, teachers, and administrators must be trained to work more sensitively and effectively with all minorities.

*Group counseling*

Group counseling is particularly helpful and effective in the field of counseling. In speaking of a group experience, one counselee stated:

> Regular visiting time should be set up like every Tuesday or Thursday just to talk, you know, like our seminar sessions, so that you know what counseling is, what a counselor is, to hear about you and your family background, so you can talk about racism, what's going on, what bugs you, what it feels like when you have to walk down in the basement (this is where all the Chicanos hang out in this school, because all of their classes are down there), how it feels to hang out by the poles (the hippies' hangout), to find out why you are failing a class, or why you do this or that, just the whole thing. . . .

This is not to say that the Chicana does not need individual counseling, but the option should be given her to select the most effective processes, namely, individual, individual and group, group alone, etc. However, group identity and association of personal and social feelings of inadequacies and insecurities become crucial and constitute a sensitive area in the group process. Furthermore, the peer group dynamics of the Chicana, particularly those of barrio gangs, provide a culturally supportive basis from which strength and security are obtained. Also, Chicanas and Chicanos have often worked problems out by themselves through their peer group and rejected interaction with social and educational institutions because of social pressures, injustices, and inadequacies experienced in the system.

When a young Chicana is struggling with her family, peers, and society, she can turn to a parent surrogate (teacher, counselor, coach, etc.) for understanding and guidance, as can most Anglo students. However, the Chicana has not always had an adult parent surrogate in the schools, because those in authority have not experienced the varying life styles of the Chicanas, nor have they been provided the training needed. Consequently, the peer group was more important in the barrio. Thus, in group counseling one is institutionalizing a process that has long been part of the barrio experience for these young girls. But one may encounter resistance by Chicanas upon intrusion into "private territory" with its own rules for achieving self-identity, social interrelationships, and sheer survival.

Counselors working with any group process must become familiar with the cultural differences of the different members. These leaders must be equipped to deal with racial biases and confrontations from the counselees. *The goal of the author was to bring the Chicanas into multiethnic counseling groups* The sequence was to work first with the counselees on an individual basis; second, to move them into a group process by utilizing the similarities of their being females of Mexican descent; third, to accept and work with them in their defined world of reality; and fourth, to move them into ethnically mixed groups in which the objective was to deal with ethnic apprehensions and misunderstanding. If the first two stages were adequately handled, the counselee was in a place to communicate and accept those of other ethnic backgrounds and to interrelate on any racial apprehensions.

As stated by several Chicanas:

> There should be seminars on all races, like what we did. I couldn't have done it any other way, like if we would have mixed first. (The first group dealt with only Chicanas.) I had to get it on with my people first and get into myself, then mixed, and be able to learn to deal with race problems of other people.

Interviews with young Chicana students and high school counselors force the conclusion that not only are more counseling groups needed, but most existing ones avoid dealing with issues of most concern for the young Chicana: drugs, homosexuality, racism, self-perception, cultural identity, poverty, and relating to the dominant culture.

Anglos make up the largest percentage of counselors in the educational institutions today. The backgrounds and environments of the majority of them are of the dominant society, white Anglo-Saxon Protestant. This can be a disadvantage in counseling individuals or groups whose values are culturally and socially diametrically opposite. If the counselors' values are controlled or nonjudgmental, they may be able to move beyond them in counseling and be successful; however, the human tendency is actually to counsel from one's own values, perceptions, cultural experiences, and societal exposure, thus limiting one's ability to relate to other cultural life styles.

This is not to overlook the fact that some Chicano counselors may at times prove less effective than their Anglo-Saxon counterparts; however, if those Chicano counselors are totally accepting of their own cultural background, they can be of great benefit to the Chicana. One young girl stated:

> Hey, man, there are some really cool white people here. They're not like most gringos; they care. You can tell. It's hard to say how you know. It's like you can just tell, you know.

## Privacy in counseling

Chicanas, like other young people, are concerned about lack of *privacy* and confidentiality in counseling. More generally, the lack of privacy in the counseling office often prevents a great deal of interaction from occurring between the student and the counselor. According to one Chicana:

> First, I would stop (the counselor) from going to all those meetings and have her give more time to the student and try to help them out. Sometimes other teachers and counselors come in when you are talking and interrupt and talk about something else and leave you there stoned, and that is what turns most of the kids off. I want more privacy, and she rarely closes the door when I talk.

Another Chicana stated:

> . . . Also, there is no privacy; the walls don't go all the way to the ceiling, and other people can hear what you are saying.

Historically, counselors and teachers have too often discussed a student's background in the hall, faculty room, or offices. If the counselor finds it absolutely necessary to discuss with a colleague, or the parent, information regarding the student, professionalism dictates that it be done in privacy and only when the discussion is productive to the student and her future. Chicanas broached the fact that counselors would gossip among themselves and destroy confidentiality by discussing information considered private and personal to the girls. Sadly enough, the author has witnessed such thoughtlessness, insensitivity, unprofessionalism, and outright inhumanness. This behavior by counselors has interfered with Chicanas (and others) seeking out counselor guidance.

Also, counselors must avoid stereotyping students' present behavior by relating to past records, previous counselors' experiences, or by relating to the records of brothers or sisters. The author once heard a counselor laughing, moralizing, and disclosing to a group of teachers her judgmental experience with a Chicana counselee. The counselor considered the student "typical for her type" (the girl identified with gang girls), namely, that she was immoral and bound for prostitution. The counselor saw no worth in the girl, no chance of any possible acceptable future for her, and she found her to be a waste of time. After discussion with the counselor, the author found that judgmental conclusions were based on feedback from previous counselors. A most damaging element was the stereotyping and judging of the Chicana based on an appearance common to many cholas: high, ratted hair, "far out" eye makeup, and mode of dress. Obviously, this can lead many Chicanas to avoid whatever counseling services are available.

## Communication skills

Counselors for all young persons need to be receptive to nonverbal communication. Calia (1966) makes the very important point:

> As counseling services are extended to less articulate segments of the population—the educationally disadvantaged, the mentally retarded, and others—we are going to have to try to discover nonverbal or at least less verbal ways for such clients to communicate with us. It is one of the challenges we face right now (p. 102).

Communicating with the poor and the minorities requires understanding of their jargon as well as the nonverbal. This entails understanding and respecting their mode of communication. The Chicana student often may have more difficulty verbalizing her feelings with educators and counselors because of her apprehensions and uncertainty of the counselor's sincerity and reactions. On the other hand, in regard to the cultural aspect, she is reluctant to share home or personal problems with someone outside her family or peer setting.

The language spoken in the barrio is composed of a mixture of Spanish and English, called "Spanglish." "Pocho" is the process used to create a new word by combining the Spanish and English: for example, market + eta = "marketa." If one is working with gang girls, one is exposed to "Calo," which can be considered a creative dialect resulting from Pochismo and Spanglish: "My wife is in the house—Mi *ruca* esta en el chante." But in Spanglish, Pocho, or Calo that is being spoken, one experiences a language that is sensitive, has feeling, and above all, is very descriptive and difficult to interpret word for word or feeling for feeling. Learning the language spoken in the barrio will not be sufficient in relating effectively with Chicana students; however, a *sensitive and sincere counselor who is bilingual* will be in a much better position than a *monolingual counselor*. The more assimilated Mexican-Americans, especially those who may be well educated, can verbalize their feelings in English more readily to a counselor than the Chicana student who does not relate or identify with the school culture.

*Community impact*

If community influence could be more effectively exerted in schools, the staff would then be more aware of the views, orientations, contributions, and needs of the immediate community. This would aid the student as well as the school staff. Barrios are very closely knit communities in which strong family and community ties are respected and perpetuated. The school would find this aspect of great benefit in maintaining a more harmoniously functioning institution. The student would see many of her community influences in the school, and this in turn would make her feel she belongs, that she is part of that school, as are her family and friends.

In effect, the school should be aware of the following forces that place certain expected behavioral patterns on the student:

(1) those set down by the school (the socializing institution of society);
(2) those set down by her family (parent culture);
(3) those set down by her peer group (identity).

The peer group identity is a role that results in forms of behavioral resistance, questionable identity factors, and need for security, because it provides survival mechanisms. In the second role, one sees the influence of the most stabilizing force in the Mexican-American culture, *the familia*, struggling for its survival. The first role is based on a preconceived behavior as defined by society and implemented by the schools. If counselors are exposed to various cultures and have a secure sense of self worth, the need to degrade or minimize others will be reduced. Thus they will be of great assistance in supporting and encouraging Chicanas toward a strong sense of well-being. Counselors will thereby develop a secure sense of appreciative values for individual uniqueness, cultural perpetuation, community directiveness, and input. The placement of more Chicanas and Chicanos in *key* administrative positions and in counselor educator programs at the university level would have a decisive contribution to multicultural counseling.

## A special approach to group counseling with Chicanas

A view of the group process approach that was used by the author may be of interest. She chose to work with a group of young Chicanas who, for the sake of security and self-identity, had no other alternative but to associate with others like themselves. Some of these groups were termed by society as "gangs," "Pachucas," "cholas," "Chicana hippies," or trouble-makers. Although the author worked with other groups, she chose to write about the process utilized with this particular group of girls because of the lack of material on the Chicanas and the poor quality or absence or services for this group. This does not imply that such a process can be standardized to be applicable to all Chicana groups. It may be that the author served as an identity model for the young Chicanas throughout the evolution of her involvement, and this role was of essential value. The author was able to develop a relationship in which the Chicanas and their families could openly relate their most intimate fears of Anglo racial hostility, self-rejection, social rejection, and value conflict.

The group selected by the author was a core group of young girls who had developed a reputation for being "cholas," or an identifiable group of Chicanas who were resistant to the societal and educational establishment. Besides this core group of girls, there were other girls who identified strongly with the "guts of the cholas" to act out negative feelings but, because of social pressures, chose not to act out their tension and frustration.

The second phase after selection was for *counseling each girl individually* before involving her in the group process. The author's main purpose was to bring the student to a point where she could communicate with others besides her peers without fearing that some of her deepest personal doubts, anxieties, and hostilities would not be understood.

The next step was to move each girl to a place where she felt secure in revealing her personal feelings in a group (all of the girls were Mexican-American and had similar environmental and family backgrounds). The author reassured each student that others in the group would be accepting of her feelings and would associate and identify with her. This often provided the supportive bridge needed in order to bring the group into a secure state of being.

The author also found that *these Chicanas needed a more personalized type of relationship,* especially beyond the school building or school hours. She provided this by spending time with them, evenings, weekends, overnight parties, skating, and parties. Visits to juvenile hall, appearance on their behalf before juvenile court judges, and direct contacts with probation officers further helped to prove the counselor's sincerity and loyalty. These moments of legal and emotional difficulty were very lonely and deeply depressing for the girls, and it was at these times that they needed a true friend.

After these *shared experiences,* the sincerity of the relationship was no longer questioned. One girl, Lucy, said to the author, "You really came through. You're not full of a lot of bull shit like the others." She paused and then turned to me again and asked why I was doing all this for her. Why did I care when no one else seemed to care? She walked away. One of the prime reasons for being supportive specifically in instances such as this was to let them know that the author and possibly other teachers, counselors, and administrators cared. This counselor realized that this was a very crucial time and utilized it to support and reassure them that they were healthy, productive, and wanted human beings. This is the period when a friend, teacher, counselor, and administrator can have utmost impact and be most productive in counseling and directing students who enter into such a state. However, the effectiveness of such counseling is dependent on the consistency, knowledge, and sincerity of the helpful leader.

Another very important step involved sensitivity, respect, and knowledge of the Mexican culture. Once the Chicanas and the author had established the trust essential to a good counseling relationship, *the counselor made contact with the family,* particularly the mother. It is important to recognize that the mother, student, and counselor were all Mexican-American females. Contact and relationship with the mother was more practical, since the father usually worked during visiting hours. The fathers were more hesitant and critical of the visit perhaps, because the counselor was young, single, and a Mexican-American female. In the author's opinion and that of other Chicano educators, the social conditioning process was such that an older married Caucasian woman's authority was less questioned by the fathers.

The mother, on the other hand, seemed to be concerned about developing a relationship that would help her understand the total impact of all forces. The father's major concern in this instance was one of a disciplinary nature.

In many instances the author was invited to showers, baptisms, and parties. Because of the author's background and community ties, the process of establishing relationships was easier. One of the counselor's goals was to make initial contact with the parents on a positive rather than a negative level. Once accepted by the family, especially the mother, the author learned a great deal about the girl, the family structure (not all Mexican-American families are alike), and some of the realities of the young girl's background having a direct relationship to her behavior in school. Many times this behavior was in direct conflict with the values at home. The author continued to visit the homes of the girls even after high school, and today she still finds some of the relationships of value. Some of the girls went to college; some are married; others are seeking menial employment. Some are attempting to survive the drug culture, while others are drifting into oblivion or simply existing.

Of grave importance in the group process is the *very first group session.* It is then that one either wins or loses the group. Therefore, the author conducted the first rap session with the Chicanas not on the school campus, but in the privacy of her home. Other sessions were held in "hangout areas" such as neighborhood parks, and eventually sessions were held on the school grounds. This process was very important to this particular group of Chicanas, since they did not relate positively to the school.

The factor the author found most trying and difficult to deal with was not her interactions with the girls, but her interaction and relationships with some educators, administrators, and counselors. Some educators and counselors persecuted these girls for their appearance, manner of behavior, and language. Unlike most educators, the author found positive aspects in all that the counselees were. In time this counselor was able to explain the reality of the "status quo appearance factor" and how they would have to confront such an issue in seeking jobs. She presented this to them as a selection of alternatives in identity projection, after continuously reinforcing them in their strength. They found that acceptance of their beauty and of themselves provided the power they needed to confront any issue that questioned their validity as beautiful and productive human beings.

### Need for change in counselor's role!

The following concept bears mentioning although it cannot be adequately elaborated here. As demonstrated in the type of group with the Chicanas above, the process of counseling is not complete if it is confined to the four walls of the counselor's office. *Total counseling* means that the counselor has got to be more aggressive within the institution as well as outside the institution. It may be necessary more often to say "no" to administrative duties and be more demanding of adequate tools, facilities, caseloads, work studies, supportive staff (such as counselor aid) and, above all, release time and/or compensation for courses, seminars, community workshops, etc., that will promote professional growth. This role may be somewhat threatening and new contrasted to past role definitions. The counselor must be more aggressive as well in utilizing and learning about the vast amount of resources, agencies, etc., in the community that can be of benefit in helping young people.

As described in the experience with the group of Chicanas, it was often desirable and essential to intervene for the girls in community agency settings where important difficulties were occurring. These difficulties certainly interfered with an effective educational experience as well as with a successful counseling experience. Counselor avoidance of help in these areas may well be seen as signs of indifference, neglect or bias in the mind of the counselee. Time in the schedule for these types of assistance should be considered essential in any complete counseling program.

## Conclusion

The author's concern is to find ways in which counselors and educators can guide and counsel the particular minority children with whom they are working.

Perhaps one approach is to have counselors reeducate themselves to the cultural life style of the students they will be counseling. They should seek ways to understand the different life and cultural styles of the students by enrolling in local colleges, by studying the particular community, and by involving themselves in the social life of the community. Areas of immediate concern are: home situation, peer relationships, language difficulties (as they relate to the school environment), crosscultural conflict values, societal alienation, identity establishment, and the different forms of anxiety release. Counselors and other educators must not only become aware of this conflict or process that is occurring within each Chacana and Chicano student but must also be sensitive to the conflict in order to adequately counsel her or him.

Some of the processes and content referred to may mean a total reassessment of the role counselors have traditionally held and the actual role with which they are faced in an everyday life orientation. Exploration might in-

*When Schools Care*

clude an introspective look at prejudicial judgment, or questioning the disciplinary role assigned by the administration. Going beyond the individual counselor, the author realizes the impact and reconstruction that would have to take place in the traditional counseling system.

Lastly, the author supports the need for a new approach and reeducation of the traditional paper-pushing counselor role. This need is based on observations made of counselors, the author's own personal evaluation of the counseling system, and the responses of students. Many students, particularly Chicanas, have not been provided adequate educational guidance and counseling. It should be obvious to any professional educator that unless students are properly counseled in conflict and role-adjustment situations, the academic, educational, and social functioning of the students will be limited and hampered, in school as well as in their life experience. The 1974 Civil Rights Commission Report indicates gross miseducation and neglect in the guidance of the Mexican-American student. Will there be change in the later '70s?

## BIBLIOGRAPHY

CALIA, V. F. (1966). The culturally deprived client: A reformation of the counselor's role. *J. of Counseling Psychol.*, 13:1, 100-105.

CICIRELLI, V. G. and CICIRELLI, J. S. (1970). Counselors' creative ability and attitude in relation to counseling behavior with disadvantaged counselees. *J. of Counseling Psychol.*, 17:2, 177-183.

HORTON, K. (1970). MMPI differences between terminators and continuers in youth counseling. *J. of Counseling Psychol.*, 17:2, 98-101.

PURKEY, W. W. (1970). *Self Concept and School Achievement.* Englewood Cliffs, N. J.: Prentice Hall.

RAMIREZ, M., III (1967). Value conflicts experienced by Mexican-American children. Sacramento, Calif.: California State Dept. of Education.

ROSENTHAL, R. and JACOBSON, L. (1968). *Pygmalion in the Classroom.* San Francisco: Holt, Rinehart, and Winston.

SANCHEZ, C. (1973). Higher Education y la Chicana? *Encuentro Femenil*, 1:1.

# PART II: C. SPECIAL TECHNIQUES

## EDITOR'S NOTE

*Most often discussion in groups of adolescents will proceed spontaneously without any need for-stimulation by any procedures introduced by the leader other than discussion-related remarks or questions. At times, a group may be stalled, out of control, or anxious in a nonproductive way. Even these eventualities may be conducive to discussion, analysis, and useful understanding by a confident, knowledgeable teacher.*

*At such times an exercise or prescribed confrontation as described by Bates (Chapter 15) and Rueveni (Chapter 35) may be useful if applied with discretion, care, and if available, supervision. There is the danger that a leader's anxiety may be masked by excessive, mechanical, or inappropriate use of such planned devices. Activity and control as a way to discharge or contain anxiety are used by adults as well as by adolescents. However, carefully used, these exercises may add depth, movement, and understanding to a group's experience when they are not used to frustrate the values of unstructured person-to-person interaction.*

## CHAPTER 15

# Confrontation in the Group Process

Marilyn Bates, Ph.D.

THE FUNCTION OF THE COUNSELOR in group work has been variously categorized as a superego, catalytic agent, and facilitator. Implementation of these roles has been through techniques generally indigenous to individual counseling. One of the unique contributions to understanding group process has been emphasizing the importance of confrontation as a means of promoting behavioral change.

It should be recognized that the use of confrontive techniques involves *risk for both counselor and counselees.* Such is the essence of encounter. It is not clear whether the intensity of confrontation is in linear relationship to the amount of risk involved, but this seems likely. The writer has chosen to make this assumption and has clearly ordered the following comments around confrontive techniques as *mild and moderate levels of risk.* The interactions may involve only group members, group member and therapist, and group members and therapist with varying degrees of risk.

*Mild confrontation techniques*

It is very likely that moving too far ahead of group members on the part of the group counselor will inhibit rather than facilitate movement toward confrontation. Thus, it is wise to proceed with caution, and the following suggestions represent only mild degrees of confrontation.

*Birth Order.* A very simple but usually productive device to encourage group members to look at themselves is to ask the group to subdivide into small groups according to whether the member was first born, last born, or

Reprinted with permission from *Research and Pupil Personnel Services Newsletter,* Office of Los Angeles County Superintendent of Schools, November, 1972.

middle born. Each group discusses problems which resulted in their lives as a result of their sibling position; then the entire group reassembles to share points of view. This technique will focus attention on present perceptions of group members as they talk about a productive topic of group counseling content—individual members.

*Territoriality.* Asking a group which has been in session a time or two to change seats after the group has started will bring up the problem of territoriality. Why did group members tend to arrange themselves in the same seating order each time? How did they feel when they saw someone else sitting in their "territory"? Who sat next to whom on the rearrangement and why? What is each member's psychological territory? Another illustration of territoriality is made by asking group members to whisper in each other's ear, and then to talk nose-to-nose. Acceptable social distances can be discussed before focusing on how close group members would feel comfortable sitting by other specific group members. The discussion of variations in distances leads to confrontations between group members.

*Interaction Diagram.* A simple sociometric device of asking group members to diagram with arrows the interactions of a given period of group discussion will call attention to cross currents within the group. Who are "stars" and why? Who were isolates and why? Have the directions of output changed as the group has been developing?

*First Memories.* The recalling of first memories may elicit mild confrontation. Members share with the group their very first memories in which there was an element of conflict. What was significant about that particular memory? Do group members perceive similarities in current behavior patterns which might create conflict?

*Free Association.* Free association can stimulate confrontation. The usual procedure is for the group leader to present a stimulus word which may or may not be "loaded" and ask group members to respond without thought going around the circle. (Split-second censoring should be noted and perhaps called to the group's attention by the leader.) This technique tends to bring out affective content and is useful as a warm-up process. "Going 'round" is seldom completed more than a time or two before the group is dealing with significant material.

*Stereotyping.* Exploring stereotyping can lead to mild confrontation. One way this might be encouraged is by asking the group to respond to a group leader's third-person comment about a group member, such as, "Mary sure thinks she is pretty good," and asking the group to share their immediate impressions concerning Mary. Then restate the comment, "Mary seems delightfully sure of herself." Again the group can react. Mary can respond with her feelings, perhaps "going 'round" giving feedback to each group member individually concerning her reactions to their comments.

*Human Potential.* The last procedure to be presented under mild confrontation techniques is a methodology rather than a technique. An entire group counseling format could be built around these principles. The human potential seminar is based on the assumption that something is right with the student rather than, as is perhaps more usual, that something is wrong. The first step toward confrontation consists of *"strength bombardment,"* in which one student volunteers to tell what his or her personal strengths are, after which the group responds by telling what strengths they see in him or her. The student then asks, "What do you see that is preventing me from using my strengths?" and again the group responds. The fourth step in the "strength bombardment" consists of group members' constructing a group fantasy in which they imagine what the target person can be doing in five years or more if strengths are used optimally. As a final step the student is asked to relate to the group how he or she felt in undergoing this experience.

The second portion of the human potential seminar consists of *"success bombardment,"* in which a student begins by telling the group about the most successful experiences in his or her entire life and then follows up by telling about three fairly recent experiences which were unsuccessful. The group analyzes the failures in light of the success or achievement pattern revealed in the strength bombardment in order to make the student more aware of the success pattern, to indicate whether failures represent nonapplication of the success pattern, and to suggest areas where potential has not been tapped.

The third section of the human potential seminar is focused on action and consists of *goal-setting experiences*. At the close of each session students in the group set individual goals which are to be accomplished before the next meeting. The goals must be expressed verbally; they must be believable, measurable, and something the students really want to do. They must be presented with no alternatives. The purpose of this procedure is to help students become aware that they can control their own lives to a far greater degree than they probably do at the present time. It also helps students become aware of their own value systems and increase self-motivation. The human potential seminar is a small group educational experience which makes use of the confrontation level of interaction in a planned sequence.

*Moderate confrontation*

The following confrontation techniques probably involve a *higher degree of risk* than do the preceding procedures, although it should be recognized that all confrontation holds risk and pain potential. The procedures to be delineated in the following section require fairly intensive involvement and move to a personal level rather quickly. They probably involve some threat as the procedures tap conative levels and/or contain some degree of possible hostility, which may bring up negative aspects of the members' personalities.

*Magic Shop.* In this first procedure the group is asked to imagine that they can shop at a magic place in which only intangibles are in stock. Any intangible, such as honesty, love, great intelligence, etc., may be purchased, but the price is something which the individual already owns, such as good health, joy of living, intelligence, etc. The magic shop is an excellent device for confronting group members with their value systems and the commitment each may have to any given set of values.

*Role Playing.* A common confrontation technique, but one which is too little used in group counseling, is role playing. An alert leader can easily find appropriate situations arising out of the content which group members provide wherein role playing can be useful. It is important to use the technique of role reversal, and it is important to provide sufficient time in the group session to explore thoroughly the implications of the role play. The insights gained through skillful use of this confrontation technique usually are most satisfactory.

*Identifying Emotions.* Two simple confrontation procedures aimed at the conative level of awareness involve emotions. The first asks group members to list quickly all the emotions they can. Lists are then compared, and differing lengths and contents are discussed relative to the affect which each group member transmits. An additional exercise involves asking group members to communicate to the group the emotion in awareness at a given time. Then the members are asked to bring up from the back of their minds the next emotion as another is brought into awareness. The purpose of the group leader is to help group members become aware of their ongoing feelings, tap their stream of consciousness, tune inward on visceral reactions, and gain in skill of verbalizing these feelings.

*Drifting.* Another possible confrontation-encouraging procedure is called "drifting." In this exercise the group leader asks the group to drift aimlessly about the room without talking. No further instruction is given, but the group can be seen to divide into subgroups—who with whom?—and some members will return to their seats more quickly than others. The ensuing discussion brings about focus on group members' tendencies toward conformity, their degree of independence, their tolerance for ambiguity, their compulsion toward goals, self-consciousness in the face of an unstructured field, and need for territoriality.

*Authority Syndrome.* Group leaders might also tap members' insights into their reactions to authority figures by asking the group to put down on a piece of paper as many or as few dots as each member wishes, then try to connect these dots in a line which does not cross itself. As the group does this, the group leaders express disapproval, shaking their heads and looking rather disgusted. They then announce that they will give the group one more trial, at which time they transmit no approval or disapproval, but merely sit indifferently by. The discussion can focus on the group members' reactions to an authority figure's disapproval concerning a task which obviously can be accomplished and the feelings this inappropriate disapproval engendered within them. Where is their locus of evaluation? Another area for discussion might be the various life styles demonstrated by group members as they approached this task—were they serious, committed, uninvolved? Did members put down many dots or few? How long did each continue under disapproval? Did the disapproval create group unity? Did behavior during the second opportunity differ from the first? Did the group leader's attitude change behavior? How do group members respond and handle authority figures?

*Autobiographies.* The capsule autobiography can be used to effect confrontation. Each group member is asked to write five or so sentences concerning his or her life history. These are read by the leader and discussed anonymously. Is there a life theme, a script? Group members will gain in understanding of the life space of other group members, some may gain insight into their own life space, and focus may also dwell on future plans. Confrontation will be gained in this exercise if the group leader is somewhat familiar with projective theory.

*Group Sociogram.* Asking the members to draw a sociogram of the group, after it has been in session at least once, can hasten confrontation as members examine interpersonal relations within the group and speculate on causes. Who are isolates? Who are stars? After a period of sessions will or did the sociograms change?

*Rejection.* An exercise in deliberate rejection can be used to dwell on hostile feelings. Group members are asked to totally ignore one member who attempts to integrate with the group, either physically or verbally. The feelings engendered in all group members are worth exploring at a confrontation level.

*Micro Lab.* The micro lab is one of the most useful exercises to encourage confrontation and can be used to initiate a series of group encounters. Each sensitivity group will be divided into two subgroups for the purpose of this exercise. Subgroup composition will remain the same for the duration of the exercise. Subgroups will be labeled "A" and "B." To begin, group A will meet for seven minutes, responding to an assignment given them by the trainer, e.g., discuss feelings here and now.

While group A is meeting in a small circle, group B will sit outside that circle, observing the members of group A. Each member of group A will have a feedback partner in group B. After group A has met for seven minutes, it will break for a four-minute feedback session, during which each individual in group A will receive feedback on his or her seven minutes of behavior from the partner in group B. When the feedback session is concluded, group B meets in the small circle, and group A observes.

When seven minutes of activity are terminated, the four-minute feedback session again occurs, with individuals in group A giving feedback to the same individuals in group B who had initially given them feedback. Partners should be changed after both have given each other feedback. After the change of partners, the process indicated above should be continued. It should be noted that before beginning the first meeting, a timekeeper should be selected for each subgroup. The subgroup on the outside times the inside group for the seven- and four-minute periods.

*Significant Experiences.* A final moderate confrontation exercise involves a "going 'round." Group members are asked to make a specified number of statements about themselves which should be personal. The group then reacts. A variation of this procedure involves the use of a timer. The leader sets the timer for a selected amount of time—perhaps three minutes—and group members use their allotted time to tell about themselves, going back to early childhood for significant experiences. If the time is not used by a group member, the group is encouraged to ask personal questions. This procedure should be initiated by the leader, who sets the stage by being the first to tell about himself or herself.

*New Ways of Behaving.* For a specified time, group members are asked to try out a way of behaving which they see as desirable, but which they have not previously seen themselves as doing. Five minutes may be sufficient for the exercise if the group is not too large. At the end of the designated time, members are asked to report to the group what "new" behaviors they observed in others, to react to their own "new" behavior and to report feelings involved.

*Psychodrama and Sociodrama.* Reporting the procedures particular to psychodrama and sociodrama are beyond the scope of this paper, but the use of this method seems to hold promise for group counseling. Some adaptation may be needed for the school setting, but much of Moreno's work seems applicable.

The preceding techniques may be useful as devices to encourage groups to focus on the "here and now," "I and thou," but the main instruments of movement toward confrontation are the group leaders themselves. If they are willing to risk themselves in encounter, the groups are likely to follow. If they are not, the groups probably will remain at a safe, nonproductive, topic-centered level.

# CHAPTER 16

# Activities of Group Leader and Group Member Clarified by Videotape Evaluation

## Kathryn Lewis, Ed.D.

GROUP COUNSELING has had mixed reception in the secondary schools. In some cases it has been regarded as a panacea for all evils, in others as faddish nonsense. Part of the problem, it seems to me, lies in the difficulty we have in deciding what we want to happen in a group and then in deciding whether that or anything else of significance has, in truth, occurred. These decisions are complicated by the fact that many practicing counselors have had little first-hand experience with group counseling in their professional training. If they have had experience in encounter or sensitivity groups, it does not translate directly to the high school situation. *High school groups do not parallel adult sensitivity groups.*

This leaves a void which has to be filled through in-service education. I believe that the planned use of videotape can help counselors gain a perspective on the group process, which can facilitate both their own effectiveness and that of their counselees. Although a group may improve its effectiveness simply by watching a replay of the videotaped session, it can make greater progress by deciding upon clearly understood, easily defined segments of behavior for evaluation. Initial viewing may well be concerned with improving communication skills, for example, which is certainly a desirable objective in any group.

One target of leaders concerned with improving such skills is their own increased ability to use words and attitudes that will foster intragroup communication. A goal of group members might well be to learn to hear more perceptively what is being said. The discussion guidelines which follow can

133

provide a basis for observing the behavior segments displayed by both leaders and group members as they communicate with each other.

Another planned sequence in the use of videotapes for in-service work with groups may center around a group self-appraisal form. As group members review their session, they may, at 10-second intervals indicated by a blip, check on an appraisal form the behavior which they observe in themselves. The patterns so recorded may provide a basis for group discussion. Counselors may use videotape effectively to broaden each other's understanding of the group process. Mr. Smith, for example, viewing portions of Mr. Jones' group tape, may be able to see that group is responding angrily to what it considers inconsistent leadership; Miss Brown, viewing portions of Mrs. Blue's tape, may decide that it is all right for a leader to act decisively. As counselors become more at ease with the use of videotape and as they discover the potential it has for effective teaching, they usually feel greater freedom to use it creatively.

*DISCUSSION GUIDELINES* for use with videotapes:

*Activities of group leaders*

One of the chief tasks of group leaders is to facilitate communication among group members. They assist them both in expressing their own feelings honestly and directly and in understanding with greater insight the feelings of others. Certain facilitating statements and questions—specific techniques—may help the leaders in this task. Some of these are listed under descriptions of what the leaders are attempting to accomplish.

The attitudes which counselors bring to the counseling relationship deeply influence the kind and quality of communication which takes place. Such attitudes are as important in the group process as they are in the one-to-one relationship. Different theorists seem to have convergent views about what constitutes facilitating attitudes on the part of counselors. These are also outlined, with specific suggestions for their implementation.

The leaders, as facilitators of group communication:

A. *Make sure that they understand what is being said—*

I don't understand what you mean when you say ...............
Do I hear you say ...............?
Am I right in feeling that ...............?

B. *Rephrase member's statement—*

In other words, you believe that .................
Your experience has been that .................
You just have never liked working with details.

C. *Put into words the emotion accompanying member's statement—*

You sound mad. Are you?
You're thinking, "I'm so ugly that no boy will ever look at me."
Could it be that deep down you're afraid you'll never be able to please your parents?

D. *Encourage specificity—*

Give us a for-instance.
Can you describe the situation in more detail?
Exactly what does he say that upsets you?
Will you clarify that?

E. *Invite role play—*

Mike, will you play the part of your father, and will someone volunteer to play the part of Mike?
If you were a teacher, how would you act in this situation?

F. *Help antagonists to listen to each other—*

Before you answer, will you put into your own words what Mary just said?
Jerry, how do you feel when John tells you off?

G. *Assist group members to talk to each other—*

Who are you talking to?
Tell Jerry, not me.
Are you talking about John or *to* him?

H. *Describe what they see—*

Jerry's doodling is getting lots of attention.
It's so quiet in here.
Mary's frowning.
Jerry, are you aware what you're doing?

I. *Point out limiting nature of many questions—*

What happens when Mary asks so many questions?
Can you make that question into a statement?
How do you feel when you ask that question?

J. *Express their own feelings appropriately—*

I'm puzzled by what's going on.
I find myself feeling uncomfortable.
I'm embarrassed.

K. *Use open-ended questions or statements, rather than those requiring "yes" or "no" answers—*

Tell us about it.
What are you feeling now?
Describe the situation.

L. *Assist group in staying with topic—*

How did we get here?
Nobody seems to want to talk about Mary's problem.
I have a feeling that we didn't respond adequately to Mary's question.

M. *Discourage subgrouping—*

I can't hear Mary.
Will you bring it to the group?

N. *Point out similarities, differences, and inconsistencies—*

Jim, you and John seem to agree that ................
At one time you feel that ................, but a little later you feel that ................
Mary believes that ................, but John ................
You say you're angry, but you're smiling.

O. *Encourage group to focus on the "here and now"—*

Even though it happened last Fall, it still makes you angry.

Leaders facilitate group communication by showing respect for individuals in the group. They (1) avoid approving and disapproving members' statements; (2) avoid being threatening—do not misuse their authority; (3) express their own feelings honestly and directly; (4) are sensitive to the distinction between prying and facilitating; (5) treat group members as equals, not subordinates; and (6) trust the group.

They show empathy toward group members: (1) take time to sense what is going on; (2) stay with the speakers, not ahead of them; (3) verbalize their responsive feelings; (4) allow silence; and (5) permit their own emotional reaction to show.

They (1) evidence warmth through facial expression; (2) exhibit postural attitudes of interest, concern, and caring; (3) communicate warmth through tone of voice; (4) respond person-to-person, rather than person-to-group; and (5) use gestures and bodily movements which include group members, not reject them.

Leaders show congruence: (1) do not unknowingly mix authoritarian and permissive roles; (2) operate within the group structure in a manner consistent with their personal philosophy; (3) are sensitive to their own feelings and do not misrepresent them; and (4) communicate any agenda they have for the group to the group.

*Activities of group members*

Group members have a responsibility both to say what they think and feel, and to listen to what is said by others. The objective of this paper is to have group members improve their listening behavior through replay of the videotape. Before the tape critique, members may discuss the points listed below, in order to provide a basis for constructive criticism. In conducting this kind of critique, group leaders should allow considerable flexibility, bearing in mind that, for the beginning group members, it is often more difficult to say what they think than it is to listen to others.

Group members' ability to hear each other may be evidenced through a word, a motion, a look, or a silence. Group members who feel that they are not heard and those who feel that they have been heard incorrectly may speak a great deal or not at all, may become angry or flippant or tearful. Sometimes members interfere with the listening of others without realizing they are doing so.

Group members may interfere actively with the listening of others by (1) changing the subject frequently; (2) bringing in unrelated material; (3) asking unrelated questions; (4) talking too much; (5) cutting off speakers; (6) reacting negatively much of the time; and (7) providing physical distractions.

Group members may interfere passively by (1) talking only to the leader; (2) speaking in a voice which cannot be heard; (3) withdrawing in some way from the group; (4) speaking rarely, if at all; and (5) giving mixed signals, e.g., smiling when angry.

Group members listen effectively by (1) looking at the person who is talking; (2) giving verbal assurance that they have heard; (3) giving physical assurance that they have heard; (4) staying with the speaker; (5) being aware of their own feelings; (6) identifying prejudices which may distort hearing; (7) responding honestly; (8) exhibiting interest (attending behavior); and (9) staying with the group physically.

## CHAPTER 17

# School Social Worker and Probation Officer Conduct a Group in an Inner City Opportunity High School

Stanley Asada, M.S.

AT ANY GIVEN TIME IN 1970, probably 70 percent or more of the students in a particular opportunity high school in the Los Angeles Unified School District were on probation, had been dismissed from probation, or were being processed for probation. Yet only a few of these were receiving ongoing probation service at the school site where they were involved in most of their daytime activities.

Searching for a way to give these adolescents more adequate help, the Mental Health Section of the Los Angeles Unified School District, acting as liaison between community resources and the schools, brought together the directors of three of the Los Angeles County probation offices, the principals of three of the boys' opportunity high schools, and administrators of the school support services. The purpose of the initial meeting, held in the fall of 1970, was to explore ways of providing a program of probation service within the school setting. It was decided by this group to conduct pilot projects in the Metropolitan,* Jackson, and California** opportunity high schools with the details of probation service to be worked out individually by each school and the local area probation office. Throughout the school year the mental health consultant would meet with the probation

Reprinted with permission from *Research and Pupil Personnel Services Newsletter*, Office of Los Angeles County Superintendent of Schools, June, 1972.

* Phased out in 1973.
** Phased out in 1971.

officers to help them plan the programs being developed in their respective schools.

The following is a report of the program developed at the California High School. Located in central Los Angeles, this school had a total enrollment of 180 boys at the time of the project. Most of the youngsters had experienced school failure, came from poverty homes, and had records of delinquency.

The director of the Firestone probation office, which served the area in which most of the students lived, worked closely with the school personnel in developing a program which would best suit the local situation. First he visited the school to meet the principal and familiarized himself with the unique problems of an inner city school established primarily to educate boys who had been in difficulty. A deputy probation officer especially suited for school service was subsequently selected to serve California High, with a major part of his work hours to be spent there. An office was provided at the school, and he was invited to use the secretarial pool. Later, the officer was also assigned a community worker in order to enable him to conduct his normal supervision case load at Firestone while working at California High School.

The services in the experimental program varied. There were times when students simply wanted to talk with the probation officer to allay anxieties related to the stresses associated with their lives. At other times he was able to settle differences that erupted between probationers attending the school or between probationers and teachers. Toward the end of the school year he helped many of the probationers to find summer employment or become involved in other constructive summer activities.

The principal contribution was the *offering of group counseling at the school,* made available to the students on school time. The mental health consultant who was coordinating the total project was a co-leader for these group meetings. The sessions were scheduled as a "mini-course" provided by the school, and group members could earn a half unit of credit for eight hours of participation. Subsequent to this brief experience in group counseling there was *some improvement in the school attendance* of a number of the students and indications of a general *upward trend in grade average.* No research was conducted to verify these findings, but it was generally felt by the staff that there was a relationship.

Some of the students indicated at the end of the semester that they had enjoyed participating in the group and that it had allowed them to *express hurt feelings against some of the social injustices* they felt they were undergoing at that time. It should be pointed out that California High was in the process of being phased out, and many of the students felt that this was unfair treatment traceable to race feelings and the school's reputation. Many of the participants seemed relieved to find that there were others among them who were experiencing similar angers and frustrations, and they expressed some security in the realization that the group leaders, who were authority figures, were not going to "put them down" for what they said. All the students who participated in the group sessions at California indicated subsequently in a simple questionnaire prepared by the head counselor that they would like to get involved in more group sessions in the school years ahead of them.

The cooperative endeavor evinced by the principal at California High School and the director at Firestone probation office demonstrated what could be accomplished for and with troubled youths in a school setting. This project seems to illustrate the simple truism that when administrators of good will, both in schools and in the probation service, sensitive to the needs of people and flexible to the stresses of the time, join hands in good faith, many hoped-for programs within schools can become a reality.

## PART II: D. BRIEF DESCRIPTIONS OF PROGRAMS IN SCHOOLS

## EDITOR'S NOTE

*The following experience (Chapter 18) illustrates the fortunate usefulness in a school of a nurse who sees herself as having the ability and option to serve as a mental health resource in the school. Of course, administrative sanction has to be present as well.*

*Parallel with a change in roles of nurses in the mental health field, there is a change in role by many school nurses (Daniels, 1966; Pazdur, 1969; Stimis, 1963). Chapters 26 and 32 describe the roles of some teachers as group co-leaders. Hopefully, the day will come when personnel not exclusively in a category called "counselor" will be associated with group or individual counseling. The ability to make a responsive, communicative relation with teenagers often is not relevant to credentialed category. The organizational aspects of compensation and flexible scheduling are obviously huge but the needs of the consumer—young people—require it.*

## BIBLIOGRAPHY

DANIELS, A. M. (1966). Training school nurses to work with groups of adolescents. *Children*, 13, 210-216.

PAZDUR, H. (1969). Innovation: The school nurse as a mental health specialist. *J. of School Health*, 5:39, 449-457.

STIMIS, A. (1963). The school-nurse-teacher's role in aiding children with emotional problems. *Nursing Forum*, 5:2, 61-86.

## CHAPTER 18

# The School Nurse Organizes a Group Counseling Program in a High School

Mina Elkin, P.H.N.

THE BASIC GROUNDWORK for this program dates back to 1966. I organized and led a mental health workshop project with required reading, guest speakers, and weekly group discussions for two hours after school. We added three no-credit sessions because of sustained interest of the teachers, and all attended. It was my first introduction to the faculty as a group leader, and it was a successful workshop.

The following year a *mental health consultant* became available through the East Los Angeles Mental Health Service, a part of the Los Angeles County Department of Mental Health. We continued to have a consultant from that agency. At first, the conferences with the consultant involved case study of individual students, whose problems were typical of many of our students. The consultant's interpretation made it possible for those present to project the same approaches in dealing with other students as well.

The next phase involved *human relations training for 54 teachers* and *staff members. Four groups were formed* and met after school; two were led by group counselors assigned that year and were federally funded; the other two groups were led by counselors on staff. While these groups were in process, many of our teachers expressed their awareness that in spite of their own conflicts, no matter how different we were in philosophy or politics, we had many similar hopes and goals for the students. Generally, the groups became more sensitized to student needs as well as their own.

The *federally funded group counseling* program for students gave us five full days of counseling time. The administrative staff recognized the value of the program. In school vernacular, it often helped the students "keep their heads together." The opportunity to rap helped them to maintain emotional stability through rough periods. Many times we were told that the groups helped them make it through school rather than drop out.

Since 1969, with *school budgets cut,* we lost the federal funds. Those of us who were convinced of the positive impact of the group counseling program would not permit this loss to our students. Our principal gave us the go-ahead sign. *Teachers and counselors volunteered* to give up their conference periods. I coordinated the program, and we started *eight groups,* each with a male or female teacher, counselor, or nurse. The health office assigned all students to groups, which met once each week. Students were taken from elective classes whenever possible; releasing the student was the option of the classroom teacher.

Our mental health consultant (Steven Jacobs, Ph.D.) has met with us every week since 1969. His skills are utilized in meetings with group leaders, with administrative staff or with any faculty members concerned with specific students being discussed. He helps us anticipate or cope with problems that come up in groups and with difficulties that are of general concern to the faculty and/or staff.

We also have the good fortune to have one of our own counselors (Dr. Vern Willey) with a doctorate in counseling. He meets with a weekly group of those of us involved with this group counseling project. We consider this group *mandatory for any faculty member* working with student groups. The only alternative is to meet regularly with our mental health consultant as described above.

We feel that this group counseling program has been our first line of defense against estrangement, alienation, drug problems, police problems, and communication problems of students. We are now working toward an expansion of this type of program to parent groups, family groups, and faculty-community groups.

Some frequently asked questions about our program may be of interest:

*Why are referrals made through the health office?* Students in therapy outside the school or with severe emotional problems may feel threatened by the group situation. Coordination is needed, and we feel emotional problems of students are generally known to the nurse.

*How are referrals made? By whom?* About 50 percent are referred by students themselves, having heard about groups from participating students or teachers. The others are referred directly by me (nurse) or by any administrator, counselor, or teacher. There have been instances where the referral was requested by a parent. Several opportunity transfer students, having heard about the program somehow, have requested referral on their arrival here.

*What is the size of groups?* We try to keep groups limited to from 8 to 10 students, usually signing up 12 for each group. With normal absence or attrition, groups are kept to optimal size of 8 to 10.

*How are members chosen for each group?* No special, single problem is dealt with in each group. We try to have a mix of students with normal problems of adolescence mingled with students referred for special problems, i.e., drugs, attendance, behavior, etc. One comment we often hear when groups get started is, "How come you mix us bad ones in with the good ones?" This awareness is no problem, and we find peer group influences toward positive goals and changes rather than toward negative ones.

*How long do students remain in groups?* Generally, we leave this up to the group leader and individual student. Also, if a student is out of an academic class by chance, after eight weeks it is put up to the classroom teacher to decide if the student is missing too much work. If so, the student may be transferred to another group. From the time our program began, the *average has been about four months.*

*Is the program publicized?* Progress reports about the program are made at faculty and parents' group meetings and at community meetings.

*Do you see any advantage to the faculty?* From the point of view of being involved in a joint enterprise, and because the teachers involved meet in a group of their own, there is a close feeling among these teachers.

*Do faculty members complain about students' being absent from class?* Students are usually assigned from minor classes. One complaint last year occurred when the student was missing a physics class. The student was changed to another group. That was one complaint from approximately 100 students involved last year. Most faculty members are convinced of the value of the groups and accept the weekly absence graciously and cooperatively. We have had many reports from teachers, vice principals, and parents of apparent changes in attitude or behavior of students involved in groups.

## CHAPTER 19

# Chronic Absenteeism Decreased by Group Counseling

Wilma Awerbuch, M.A., L.S.P., and
Kathryn Fraser, M.A.

CHRONIC ABSENTEEISM increasingly frustrates students, teachers, and school officials. In the past, economic and occupational conditions, plus a lower compulsory attendance age, seemed to justify some degree of absenteeism. Also, relatively few students were involved. Today, the law, parents, educators, and employers all put pressure on students to stay in school, but they leave in increasing numbers. Why?

This was the perplexing question that prompted the experimental project here. Observing that the traditional punitive treatment of students with chronic attendance problems was not effective, group counseling was offered on an experimental basis to selected students. The goals were: (1) to improve attendance; (2) to raise academic performance; and (3) to determine what common factors, if any, were a part of the behavior patterns of the participants.

*Procedure*

A list was compiled of *students known to have both severe attendance and academic problems.* Those having average ability and adequate reading achievement as measured by standardized group tests were identified, and 15 were then selected for individual interviews. The purpose of the group, its goals, and tentative plans for the meeting time and place were discussed.

Reprinted with permission from *Research and Pupil Personnel Services Newsletter,* Office of Los Angeles County Superintendent of Schools, June, 1974.

The voluntary nature of participation was also emphasized. *Thirteen students* agreed to participate. Letters explaining the project and containing permission slips to be signed were then sent to the parents.

Before the first group session, *an orientation meeting was held for teachers of the students involved.* The project was explained, and the need for participation of the teachers in the evaluation procedures was presented. Also, the problems inherent in having students make up class work were discussed. Most of the teachers expressed interest in the project, a willingness to cooperate, and no resistance to the loss of one class period a week for the students involved.

*Second period, Monday morning,* was designated for meetings in the hope that the group experience would increase attendance on the first day of the week and provide some support for continuing through the next four days.

The *kitchen in the homemaking department* was less than ideal as a meeting place, but it did provide privacy, space for flexible chair arrangement, and the opportunity for occasionally serving food. It also lacked association with a formal classroom atmosphere.

*Measurement instruments*

1. A *behavior checklist* to be completed by the teacher of each participating student, at the beginning and at the end of the project. This form, used in the district special education program, was adopted because it provided a quick, convenient check list of behaviors: independence while working, work habits, self-control, activity, attendance, promptness, reaction to authority, temper, tension, learning attitudes, and observational assessment of learning skills.

2. A *self-assessment attendance chart* using symbols to provide a line graph record of attendance. This provided a means of recording the decision of whether to go to school and the feelings involved, e.g., "Didn't feel like going to school but went anyway."

3. *Individual and group charts* for comparing attendance, grade point average, effort and attitude ratings, and percentage of classes passed, for the 12 weeks of school prior to the project and the following 12 weeks during which the project was conducted.

4. A *student questionnaire* used at the end of the project to explore feeling change toward the group, self-evaluation on attendance and school performance, feelings toward other significant persons, and comments and suggestions about the group experience.

*Objective results*

1. Grade Point Average          Improvement  .732 (on 4-point scale)
2. Effort ratings              Improvement  .63  (on 4-point scale)
3. Attitude ratings            Improvement  .07  (on 4-point scale)
4. Classes passed              Improvement  18.7%

5. Absences

|  | *All-day* | *Part-day* | *Tardies* |
|---|---|---|---|
| First Quarter | 15.1 % | 10.5% | 3.2% |
| Fourth Quarter | 9.99% | 5.2% | 2.6% |

It had been predicted that attendance would improve on "group day" with minimal change in the usual pattern for the remainder of the week. The records showed better than average attendance on Monday, with *improvement in attendance also occurring on other days.*

It had also been predicted that the greatest change would occur in effort and attitude marks of the students and that improvement in academic grades would be minimal. This anticipated outcome was reversed. Teachers' comments about behavior changes were more reflective of the prediction than were the marks they assigned on the report cards.

*Observations of behavior change*

An *observable change took place in the behavior* of members between the first and final meetings of the group. At first they were uneasy and reluctant to talk. Passivity was a common denominator. The students appeared to have little recognition of their ability to make changes and control things which were happening to them. As the meetings continued, they progressed from reluctance to talk to active participation and from uneasiness to apparent comfort. Students' responses on the evaluative questionnaire substantiated the observations. Some improvement was reported in their relationship with peers, teachers, and administrators. *Only in their relationship to their parents did they report no improvement.** This could be attributed to: (a) The goals, objectives, and methods used in counseling focused on school-related problems. When home-related problems were brought up, no attempt was made to deal with them except in reference to school performance. (b) The relatively short duration of the series of meetings precluded any significant or observable changes in established family behavior patterns.

---

* See Chapter 29.

*Recommendations*

1. Continue to expand the group counseling program.

2. Begin with 15 members, so that attrition will not jeopardize the effectiveness of the group.

3. Continue the volunteer participation.

4. Expand the offerings in group experiences to career concerns and to personal and academic problems.

5. Include students in the groups with a mixture of abilities and problems.

6. Continue the use of an experienced leader with one who is not experienced for staff in-service education purposes.

7. Conduct parallel parent groups.

8. Continue to schedule the group meeting early on Monday morning.

9. Hold the sessions in a room of appropriate size and range of use.

10. Consider opening a rap room available to groups of students during lunch time and coordinated by trained counselors on a rotating basis.

*Conclusion*

This report was written in September of the school year following the one during which the project was conducted. It appears that the *summer vacation has magnified rather than diminished the positive feelings and the improved attendance* of the students involved. With two exceptions, the members of the group have attended school almost every day, have shown enthusiasm in their attitude toward school, and seem committed to new patterns of involvement this year. *They appear to feel they belong,* in contrast to their former feeling of being on the periphery.

## PART II: D. BRIEF DESCRIPTIONS OF PROGRAMS IN SCHOOLS

### EDITOR'S NOTE

*The following description of a time-limited, task-oriented group procedure illustrates another facet of the potentials in guided group interaction. This experience demonstrated a direct, immediate facilitation of the educational process. Many sensitive teachers probably use some alternation of group interaction and concentration on content to optimize class attention span and involvement. The use of this type of counselor assistance in the classroom is a step which may be worthy of wider consideration, depending on teacher comfort.*

CHAPTER 20

# An Experiment in the Use of Group Guidance to Improve Classroom Control

Muriel Thomson, Ed.D., and
Gerald F. Jones, M.S.

AN EXPERIMENT IN HELPING STUDENTS in a tenth grade algebra class resolve a problem of classroom control through small group guidance sessions was conducted recently in a high school in Los Angeles County. The class was composed of students of average academic ability, who were either repeating the course or had just earned the necessary qualifications for registering for it. Most were under pressure to complete it satisfactorily to fulfill college entrance requirements. Classroom behavior was generally restless and disruptive.

*Procedure*

The teacher asked two counselors—a man and a woman—for help in evolving an approach to working with students on the problem. The method selected was that of small group discussion, involving all members of the class working with the counselors.

Three groups were arbitrarily formed by first numbering the alphabetical class list by threes and then assigning the numerical groups to meet on successive days. All those with the number *1* were to meet in a discussion

Reprinted with permission from *Research and Pupil Personnel Services Newsletter,* Office of Los Angeles County Superintendent of Schools, April, 1967.

group on Wednesday instead of attending class. All those with the number 2 would meet on Thursday and those with the number 3 on Friday.

The discussion groups met regularly for six sessions with both counselors in attendance at each session. The purpose of the meetings was presented by the counselors as an opportunity for the students to talk about the behavior in the classroom and how it might be improved. At the conclusion of the fifth session the students were asked to evaluate the process by writing whatever they wished on "How I Felt About the Group." The papers were anonymous, and the students were informed that they would not be read by any staff member but would be read by a consultant from the county office, who would report the results to the school guidance staff in order to help them plan increasingly effective programs for helping students.

### Results

The primary focus of the students' responses was on the relationship of the group's interactions to the behavior in the algebra class. Many felt that the purpose of the groups had been achieved after the second session, when some resolution of the stated problem seemed to have been reached.

Several students expressed the feeling that the group meetings had forced them to recognize a class problem which affected them through their grades, and so they were motivated to work on that problem. Others thought that the noisy class was only a pretext to form them into groups, but they said they were unable to guess what the teacher might have in mind as the ultimate purpose of such a group.

There were opposing reactions to several factors related to the group process. There was a decided difference of opinion on whether the group had actually solved the problem. Some believed the class was quieter as a result of the group meetings, and others felt that the groups had made no difference. A few said that it was a relief to break the classroom pace and to be with fewer students for part of the time. Some said they thought it was a good idea to be in a group with friends, while others thought that it was not. There were opposing feelings about having the group in a public school setting rather than under church supervision.

Reaction to the group process itself was expressed by several students. Some said they believed the technique was a useful one, and some of these said that even though they felt the present problem had not been solved, group interaction was a good approach when several people shared a common problem. None of the students suggested that, now that they were a problem-solving unit and had already successfully worked on a problem, they might go on working on problems of their own definition.

The experience was described by some of the students as follows:

"Some of it was fun, and some was boring."

"It did not solve the stated problem, but I enjoyed learning about other students."

"When I would start to talk in class, I would think about what the others said, and then I would be quiet."

"I became more concerned about others."

"I have the best view anyway, so listening to their views didn't help."

"Even if you don't talk, the group is valuable because you learn by listening."

"Others didn't care what I said, but I was able to be free."

## PART II: D. BRIEF DESCRIPTIONS OF PROGRAMS IN SCHOOLS

### EDITOR'S NOTE

*Rap rooms began as a response to needs of students, especially in high schools, in the late '60s. These rooms varied in makeup, values, and services offered with each school and its administrator, as the following survey of five rap rooms will show. Generally speaking, such rooms can range from offering a solicitous, emotional, first aid, nursing-office-type walk-in clinic to a low-pressure study hall.*

*Rap rooms thus can offer significant counseling individually and even in groups, depending on the skills or wishes of the school personnel present. However, in rap rooms the formal aspects of group counseling, namely, consistent time and duration of meeting or stable membership of group, will usually not be present.*

*Many administrators and school districts feel a concern about the rap room's becoming a place for "goof-offs" or troublemakers rather than a place for valid assistance to students momentarily and briefly disturbed during the day at school. This possibility needs appropriate awareness. Yet, many students have received important help in some rap rooms, for personal as well as school-related difficulties, as the student attitude survey in Chapter 21 does demonstrate.*

## CHAPTER 21

# A Survey of Rap Rooms
# in Five High Schools –
# and Some Student Attitudes

Philip A. Smith, Ph.D.,
William O'Rear, M.A., and
Alva Cashion, P.H.N.

WHEN CONSIDERING A REQUEST that a rap room be opened at El Camino Real High School recently, the principal sought pertinent data on the operation of such rooms in nearby schools. He was particularly concerned with the identification of those factors which contributed to the success of these rooms or to complications in their functioning. Therefore, he invited a team composed of the head counselor and the school nurse of the school and a consultant from the Los Angeles County Department of Mental Health to gather the necessary information and to make recommendations. The following is the report of this committee.

*Preliminary steps*

Before initiating the project, conferences were held with two of the administrative staff of the El Camino Real High School: (a) the girls' vice principal, who reported her experiences with rap rooms in the inner city schools and raised questions regarding ground rules covering confidentiality of information, time commitments, attention to academics, and the mechanics

Reprinted with permission from *Research and Pupil Personnel Services Newsletter*, Office of Los Angeles County Superintendent of Schools, November, 1972.

of referral; (b) the dean of girls, who brought up the issues of parental authority and responsibility, training for rap room leaders, school referral channels, and the handling of communication among students, parents, and school staff.

Following these discussions, an exploration was undertaken of how the many issues pertaining to rap room are being met by five representative high schools in the San Fernando Valley area.

## Schools visited

All schools visited were in the San Fernando Valley. They ranged from a mid-valley high school with a transiency rate of 65 percent and a substantial Spanish surname population to a west valley high school similar to El Camino Real in terms of educational objectives, student characteristics, ethnicity and community environs. Data from these schools relating to rap rooms are shown in Table 1.

## Characteristics surveyed

The following variables were assessed:

- History and inception of the rap room project at the school.
- Approach to orienting teachers, community, and students regarding rap room objectives.
- Rules for operation, including such details as procedures, time of operation, methods for handling confidential material, legal and ethical constraints, and use of student aides.
- Selection, training, and supervision of leaders.
- Physical arrangements and furnishings.
- Nature and percentage of students using the rap room.
- Special problems encountered by the school in implementing or maintaining their rap room.
- Evaluation studies of rap room effectiveness.

## General findings

1. The sentiment of the school principal regarding rap rooms appears to be the determining factor in whether or not a school institutes such a room. His or her critical judgment and timing in securing the cooperation of community groups, interested parents, and faculty advisory groups is instrumental in helping such a project develop smoothly and rapidly.

2. The counseling, advisement, and assistance provided to students in the rap room do not differ in principle from those functions already pro-

vided by the school. However, many persons believe there are both quantitative and qualitative differences, including increased effectiveness of counseling services, greater timeliness, and differences in the type and numbers of students reached. The easy informality and acceptance of the rap room contrasts with the scheduled appointments, busy clerks, crowded office cubicles, or the blatant statement of a desk crowded with papers which sometimes intervene between staff members and students. In some of the schools surveyed, a few teachers have begun to modify their classrooms in an effort to create better learning environments, modeled after the comfort and informality of the rap room.

3. Those rap rooms which have been most successful are under the leadership of personnel who can be characterized as having judgment and commitment, qualities which are not guaranteed by any one state credential. In this survey, effective leaders were found who had been recruited from the ranks of teachers, counselors, PSA* workers, and graduate students enrolled in training programs in the human services. High school teacher assistants were also used in some rap rooms, but they were supervised by the leader. All schools agreed that the choice of the leader is critical.

4. In addition to working well with students, the rap room leader must be able to work effectively with the administrative staff and must have their trust and confidence. It appears that it is fairly easy to find leaders who are strongly student centered, or who are strongly staff oriented, but it is difficult to find a leader who can move back and forth smoothly between these groups and strike a fair balance. Close coordination between rap room leader, faculty, and administrative and support staff is particularly essential in the case of students in crisis or students who constitute a threat to themselves or others.

5. In general, most of the problems which it was anticipated would accompany the presence of a rap room in a school have not materialized. The sessions have not become a forum for student tirades against the school, for sharing information about illegal activities, for gaining illicit information, for circumventing school procedures, or for other abuses of the privilege of relative privacy and confidentiality. Use of the rap room as a crash pad for drug users had not occurred at any of the schools visited.

6. One high school reported a substantial decrease of drug incidents on campus since initiating their rap room, although this decrease could be due to other factors. All schools reported that students obviously under the

---

* School Pupil Service and Attendance personnel.

influence of drugs were referred to the usual school channels rather than allowed access to the rap room. The students were invited, however, when free from the influence of drugs, to attend the rap room to discuss the reasons for their drug use. Problems related to pregnancy and abortion were usually handled in coordination with the nursing staff.

7. The problems presented by students were reported to be primarily alienation, feelings of futility and failure, poor peer relationships, troubled home relationships, and life crises.

8. In general, it appeared that effective rap room leaders worked to increase communication between students and teachers, between students and parents, and between students and their peers. They also worked to help students assume personal responsibility for their actions and thereby helped to delay or inhibit the tendency toward their impulsive discharge. The rap room used in this way became a tool to increase the students' capacity to control their own behavior rather than a place where uncontrolled activities were condoned or fostered. There were occasional abuses of academic responsibility both by students and by teachers, but these were usually easily detectable and remediable.

9. At one school, use of the rap room will be expanded by making it also an orientation and friendship center for new students. It is hoped that this will ease the adjustment problems posed by the transfer students. The high transiency rate of this school suggests that a large and constantly renewing pool of students will be served by this device.

10. Evaluation studies have been limited but, on the whole, responses have been positive. At Cleveland High School, group interviews were conducted and responses to a student questionnaire after one semester yielded favorable replies. Granada Hills High School reported excellent student feedback and, at a meeting convened for off-campus representatives to review school problems, there were generally favorable findings with respect to the rap room. Monroe High School reported that average daily attendance was up and that the truancy rate was lower during those periods of the day when the rap room was in operation. Another school also reported that arrests had dropped from 50 one year ago to none during the fall semester of 1971.

## Recommendations

If a school elects to implement a rap room, the committee recommends the following:

1. *Name.* That a designation other than "rap room" be selected. Several schools surveyed believe this title has unwanted overtones and may be mis-

TABLE 1

School Data

| High School | Rap Room Since . . . | Periods Open | Staffing | Student T/A[1] | 1970-71 Transiency |
|---|---|---|---|---|---|
| Cleveland | Spring 1971 | 4 | Nurse, counselor, faculty rotation | No | 62% |
| Granada Hills | Summer 1971 | 3, 4, lunch | Health Science teacher | Yes | 34% |
| Monroe | Fall 1970 | 10 am-1 pm. | 2 PSA[2], CSUN[3] volunteers | Yes | 45% |
| Taft | Spring 1971 | Lunch, 7th | Volunteer, BVP[4] supervn. | No | 45% |
| Van Nuys | Spring 1972 | 4, lunch | Counselor, PSA rotation | — | 65% |

1. Teaching Assistant;  2. Pupil Service and Attendance worker;  3. California State University at Northridge;  4. Boys' vice-principal.

perceived by students and community alike. Alternate suggestions include "student center," "counseling annex," "student forum," "student-faculty center," or "student workshop." These titles all carry the thought of work in progress.

2. *Faculty involvement.* That an assessment of faculty opinions and recommendations about rap rooms be made before one is instituted.

3. *Community sanction.* That the community advisory committee, PTA, and community leaders be kept informed and their collaboration be solicited.

4. *Leadership.* That a suitable leader or leaders be nominated and given orientation about existing school procedures for handling student problems. Some means for continuing liaison with other staff members, whether formal or informal, also must be established.

5. *Space.* That a suitable location for the student center be determined and students be given the responsibility for furnishing and maintaining it within the limits of reasonable constraints established by the school.

6. *Controls.* That teacher permission for attendance be required and a sign-in procedure be followed. Such a system would permit faculty control, limit student abuse, and permit logging of data for research and evaluation purposes.

7. *Time limits.* That, initially, the student center be available during periods 3, 4, and lunch. On a trial basis it might be limited to those students who have an open period at that time. Later it could be extended to students with classes during third or fourth periods.

8. *Evaluation.* That student and faculty opinion regarding the value and effectiveness of the student center be surveyed after a trial implementation period, and adjustments in procedure considered at that time.

### Student attitudes toward a high school rap room

A high school located in an upper-middle-class area of Los Angeles hesitantly offered a rap room program for students, led by a team of counselors from the community. After the rap room had been in operation for eight months, the anonymous opinions of student participants were surveyed. The following is a summary of those findings, made in June, 1971.

The great majority of the students were favorable in their comments about the rap room. They were mainly concerned with having an opportunity on the school campus for openly expressing feelings and for improving interpersonal relationships. The word "feelings" was frequently used in their answers to open-ended questions. Somewhat surprisingly, the subject of drugs, which had been a prominent administrative concern, was not mentioned. Students also reported that the rap room privilege was not abused by students seeking to escape exams or recover from drug ingestion. They also noted long-term favorable effects on nearly all participants and recommended that the room be available on an all-day basis.

*Summary of survey findings*

Twenty-one students responded to the rap room questionnaire on the day of the survey. Two-thirds of this number had been attending for three months or longer. Heaviest usage of the rap room was during the noon hour and the period following lunch. The ratio of boys to girls was 4:3, and all grade levels were tapped. The ratio of Sophomores: Juniors: Seniors was approximately 2:2:3. For the most part, survey respondents were "B" students.

*Response to questionnaire*

How many months have you been attending the rap room?

| | |
|---|---|
| Less than 1 month | 15% |
| 1 month | 9% |
| 2 months | 15% |
| 3 months | 19% |
| 4 months | 9% |
| 5 months | 24% |
| 6 months | 9% |

How frequently do you attend?

| | |
|---|---|
| Less than once a week | 0% |
| About once a week | 0% |
| About half the time | 0% |
| Most of the time | 48% |
| Every day without fail | 52% |

What topics are discussed (all that apply)?

| | |
|---|---|
| Drugs | 5% |
| Peer relations | 100% |
| Parents | 100% |
| Teachers or school | 43% |
| Politics | 5% |
| Other topics | 76% |

What other topics are discussed?

*Other topics discussed are:*

> personal hang-ups
> feelings about self; self-image
> outlook on life
> what we would like to be

What is the chief value of the rap room?

*The majority of the students seemed to express two main values of the rap room:*

> to become aware of and communicate one's own feelings
> to improve relations between people.

*Others mentioned:*

> to speak frequently without fear of being rejected
> to relieve pressure
> to give hope but not necessarily solve problems
> to make life happier.

Do any students abuse the rap room? For example, use it to take drugs, avoid exams, etc.

> There was unanimous agreement that the rap room was "rarely or never abused."

Has the rap room had any bad effect on anyone at any time this year? (Explain).

> All students agreed that the rap room had "no bad effect on anyone this year." However, many of the "no's" were qualified by saying that there were short-term bad effects but in the long run there were none.

What changes should be made in the rap room next year?

*The two changes suggested most often were:*

> room should be open all day
> room should be more publicized.

*Other changes mentioned:*

> more non-verbal communication
> more open to newcomers
> encourage more students to come
> separate sections for different discussions.

Any other comments.

*Other comments*:

    really great
    made friends
    everyone should have one.

# Part III

## MENTAL HEALTH PROFESSIONALS FROM OUTSIDE THE SCHOOLS ASSIST SCHOOL PERSONNEL IN CONDUCTING GROUPS

A. General Articles

B. Collaborative Assistance

C. Consultative Assistance (without Collaboration)

D. Other Useful Groups in Junior and Senior High Schools

CHAPTER 22

# The Consultative Role of Mental Health Professionals in Schools

Irving H. Berkovitz, M.D., and
Muriel Thomson, Ed.D.

MENTAL HEALTH PROFESSIONALS AND EDUCATORS have cooperated in developing a mutually helpful exchange of knowledge about children for the past half century. Procedures have included the traditional case consultation as well as mental health education, supervision when new techniques such as group counseling are being taught, collaboration when formulating new projects, personal development groups, and programs of in-service education designed to meet specific district mental health needs. These services might best be described by the term "psychoeducational assistance," with traditional consultation as one form of this help.

Traditional mental health consultation has been described as a communication process taking place between a mental health professional, the consultant, and an independent person or group, the consultee(s). The consultation process between the educator-consultees and the mental health consultant is designed to achieve a dual goal for the consultees: to help them deal constructively with a current problem and also help them build a rationale for ways of operating that will be useful when they are faced with similar problems in the future.

In one program during 1960-1974, some 50,000 hours of mental health professional time were provided by the Los Angeles County Department of Health Services, Mental Health Services Division, to approximately 50 school districts in Los Angeles County. Other agencies provided additional hours.

The consultant group included psychiatrists, psychologists, social workers, public health nurses, rehabilitation counselors, and others. All had mental health training and experience, and most had training in consultation with school personnel. This service was provided to the full range of school personnel from teacher to superintendent, either in individual conferences or group sessions.

Commonly, the focus of the meetings was on children's needs, concerns in communication among staff members, problems within the school, or philosophical issues basic to school practices. Members of the staff of the office of the Los Angeles County Superintendent of Schools, especially consultants of the Division of Research and Pupil Personnel Services, were of critical value in publicizing and expediting these services in several districts.

Services in the Los Angeles program fell into five major categories: (1) the *case discussion,* a favored format between mental health professionals and educators; (2) assistance to school personnel in regard to *programs of group counseling* and group discussion in schools; (3) *group discussion among staff members* designed to improve their intercommunication; (4) service to *teachers of children with unique needs;* and (5) consultation especially with *pupil personnel services workers.* At times collaborative in-service education workshops were developed.

While the assistance to group counseling programs is of most interest here, a few words about the other types of services may also be relevant. Often these other types of services preceded or were concurrent with those concerned with group counseling. At other times only assistance to group counseling was desired.

*Case discussion* at one time involved one educator with one mental health professional. In recent years group sessions with a mental health consultant have been more widely used. Meetings have usually been scheduled on a weekly, biweekly, or monthly basis with sessions usually lasting for an hour-and-a-half. Attendance of participants has been voluntary and has usually been consistent. Groups varied in size from 6 to 15 members. Many of the groups met for a minimum of eight sessions in one semester, and others have continued from one school year to the next. Initially, there may be concerns about time taken from other duties, meeting after school hours, or the time necessary to orient the consultant to the school. Usually, however, by the time a group had met for three months these concerns had become less prevalent, and the meetings were an accepted part of the school staff's activities.

In these meetings it was often striking to note the beneficial sharing of thought on solutions to problems. The presence of a *consultant who had no judgmental or administrative role in the system* seemed crucial to this type of sharing. There was strong suggestion that previous methods of communication which are common to all schools, such as faculty or administrative meetings, lunch room or corridor discussions, had been useful but had not provided fully for staff needs.

Discussion focusing on *staff relationships* is also known as personal development or communication discussion. When a group has met for a series of case-oriented discussion meetings and has reached a fairly stable state, members have occasionally expressed the wish for deeper consideration of the significance of attitudes of individuals as they affected the school children and each other. At times this kind of discussion was then agreed upon by the consultant and the group.

After variable periods of discussion meetings with administrative and teacher groups, several of the districts reported noticeable improvements in communication. Such reported benefits did not imply that severe problems had existed prior to the consultation, but simply that in any large organization communication efficiency is often taken for granted with the result that major or minor difficulties may be ignored or tacitly accepted as unchangeable. The group method has proved noticeably effective in many such instances.

The ideal mental health climate in a school would be that which provided a success experience for every student. The student would then enjoy learning, gain pride in competency and self-esteem, and build the feeling that people in the world could be truly loving and helpful. Unfortunately, this ideal is often difficult to realize because of factors present in the pupil or educator, or because of social and financial limitations. In the case of the educator, some of these factors are not difficult to trace. Adequate knowledge of child development is not always provided in the teachers' or administrators' preparatory program. Many mental health concepts are confusing or contradictory when learned from popular media without a chance for discussion. Subtle attitudes of relating or communicating with children and peers are often not readily perceived without outside assistance. Of paramount importance is the fact that some children are emotionally disturbed and seriously tax the teacher in a class of 25 to 35. Sometimes minimal new knowledge from professionals or peers can strengthen the educator and bring the ideal experience closer for more children.

The problem of the disturbed and disturbing child is particularly pressing. Direct treatment for such children, individually or in groups, by school health personnel or outside clinical facilities is not always available. Also, except in the most severe cases, treatment of the children in their usual social milieu is preferable. A mental health professional can provide specialized knowledge and encourage the participants to use their own intrinsic, intuitive resources.

## PART III: A. GENERAL ARTICLES

## EDITOR'S NOTE

*The following chapters provide examples of the valuable interchange discussed in the preceding pages. Some also describe experiences of mental health professionals organizing a group communicative experience to help improve school milieu, and not only to help disturbed students. Outside professionals may have had an advantage over the regular school personnel in providing these procedures. For example, the communication seminar in a junior high school could have been offered by school personnel, but perhaps without the same objectivity as professionals who do not have a defensiveness about the school. In most other chapters, however, the goal was to introduce new concepts and practices to school personnel. At times, understandably, the school personnel would have liked to retain the mental health professional as a regular member of the school staff, especially when the service came without the requirement of any school budget. This may suggest a model of public assistance to schools justifying future legislation.*

CHAPTER 23

# The School Mental Health Consultant as a Coordinator: A New Role Concept

Edith Hill, A.C.S.W.

IT IS A FORTUNATE OCCASION when community professionals volunteer to. meet a school's needs in such volume that the school personnel are hard pressed and overwhelmed to coordinate the flood of riches. In some cases, the result may be confusion, discouragement, and loss of useful community professional assistance. On the other hand, the constructive utilization of this volunteered expertise can have long-range benefit for the youngsters served, the school personnel involved, and school-community relationships.

The setting in which the program described below evolved was an urban high school in a socioeconomically rapidly changing neighborhood. Following the suicide of a student, parental concerns mobilized some volunteer professional talent to offer a counseling program in a church across the street from the school. There was racial friction and some confrontations between various community powers, but this did not deter a committed, involved school administrative team from exploring steps toward a solution of the problems.

The counseling center was not enough. The school administrators decided to look for more help. The department of community psychiatry of a nearby medical school and the regional office of the Los Angeles County Department of Mental Health were contacted and were instrumental in the setting up of a *school-wide convocation*—a meeting which involved groups of all the students in the school, all the teachers, and many parents. Each group had, as a facilitator, an experienced volunteer professional from the mental health field. The findings of the convocation pointed to a need for more group counseling, more open discussions of racial issues, and more emphasis on human relations.

Fortunately, *two mental health consultants,* a psychiatrist and a social worker, had been working with the school administrators and counselors even before the convocation. When the community professionals offered their help following this mass meeting, the consultants were there to provide the leadership and fill the obvious need for coordination.

In 1970, the first year after the convocation, a score of professionals from several nonprofit agencies, as well as the school itself, provided *individual and group counseling* to many students on school grounds during school hours. The social worker of the mental health consultant team became the pivotal person who assumed responsibility for coordinating these efforts. She screened the volunteers, established guidelines, and helped the school administrators trust the mental health professionals while structuring the clinicians to work within the framework of a public school. Originally, as a traditional school consultant, her interaction had been with administrators and counselors, but this changed when she became a coordinator-consultant.

Coordination might be looked at as a novel role for a consultant. In this case it took both clinical and administrative skills. There was a need to relate to a total system and in this way be willing to perform many tasks not always traditional for a consultant; for example, if a clinician was committed to do group counseling with a group of youngsters and had to leave in the middle of the term, it was the job of the coordinator to secure a replacement. If the administrator had concerns or hesitations about a professional's stance with the youngsters, the coordinator had to bridge the gap. If a volunteer clinician was confronted with a psychiatric emergency while at the school, the coordinator had to be able to offer back-up services. Parents who were pleased or became disgruntled also needed to be heard.

In 1970 or 1971, 27 professionals from agencies worked within the high school described, providing individual and group counseling to students.

In the spring of 1972, the school principal wanted to explore a *comprehensive human relations program* to be offered to the whole student body. This was a departure from the program described above, because it would be offered in the classroom and therefore would involve classroom teachers with their own students. In the individual and group counseling program, service was provided by professionals upon the request of the students and with their parents' permission. The human relations program was to become part of the classroom's teaching content.

Again the coordinator-consultant was involved, this time to find between

20 and 24 trained mental health professionals who could work with 10 English teachers on a once-a-week basis helping discussion in the classroom. The purpose of the program, and essentially the reason for putting it into the tenth grade, was to help the new high school students with their adjustment to an integrated setting; to help them become aware of their fears, prejudices, and concerns; to help them appreciate the variety of ways in which their peers perceived them and responded to situations; and, above all, to establish healthy and open channels of communication among the students. These students, for the most part, arrived at their new school full of distrust, if not open hostility.

The coordinator-consultant recruited and screened the volunteer mental health professionals who were to work in the classrooms as consultants to the teachers. Meetings were held to pair teachers and consultants, lay ground rules, and establish goals. Finally, the coordinator prepared an evaluative instrument to measure the success of the human relations program.

In all, the coordinator-consultant created a role new to the school as well as to the county regional mental health service. The work took time and endless telephone calls and meetings but was most rewarding. It has been an outstanding example of a mutually beneficial partnership among the school, the preventive service component of the mental health facility, and the community in transition.

CHAPTER 24

# Advantages and Problems of Interdisciplinary Collaboration in School Group Counseling

Celeste Kaplan, A.C.S.W.

WHEN EDUCATORS AND SOCIAL WORKERS (from a community social agency) conduct groups together, collaborative complexities are to be expected. However, the values of this interdisciplinary collaboration were far more significant, as illustrated in the following account of experiences in 48 Los Angeles area schools during a four-year period. During this period 200 counseling groups, with students ranging from first and second graders through graduating senior high school students, were sponsored and led jointly by school staff and agency workers. At all stages, from planning to conducting the groups and then evaluating their effectiveness, problems of interprofessional and interagency relationship arose. Solving these problems required special sensitivity and thoughtfulness and was vital to the success of the program.

Three main problem areas emerged in which awareness of divergent professional backgrounds and approaches was especially required: (1) definition of the objectives of school group counseling and evaluation of results; (2) content and technique in groups led jointly by school and agency personnel; and (3) relation of school administrators and faculty to the group counseling program. Examination of these issues will follow a brief description of the four-year program.

Collaboration between the schools and the Child, Youth and Parent Counseling Agency occurred initially in the spring of 1970 when the agency agreed to supply some of its psychiatric social workers as co-leaders for groups in two schools. The agency (also known as the Council of Jewish

Women of Los Angeles, Inc.) has for many years received referrals from the schools on a non-sectarian, interracial basis. But the increase of self-destructive and antisocial behavior among boys and girls at all age levels has made the individual referral system seem like bailing out a boat with a teaspoon. It therefore made sense to offer direct service in the place where most girls and boys are found—the schools.

Meanwhile, administrators, teachers, and other school personnel are daily encountering troubled young people whose problems block their constructive use of a school's offerings. In addition to urgent issues of curriculum change and effective pedagogical methods, schools face the almost insurmountable task of successfully teaching young people who are using drugs, stealing, absenting themselves from school, or in other ways acting out unresolved emotional, interpersonal, or social difficulties. Educators are more frequently encountering hostility and defiance, or depression and withdrawal, which most often stem from sources outside the classroom. Measures from within and without schools are required to deal with problems of such scope. A growing number of educators see the value of providing some on-the-spot help to their students. Unfortunately, school resources alone do not suffice. The problem requires community resources as well.

Our first experience was in 1970 in a junior high school with which the agency had especially good prior working relationships. When one of the counselors expressed interest in starting group counseling, we suggested that the groups be led jointly by school and agency personnel. This proposal was supported by the girls' vice-principal, the head counselor, and then the principal. Two groups of girls were organized in March and continued through the semester. Similar services began also at a senior high school in a middle-class neighborhood facing problems of transition in ethnic composition.* In both schools, school personnel participated as co-leaders.

The experiment grew! Within four years, the agency was providing leaders for jointly led groups in 6 senior high schools, 16 junior highs, and 26 elementary schools. These schools were located primarily in working-class and lower-middle-class areas with varied ethnic composition. Some 2,000 students ranging from first graders to seniors in high school were involved in 200 groups. In addition, 22 groups for parents of elementary school children were organized. Almost every group was led jointly by an agency social worker and a member of the school's professional staff. The latter

---

* See Chapter 23.

included school counselors, teachers, pupil and attendance workers, psychologists, and school nurses. Agency representatives also spent many hours with school personnel in planning, organizing, and evaluating the groups.* This rich variety of interdisciplinary experiences made possible some tentative conclusions about the three problem areas cited above.

### Defining objectives

Definition of objectives for group counseling inevitably reflected the respective purposes and professional "set" of agency and school personnel. Agency social workers were geared to the aim of helping troubled young people find better ways of dealing with their difficulties in interpersonal relationships and with their inner emotional problems. School personnel tended to be concerned with improving school behavior and academic achievement, although many educators proved very responsive to the more inclusive developmental problems of young people. In every school these two approaches were combined into a general objective for group counseling: the emotional and social growth of students, which should be reflected in better use of school experience.

The way in which the two professions (social work and education) have moved toward each other was indicated by a change in the wording of a letter to parents from grade counselors explaining the purpose of the group counseling program. The first letter stated, "We are beginning a program of counseling to help . . . students develop attitudes and work habits which we hope will enable them to improve their academic achievement." By the next year the letter began, "This year we are continuing a program of group counseling designed to enable our students to have a successful school experience." This was not a minor semantic change. It corresponded to an enlarged view of the program's goal.

During the first year at that school, participants in the groups (then only girls) were referred by counselors or the girls' vice-principal because of problems quite evident to school personnel: truancy, defiance of school rules, fighting, probable drug use, underachievement, social immaturity, depression, and/or withdrawn behavior. In the second year all eighth grade girls who felt they had personal, social, or school problems were invited to request group counseling. *The response was overwhelming!* Eighty girls applied. These included not only virtually all the girls in that grade whom school personnel would have referred; *in addition, at least half the applicants were*

---

* Evaluation is described in Chapter 29.

*excellent students with impeccable records.* The latter, as they were interviewed, verbalized many serious, unresolved problems, which were either internalized or simply not evident in the school setting. This was something of a shock to school personnel, who certainly had enough on their hands with those students in more overt trouble. However, the school and the agency honored their commitment to offer help to all girls who requested it.

As school personnel and social workers learned from each other, group counseling developed more specific goals in the schools, pinpointing a particular type of problem or population. For example, in several elementary schools, groups were established for fifth and sixth graders who needed special help to be ready for junior high school, usually because of their social immaturity. In another elementary school, group counseling was provided weekly for an entire opportunity room class with the aim of helping its members (mainly fourth grade boys) return to regular class. Group counseling was considered for continuation school students and classes of physically or emotionally handicapped youngsters. In all these groups, educators and outside professionals merged their skills to define specific objectives within the general goal of personal and social growth.

*Evaluating results*

In the third year, a systematic method of evaluation was developed through questionnaires to be answered by group leaders and other agency personnel. The agency was basically concerned with whether such a group counseling program was helpful to the young people involved. The questionnaires used at the end of the 1972-73 school year asked group leaders (both agency- and school-based) to evaluate each group member's use of group, and especially whether the student had made progress in the problem area involved in the referral or self-referral. For each group member, a member of the school staff who knew him or her well was also asked to make a similar evaluation, including an opinion as to whether group counseling had been helpful to the partcular student. The analysis of data thus obtained (for nearly 500 students in 47 groups), with our conclusions, is contained in a mimeographed report entitled, "Evaluating an Agency-School Group Counseling Program" (an exploratory research project). The study indicated a positive reply to our basic question—Is the program helpful to young people? It also contains a breakdown of outcome by school levels, problem areas, age, sex, ethnicity, and times attended group (see Chapter 29).

*Content and technique: differences in attitude between agency
and school personnel*

The divergence of professional training and its impact on content and
technique arose in sharpest form when group leadership was shared by an
agency worker with no prior school background and a teacher or school
counselor with no previous experience in group counseling.

*Social workers* from this particular agency are oriented to examination of
feelings as a major determinant of behavior. They attach considerable importance to implicit meaning and respond to nonverbal cues by turning the
group's attention in that direction. They try to sense where the group is at
each group meeting, moving freely toward those concerns which seem
pivotal at the time. Their approach tends to be unstructured, and group
process rather than leader authority is used to set limits and determine
direction.

On the other hand, *teachers and counselors* have been trained to deal with
young people largely in terms of structured learning and intellectual communication. Concern is mainly with overt behavior, while feelings are rarely
dealt with in an explicit way. Authority and control are exerted directly by
the adults in charge, with little or no utilization of group process. Normal
procedure for group discussion would involve selection of a specific topic
for discussion, either in advance or at the outset of a meeting.

It was hardly surprising with these two divergent attitudes that members
of both professions viewed their impending collaborative efforts with apprehension. One might well regard such a combination for co-leadership as an
invitation to disaster, given all the strictures about the importance of com-
patibility of approach for group co-leaders. To the contrary, what occurred
in nearly every instance was a process of mutual learning in which both
leaders grew closer, with real benefit to the group members. We believe this
occurred because of *one basic common denominator: their mutual genuine
concern for troubled young people* and their joint determination to find the
most useful ways of helping. The process is illustrated by a social worker's
observation about her initial experience:

> Our first group meeting of seventh grade girls was in a laboratory;
> no other space was available. I had never met the girls who had been
> interviewed and selected by the grade counselor who was co-leader—a
> warm, strong woman whom the girls obviously liked. As we seated our-
> selves in a circle, some of the girls began fooling around with lab equip-
> ment, and Mrs. H. told them firmly that they could not handle it.
> Several of them then began to flick their fingers and hands on each

other's arms and legs, while a general air of restlessness pervaded the circle. Mrs. H. looked at me, and I read her question clearly. Should she intervene again? I asked if the girls knew why they were here. Some said Mrs. H. had asked them. More flicking, changing into hitting. I asked what they were saying with their hands and feet. This appeared to startle them. One girl said, "Nothing. We do it all the time." I pressed further, and a discussion developed about how they express friendliness this way. They also agreed maybe it was a way of handling embarrassment at being here. This moved into a further discussion of how sometimes it ends in fights (which was one of the reasons some of the girls had been referred for group). Meanwhile, as the group talked about it, the actual behavior ceased. I breathed a sigh of relief that what I thought I knew about group process and feelings had worked at this crucial moment. Later, Mrs. H. and I talked about what happened in terms of when one had to use direct adult authority to control a group (safeguarding property and preventing personal injury, for instance) and when and how group process could be developed to deal with issues. Mrs. H. said this was new to her, but she was quick to grasp the idea and soon began to direct her remarks to promoting group participation and involvement.

Discussion occurred usually after each group meeting. Agency workers learned the value of offering their co-leaders a minimal explanation of their own rationale for group and began to make books and articles available while still offering themselves as one kind of model. This, of course, required conscious conceptualization by social workers, in itself a step toward the positive values of professional educators. For example, agency workers found themselves struggling to explain the whys and wherefores of enabling young people to air their negative feelings about trusting either adults or peers, a procedure some teachers and counselors found upsetting.

Frequently, school personnel would feel that we were pushing too hard for feelings in a way they experienced as intrusive. Yet, over a school semester or school year there was usually a *noticeable shift in their own readiness to deal with feelings* and their comfort in doing so. In a similar fashion, social workers' emphasis on process in group required continuing explanation.

Social workers also learned a good deal from school personnel, for example, the reality of the school situation within which students and teachers live. The educators knew when students faced situations that were actually not of their making as opposed to those which resulted from their own behavior. Many *teachers and counselors were very effective in confronting students* with their responsibility in learning how to handle school problems in a more effective way. They would not let students off the hook just because the problem had been created by others or because it was understandably upsetting. To illustrate:

> A very bright, capable, and attractive black girl had come from an almost wholly black elementary school to a junior high school comprising many ethnic groups. When she entered group, she was underachieving and in difficulty because of open hostility to her teachers, who she felt were prejudiced. She expressed hatred for her new school and a desire to go to an all-black junior high school. The group, which was ethnically mixed and co-led by a black counselor and a white social worker, repeatedly discussed the whole problem, separating out its various aspects and focusing on what Althea herself could do about it.
>
> The school counselor was aware of prejudiced attitudes on the part of some teachers, yet she did not permit this to be used as an excuse for self-destructive defiance or withdrawal. She both supported and confronted Althea in group and out of it. Eventually, Althea became much more self-assured and comfortable in dealing with students and teachers of other ethnic backgrounds (Anglo, Chicano, and Japanese). Her academic work improved, and she eventually emerged as one of the natural leaders of the school. In all of this, the ongoing understanding and intervention of the school counselor was of crucial importance; there was no substitute for this. A group led wholly by nonschool personnel could not have played the same role.

A certain natural *division of labor also developed between agency workers and school personnel,* based upon their respective areas of professional expertise. This is well illustrated by our experience in a group of ninth grade boys with quite serious problems, who were going on to senior high school the following year. The group, led by a man who was the school's head counselor and a woman social worker from the agency, went through a great deal together. Topics dealt with relations between students and school personnel, fighting in and outside school, family problems, stealing, drugs, and sex. A trust developed, group members spoke more and more openly about some very serious problems in all these areas.

One central, recurring theme was the sense of utter powerlessness over their own lives which these boys experienced. During the group's beginning period, this had been hidden under a mask of swaggering braggadocio, which the boys finally laid aside after much testing of the group leaders and each other. A major objective shared by the two group leaders was to help the boys recognize those areas of living over which they could have some control and assume greater responsibility for their own behavior.

As graduation approached, group members had developed a great deal of trust in each other and in the group leaders, to whom they turned for assistance and support in facing the new responsibility of senior high school. They opened this area of concern by anxious inquiries about many practical facets of the admission process. When would they be seeing the counselors from the senior high school who were due to visit their classes? Should they attend summer school? What were the requirements for high school graduation? Would their conduct record from the vice-principal's office be sent to the new school? The *counselor dealt with these matters factually* and with a wealth of knowledge which the social worker did not have. He also set a supportive but realistic tone in telling the boys that the reports of misconduct kept by the vice-principal did not ordinarily accompany the student's official record but that they would probably be communicated to the senior high school if the student got into difficulties there. In that event the senior high school would usually call up the previous school to ask about the student's conduct in more detail.

As these factual questions were dealt with, the *social worker brought up related issues involving goals and values as well as feelings of anxiety.* She inquired about the more long-range work plans of each boy; in many cases they had never really considered the future, and this in turn resulted in discussion of their feelings about the difficulty of planning ahead. These boys as a group tended to be wholly oriented to the present. The discussion which ensued was of great importance, harking back to their earlier expression of feeling powerless in the face of a world which they experienced as chaotic and "dog-eat-dog." The counselor and social worker together were able to help group members see that in this area of living, at least—work and preparation for it—they need not be wholly without power but could indeed make certain realistic and significant decisions which would affect their subsequent lives.

They related the boys' work objectives, such as auto mechanics, motorcycle building and repair, architectural drafting, and professional athletics, to the opportunities offered in high school. It was perhaps the first time these boys ever viewed school as offering them something which they could really use, beyond English and arithmetic, which they had earlier agreed everyone needed. Their responsibility for making sound decisions was specifically outlined. The group thus ended on a note which marked the boys' development over the school year: from brag and bluster as a cover for powerlessness to at least a partial realization that they could have the power of real action to influence, if not wholly determine, their present and future.

The point to be stressed here in terms of interprofessional collaboration is very important. For such boys to take more responsibility for themselves involved not only helping them with feelings but also giving them input of knowledge which they lacked. The *combined know-how of social worker and educator* effectively met this need.

### Difficulties for school personnel

Teachers or counselors are at the school every day; in a crisis the group members can and do run to them. This is invaluable in many situations, but it also poses certain difficulties. In some cases, students may seek *inappropriate personal involvement with the leader* outside of group, although in our experience this has rarely occurred (see Chapter 7).

A *certain role confusion* has also sometimes developed in groups when the school-based group leaders are classroom teachers and the groups include students from their classes. Several teachers have reported that the students attempted to bring the more informal group atmosphere into the classroom in what seemed an unacceptable and disruptive fashion. In other cases, students have used group to criticize and attack teachers' methods and style in their classrooms. We concluded that it is preferable to *limit membership in groups co-led by teachers* to students not currently in the teachers' classes. If this is not feasible, the problem should be discussed openly at the outset of the group and dealt with whenever it surfaces. The same difficulty does not usually arise with counselors. They are also in a better position to deal with parents when this seems indicated.

Students *tried to use leaders in a manipulative way* to deal with situations that had arisen as a result of the students' own conduct. For example, students may try to evade disciplinary action which is actually appropriate for their behavior. School group leaders have to avoid being misused in such situations. On the other hand, they can certainly offer to help the students deal with such problems in a new and more constructive way.

### Contribution of community agency workers

The participation of *community agency workers as co-leaders added important elements:* specific expertise in interpersonal relations and community resources, and a certain freshness of viewpoint. They are comparatively free both from prior alignments or involvements in the school's internal life and from the pedagogical approach. For example, it may be easier for an agency worker initially to see and to challenge efforts on the part of students to misuse or manipulate the educator co-leader, a protection and back-up for the more exposed school-based leader.

### Collaborative issues in selection of group members

It is proverbial that proper selection of group members is a major determinant of group outcome. Through a process of trial and error, agency workers learned to modify and adapt our agency experience to the school setting.

There was the classic episode of the elementary school group in which the co-leaders spent much of their time chasing after six hyperactive little boys. We were too ready to accept the school's proposals for group members. What we forgot was the importance of a balanced mix of problems and personality, something we had known from long and difficult agency experience. In several secondary schools we made the mistake of trying to handle group selection and admission with the same procedures used at our agency, namely, individual interviews of a fairly extensive nature. This procedure proved to be inordinately time-consuming for both school and agency personnel.

We subsequently developed a clearer division of labor between agency and school personnel. Agency workers took the responsibility for explaining the importance of balanced group membership, including diversity of problem and personality types, as well as ethnic composition. The questions of coed or one-sex groups were decided by school personnel. Age range ordinarily embraced only one or two grades.

The responsibility lay with the school personnel for selection and assignment to group from the pool of referrals. These referrals were wholly by school personnel or included student self-referrals, especially in junior and senior high schools. In some secondary schools the final selection was the responsibility of the head counselor and/or grade counselor who served as group co-leaders; in others it was handled by the school nurse, who served as a routing agent for students. Interviews were generally much briefer than in agency practice. This did not appear to have negative results. Even if one or both group leaders did not know their group members in advance, this was quickly remedied as the group got under way.

Outside professionals can and should bring to the school their own knowledge and skills in matters of group composition, but school personnel have the ability and knowledge to assess their own students.

## Dealing with administration

*Support by school administrators is essential* to the success of a collaborative group counseling program. Principals and other administrative personnel need assurance that the agency and individuals involved are professionally competent as well as sensitive to the characteristics and problems of a school setting. Schools having prior experience with our work around individual children were more prepared to open the door to a jointly sponsored group counseling project. As our work in group counseling expanded, administrators in schools new to us checked out our agency with those with whom we had already collaborated. *Community situation* around the school influenced administrator attitudes. Receptivity to group counseling seems to have been more marked in schools which were faced with new, greater stress from changes in ethnic or economic groupings in the school population. Also, many administrators were prepared to have their schools become more involved with the community.

It was *important to work with all appropriate administrative sectors* from the beginning. In one school the idea of group counseling was initiated by the principal; however, the counseling department had not been consulted at the outset and subsequently blocked the development of any joint program. Planning with counseling departments without involving principals and/or vice-principals could be equally self-defeating.* In several schools the school nurse played an important role in launching the program. The initial approach may come through any of these personnel, depending largely on the agency's earlier relationships with the school. The agency representative needs to be sensitive to the various levels and differing reactions within administrative circles.

The special problems and particular administrative relationships in each case have to be taken into account. This requires awareness and understanding of a rather large and complex setting, together with an appreciation of pitfalls to be avoided. One of these is inappropriate involvement in differences or conflicts between individuals or groups of school personnel. A certain amount of tact and plain common sense is essential.

## Obtaining faculty support

*Faculty support* of a group counseling program is in some ways a more complex and difficult problem than securing administrative backing. There are more teachers than administrators, and it is usually not easy to have direct access to all of them. Commensurate with their numbers, they hold widely diversified views on all questions connected with school policies and

---

* See Chapter 31.

programs. Securing faculty support is extremely important, since group counseling works best when it is scheduled during the school day. Requiring students to come before school, stay after school, or use lunch periods has not worked as well for the less motivated. This requires that students miss certain classes.

A flexible approach in each individual school is necessary to present the program to the faculty. In some cases it has been briefly outlined at a faculty meeting by a principal, vice-principal or head counselor; in other cases it has been written up in a school bulletin or letter to the faculty. Teachers were often asked to make referrals of students to the program. In some schools, teachers were invited to volunteer as group leaders; in other schools, counselors or other school personnel served as group leaders. The decisions on such issues were ordinarily made by the school administration, sometimes in consultation with agency representatives.

In all schools, it was necessary to work out with teachers a way of handling student absence from class to attend group. Individual discussion with those teachers who had some objection to the procedure was very important. Usually, the school-based leader took the responsibility for this. Involving teachers in evaluation of student growth was useful both to the group and to the teacher. This was easiest to do in elementary schools, but not impossible in junior or senior high schools. Agency workers found that informal discussion of the program with teachers they met at lunch or coffee breaks was mutually helpful. As classroom teachers understood more about the aims of the program and perhaps experienced better relations with students involved in it, their attitude was naturally more receptive. Agency workers had to be aware of the problems teachers faced.

## The future of collaboration

One final word on the position of interdisciplinary school group counseling in the school structure: We believe the need for such a program will continue and expand in the foreseeable future. At first, we thought community agencies might be utilized in a rather temporary way, pending the inclusion of group counseling as a basic feature of the educational system itself. Now *we believe our involvement will not necessarily be short-lived,* even though there has been a growth of skills in school personnel to the point that several are now confidently handling group counseling on their own. Continuing cooperation of agency and school personnel offers both a qualitatively valuable and quantitatively economical method. This collaborative way of meeting the ongoing needs of troubled young people may keep school counseling groups flexible and open to constant evaluation and change.

CHAPTER 25

# Mutual Learning by High School and University Students in a Group Counseling Program

Evelyn Cohen, M.S.W.

IT WAS OF INTEREST in the group counseling to be described here that an important value of the project was the mutual growth which developed in the interaction between students of two institutions—an inner city high school and a large university (psychology and social welfare graduate programs).

*The setting*

The group counseling program was part of a special four-year project known as Area Program Enrichment Exchange (APEX), a federally funded demonstration project by which secondary schools in the central part of Los Angeles were provided with additional staff and funds to improve school services. At Crenshaw High School, the guidance and counseling staff was augmented by the school group counselor, who supervised the group counseling program and coordinated it with UCLA* psychology clinic personnel. This satisfied the school district regulations relating to the use of certificated personnel in direct contact with students and the confidential nature of student records.

Crenshaw drew its students largely from a neighborhood of middle- and working-class families in Los Angeles. The enrollment of 2,750 students was predominantly Black, with approximately two percent from other racial groups, chiefly Japanese-American and Mexican-American. During the first

---

* University of California at Los Angeles.

year of the project the school was like an armed camp. Police and plain-clothesmen carried loaded weapons. Some students brought arms to school with them that were confiscated by the vice-principals. Many students were heavily drugged on "pills." Fires broke out in wastebaskets in rest rooms and on the school grounds. Gangs on the street and on school grounds openly challenged the police and the school authorities. As students shared with us their apprehension about coming to school under these conditions and parents demanded that the police and plainclothesmen not carry loaded weapons into the school, the situation changed. Parents volunteered to maintain order on the school grounds, if the police would control the activity on the street.

## The graduate students

The UCLA staff consisted of one supervisor and two graduate students the first two years, and two supervisors and four graduate students the last year. These students conducted weekly counseling groups from February 1968 to May 1970. The school group counselor served as a co-leader in several groups during the entire period. An additional counselor was given time to serve as a co-leader in the last semester. Whenever possible, we teamed a male and female, a Black and a white as co-leaders of the counseling groups.

Following each group meeting the group leaders met with the UCLA supervisors to discuss the session specifically, including issues of group dynamics and processes. Each group was composed of a maximum of 12 students. The program entailed the identification, referral, and summoning of each of the 50 students who were participants in the program. Twenty-five of the 50 constituted a control group. The members of the control group were identified and interviewed but did not participate in the group counseling experience. New participants were chosen each year to keep groups full.

## Group members

The group members consisted of underachievers, first offenders in behavioral difficulties, a number of hard-core multiproblem students, and some young people who were struggling with problems that interfered with effective utilization of their capacities, both socially and academically. These students had been referred either to the group counselor's or the vice-principal's office because of truancy, underachievement, drug abuse, or excessively hostile behavior.

The groups were *time limited* to a series of 17 meetings. Before the groups began, a preliminary meeting with the school group counselor was held to give the UCLA staff the necessary demographic information about the school, the characteristics of the young people who were about to be involved, and the nature of the surrounding community.

## Selection and preparation of members

Students were interviewed individually and offered the opportunity to participate weekly in a group, where they could talk about anything that bothered them, at home or at school. Attendance was to be voluntary. Ninety percent of the students interviewed agreed to come and try the group for a few weeks. Eighty percent of those who agreed to come continued to attend for the balance of the school year. However, attendance was quite irregular because of conflicts with academic and other school activities. To avoid having students miss academic work, the groups met at a different period each week, alternating between second and fifth periods.

Group sessions lasted 45 minutes. The group counseling method was eclectic, borrowing from education, casework, counseling, and psychotherapy. Leaders often provided psychological information, education about sexual behavior, human development, and career data. They engaged as well in role playing and modeling-feeling expression patterns.

*Group leaders received ongoing feedback* from the school counselors, administrative personnel, and students about the impact of the program. The program extended over three years to more than 100 students.* Personnel involved 10 advisors, two clinical supervisors, and two school group counselors. Nine masters and doctoral candidates from the schools of Social Welfare and Psychology participated in leading nine groups (two or more per year).

## Development of involvement and trust in the groups

The first concern in the group counseling was to develop motivation and involvement in the group counseling process. These adolescents, as are most, were reluctant about asking for help, since this was perceived as a frightening concession of weakness. However, when the leader reached out to the student, and expressed a warm interest in understanding and helping, most responded and began to relate, though cautiously.

---

* Editor's Note: Actually, many more than this number were helped in (1) individual crisis interventions by the graduate students related to group involvement or without group involvement and (2) a group of counselees who moved into a group (not described here) where peer-counseling was discussed. In addition, there was a group for teachers (Jim Burt).

However, for most adolescents the idea of receiving help as a member of a group is usually less threatening than receiving help as an individual. It is comforting to know that others have problems and feelings similar to their own. Yet it was difficult here to develop a sense of group unity. The group members feared that the fact that they were in a counseling group in school might cause them to lose status with peers. Other young people might suspect that they had problems or were "crazy." They were often dubious about their own participation in the group and reluctant to identify with other members whom they perceived to be odd or funny. They feared others would interpret their involvement in group counseling as weakness and dependency upon an adult, both of which are contrary to adolescent values.

Another obstacle to group solidarity was the *deep distrust for the leaders,* one of whom was usually white or of the opposite sex. Students continually anticipated criticism and punishment from the leaders similar to their teachers' reactions. The members tested the leaders and the other group members over and over again on this score.

The counselees were suspicious of the project and the University people. They stated that they were not sure that confidences shared in the group would not be turned over to the police or the administration. There were several members of the Black Panthers in the groups and it took months before they accepted our motives and purposes and the idea that we were "not out to get them." They had difficulty in trusting the Black graduate students, who they said "had sold out to Whitey." In the divided society of then and today, it is, and was rare to see "whites" in an all-Black high school, especially whites who wanted to be there. Many Caucasian teachers were requesting transfers to schools in other areas.

Group members tried to ascertain whether their free expression would lead to self-incrimination, criticism, and punishment by the leaders or school authorities. When they had reassured themselves, they tested to see what advantages they could derive from the therapy situation. Could they get an extra pass to stay out of class? Also, they used the group freely to abuse authority figures at great length and with much pleasure. These included teachers, principals, and parents. As well as their distrust of the adults, *a significant obstacle to the development of group unity* was the lack of empathy on the part of individual members for each other. This usually changed by the fifth session.

Entering high school students are painfully uncertain about their relationships not only with adults but also with the new and greater number of peers they are suddenly required to encounter. Group counseling was a means of expanding the students' repertoire of responses to other students and authority figures.* The groups provided a rich atmosphere for peer learning and teaching, through modeling and role playing. When the cohesiveness of the group was high, approval and disapproval of other group members served as effective control, particularly in the case of drug users.

Some of the *issues raised* and discussed in the groups were: Do I have the freedom to choose the type of relationship I want with my parents? Do I trust other persons enough to be able to listen to them and express my inner feelings to them? Am I able to exercise some initiative in my family without feeling guilty about it? How should I respond to my parent who says, "This is the way it has always been done; therefore, this is the way it must be done now"? Our group experience was seen to have some relevance to the *dropout* problem as well. The high dropout rate grows out of students' not perceiving the schools as providing them with what they think they need in order to achieve or even to survive in the society they will soon have to enter. Students seem to want the high schools to help them find themselves personally as well as vocationally, to help them understand their abilities, to give them some idea of their potential, to concentrate on their feelings, and the caring aspects of human relationships. They want to know that in some way they matter, that they exist, and that their wishes for themselves count, to others as well as to themselves.

It is our impression that the group experience in the school provided the members with a peer group that was openly concerned with them, their present, and their future. The group felt with and cared about them. Each week they brought their worries, fears, doubts, and achievements. They shared their joys and woes with their group; the other members confronted them with their strengths and weaknesses, and they learned to do the same for the others.

*Sex education* was another conspicuous area of need. Most students were full of misinformation. They were frightened, frustrated, and curious. Many had been offered opportunities for prostitution which frightened and attracted them. Some girls were adding to their allowances in this manner. One girl was involved with her mother's second husband and subsequently became pregnant with his child.

It was the impression of the supervisors and group leaders that students, as a result of the group experience, began to function with greater independence. They were able to feel and express concern for each other. They

---

* See Chapter 23.

clarified for themselves to different degrees their goals and values, and gained some greater insight into their parents' goals and values for them. They seemed better able to evaluate what they wanted for themselves and openly experienced differences and similarities among them with greater tolerance and better understanding.

### Activities of group leaders

The group leaders accepted the students' feelings, but they did not permit themselves to be manipulated by members or seduced into agreeing with complaints. Common emotions underlying the members' symptoms were frequently pointed out to the group members. This facilitated identification and mutual support. The leaders displayed an attitude of understanding but did not condone antisocial feelings. Interpretation of symptoms stressed immediate causes rather than roots in the unconscious infantile needs of group members. For example, stealing was interpreted as the result of present anger or deprivation rather than as the result of feeling unloved as a child.

A prerequisite for effective group counseling was the *understanding and support of the teachers and school administrators*. Two-way communication was essential. Information was shared between leaders and teachers, coaches, nurse, and vice-principals without revealing the specific experiences or feelings the group members had expressed. A separate group consisting of teachers was helpful.

The *role of the leaders was necessarily more authoritarian* and less permissive than in group therapy. Students' expectations of the leaders' role followed from the teaching model; therefore, it was essential that the members respected the leaders and knew that they were in control of the group. The leaders were active in beginning and maintaining the group process. Nevertheless, the leaders indicated that group members were not helpless and were responsible for their behavior—that they were capable, at least potentially, of self-control.

The perceptions of the adolescents tended to be stereotyped. They often saw adults as either "dangerous" or as "suckers." They saw their peers and themselves as "tough" or "weak." The leaders offered alternative views to these distorted perceptions of roles and encouraged empathy with others by reacting with empathy.

The most common countertransference problem was to deal with feelings of hurt after *injury to the leaders' narcissism*. Adolescents lack the usual faith in the group process or respect for the leaders. Many group members kept complaining that they were not being helped. Many felt differently by the eighth or ninth sessions. It was helpful to the leaders to recall their own adolescent conflicts, and the co-leaders helped each other maintain the capacity for empathizing with the group members.

### The mutual learning experience between the high school and graduate students

Most of the graduate students had some theoretical cultural and ethnic information about the population in the school. However, in the groups they had an opportunity to hear directly from the counselees about their parents, the child-rearing patterns and marital and family arrangements as well as their life styles. They also were given an opportunity to speak about their own, as they were questioned by the high school students.

As the counselees began to trust the counselors they gave evidence of their hunger for knowledge and information about the world of the University and the community that many of them knew very little about. Many felt that they had been bright as younger children but that they had been doing very poorly since junior high school. Most students underrated their abilities. A few, it seemed to us, were very unrealistic about their futures. A handsome, quiet student with superior intelligence was a leader in the Black Panthers and planned to become an organizer when he graduated. At the end of the semester he decided he could be of more help to his people if he went to college and continued his education.

The counselors became confidants, friends, and models as the project evolved. At the end of the second year the high school students came to visit the University. For most of them it was their first exposure to a university campus. As they toured the campus many determined to return on their own some day. Termination was difficult for the graduate students as well as the counselees. Their evaluation indicated that for some this had been one of the most significant learning experiences they had had since coming to the University.

### Evaluation*

Fifty students were randomly selected from the tenth grade class. Twenty-five were involved in group counseling, and 25 were treated as a control group and not invited into the groups. Self-rating inventories were administered to both groups in order to obtain pre- and post-measurements of

---

* See Chapter 29.

interests and self concept. A sample of each group was interviewed at the middle of the second year. In reviewing the changes in both groups it was found that the *experimental group did not do as well as the control group in academic performance after one year*. However, the group that had the group counseling showed *generally higher interest scores* on the self-rating inventories, *more involvement in extracurricular activities*, and *more satisfaction with peer relationships*.

The counseled group generally showed changes in a negative direction on the self-rating scales, and this may reflect the development of greater self-awareness in this group. Although the objective of increasing academic performance did not manifest itself at the time of the statistical evaluation, it was strongly indicated by the group discussion that many of the *students who had remained in groups for the two-year period began to be much more serious about their academic performance*. They were seriously concerned about grades, not missing classes, and going on to college. They were concerned about each other, tried to help others obtain after-school jobs, and aided in handling conflicts with parents and teachers.

The issues of *white leaders working with Black students* remained alive and unresolved for the total time.* Verbalizations of trust were questioned, but warm, affectionate behavior seemed to indicate that color differences were erased by understanding and familiarity. At times the leaders felt they did not know how to communicate openly with group members and that they were not trusted or believed. When they confronted members with their feelings of frustration and rejection, the young people denied that they were rejecting or distrusting because of color differences, but at times they admitted they were not accustomed to trusting white people. They rarely communicated openly with white authority figures. Trusting people over 30 was difficult, and most of all it was difficult to trust their own feelings, which were often mixed and uncertain.

The leaders and co-leaders of the groups were unanimous in their agreement that they had learned a great deal about themselves in relation to high school students and especially this ethnic population. The feeling of acceptance, personal significance, and social comfort which the students developed from belonging to a group of adults and fellow students seemed to be a valuable educational experience for this group of students.

---

* See Chapter 28.

## BIBLIOGRAPHY

BUNT, M. E. (1968). Ego identity: Its relationship to the discrepancy between how an adolescent views himself and how he perceives others view him. *Psychology*, 5:3, 14-25.

ERIKSON, E. H. (1956). The problem of ego identity. *J. Am. Psychoanal. Assn.*, 4, 56-121.

GILLILAND, B. E. (1968). Small group counseling with Negro adolescents in a public high school. *J. of Counseling Psychol.*, 15:2, 147-152.

GITELSON, M. (1948). Character synthesis; The psychotherapeutic problem of adolescents. *Am. J. Orthopsychiat.*, 422-431.

OHLSEN, M. M. (1970). *Group Counseling*. New York: Holt, Rinehart and Winston.

SHULMAN, I. (1959). Transference, resistance, and communication problems in adolescent psychotherapy groups. *Int. J. Group Psychother.*, 496-503.

CHAPTER 26

# Teachers and Mental Health Professionals as Co-Leaders in High School Groups

Zanwil Sperber, Ph.D., and
Deborah K. Aguado, M.S.

IN THIS STUDY, two mental health professionals* from different agencies were collaboratively involved with teachers on the campus of an urban high school attended by 3,000 students. The school population had a large number of students from families whose parents had valued education as a way toward occupational, economic, and personal advancement. Some of these families had achieved a substantial degree of success and affluence from adhering to these beliefs. Nevertheless, many of the students from these families joined with classmates from lower classes and other cultural groups, who had not experienced that value system, in finding the school and the curriculum of dubious relevance. They, as well as the faculty, often doubted the value of what they were doing.

In addition, affluence and drugs provided more dramatic and potentially more dangerous ways for acting out against boredom, or for distracting one-self from the pains of unresolved personal and familial problems. The traditional signs of distress—somatic symptoms, anxiety, depression, and intense love-hate emotions related to the agonies of teen-age social development—

---

* Many colleagues participated in the program described. The sensitive, thoughtful observations of the teachers and professional psychotherapists who committed time and energy beyond their regular hours to this project are appreciatively acknowledged. We especially wish to thank Maxine Wainman, R.N., M.S., the high school's nurse, for the many vital contributions she made to the program.

were also often visible to be picked up by concerned and sensitive peers, teachers, the school nurse, and parents.

## The school

In addition to these problems, pressures came into the school that were associated with the changing racial mix of its population. The surrounding business and parental community reacted with anxiety to real or fantasied dangers attributed to the recently increasing proportion of Blacks in the school's student body. At this same time the school was moving toward use of a more flexible (block) method for scheduling classes, and this required increased teacher cooperation. It was hoped this plan would make educational possibilities richer and more gratifying for teacher and student. Unfortunately, it was implemented in the period after a teachers' strike, which left a residue of bitterness between those who had struck and those who had not.

For some time, one of the authors (Aguado), a consultant from the local county mental health office, had been working with key school personnel as a regular member of an ongoing intercultural committee involving faculty, administration, and students. This committee was designed to deal with the above tensions and to set up a mechanism for developing services helpful to the overall school and community groups. The other author (Sperber) represented a nearby mental health hospital-clinic service with an established reputation for serving youth. In February 1971 an earthquake damaged a second nearby high school, necessitating that the almost all-Black student body move into the undamaged, more middle-class Caucasian school. Both schools continued to function as separate bodies, using the same plant sequentially with a "buffer zone" of a half hour separating them. We reached out to principals of both schools, offering our services as human relations experts to facilitate communications which might prevent conflicts. Our proffered service was gratefully appreciated but termed unnecessary by the principal of the wrecked school. The other principal referred our offer to his school's intercultural committee.

## The students and teachers

Conditions of tension, frustration, and despair characterize the experience of many students who feel trapped in a high school setting where the courses imposed and the grades and evaluation associated with them are beyond their control. These conditions also seem to apply to the teachers, who experience a similar feeling of isolation. Sarason (1971) described the "behavioral regularities" observed in the average school system, where, in general, students sit passively in the room in front of the one adult, who does most of the talking. However, teachers also cannot readily go to the principal because he evaluates or grades them. Merely to ask for assistance or supervision often implies failure. In a school in which some of the teachers had so recently been on strike and some had not, it was difficult to have the trust to seek support in informal exchanges with one's colleagues. In this particular school there was not even a teacher's lounge where this kind of interchange could take place with any degree of privacy or comfort, if one felt motivated or trusting enough to do so.

In these situations there is a tendency for teachers vis-à-vis the principal and other administrators, and students vis-à-vis teachers, to assume that the one next above them in the hierarchy has tremendous power. The students felt that the teachers had the right to change the curriculum, while at the very same time the teachers felt compelled to stick closely to lesson plans, because achievement test scores would be used to prove their adequacy as teachers. Similarly, when teachers sent students to the vice-principal for discipline, they expected the youngsters to be suspended or their parents called in. If the students merely returned to their next class, the teachers felt unsupported.

### The groups

In this context 6 groups of students, each co-led by a mental health professional and a teacher, began meeting after the spring recess of 1971. In 1971-72, 10 groups were regularly attended by some 90 to 100 students. The fundamental contribution of these groups to mental health was the provision of a place where feelings, words, thoughts, and doubts could be expressed and where members at two levels of the educational hierarchy, teacher and student, could more realistically share where they were and what their limits were.

We were pleased to note that students could freely express themselves and ventilate in the groups on campus. There was little apparent fear that what they said, even if directed against their own faculty and school administration, would be used negatively against them. The problems discussed often were very similar both in intensity and even in content to those bothering adolescents in group therapy in a psychiatric clinic.

While the concerns of youth are frequently socially constructive, the substance or content of their concern often may generate *anxiety in adults.*

This anxiety can make it difficult for the adults, particularly when they are tied to the culture and rules of an institution, to respond directly. As the adults "fuss," the students are often left in an ambiguous void and can readily assume that no one had really listened. For example, students and adults in the school had indicated a desire to prevent venereal disease and unwed pregnancy. However, when *they asked for sex education,* including birth control information, and suggested that birth control equipment be dispensed on the school grounds, the adults and the school with its legal strictures were unable to generate a direct response. From the point of view of the students, adults in the school may then appear unaware, uncaring, or critical of the students' needs or impulses.

With reference to the particular problem of sex and sex behavior, dramatic changes obviously have occurred since the teen years of today's educators, alienating them at times from the teen-age students of today. The following is an example of one of today's teen-age situations: In one group a young male student took the lead in discussing his feelings about being cut off from expressing his concern and affection for the girl he impregnated because she had excluded him from making any of the arrangements for the abortion. His girl friend had, however, involved another boy, who was known to our group member and also to a girl in the group, to convey the message, "When he got me pregnant he wasn't available to help me." In the discussion other girls helped the boy understand the possibility that his girl friend might have feared his rejection and therefore defensively ruled out asking for his assistance. He was encouraged to leave the group session early so that he could wait outside his girl-friend's classroom to tell her how much he cared and offer his help.

Examples such as the one above, of *support, warmth, and empathy occurred frequently.* One group, for example, dealt supportively with a girl about to graduate in mid-year. She did not feel ready to go immediately into college but felt she could not withstand the pressures from her parents to do so. The group chose to meet during the Christmas vacation so this issue could be discussed further. In this way they helped the girl find a way to speak to her parents so that they could accept her desire not to emulate an older sibling by rushing so quickly into advanced education. This girl was among two or three group members who continued after graduation to return to campus for participation in the groups.

However, the *groups were not universally successful* in facilitating communication. A frequent problem was the stance of someone who came to the session but handled possible tensions by responding to every voiced difficulty with an assertion that it was no problem for him or her. The participating mental health professional often suspected that the student was avoiding discussion of a feared problem, but intervention was impossible, since the student might sheepishly begin to blush and then remain silent. At times like this the *teacher co-leader was of great value* and provided something which the mental health professional alone could not offer. The teacher and student shared an ongoing membership in the school community, and their lives converged on the same space five days a week. Seeing the student later on campus and noticing troubled looks of sadness, the teacher could walk up to the student and say with some sympathy, "You still look kind of bothered." An invitation to return to the group could be repeated at periodic intervals, and many students who dropped out of group did return some weeks later.

We have also found *peer "networks" operative* (Sugar, 1971). Sometimes two or three students who were close friends off campus would come into a group together. They would often use their friendship not only to facilitate certain conversations, but also to protect each other from taking the next painful step, i.e., facing the difficulty long enough for it to be understood and resolved. Unfortunately, when two adult co-leaders function as relatively silent listeners during sessions, they may generate the effect that they have their own private secrets. This may then encourage communication blocking, defense-supporting whispering or giggling among the groups of friends. One of the ongoing groups had a strong subgroup friendship network within a larger group. The leaders devoted a good deal of their activity to discussion of the communication-thwarting effect of subgroup separation. To the surprise of the leaders, a situation developed in which the whole group worked together to set up a trial against the two adults, with the charge: ". . . accused of not talking! You just listen!"

The substance discussed in many of our groups and the intensity with which emotions were expressed encouraged us to feel that something real and meaningful was occurring. This belief was supported by the instances in which students returned to the group after graduation or wrote letters if they had moved away. On the other hand, certain serious and painful problems might come up for discussion, but the member would fail to return for a period of weeks, or perhaps not at all. However, this discouraging *phenomenon of dropouts* now seemed to be of less concern, since meeting group members in the larger school group community allowed expression of concern and encouragement to members to return. Unfinished business which was started in the group continued to be discussed even when the person had left. Some remaining members apparently then felt able to take responsibility for seeking out the lost persons to invite them back.

The experiences generated by group participation appeared to affect group members, setting up *motivation for further participation*. Many of the eleventh graders from the spring 1971 groups returned as group members at the beginning of the 1971-72 school year. Apparently, desires for introspective self-reflection or interpersonal sharing were strengthened and led to the determination to continue. This perpetuation of membership patterns was often extended when existing members invited friends from their own network to join them in the group.

*Results and conclusions*

Some *overall statistics** might be of interest. Of the 90 to 100 students regularly utilizing the 10 groups in 1971-72,, approximately 60% were female and 40% male. Nearly all the group members were eleventh and twelfth graders, with very few tenth graders participating. The campus student population was now 79% Caucasian, 17% Black, and 4% Latin American, Oriental, or other backgrounds. In terms of group membership, the proportion of Blacks was slightly underrepresented, with only 11% of the students regularly attending the groups being Black. About 2% of the students attending the groups had Latin surnames. It was also our impression that students attending the groups tended to be from the middle-class segments of the student body, with working-class and very poor students underrepresented. This social-class bias in group use appeared to be true for both Black and Caucasian members.

The question arose as to *why teacher-selected or school nurse-selected referrals did not bring in more minority members* from the low socioeconomic, Black, Chicano, and other segments of the school population. One speculation to answer this derived from an observation of the kinds of symptomatic behavior associated with lower- versus middle- and upper-class cultures, or with membership in the Black culture versus the Anglo culture. It could be that when the population of the high school was familiar to the faculty and its administration, because the students came from the same middle-class, achievement-oriented background and often from the same religious beliefs as the teachers, difficult students could be more comfortably defined as having an "emotional" or "mental health" problem. That is, referral of a "familiar" student to a mental health system would follow

---

* See Chapter 29 for additional statistics.

more readily. More members of the current student body appear to express their difficulties by hostile, aggressive, or disrespectful behavior. The adult's reaction then might more often be a biased one in which the student would be viewed as "bad" and be sent to the vice-principal for entry into the disciplinary system, rather than to the school nurse for entry into the mental health system available on the campus.

Indeed, it has been our impression that teachers, sensing threats to their authority and to their functional role in the system (teacher as communicator of valued information to student) begin to see the problems not in terms of a breakdown of interpersonal communication, but in terms of a *power struggle*. When we attempted to work in a group with teachers who were not co-leaders of groups, we noted that they were caught up in this issue. They were prone to talk not about their feelings in dealing with these literally challenging students, but rather about their anger at the school administration for not supporting them.

*Teachers who worked as group leaders* with the students frequently reported that the experience was "the high point of my work." Issues of *emotional overinvolvement* became apparent for the co-leaders. For example, one teacher offered a home for a weekend to a student who said she could not bear the familial distress of living with her mother. Other issues which arose for the teachers were fear of loss of authority and problems in sharing caused by fear of establishment of reciprocity between adult and youngster. This reciprocity issue was illustrated in a group in which the teacher was alert intellectually to the need to be open about one's feelings of distress. She also was aware that a personal conflict can often be so anxiety-inducing that it distracts one from doing usual tasks, making academic work difficult. She was very understanding and supportive of students' claims that their worries were affecting their grades. However, in one session when the teacher was preoccupied with an illness in her family, she was invited to discuss her preoccupation and sad look. She verbally refused to do so. She withdrew to the periphery, apparently needing to feel either that an adult has no right to express feelings of need to a younger person, or defensively believing that it would be demanding for an adult to try to account for a changed level of performance.

At the current level of collaboration between mental health worker and teacher we felt free to encourage close work, exploring the implication of personal discoveries such as the one above. We also provided a co-leader teachers' group as a setting for the discovery of the cost as well as the opportunities associated with freer emotional involvement with students.

We were aware that we were regularly serving only 100 students of a far larger student body and that this program consumed a number of professional mental health hours that could not readily be funded if they were not being provided free by a mental health training center and a county agency. However, *the teachers themselves were beginning to find ways to expand the program.* Although they did not yet feel ready to work with an inexperienced teacher as co-leader, present teacher co-leaders felt, by the last meeting, that two of them together might be able to conduct a group the next year without the presence of a mental health professional. We were encouraged by the thought that interested regular members of the staff would develop a commitment to permit the program to operate on a self-maintaining basis. This might be insured if, as one of the co-leading teachers suggested, the time in group leader activity were compensated by a reduction in teaching load. In a sense, the recognition of the value of rap group activity might be equated to what other teachers receive for athletic coaching endeavors. The added extrinsic reward would combine with the real intrinsic satisfactions teachers experience when having a meaningful, ongoing involvement with their students as persons, not as passive vessels to be loaded with a predetermined cargo of facts—the curriculum.

## BIBLIOGRAPHY

SARASON, S. B. (1971). *The Culture of the School and the Problem of Change.* Boston: Allyn and Bacon.
SUGAR, M. (1971). Network psychotherapy of an adolescent. In S. C. Feinstein, P. L. Giovacchini, and A. A. Miller (Eds.), *Adolescent Psychiatry,* Vol. I, pp. 464-478. New York: Annals of the American Society for Adolescent Psychiatry and Basic Books.

CHAPTER 27

# Structured Problem Solving to Improve Participation in a Large High School Group

Harry Pannor, A.C.S.W., and
Nora Nicosia, M.S.

HAMILTON HIGH SCHOOL in Los Angeles was considered a school in transition in 1969 because it was rapidly changing from a middle-class, largely Jewish community to one which comprised about 41 percent Black youngsters, a growing number of Mexican-Americans, and a dwindling Jewish, middle-class population. The newer students came from very diverse socioeconomic backgrounds. For four years this school in transition has faced all the recent problems of most urban schools.

For the minority population there were tremendous feelings of alienation. Many students had difficulty competing scholastically and, in fact, constituted the majority of many of the slower academic classes. The school had not been able to provide sufficient remedial assistance for these students, and the need for additional resources constantly existed. Even outside the classroom there was not a real social mixing of the groups. Some minority students, who found it difficult to compete scholastically, used a more familiar means to find a measure of success, namely physical abilities in athletics. A very small, although highly visible, group used less constructive attention-getting behavior, such as extortion and fighting.

A schism also existed in the goals of these two groups. Many minority students were striving for middle-class values. As a result they could not understand the alienated behavior of some of the middle-class young people who were not interested in academic or material success, or the social life around school, including extracurricular activities and sports. Having had limited experiences with minorities, except perhaps as servants in their homes, many white students in their desire to get along used methods familiar to them, attempting to talk, finding compromises, and sometimes even "bending backward" out of feelings of guilt.

*The staff* experienced tremendous feelings of frustration. The old methods of teaching were not working. Many teachers lacked a repertoire of skills to approach the new cultural groups. The unknown produced anxiety and resentment about the changes. Some of the more aware personnel were frustrated because the school was not meeting the changing needs fast enough. Administrators were often not successful in providing solutions. Some staff also feared the violence and were frustrated by their inability to handle the situation. Many students picked up on the insecurity demonstrated by staff members.

*Parents* of the students attending Hamilton also experienced anxiety and frustration. Some of them, particularly the white parents, felt fear of physical harm to their children, depreciation of land values, and lowering of academic and moral values for their children, most of whom were college bound. The conflict between the adolescents and their parents became involved with and accentuated around the issue of Black-white relationships. Although many of the parents professed liberal attitudes, they became fearful and apprehensive when faced with the reality of mixed socialization. In many instances the students were socially more aware and accepting of this mixing between the ethnic groups than were their parents.

As the school became aware that the situation was more than it could cope with, the *principal reached out for help to the community* and, more specifically, to various social agencies that he felt would have concern and appropriate resources. As a result of meetings between school and agency representatives, it was decided that the main thrust in trying to help the school would be through the use of counseling groups and a limited amount of individual counseling.*

The school had to accept its role, not only for education but also for handling of psychological problems, because this is where the young people were. This is where many of the latent problems surfaced because of the pressures of achievement; this is where they struggled with acceptance, feelings of isolation, and anxiety. Group discussion can elicit movement towards help and provide constructive experiences in a time of tension. The chance

---

* See Chapter 23.

to ventilate school and personal problems can contribute to the general welfare of the individual student and the school, even as far as helping the school to run on a more even keel.

*Advantages result for the community agency* as well as the school community when agency personnel can bring their expertise into the school. For many years agencies were not reaching large numbers of students and their families. This has been particularly true with minority people, many of whom have had negative experiences with social agencies. These clients often lack confidence and trust in the agencies when they are primarily staffed by non-minority workers. Many families and their adolescents are reluctant because they associate the agencies with emotionally sick or "crazy" people. In addition, many agency personnel are aligned with the adult world and less able to understand youthful individuals.

*The advantage for the school community* is that groups located on the school grounds are able to relate the counseling to the daily living milieu of the students. Another important advantage is the opportunity to assist in developing counseling expertise among school personnel, such as counselors, nurses, and teachers. This in turn could move toward an ongoing mental health program led by school personnel when and if these outside agencies could no longer participate within the school setting. Also, agency personnel would be available for consultation and referral for students and families who needed additional help.

## Goals of groups

The prime goal was to help students find relief from personal problems, so that they could evidence positive changes in social and academic behavior in school and also get in touch with underlying positive feelings. Other goals were: to help students understand similarities of their problems despite basic cultural differences; to appreciate and understand how differences in behavior and attitude were affected by culture; to provide an opportunity to understand various aspects of cultural behavior with respect to parents, sex, peers, vocational goals, values, and boy-girl relationships; to help students develop better self-image; to provide a more positive view of the school as interested in their personal welfare; to offer them an experience in an open, warm, close, safe setting to deal with feelings of loneliness and alienation; to help their students develop listening and communication skills, a sense of commitment, and responsibility; to provide models to emulate for new ways of coping as they listen to other members describe successful behavior in dealing with past or present problems; to provide new behavior techniques, which could be tested immediately in the school setting in and outside of classes.

*Selection of group members*

Groups were selected to include students whose personal problems appeared to be interfering with their social or academic functioning. Group members were balanced in relation to sex and cultural and economic backgrounds; each group included Black, white, and Spanish-speaking (Mexican, Cuban, and South American) students who demonstrated scholastic underachievement.

The *screening was done by the counselor* from students with whom she dealt regularly, others with whom she had contact, and those referred by other faculty members. At an individual conference with each student, the nature of the group was explained, questions were answered, and feelings were discussed. The group process was described as one of verbal communication, but students were reassured that no one would be pressured to talk. The counselor further reassured the students that they were being invited to join not because they were "problem" or "sick" people, but rather because the counselor felt they could benefit from and contribute to this type of experience, reinforcing their self-esteem. Hesitant students were encouraged to risk joining, and most of those invited agreed to participate out of trust already established with the counselor.

In order to meet administrative guidelines for group membership, students were given consent forms to be signed by their parents. However, if youngsters felt ambivalent, they could attend the first session without returning these forms, so that their decision would be based on their own experience with group process. Following the student-counselor conference, the counselor and the social worker discussed each member in relation to the group.

*The groups*

Since spring 1969, the authors have led four groups. Each one had some significant differences from the others and provided a learning experience. While we will explore aspects of all four, there will be greater detail about the third group, which, we feel, was the most successful for a school setting.

Our *first group* was scheduled to begin in March 1970. Because of a teacher strike in the city, the group did not start until May and ran only for the very brief period of five one-hour weekly sessions. This group was limited to 10 students. After the first session new members and drop-ins were discouraged. One student did drop out. An extremely significant aspect of this group was that it met during the sixth period of the regular day, between 2 and 3 p.m. Students were excused from classes with the understanding and agreement of the subject teachers. The attendance record was very good, and students quickly formed a cohesiveness. At the last session the leaders asked for a written evaluation from each student. The written feedback confirmed the leaders' evaluation that the group had provided a positive experience despite its extremely brief duration.

The *second group* ran into a circumstantial interference. The high school schedule had been modified drastically, with the school day ending at 2 p.m. Most students left school as soon as possible; in fact, many students who did not have afternoon classes on alternate days left school at lunchtime. The leaders of the 12 counseling groups then on campus were not surprised to find that members attended erratically, with a general falling off of attendance. The general conclusion was that reaching students within the framework of the regular school day provides a minimum number of obstacles and is important in order to reach the more resistant students in greater need of help. Students, like other workers, seem to feel a desire to leave the school grounds as soon as the school day is over.

The *third counseling group* ran from February 1971 to the end of the semester. Twelve students were invited to join, and again the group was balanced in membership based on our criteria. Substantial modification of the school schedule called for a new study period at 10:30 a.m. after nutrition, instead of the activity period at the end of the day. The 20-minute study period, combined with the 20-minute snack time, provided a 40-minute period. Counseling groups meeting during this time were excused from their study centers and voluntarily gave up their nutrition. Since most students were bored in their study centers, they welcomed any diversion and began to drop in to group sessions with friends. Thus began a *self-referral process* that resulted in an ever-increasing group, often consisting of *as many as 25 members*.

As members of the initial group began to bring friends with them, the leaders discussed this phenomenon. Several important student motives and needs emerged: inclusion of some friends with whom they wished to work out problems; to share the experience with other friends; desire to be with peers in order to feel more secure about group participation; or the wish to help peers. It was interesting that the invited friends were always of the same sex. We decided to accept any drop-ins and the self-referred friends of members of the group.

The group *convened in the school dining room,* where two soft couches and movable straight chairs were arranged in a circle and leaders sat away from each other as part of the group. In order to help members begin to feel more at ease, leaders explained the following *method of introduction:* Members were to combine in pairs and share with each other something that they would then share with the group as a way of introduction. Specific instructions were that the members should share something positive that they wished group members to know about them. We found that this method was not effective with this group, as it seemed to inhibit students and make them feel as though they were put on a spot. Many appeared to be uncomfortable about emphasizing their good qualities. For adolescents with feelings of low self-esteem this may be too difficult a task for starting a group experience.

The counselor then briefly explained some of the purposes of the group: self-awareness, sharing of problems, use of feedback, and the need for trust and confidentiality. She de-emphasized diagnosis or history, because this was not a therapy group. Limits were few; members had freedom as long as they did not interfere with the freedom of others. At the first meeting we asked the members individually what they personally wanted from the group experience, but we found that the students were so unsophisticated in group process they were either unable to verbalize ideas or actually had no real concept of what they expected. We therefore eliminated the question from subsequent groups.

## Use of structure in sessions

The students required at least 5 to 10 minutes to assemble and settle down. *Because of the time limitations of a 40-minute session, greater structuring seemed to be indicated.* After the fourth session the leaders evolved a more scientific problem-solving technique for handling reality problems. Focus was on the most pressing matters, and the aim was to *achieve maximum participation* in such a large group, with maximum growth experiences for each member. Without being heavy-handed, one of the leaders intervened to subdivide the limited time into certain basic areas. *First* came a *statement of the problem,* ("Does any of you have something you want to discuss with the group?") in which a member would state a problem as he or she saw it. *Second, clarification of the problem:* The group questioned the member for greater clarity, providing an opportunity for group interaction and assisting the person with the problem to see it more clearly.

*Third, discussion of similar experiences:* Members reacted to feelings activated within them in response to this shared or common problem area. Discussion of values and attitudes generally followed, and similar problems were shared. *Fourth, how can we help?* Members were encouraged to think creatively about alternative ways of behavior to be considered, to provide emotional support, and to show that they cared. *Fifth, how do you feel now?* This was directed to the member with the original problem. It presented an opportunity to share feelings at the end of an experience, and it also afforded the leaders the possibility of determining whether the member felt satisfied or if loose ends required follow-through. The very brevity of the sessions made this important, but members were not pushed for decisions about changes in attitude or behavior.

*Sixth on the agenda was "stroking time."* The leaders used this short period to pull together significant ideas and to focus on strengths, reinforcing and validating successful coping behavior alluded to by members during the session. Any member who appeared upset was asked to remain after the session for a determination as to whether a problem needed immediate attention. *Seventh, follow-through:* At the beginning of the next session, one of the leaders would ask students who had problems the week before, "What has happened?" Significantly, in most cases the problem was no longer important. (The follow-through is important in terms of helping the adolescent get a feeling of continuity in life process, rather than emphasizing that many of them seem to have immediate here-and-now experiences without any relationship to consequences or future goals.)

ILLUSTRATION

A description of one group session will illustrate our technique in action. After the group of 17 students was settled in its usual circular seating arrangement, one of the co-leaders asked for feedback from the previous session. When he received no response to this, he asked if anyone in the group had a problem to share.

*Statement of problem*

Janie promptly answered that she was upset about school. She had received three *D*'s on her midterm report card, and she was worried about her parents' reactions as well as the effect of the low grades on her plans to graduate at the end of the next semester. Another student interjected that something was bothering him but that it could wait until next time. Janie proceeded to discuss her problem, saying that she had to work after school and felt too tired to study when she got home and that this was the reason for her poor grades.

*Clarification of problem*

When one of the leaders asked whether the group wished to know more about Janie's situation, several members spoke up. One of them commented that working and going to school certainly wasn't easy, but he wondered if there weren't other things bothering her. She promptly responded that the situation at home was not good for her because her parents were constantly putting her down. For example, her mother would say, "Why don't you continue on your job and make it a full-time career, because that's all you're capable of doing, anyway." Someone asked, "Do you mean your mother wants you to quit school?" Janie admitted that she was confused about the messages her parents were giving her. On the one hand she felt her father was serious about her quitting school and going to work full time, whereas she felt her mother's sarcasm was primarily to motivate her to continue her education.

Another member remarked, "It seems your problem, Janie, is that you seem mixed up about what you want for yourself in school, and the hassle with your parents." Janie continued pouring out her feelings of confusion, disappointment, and anger toward her parents, and someone asked her *what she wanted for herself* in regard to her education. As she began to look at her situation, her conflicted feelings became obvious to her. She wanted to finish high school, but she didn't want to leave her job because she wanted a car. But if she continued on her job, she stated, "I would be too tired to study."

*Discussion of similar experiences*

At this point there was a lull, as if members were responding to their own reactions to the discussion. One of the leaders suggested that this would be a good time to share what the group was experiencing. A boy who had been quiet in previous sessions said he had had a similar experience during the preceding semester. He was holding down two jobs, and his grades began to fall. He said he could understand what Janie was going through. A girl in the group, whose facial expression showed real concern as she listened, commented, "It's terrible to be put down by parents." She explained that at home she was constantly criticized and wondered if she could do anything right. A boy who was visiting a session for the first time at the invitation of a friend remarked that he used to have the same hassle and put-downs from his parents, but he had learned to tune it all out and to go about doing his own thing. A girl, looking somewhat sad, said she was not able to do that, and her studies were very much affected by the problems she was having at home.

Group discussion seemed to center around the effects of friction and conflicts at home in relation to school work. This elicited anger at parents, mainly by the white students. As they verbalized this with intensity, some of the Black students laughed. One of them remarked that she was taken aback by the amount of anger and hostility that Janie ventilated, particularly in regard to her mother. The laughter seemed to be a cover-up for anxiety. A co-leader asked some silent youngsters how they felt about all this. One Black student commented that he would never talk about his parents that way.

### How can we help?

As no further responses seemed to be forthcoming, one of the leaders asked if any member had ideas that could be helpful to Janie. The student whose two jobs had affected his grades reported that he solved his problem by quitting his job and that he was currently "zeroed in" on school, because "that's where it counts" for him. The new boy suggested that Janie was too much involved with her parents and that she should begin separating herself from them and do as he did, put his "own head together." Janie declared that it was not easy to separate herself from her mother. "She is lazy, sits around the house and does little, yet expects me to do well." Several Black students commented that their mothers worked very hard, and it seemed only fair that their mothers expect things from them. The discussion now appeared to center on separating oneself from parents. Most group members seemed to identify with this difficult problem area.

### How do you feel now?

As the session was nearing the end, the counselor asked Janie how she felt. Her reply was that she was glad she had talked about her problems and that some of the comments were useful.

*"Stroking" time*

In the few remaining minutes, the co-leader commented generally on how open members had been in the discussion. He emphasized the difficulty that besets many young people and their parents in this separation process called emancipation, and the movement already made by some members in this area. As the bell rang and the group dispersed, one quiet member remained to speak to the school counselor about a problem she felt she could not share with the group. It involved severe depressive feelings and suicidal thoughts which required immediate handling and follow-through by the counselor.

The *most significant aspects of this group* were its large number of members, the short 40-minute meeting time, and structured problem-solving technique. Allowing students to bring in peers seemed to give them a positive feeling of being responsible for group organization. The leaders and group demonstrated respect for members who chose new recruits, enhancing self-esteem. A larger group had less depth but was easier for the student who was not ready for exposure; smaller groups seemed to exert greater pressure for interaction.

*Leader activities*

The leaders met briefly after each session to review what they felt had occurred, to share feelings about content that had gone well, and to determine problems that needed attention.

During sessions the leaders consciously attempted to help members develop skills in communication and expression of feelings when appropriate during sessions by reflecting feelings, modeling, or simply illustrating. They tried to function by serving as models in many life roles—adult, mother, father, counselor, social worker, or group member; participating without taking over —less as time went on—appropriately but not omnipotently; structuring sessions—low key; reflecting feelings, a technique learned by members as time went on; emphasizing members' strengths and helpful coping mechanisms successfully used in the past; encouraging participation of nonverbal or shy members; when appropriate, going around circle with "How do the rest of you feel about this?" or "How would you handle this problem?"; redirecting questions to group first unless related to their adult roles; giving support when not forthcoming from group; speaking in the first person, "I" rather than "they"; talking about leaders' feelings rather than thoughts, tuning in on oneself; looking directly at person to whom one is talking;

responding to other person's feelings rather than interrupting, tuning in on others; responding to verbal and nonverbal cues; not intellectualizing; making statements instead of asking questions to make a point; becoming sensitive to feedback from others; repeating what is said to be sure one understands, and requesting others to repeat one's conversation if they do not seem to understand; acknowledging underlying feelings by reflection in accepting way; challenging in a caring manner the member who distorts reality—this seemed to be more acceptable when coming from peers than from leaders; role playing—useful in dealing with problems with parents.

One of the most important work areas was in learning to listen. Leaders became aware that many of these students had not experienced being really listened to and understood. They became participants in the reciprocal listening experiences.

### Problem areas mentioned by students*

Areas of difficulty included: *peers*—a desire for acceptance, the reaction to rejection, expectations of each other, closeness, and, at times, overdemanding relationships, which often led to involvements beyond the coping ability of the adolescent; *school*—areas related to feelings about teachers, general school administration, and reflections on the curriculum, social life and reactions to structure, such as open campus; *sex*—feelings about morality, double standards, sexual responsibility, pregnancy, and abortion; *emancipation*—feelings about the struggle to emancipate from parents and develop individual life styles, with discussions in this area relating to options upon graduation such as work, leaving home, getting one's own apartment; *drugs*—feelings about the use of drugs, police, and the experiences of overdosing and being busted; *identity*—Who am I? What is my relationship with my parents? How do I separate myself from them?; for the seniors, anxieties related to moving into the new young adulthood phase of life. Other problems involved: *confidentiality and trust*—ways of dealing with these qualities within a group, at home, in school, and with intimate relationships; *violence*—if turbulent episodes occurred during the time that groups were meeting, these episodes generally became stimuli for group discussion.

### Conclusions and recommendations

In working with groups we needed to be very flexible and not locked in by conventional group processes, which in many instances have been devel-

---

* See Chapter 29 for a slightly different set of problem categories.

oped in conducting groups with middle-class adolescents. For example, we found that it was extremely *meaningful to permit adolescents to bring friends* and, with group permission, to allow other adolescents to drop in and attend whenever they felt the need, and we accepted the lack of weekly commitment.

Our experience has been that the use of *co-therapists* from school personnel and outside agencies provides maximum balance and the best potential for utilizing existing resources and expertise in a cooperative relationship.

Although the *40-minute session* was experimental and had shortcomings, we found that it could be effective, but *required greater structuring* than the usual group setting. With this shorter time period it is important to have time available for dealing with students who require additional help after the group session, as well as someone on campus between sessions, such as the counselor, to whom a youngster may turn with unresolved feelings.

For mental health programs to be effective in a school setting it is crucial that the *school administration* and other personnel recognize the importance of such an undertaking and be committed to this kind of program. Our experience shows that groups have the greatest potential for success, that is, in terms of numbers of students reached and sustaining attendance in the group, when the groups are conducted during the regular school day. This is of particular significance in efforts to reach the less motivated students who are in need of mental health programs. Groups are least effective, in our experience, if conducted during lunchtime, or before or after school. This may be related to the desire of students to leave campus as soon as possible, just as people like to leave their jobs. Youngsters prefer to socialize and do other things during lunch and nutrition times, which, for many, have a priority over the unknown of mental health group situations. The same difficulty in mobilizing oneself to attend a group prior to school exists for students who have general motivation problems in getting to school in the morning. Most people show resistance, defensiveness, and fear in getting involved in mental health programs. For the adolescent this becomes greatly intensified and exaggerated, and minimal numbers of obstacles should stand in the way of providing mental health services to them.

We feel it is pertinent for schools to see themselves as actively involved in providing mental health services to students. The concept of *referring students who need help to agencies outside of the school no longer appears feasible*. This is particularly true in the areas of crisis intervention, extending service to students who would ordinarily not accept referral to outside agencies, and dealing with the normal tensions and pressures that adolescents present constantly in most school settings. We also feel that the group is one of the most constructive ways of effectively dealing with the myriad problems seriously affecting our inner city schools today. Although this chapter is concentrated on the high school student, it is obvious that these services are necessary in, and can be adapted to, the elementary and junior high schools. Many of the students who evidenced problems in high school were identified as having had difficulties in the elementary grades. Mental health services in varying degrees should be given consideration as an integral part of the school system for all children, beginning with kindergarten.

CHAPTER 28

# Ethnic Issues in School Group Counseling

Celeste Kaplan, A.C.S.W.

ETHNIC ISSUES are of crucial importance in many instances of school group counseling. This was a striking conclusion from a four-years' experience of groups conducted collaboratively by a community social service agency and personnel of 48 schools in the Los Angeles area.*

These ethnic issues arose in a variety of ways in the counseling groups. Their character and impact depended in part on the ethnic and social composition of the particular community, school, and group; in part on the students' developmental level; and in part on the ethnic background and attitudes of the group leaders. The 48 different schools in the Los Angeles area in which we have led counseling groups ranged from virtually all white to all Black, and included many with an ethnic mix which embraced, in varying proportions, Black, white, Asian, and Latin-American students.** Their social composition varied primarily from lower working class (including families on public assistance) through middle class. Agency and school personnel made conscious efforts to insure that counseling groups and their leaders generally reflected the ethnic composition of each school. Fortunately, Black, white, and Asian group leaders were available from both the schools

---

* The agency is Child, Youth and Parent Counseling Agency (also known as Council of Jewish Women of Los Angeles, Inc.). For a description of the agency's school program, see Chapter 24.

** The Asian population is primarily Japanese-American but also included students of Chinese, Filipino, and Korean background, as well as a grouping from Guam and Samoa. Latin-American refers mainly to Mexican-American or Chicano but also includes students from Cuba and Central or South America. See Chapter 14 for attitudes in counseling Chicana girls.

and the agency; the greatest lack to date has been in availability of Chicano group leaders.

The stated purpose of our school group program was to give troubled students an opportunity to deal with their own problems (including, but not confined to, school difficulties) in a group of peers, under the joint leadership of an agency social worker and a member of the school staff. It therefore was not a substitute for a broadly based human relations program which would deal directly with ethnic attitudes and relationships throughout the entire school. However, our agency's experience demonstrated that ethnic issues often affected group members deeply and had to be dealt with on a number of significant levels if personal growth was to occur.

*Ethnic background stands as an intrinsic aspect of young people's intrapsychic development;* ethnic similarity and difference affect interpersonal relationships both within and outside the counseling group; and the ethnic structure of our society constitutes an important feature of the objective social reality, including the school system, with which each student must cope. Ethnic considerations also enter into the role of group leaders, in both their relations to each other and their interaction with the group.

Group members, especially in mixed groups, found it more difficult to talk about their feelings in these areas, at least initially, than to discuss what appeared to be much more personal matters. As group members got to know each other and found areas of commonality in their individual lives and problems, they became more able to open up what they felt was divisive between them. In most instances, feelings were first directed toward experiences from outside the group; members found it very difficult to deal with each other directly in terms of their ethnic feelings towards each other. This reluctance is not unique to ethnicity, but we have found ethnicity to be an area in which feelings are especially deep and sensitive and usually opened up with great caution. Eventually, however, the themes mentioned above emerged.

### Ethnic identity

Personal identity, the development of one's sense of self, was dealt with recurrently from first-grade groups on through those composed of graduating high school students. *Feeling about one's ethnic heritage was an important facet of identity.* We found early awareness in this area, especially among children of minority groups. This awareness was intensified as students moved into junior and senior high school.

Group members from every ethnic minority characteristically expressed anger at, and rejected, stereotypes. For example, in one racially mixed senior high school group, Black and Chicano students voiced their resentment of expectations that they would be D or F students, while Japanese-American students equally resented pressure to live up to the model student role assigned to them. Variations on this theme have appeared in many groups and are frequently coupled with expressions of pride in a particular identity, especially by Black and Chicano students. Such expressions were often verbal; in other cases they were conveyed in another way, for example, through distinctive hair styles, special hats, or other types of ethnically identified clothing. Group members, who often suffered from low self-esteem, utilized such positive identification as a point of departure for developing a stronger and better sense of self. Seen from this vantage point, the growth of ethnic pride and assertion within Black, Mexican-American, and other communities represent a positive influence for the children of these groups.

On occasion, negative feelings about ethnic identity were also expressed by minority group members. For example, in the high school group referred to above, several Black students voiced distaste for dating Blacks whom they described as being too rowdy; their attitude actually reflected social and individual differentiation within the Black community, but it seemed subjectively experienced as a negative aspect of Black identity. In the same community, Japanese-American students in both junior and senior high school groups frequently expressed anger over the conforming attitude and high achievement expectations held by their parents, whom they saw as characteristically Japanese. The parents, on the other hand, seemed often to view achievement as the road to acceptance by the majority culture. This viewpoint was often not shared by their children. It was even rejected.

Their struggle for independence thus contained an added element which may have hampered positive internalization of an ethnic identity. This feeling was reminiscent of that of many second generation young people of European parents. In addition, many young Japanese-Americans felt resentment and anger over the special oppression experienced by their parents' generation, including the confinement to detention camps in World War II. This issue is openly discussed today by politically aware and active young people. Such young people insist upon a more assertive stance by the Japanese-American community against discrimination, holding that personal achievement alone will not guarantee acceptance. Although this latter issue rarely arose explicitly in counseling groups, it often formed an unspoken emotional background.

On the other hand, most Caucasian youngsters seemed to internalize their ethnic identity without consciousness or conflict. Basically, there were no social penalties or problems connected with it, since it is the identity of the dominant majority. Greater awareness appeared and was expressed in counseling groups as minority families moved into previously white or "Anglo" neighborhoods. It often came out negatively as fear of, and hostility to, the newcomers rather than being expressed in terms of feelings for positive values.

Differentiated groups within the white community became apparent. Some were ethnic in character, others more sociocultural and economic. In two ethnically mixed high schools, group members who came from a Jewish background reflected a wide spectrum of feeling about their Jewish identity. Some saw it as primarily religious, others as cultural and/or political. A few denied it any significance (usually in the context of conflict with their parents over other, often unrelated issues). Meanwhile, Black and Chicano group members tended to view Jews as simply part of the dominant white or "Anglo" majority, or at least as a minority that "had it made," with little cause to worry about discrimination or oppression.

In other schools we encountered a white minority group made up of families from small towns and rural areas of the south. Members of this group expressed their negative feelings toward other ethnic groups more openly and frankly than those from middle-class, liberal white homes. At the same time, they often had a more realistic appreciation of the meaning of deprivation.

In some instances, a white or "Anglo" boy or girl deliberately identified with a particular ethnic minority (usually Black or Chicano) and selected members as a peer group. Often this tended to include only the more acting-out or delinquent members. Such identification was generally an expression of rebellion against parents, whom such youngsters struck at through their ethnic prejudices. Unfortunately, this choice did not really represent freedom from ethnic bias on the part of the white boy or girl. Frequently, low self-esteem was present which involved feeling unacceptable to the dominant (and secretly preferred) white majority. The inner feelings of these young people had to be clearly differentiated from those of more emotionally secure boys and girls whose personal strength and genuine conviction permitted them to relate well to those from other ethnic groups. This more secure type of young person was not usually found in our counseling groups.

*Young people of mixed background*

We found that the most *severe inner conflicts* over ethnic identity seemed to be experienced by *young people of mixed background.* In one junior high school group a girl whose parents were both of Japanese-Caucasian extraction spoke angrily of hating the "goody-goody Japs." This reflected her own struggle over whether to continue her self-destructive, increasingly delinquent behavior, or to move toward a more positive attitude to herself and her own future. While she used the stereotype of the high-achieving, conforming Japanese in part to evade this underlying issue, it was at the same time a real aspect of her internal dilemma. Interestingly, her negative remarks about being Japanese were challenged by a Chicano student who asked, "How come you put down your own people?" In another instance, a girl of Black and white parents told of her feelings of rejection by peers of both ethnic groups and of her own desperate effort to establish some positive sense of who she really was. The same internal suffering was verbalized by a youngster of Japanese and Black parentage; tears streamed down her face as she talked of her experience and her unhappy feelings.

Working through such conflicted feelings was crucially important for certain group members in terms of achieving a more secure sense of personal identity. One apparently satisfactory synthesis was achieved by a girl of mixed Irish and Black parentage; she felt pride in having an inheritance of rebellion against oppression from both parental lines. Other group members picked one side or another of their ethnic mix with which to identify. Generally, however, young people of mixed background could not readily work out their identification. They were facing within themselves a reflection of tensions which exist in the world, complicated by their own distinctive, individual life experiences.

The other side of identity is difference, and this, too, was a recurrent theme in our school groups. How does one deal with those who are perceived as ethnically different? In a few instances this question had arisen early in the group's life. One example involved the feelings of a Black junior high school student who was attending her first ethnically mixed school. She was strong enough to tell the group openly of her preference for an all-Black school, as well as to express her resentment of the prejudiced attitudes of some teachers and students. The group, which had both a Black and a white leader, acknowledged the reality of these difficulties and helped her consider appropriate ways to handle them. Her participation in group helped her cope more effectively with a new life experience. She was liked and respected by the other group members and went on to become one of the school's recognized leaders.

In another instance, a white "Anglo" student asked the group, during its initial meeting, to help her with her perceptions of other ethnic groups, especially Chicanos. This was a girl who had been referred for her overall difficulties in peer relations, stemming from her hostile attitudes to others. Her request was verbalized in a description of her own view of the Mexican-American family next door, with whose children she wanted to be friends. She counterposed her own feelings and desires to her parents' negative views of this same family. It became evident that she was using the group to check out her family's hostile and basically fearful attitude toward "others" as against her own innate sense that perhaps this was not an accurate view. Unfortunately, as she began to change her perceptions, her mother asked that she be taken out of the group—a left-handed and sad tribute to what she was gaining from it.

Nor were such experiences confined to junior and senior high schools. In one elementary school which had previously been all white, a relatively small number of Black students were bussed in from a school being rebuilt after earthquake damage. Two of these students were referred to a third- and fourth-grade group, which had just started and which, up to that point, had included only white students. The worker used the opportunity to talk with the group about whether they had ever had to go to a new school or to a new neighborhood and how they had felt about being new or different. She was able to help them welcome the new group members. Feelings were openly dealt with, and the experience became a positive one for both the white and Black children.

Usually, however, *open verbal expression of feelings* toward those who were ethnically different did not occur until group members had come to know each other somewhat and had felt each other out in various ways. In mixed groups the *initiative was almost always taken by the minority group students* who spoke bluntly of resentment and anger over discrimination within the school. Group members were slower to take on directly members of another ethnic background whose attitudes they questioned. Rather, they began by exploring the differences in the social life and experiences of others. In several junior and senior high school groups there were comparisons of the kind of parties whites, Blacks, or Chicanos had, including the music they played, their style of dancing, and the like. In junior high school, especially, discussions of different peer groups often included "low riders" (predominantly Chicano), "surfers" (predominantly white Anglo), and Blacks.

In connection with such discussions, feelings of curiosity as well as anger and fear surfaced.

*In mixed groups, white students were usually more reluctant to deal openly with ethnic feelings* than were minority group members. Overt attitudes of white group members ranged from a verbal denial of ethnic difference, couched in liberal terms, to a blatantly racist attitude which usually remained unspoken in mixed groups but was voiced outside. Underneath there was much fear of minority groups, specifically fear of violence and gangs. In some cases, white students may have experienced threats and intimidation by hostile Blacks or Chicanos. As the group progressed, white students finally voiced their fears. Often they asked for advice from minority group members about how to deal with such threats and were generally encouraged to "learn to stand up" for themselves.*

What was notably lacking for all students was a sense that contact with another ethnic group could be a positive, enriching experience. *Ethnic difference almost without exception was felt only as negative, threatening, and bad.* This, of course, is a commentary upon the social reality with which all our children grew up, including their experience in schools.

Helping group members deal more effectively with reality in their school and personal lives was one of our dominant aims. This required that group leaders themselves understood and faced what this reality actually included, namely, discrimination, injustice, and economic deprivation as everyday experiences. Difficult family problems could not be separated from these larger difficulties.

The children and adolescents who were referred (or self-referred) for group counseling were characteristically not those who were involved in social or political activism.**Our aim was to help them assess their own situations more clearly and help them to develop more effective means of coping with whatever problems they faced. For instance, in one ethnically mixed high school, several group members voiced bitter complaints about the domination of school clubs by one particular ethnic minority. The members of the group were helped to talk with one of the school administrators about possible ways of changing the situation, so that all ethnic groups could participate in school activities. This occurred when others, too, were pressing for change; group members learned that they were not alone or helpless and that there were ways to tackle discrimination within the existing school structure.

In another instance *eighth grade Chicano students in a junior high school*

---

* See Chapter 10.
** See Chapter 36.

*group* objected to the expulsion of several Chicano students who had been in a "low rider"-"surfer" fight, pointing out that only the Chicanos were so treated. The group encouraged these students to talk to school administrators. It was their first experience of this sort, and it actually took much support and discussion of how to handle it before they felt able to go to the vice principal and principal. Although the ruling was not changed, the students were received respectfully and heard out—an entirely new experience for them and an indication of changing attitudes within the school itself.

This is not to say that school counseling groups can or should, in themselves, be a vehicle for organized student action; but they *can help personally troubled students feel less powerless* in some areas of their lives and can open up new, more constructive approaches than taking drugs, dropping out, or other ways of running away from troubles. It should be added that school administrations which supported group counseling programs were generally more open to approaches by students such as those described above.

### Ethnic issues and group leaders

*What does the handling of ethnic issues require from group leaders?* In a general way, the same qualities and approaches are needed as for successful group counseling in any area, namely, a genuine openness to a group member's feelings and a willingness to use oneself to help the group face and deal with these feelings constructively. This necessarily involves a readiness to face one's own feelings about ethnic differences, as with any deeply sensitive area.

One thing which will block any possibility of dealing with ethnic issues—and will even destroy a group—is a really bigoted and/or dishonest attitude on the part of either group leader. I state it in this way because no one in this white-dominated society can be *wholly* free from its prejudicial impact. What is required is an honest effort to face one's feelings and deal with them. Group members will judge us by what we are in this area, not just by what we say. Young people have an eagle eye for hypocrisy.

*School personnel today face much the same challenge* on an even larger scale. Fortunately, the teachers, counselors, or other school staff members who agreed to be group co-leaders usually had an open attitude toward feelings to begin with and were as ready to learn as we were. In a very few instances this was not the case. Not surprisingly, school staff members who held openly hostile attitudes toward various ethnic groups were usually unable to respond positively to young people's feelings in other areas. In one or two situations it was necessary to ask help from school administrators to change group leader assignments because of this. In the vast majority of cases, however, both school and agency personnel were open to dealing with ethnic issues.

Group leaders had to be not afraid to help group members look at the anger around ethnic relationships, as well as the hurt and fear that underlie the anger. This meant helping white students understand something of the deep hurts students from other ethnic backgrounds have suffered at the hands of whites or white-dominated institutions. It also meant surfacing the fear that white students felt resulting from recent traumatic experiences with angry, hostile Black or Brown young people.

In schools with mixed population, it was especially helpful to have *co-leaders from different ethnic backgrounds,* who could provide a positive example of interpersonal relationships. More than this, the presence of such leaders provided emotional support and opportunity for appropriate confrontation to both minority group and white students in raising ethnic issues.

However, ethnic issues were often successfully dealt with even when the co-leaders were not of different ethnic background. For example, in a group of Black, Chicano, and white junior high school girls, the ongoing leaders were both white. One had replaced a Black group leader who had been unable to continue after the first group meeting. The new group leader openly commented upon the probably disappointed or angry feelings of the Black group members at the loss of the Black leader. While they initially denied such feelings, her open handling of the matter set the stage for a really important confrontation between one of the Black members and the other group leader at a later date. On this occasion the group member challenged the group co-leader with being friendly in group but not at all the same in the halls or classroom. It was possible to work out a piece of role playing in which the white leader voiced what she felt to be the hostile feelings of the member about "that white bitch," while the Black member grappled with the leader's role in attempting to reach out to her. This whole interchange was extremely significant for the group as well as for the individual girl involved and underscored the importance of openness on the part of group leaders.*

On the other hand, the absence of mixed group leadership at times made it difficult to retain minority students in the group. One such instance in-

---

* See Chapter 12.

volved a group of ninth grade junior high school boys, which included two Black students, five white boys, and two of Asian background (one mixed Asian-Black). Unfortunately, both leaders were white. Though this issue was raised, the group did not respond. The two Black students remained aloof and dropped out after two meetings. As the group progressed, the leaders found that they had on their hands some of the most militantly anti-Black students in the school, and the Black students' reasons for departure became quite clear.

As the prejudices of the white students were more openly expressed—without challenge even from the remaining minority group members—the agency worker decided it was necessary to take an open stand. This was one instance when it was important for the leaders to represent other, different values from those the boys had acquired. With the group leaders' example, several group members found the courage to challenge the blatant bigotry of others. In this case, the presence of one Black leader might have been even more effective, and the Black students might have remained, providing a very different experience for the whole group.

*Schools of single ethnic composition*

Most schools of this type with which we have worked were elementary schools. There was less raising of ethnic issues directly than in mixed elementary schools. In schools located in white communities, such issues generally arose as children from other ethnic backgrounds began to move in. We described one such experience above, where Black students were bussed to a white elementary school.

In many Black communities, especially in low-income areas, the experiences of Black youngsters posed some very important problems for group leaders. In such schools the administration and faculty were generally very concerned about the degree of violence to which children were exposed. This seemed to be expressed in a high level of physical conflict within such schools, both among the students themselves and between students and faculty. Group leaders, of whatever background, had to face the reality that for many of these children *their ability to fight and defend themselves physically was an essential survival trait.* The broader truth was that many of these children were wiser in the ways of their particular world than the group leaders would ever be. At the same time, physical battles within school grounds certainly impeded learning, if they did not make it entirely impossible.

Under these conditions, group leaders tried to help group members develop a *selective approach to fighting:* They helped youngsters to *broaden their behavioral repertoire* to include additional ways of coping, especially within the school, and attempted to *help them discriminate* as to what was appropriate under varying circumstances. What they did *not* do was to try to remove what for these children may be an essential means of defense. They did not try to impose upon them certain middle-class values (white or otherwise). What was achieved in some schools was a better atmosphere in which both faculty and students could proceed more effectively with the process of teaching and learning.

## Conclusions

All of the foregoing is only a first attempt to evaluate four years of experience in a variety of schools. Out of it has come a firm conviction that *ethnic issues constituted one of the important wellsprings from which themes developed in school counseling groups.* We needed to give continuing serious attention to the many implications of this, particularly as they affected the selection, role, and responsibilities of group leaders, as well as the structure and functioning of schools as a whole.

While group counseling cannot substitute for broader, many-sided approaches to problems of ethnic identity and conflict within our schools, it can help to create a better climate based on the experiences of group members. This indeed proved to be one of the significant spin-offs of our group counseling program. For example, one administrator in a very large, multi-ethnic junior high school said bluntly that the group counseling program was a major factor in preventing an explosive growth of ethnic tension and conflict within the school.* Meanwhile, attention to ethnic experiences and feelings helped individual students deal with what was often a significant strand in their personal development and growth. Our personnel found new sources of understanding and strength as well.

---

* See Chapters 10 and 37.

## CHAPTER 29

# Evaluation: Twenty-Seven Agency-School Counseling Groups in Junior and Senior High Schools

---

### Celeste Kaplan, A.C.S.W.

EVALUATION OF THE GROUP COUNSELING PROGRAM jointly sponsored by a community social service agency (Child, Youth and Parent Counseling Agency, also known as Council of Jewish Women of Los Angeles, Inc.) and a number of schools in the Los Angeles area was undertaken in 1973. The study covered 495 members of 47 counseling groups in 21 schools during the 1972-73 school year.*

*Purpose of research*

We wished to answer the following questions: (1) Is our group counseling program really helpful to the boys and girls it serves? Is it more useful to some kinds of young people than others? Is it more helpful around certain kinds of problems? (2) Does the program warrant the time and money devoted to it? Is it an efficient, economical way of delivering service to an important population needing such help?

*Method of research*

We decided to focus on whether or not group members showed improvement in the problem area for which they were referred (or referred themselves) to group. Group leaders (one from the agency, one from the school) evaluated jointly, using a scale of retrogression, no change, or improvement.** An independent evaluation was also requested of a second person

---

* For fuller descriptions of the agency's program see Chapters 24 and 28.
** See Section V, "Record-keeping."

on the school staff who had a good knowledge of the student. In elementary schools, this was the classroom teacher; in junior and senior high schools it was the grade counselor, a vice-principal, the school nurse, or even a teacher who was close to the student. Such a study told us the nature of the problems for which students were being referred and permitted some comparative study of outcome by problem areas.

Evaluators were free to work out their judgment from any and all sources they might have; they were, however, asked to indicate the bases they used for evaluation. For example, group leaders were given a listing of possible bases for judging outcome. These included: (1) the attitude and behavior of the students as observed within the group; (2) the students' own report of behavior and attitudes outside the group; (3) the opinions or reports of other group members; and (4) reports of other school personnel. There was space to indicate other bases they might use, such as reactions received from parents or collateral evaluators. These specifically included grades and attendance.

### Limitations of the study

Quite obviously, this is a descriptive, exploratory study. It is not a rigorously designed experimental project which would involve control groups, pre- and post-testing, and other more rigorous research techniques. However, a preliminary study could tell whether the program seemed to be justified and headed in the right direction. We managed the study through the devoted efforts of our own clinical and administrative staff, our school colleagues, and a hard-working committee of agency board members, together with the knowledgeable and generous assistance of the United Way Planning and Research Department. Other than this substantial investment of time and energy by all concerned, there was no direct additional financial cost to agency, school, or the United Way.

### Population studied

The number of young people for whom we have data totals 495. Of these, 184 were elementary school pupils who participated in 20 groups at 10 schools. The largest number, 240, were junior high school students, members of 20 groups in 8 schools. The smallest number were in senior high school, 71 students in 7 groups at 3 schools. All involved schools were part of the Los Angeles Unified School District except for 3 in Lennox School District.

Most schools were ethnically mixed; a few were virtually all Black and two were nearly all white.

Overall *ethnic composition* included: 230 Caucasian students (41%); 166 Black students (33.5%); 71 with Spanish surnames (14.3%); 31 Asian students (6.2%); 12 "other"; and 12 not identified. Spanish surnames included not only those of Mexican-American background but also students of Cuban, Central, and South American extraction. There were 296 girls and 226 boys. Referrals for group by school personnel totaled 404, while 87 were self-referred; one was in both categories, and for three we did not have this information. However, membership in group was voluntary for all students.

## Problems at referral

The problems for which students were referred proved to be extremely varied, ranging from poor school performance through serious acting out, to depression and even suicidal tendencies. We did not designate fixed problem categories in advance but derived them from data. We found they could be grouped under 19 specific headings which in turn fell naturally into 5 main clusters. These categories and clusters are given for each school level in Tables 1, 2, and 3.

Important differentiation in reasons for referral emerged between the three school levels. The shift in rank order of problems and problem clusters quite clearly paralleled the developmental tasks specific to each of the broad age levels involved. As young children leave home to attend school, their key problems naturally center around adjustment to this new world—both classroom and new peer group. Many of the children in group were referred because they seemed to have special difficulties with this change in their lives. *In junior high,* school and peer difficulties remained, but the focus was more on problems of achievement and difficulties with adult authority, reflecting in part the *early adolescent rebellion that comes with onset of puberty.* At this age, too, *family problems* rise in importance, suggesting the exacerbation of parent-child conflicts connected with the same rebellious thrust. The young people referred to group were less able to resolve these conflicts than were other boys and girls. In *senior high school,* personal, emotional, and developmental problems took first rank, pointing to the key developmental *task of working out one's identity,* while family problems mounted to second place, often connected with the older adolescent's *struggle for independence.* Once again, students referred to groups were those who found

## TABLE 1

### Elementary Schools—Referral Problems by Categories and Clusters

| PROBLEMS (Categories and Clusters) | Rank | CATEGORY No. | % | Rank | CLUSTER No. | % |
|---|---|---|---|---|---|---|
| *School Centered Problems* | | | | 1 | 88 | 47.8 |
| Immature Behavior in School | 1 | 52 | 28.3 | | | |
| Poor School Performance | 3 | 19 | 10.3 | | | |
| Problems with School Authority | 4 | 16 | 8.7 | | | |
| Poor School Attendance | 12 | 1 | 0.5 | | | |
| *Difficulties in Peer Relations* | | | | 2 | 54 | 29.3 |
| Difficulty with Peers Due to Hostile or Negative Behavior | 2 | 42 | 22.8 | | | |
| Absent or Inadequate Peer Relations | 6 | 12 | 6.5 | | | |
| Too Easily Influenced by Peers | — | — | — | | | |
| *Individual Emotional or Developmental Problems* | | | | 3 | 25 | 13.7 |
| Problems of Identity, Self Understanding or Self Assertion | 7 | 8 | 4.3 | | | |
| Depression | 8 | 7 | 3.8 | | | |
| Excessive Anxiety or Tension | 9 | 4 | 2.2 | | | |
| Excessively Withdrawn | 10 | 3 | 1.7 | | | |
| Physical Problem with Emotional Component | 10 | 3 | 1.7 | | | |
| Difficulty in Expressing Feelings | — | — | — | | | |
| *Problems of Impulsivity, Acting Out, or Anti-Social Behavior* | | | | 4 | 13 | 7.1 |
| Poor Impulse Control | 5 | 13 | 7.1 | | | |
| Serious Acting Out | — | — | — | | | |
| Manipulative Behavior | — | — | — | | | |
| *Family Problems* | | | | 5 | 3 | 1.6 |
| Difficulties in Family Relations | 11 | 2 | 1.1 | | | |
| Death or Loss or Serious Illness of Parent or Sibling | 12 | 1 | 0.5 | | | |
| *Other Problems* | | 1 | 0.5 | | | |
| TOTAL | | 184 | 100.0 | | 184 | 100.0 |

TABLE 2

Junior High Schools—Referral Problems by Categories and Clusters

| PROBLEMS (Categories and Clusters) | Rank | CATEGORY No. | % | Rank | CLUSTER No. | % |
|---|---|---|---|---|---|---|
| *School Centered Problems* | | | | | | |
| Poor School Performance | 1 | 57 | 23.7 | | | |
| Poor School Attendance | 2 | 44 | 18.3 | | | |
| Problems with School Authority | 4 | 17 | 7.1 | | | |
| Immature Behavior in School | 5 | 16 | 6.7 | 1 | 134 | 55.8 |
| *Difficulties in Peer Relations* | | | | | | |
| Absent or Inadequate Peer Relations | 6 | 15 | 6.3 | | | |
| Difficulty with Peers Due to Hostile or Negative Behavior | 8 | 10 | 4.2 | | | |
| Too Easily Influenced by Peers | 10 | 4 | 1.7 | 2 | 29 | 12.2 |
| *Family Problems* | | | | | | |
| Difficulties in Family Relationships | 3 | 23 | 9.6 | | | |
| Death, Loss or Serious Illness of Parent or Sibling | 12 | 2 | 0.8 | 3 | 25 | 10.4 |
| *Individual Emotional or Developmental Problems* | | | | | | |
| Problems of Identity, Self Understanding or Self Assertion | 7 | 12 | 4.9 | | | |
| Depression | 10 | 4 | 1.7 | | | |
| Difficulty Expressing Feelings | 11 | 3 | 1.3 | | | |
| Excessively Withdrawn | 13 | 1 | 0.4 | | | |
| Excessive Anxiety or Tension | 12 | 2 | 0.8 | | | |
| Physical Problem with Emotional Component | 13 | 1 | 0.4 | 4 | 23 | 9.5 |
| *Problems of Impulsivity, Acting Out, or Anti-Social Behavior* | | | | | | |
| Serious Acting Out | 8 | 10 | 4.2 | | | |
| Poor Impulse Control | 9 | 8 | 3.3 | | | |
| Manipulative Behavior | 10 | 4 | 1.7 | 5 | 22 | 9.2 |
| *Other Problems* | | 7 | 2.9 | | 7 | 2.9 |
| TOTAL | | 240 | 100.0 | | 240 | 100.0 |

## TABLE 3

### Senior High Schools—Referral Problems by Categories and Clusters

| PROBLEMS (Categories and Clusters) | CATEGORY Rank | CATEGORY No. | CATEGORY % | CLUSTER Rank | CLUSTER No. | CLUSTER % |
|---|---|---|---|---|---|---|
| *Individual Emotional or Developmental Problems* | | | | 1 | 22 | 30.9 |
| Problems of Identity, Self Understanding or Self Assertion | 2 | 15 | 21.1 | | | |
| Excessive Anxiety or Tension | 7 | 3 | 4.2 | | | |
| Depression | 8 | 2 | 2.8 | | | |
| Difficulty in Expressing Feelings | 9 | 1 | 1.4 | | | |
| Excessively Withdrawn | 9 | 1 | 1.4 | | | |
| Physical Problem with Emotional Component | — | — | — | | | |
| *Family Problems* | | | | 2 | 18 | 25.4 |
| Difficulties in Family Relationships | 1 | 18 | 25.4 | | | |
| Death, Other Loss or Serious Illness of Parent or Sibling | — | — | — | | | |
| *School Centered Problems* | | | | 3 | 16 | 22.5 |
| Poor School Attendance | 4 | 6 | 8.5 | | | |
| Poor School Performance | 6 | 4 | 5.6 | | | |
| Problems with School Authority | 6 | 4 | 5.6 | | | |
| Immature Behavior in School | 8 | 2 | 2.8 | | | |
| *Difficulties in Peer Relations* | | | | 4 | 9 | 12.7 |
| Absent or Inadequate Peer Relations | 3 | 8 | 11.3 | | | |
| Too Easily Influenced by Peers | 9 | 1 | 1.4 | | | |
| Peer Difficulty Due to Hostile or Negative Behavior | — | — | — | | | |
| *Problems of Impulsivity, Acting Out, or Anti-Social Behavior* | | | | 5 | 6 | 8.5 |
| Serious Acting Out | 5 | 5 | 7.1 | | | |
| Poor Impulse Control | 9 | 1 | 1.4 | | | |
| Manipulative Behavior | — | — | — | | | |
| *Other Problems* | — | — | — | | | |
| TOTAL | — | 71 | 100.0 | — | 71 | 100.0 |

it harder to deal with these problem areas than their peers. In other words, our data appeared to coincide with our clinical experience which found troubled young people (and young people in trouble) to be those who were not grappling successfully with their maturational tasks.

It is likely that the rank order of referral problems, especially in junior and senior high school, did not fully reflect the proportion of students in groups who were impulse ridden or involved in acting out and antisocial behavior. A more accurate picture could have been obtained by including students who revealed such problems in the course of group, although they were referred for other reasons initially. At referral only 41 students fell into this specific cluster; but later on, 55 students were seen as having problems in this area, nearly all of them having been referred for other difficulties, such as poor school attendance or performance. Including this additional number, we estimate that nearly *one-fifth of all students in group had problems with impulse control and/or acting out.* The proportion was higher in junior and senior high school groups, where it totaled closer to one-fourth of all group members, and was lower in elementary school groups where referring problems rather included difficulties that might later lead to acting out. No doubt our groups would have had an even greater percentage of such boys and girls had it not been for our emphasis on the need for problem "mix" and the inadvisability of placing too many acting-out or impulse-ridden young people in the same group, where they would simply reinforce each other.

Finally, many students were seen even at referral as having problems which fell into more than one category or cluster. However, we asked that the group leaders single out the *main* reason for referral as the basis for evaluating outcome, and this was frequently seen as a school problem. Since most referrals were by school personnel, it was understandable that the problems most salient for them were school centered. However, teachers, counselors, and administrators usually understood this to be only the tip of the iceberg, and in many cases were able to refer students on the basis of deeper, more pervasive difficulty.

### Evaluation of outcome

Evaluation of outcome is summarized below; more detailed data are contained in our full report which is available through our agency office.

First, our study clearly indicated that group counseling was seen as helpful to a majority of the 495 students evaluated. The most conservative figure in our research showed that group leaders and collateral school evaluators (who made independent judgments for 366 students) agreed that 62.9% *of these group members showed improvement* on the problems for which they were referred. They also agreed that 8.2% showed no change, while 1.6% were seen as retrogressing. This means that all three evaluators were in agreement on outcome for 72.7% of the population they evaluated. There was sharp disagreement around only 4.1% of the students (i.e., retrogression versus improvement). Evaluation of the remaining 23% showed only one degree of difference between co-leaders and collaterals (i.e., retrogression versus no change, or no change versus improvement). For the other 177 group members we had only co-leaders' evaluations. For this grouping the percentage seen as improved was slightly higher, totaling 68.4%.

The *highest percentage* of students *showing improvement was in high school* (66.6% as judged by group leaders and collaterals, and 92.9% by co-leaders only). Almost as large a percentage of elementary school students showed improvement (65.3% as reported by co-leaders and collaterals, and 73% by co-leaders only). The *lowest* percentage of students improved was *in junior high school* (57.6% as seen by co-leaders and collaterals, and 60.6% by co-leaders only).* The latter figure was no surprise to either school personnel or agency workers; this represents the age group which is in the most turbulent period of change and subject to the greatest swings in behavior and mood.

There appeared to be only minor differences in outcome by sex. However, there was significant variation by ethnic groups. *Black students showed the largest percentage improved* (over 80%), followed by Spanish surname (73.2%), and then Caucasian (72.4%). Asian students had the lowest percentage (66.7%) showing improvement. The concept that group counseling is helpful only to white middle-class youngsters therefore does not appear valid; evidently it is useful in virtually any school setting and at any grade level.

Another significant finding was that the percentage of group members showing *improvement rose steadily in proportion to the number of group meetings attended*. Among those attending 1 to 5 meetings, 40% were reported improved; 6 to 10 meetings, 65.2% improved; 11 to 15 sessions, 73.1% improved; 16 to 20, 82.4% improved; and over 20 (generally only 21 or 22 meetings), 84% improved.

---

* Editor's Note: Possibly different criteria for improvement may be necessary for this age group, or different procedures in groups.

*Outcome by problem categories*

Outcome by problem clusters for all school levels is given in Table 4. Outcome for the three largest problem categories in each school level is shown in Table 5.

The *most difficult problem area proved to be acting out, impulse-ridden and/or antisocial behavior.* This would fit with the knowledge that this type of behavior is the problem of least concern to the boys and girls involved, as it may yield them considerable gratification rather than anxiety or other negative feelings. Under these circumstances, improvement for 63.4% of students referred for difficulties of this type was not a poor outcome; however, it pointed to the need for continuing examination of ways in which these boys and girls could be reached more effectively.

Students showed the highest percentage of improvement around presenting problems that involved emotional or developmental difficulties in peer relations, running in the 80% to 100% range. This would confirm that counseling groups offer substantial help to students grappling with internalized problems or peer difficulties.

*The real surprise was the comparatively high percentage of students judged improved in family problems.* This totaled 71.8%, including all school levels, running slightly higher for junior and senior high school group members. Very few parents or families of these students were involved in any form of ongoing counseling. We conjecture, therefore, that through the group, members may have learned to view and even handle family relationships in a somewhat different and more effective way.*

*School-centered problems show a similar level of improvement,* 71.9% for all three levels combined. The percentage of improvement was noticeably higher, however, in one particular aspect of school problems, that is, immature behavior in elementary school, which was reported as showing 84.6% improvement.

We want to add our impression, based on staff discussion, that *problems which could not be effectively handled* in group were distinguished not so much by *type* as by *severity* or pervasiveness. For example, group proved to be very helpful to youngsters who were withdrawn and perhaps overly involved in fantasy; but if the *degree* of withdrawal was very severe and quite pervasive, group was inadequate to help the youngster—or maybe even contraindicated. This particular aspect of problem appropriateness was not directly dealt with in our current research. However, our staff was aware of

---

* Contrast Chapter 43.

TABLE 4

Outcome for Three Main Problems Within School Levels

| Problem | Total in Given Problem Area | | Retrogression | | No Change | | Improvement | |
|---|---|---|---|---|---|---|---|---|
| | # | % | # | % | # | % | # | % |
| *Elementary School* | | | | | | | | |
| Rank 1—Immature behavior in school | 52 | 100.0 | — | — | 8 | 15.4 | 44 | 84.6 |
| Rank 2—Peer difficulty due to hostile or negative behavior | 40 | 100.0 | — | — | 8 | 20.0 | 32 | 80.0 |
| Rank 3—Poor school performance | 19 | 100.0 | — | — | 6 | 31.6 | 13 | 68.4 |
| *Junior High School* | | | | | | | | |
| Rank 1—Poor school performance | 55 | 100.0 | 3 | 5.4 | 15 | 27.3 | 37 | 67.3 |
| Rank 2—Poor school attendance | 42 | 100.0 | 6 | 14.3 | 9 | 21.4 | 27 | 64.3 |
| Rank 3—Difficulties in family relationships | 22 | 100.0 | 2 | 9.1 | 4 | 18.2 | 16 | 72.7 |
| *Senior High School* | | | | | | | | |
| Rank 1—Difficulties in family relationships | 18 | 100.0 | — | — | 5 | 27.8 | 13 | 72.2 |
| Rank 2—Problems of identity, self understanding or self assertion | 15 | 100.0 | 1 | 6.7 | 1 | 6.7 | 13 | 86.0 |
| Rank 3—Absent or inadequate peer relations | 8 | 100.0 | — | — | — | — | 8 | 100.0 |

TABLE 5

Outcome for Problem Clusters Including All School Levels

| Cluster | Total in Cluster | | Retrogression | | No Change | | Improved | |
|---|---|---|---|---|---|---|---|---|
| | # | % | # | % | # | % | # | % |
| School centered problems | 235 | 100.0 | 15 | 6.4 | 51 | 21.7 | 169 | 71.9 |
| Difficulties in peer relations | 89 | 100.0 | — | — | 16 | 18.0 | 73 | 82.0 |
| Individual emotional or developmental problems | 68 | 100.0 | 1 | 1.5 | 6 | 3.8 | 61 | 89.7 |
| Family problems | 46 | 100.0 | 3 | 6.5 | 10 | 21.7 | 33 | 71.8 |
| Problems of impulsivity, acting out or anti-social behavior | 41 | 100.0 | 5 | 12.2 | 10 | 24.4 | 26 | 63.4 |
| | 483 | | | | | | | |

the need to watch for such indications and was trained to make these necessary distinctions affecting referral to group or responses within the group. There were several instances in which additional or alternative types of help (including hospitalization) were worked out (with child and parents) as the result of agency workers' clinical judgments. We feel this represents another valuable aspect of collaboration between school staff and clinical social workers, one which may deserve further study in its own right.

What about the *relative value and cost of this program?* Did it warrant the time and money devoted to it? Was it an efficient, economical way of delivering service to an important population? Our research was aimed at evaluating outcome and did not include analysis of the time and money required. However, certain facts could be summarized here without extensive documentation. To begin with, we know the approximate worker time required for such a program. Each group needed about an hour-and-a-half weekly. At the beginning of the school year or semester, this time was used for screening group members and other essential preparation, including discussions between co-leaders. Later, this time was used for the group meeting itself (50 minutes to 75 minutes, depending on age level) as well as for weekly conferences of co-leaders, and less frequent meetings with other school staff members, such as teachers, counselors, or administrators. Through this hour-and-a-half, help was provided to an average of a little over 10 students (smaller numbers in lower grades and larger numbers in junior and senior high).

A single worker carrying only school groups could probably handle 3 a day, or 15 a week. Time must obviously be left for supervision, travel, staff meetings, in-service training, outreach to parents on a selective basis, and just plain thinking—if quality of service is to be maintained. Three full-time workers responsible for school groups on this basis could handle 45 a week, in this way serving about 450 boys and girls. If even half, or 250 youngsters, were served on a one-to-one basis with counseling services, a minimum of four workers would be needed. The *whole 450 youngsters would need between seven and eight caseworkers, as opposed to the equivalent of three caseworkers used for the groups.* We must conclude that as a method of serving children with problems, *school groups are very economical.*

In actual practice, we did not limit leadership of school groups to three or four workers; nearly all our workers were involved in the program. In the 1972-73 school year, *eleven workers and two post-graduate trainees* carried the 47 groups in our research project, serving 495 boys and girls. The smallest number of groups carried per worker was two, the largest, five. (Parent groups, which were organized in several elementary schools, are not included here). This arrangement preserves the economical cost referred to above, while spreading it over a larger number of workers who carry additional assignments in our residential treatment program or agency counseling service to children and their families. Moreover, the quality of service to the boys and girls in school groups was thereby enhanced, since agency workers were able to constantly improve their clinical skills through their varied professional experience, utilizing a whole range of modalities. Indeed it was this high level of professional training which we contributed to the program.

An additional word should be said about the *school's contribution to the program*. We cannot presume to speak for reactions of school administrators with whom we collaborated. The school personnel provided time which was roughly equivalent to that from our agency. It was our understanding that this had been made available primarily through shifting staff responsibilities and rearranging schedules. In some cases the program required a heavier work load for individual counselors, teachers, or other staff members for whom this became both a voluntary contribution and a learning experience. We hope that schools in the Los Angeles area will find additional ways to expand group counseling, drawing on both their own staff and that of our agency, or other agencies who may be able to offer them help. We ordinarily could not offer an individual school more than two groups, given our own financial and staff limitations. If schools in the program wanted more time, or if new schools asked for our help, we were compelled to say that we could provide this only if they contracted for services with us using whatever special funds were available to them.

*To conclude:* In view of the findings of our research, we feel we have demonstrated that a high quality of service can be provided to an important population group, i.e., children with problems in coping, at minimal cost to the community, through the medium of agency-school collaboration.

# PART III: C. CONSULTATIVE ASSISTANCE (WITHOUT COLLABORATION)

## EDITOR'S NOTE

*The previous chapters described collaborative group counseling where training was provided to school personnel in the course of co-leadership of groups. This, as described, can be a valid and useful format for learning while doing.*

*Yet many school personnel express a desire for more didactic training or even demonstration prior to proceeding with a group. In many cases, this may express a fear of first-hand experience, although it may also be an expectation of learning before doing, a more traditional educational sequence.*

*Which sequence is more effective for developing good counseling or even for encouraging beginners is not conclusively certain. The next three chapters show results from the use of more didactic methods.*

*Chapter 30 deals with counselors doing group counseling for elementary school children, and illustrates some dynamics encountered in other school staff in reaction to a school counseling group. Similar reactions may be more diffused or hidden in the staff of the larger secondary school but still may be covertly creating interference to success of the group. The types of feelings reported by the elementary school counselors are often reported as well by counselors in secondary schools.*

*Students in secondary schools do not discuss feelings in the same way as younger children, but the difference is often more a difference in quality of vocabulary than in quality of feelings. Therefore, it is valuable for all those conducting groups to have some knowledge of what occurs in groups at other age levels.*

## CHAPTER 30

# Support of Group Counselors' Feelings

Lillian B. Vogel, Ph.D.

IN VARIOUS SCHOOL DISTRICTS of Los Angeles County, the Department of
Mental Health provided consultants to confer with counselors who wished
to develop skills in group work. In one district, pupil services and attendance
counselors (PSAC) were invited to participate in a workshop designed to
help counselors who had a group in process or who were being pressured by
their principals to start a group. Of the 10 participants, 4 men and 6 women,
one had considerable experience in leading children's groups, while the
others had little or no experience. All had formerly been teachers and were
currently primarily engaged in individual counseling with children who presented attendance problems. The workshop met for 21 sessions in the winter
and spring of 1973. Attendance was fairly regular throughout, and the
membership of 10 was maintained.

*Reactions of other school personnel**

Problems in dealing with school personnel, particularly *the principals,*
required repeated attention throughout the workshop. It was reported that
several principals wanted to have groups in their schools, even though they
were unfamiliar with the goals and procedure of a counseling group. Counselors seemed impelled to have a group in their school because it had been
suggested by supervisors. In some schools, counselors were presented with
lists of acting-out boys, with the implication that the counseling group was
to be the correcting "institution."** One of the counselors expressed considerable anxiety about not doing what was requested by the principal, even

---

* See Chapter 3.
** See Chapter 1, "but with a caution."

though it was apparent that this principal needed information regarding groups. Another counselor, who felt much more secure, countered with, "Don't allow him to stampede you into doing what he wants."

Each counselor was responsible for several schools. With this large an assignment they were uncertain about the number of cases they would have to handle in the assigned schools. Frequent emergencies arose which the administrator felt must be dealt with immediately. In the workshop there was a question about whether a group meeting should be postponed to meet such emergencies or whether it should wait for an hour. A parallel question concerned the right of the counselor to set aside a block of time for groups even in the face of other demands. The possibility was presented that poor time management or avoidance of a threatening situation might be involved. The counselors did not feel full value in the procedure of leading a group.

One leader talked of feeling insecure when her group was observed by a principal. It turned out that this principal was interested in group dynamics and not at all critical about what was happening. Another leader was defensive when her group, which met within hearing of the vice-principal's office, was particularly noisy. A leader who felt it valuable to take his group outdoors to play ball felt threatened when questioned about this by the principal. Still another leader talked about having felt hurt and angry that she was not given respect for her professional position when a boy whom she was about to place in a group was expelled from school without her advice.

*Dealing with teachers* was often difficult. Some of them were enthusiastic about the possibility of providing for change in their problem children; but others felt that having a child referred to a counseling group might be a reflection of their own incompetence. One teacher saw the group as too pleasant an experience for children who were classroom disrupters. She found it hard to accept that their lack of cooperation should be so reinforced. Her cynicism was reflected by ". . . sure, if I let them do nothing but play. . . ."

It was apparent that school staff members needed orientation to the goals and procedures of a counseling group. It may be incumbent upon the counselor to make certain that school personnel are regularly informed. This could insure the smooth running of the mechanical aspects of a group and thus allay anxiety in the counselor and the teachers.

## Parental consent

The need for parental consent for a child to be in a special activity is a school regulation. Usually, little resistance was encountered when a written form was sent home with the child. However, some of the counselors felt this was too impersonal a way to acquaint a parent about a group. When a personal phone call was made, a feeling of caring and concern for the child was transmitted. A personal visit by the counselor to the home was still better. When the basic goals of the group were presented to the parents at their level of understanding, the likelihood of ongoing cooperation was increased. Secondary school children may resent a home visit, and so student approval is desirable if a home visit is contemplated.

*Feelings of the counselors as group leaders*

To have worked out one's own feelings in interaction with others is no doubt the best training for group counseling. Experience in sensitivity training, encounter groups, and especially group therapy contributes greatly toward understanding the basic concepts of group dynamics. The expectation is that as counselors participate in a group, they develop increased awareness and sensitivity to their own feelings as well as to the feelings of others. Effective leaders *must identify with the children's feelings and at the same time maintain their own identity.*

Some consultation groups can function as group encounters in themselves. In the consultation sessions described here we did not deal directly with the encounter experience of the participants. Ostensibly, we were dealing with the development of skills in leading children's groups. However, because pervasive anxiety was expressed about all aspects of counseling, we were made aware that inherent in the process of skill development was the necessity for a focus on self-awareness, sensitivity to one's feelings in response to what is occurring in the group, and sensitivity to the needs and reactions of the children.

In the earlier sessions *multiple uncertainties* were expressed. Questions asked were: Am I being pushed into developing a skill whether I wish this or not? What if I'm not good at this? I enjoy what I'm doing, that is, seeing children and families in individual counseling; now I'm put into the position of a changing role. Several of the counselors made it clear that they had come into the workshop because they felt an unstated expectation that it would be wise to do so. Also, there was a feeling of being threatened by incoming paraprofessionals who might become so competent that they would take over the role of the professional counselor.

As the workshop progressed, emphasis was continually placed on the value of being open about one's anxieties: that there was no need to be fearful of revealing ineptness in front of peers; that this could be the first step toward growth in the desired skills. Rogers (1961) stated that as one accepts oneself as one is, one moves forward in the process of becoming.

The idea was stressed that even those with experience were not always sure of themselves or of what they were doing when leading a group. One need not be burdened with the feeling that "I should be solving all of these problems." "Because the children in the groups are often from homes where there are multiple problems, you alone as a counselor can't solve them all." However, the group just might help to create sufficient momentum to start a growth process in a particular child. In some other cases there may be no clear result. Increased negative behavior during the time the child is in the group is a possibility because of the existence of so many variables over which we have no control.

Anxiety was expressed by one counselor upon starting his first group. "I had the feeling right from the start that my group would be bankrupt. I felt like I'd used all of my assets in the first two sessions, so I discontinued the group and told them I'd see them individually." Actually, he had accepted his group without adequate selection. It was pointed out that perhaps he had acted too quickly in response to his feelings of failure and that if he had brought his insecure feelings to the consultation group sooner, we might have been able to help him. He was not expected to know all the answers. *There is no one answer in dealing with a group;* there are many alternate methods that could be used; it takes time to develop competence.

Several weeks later, one of the other leaders, also inexperienced in groups, reported that after hearing of the above experience she became aware that her own group was weak, and she, too, was anticipating failure. She began to accept the idea that as a beginner she did not have to be totally competent. As she became better able to deal with her feelings of anticipating failure and disappointment, she was able to sense change and growth in herself. Taped statements of the children at the last meeting of her group indicated that positive changes had occurred.

## Techniques and procedures in the groups

Once the preliminary considerations of administration and participant selection were dealt with, many questions arose which reflected uncertainty about starting a group. How is behavior within the group managed? How much control should be imposed? What happens when you run out of things to do? What if they are bored? What if you can't get them to talk about their feelings? What kind of activities and materials are brought into the group? What subjects are they allowed to talk about?

Since all of the counselors had formerly been teachers, their experience in dealing with a group of children was, in the most ideal sense, that of the benevolent authoritarian whose job was to have the class learn what was prescribed by the authorities to whom a teacher is responsible. Leaders of small groups of children with the goal of modifying behavior fulfill a role which can conflict with their own childhood training and experience. In the group it is important to assume a permissive, nonauthoritative role which will convey complete acceptance of a child: "No matter what your behavior has been heretofore, I care about you; you are important here; we want you to come."

At the first meeting the children need to be told that whatever is said in the group is confidential. They may feel free to talk about anything that is on their minds, and it would be expected to remain only within the group. Children usually reacted positively to this, as though they were in a secret club. However, all were aware that many children might not adhere to this confidentiality but might talk to their peers or parents about what went on in the group. It must also be stated that no child will be allowed to hurt himself, to hurt others, or to deface or destroy property while in the group. Any other ground rules concerning interrupting, not listening, grabbing, etc., are most effective when established by the members.

Are there any taboo subjects? One articulate child gave a vivid description of parental fights, violence, and alcoholic bouts. If the child's daily problems are being discussed, expression of such feelings should not be curtailed. One must take some risks, even with the possibility that some parent might know what went on and voice disapproval. Others felt that the school was no place for such discussion. It was suggested that if the counselor became uneasy with such topics, it might be best to arrange for an individual session.

A taped session played in the consultation group demonstrated the characteristic darting from one subject to another which so often occurs in a children's group. This led to the question of the extent to which the group discussion might be directed. For example, in one group five of the six children were from divorced homes. Gardner (1972) wrote of the universality of some feelings of children whose parents are divorced and the great need they often had to talk about this. Another crucial area pertained to children's fears, particularly the fear of death. Accepting that such concerns may often be with a child, how might they be introduced? Suggestions were made to use pertinent pictures or stories which stimulate specific feelings.

Specific techniques for appropriate age levels evoked extensive discussion.* Generally, the younger the group the greater the number of planned activities that are desirable, and the avowed goal for a particular group might suggest certain activities. For example, a group of first graders, who were all very shy, showed increased interaction when they engaged in any activity that introduced body contact.

A series of questions may be used which could start a discussion: Whom do you trust? Why is it desirable to be a good listener? Why would you want friends? One counselor reported bringing some magazines to the group and asking the children to find pictures of people who look as though they have feelings that were listed on the board. Then she suggested that they tell a story about an animal or a person having such feelings. Another leader started a group with the question, "What could you do to feel better inside?" As she listed these responses, she tried to elicit specific activities and feelings around these events. Selection of the activity to introduce into the group depends upon the sensitivity of the counselor as to what might be appropriate at a particular time.

A *focus on the "here and now"* process is a fundamental group technique. When one regards the group as a social microcosm, then the interpersonal behavior and feelings within the group may be seen as representative of behavior and feelings outside the group. When one responds to the "here and now" with a child, it can elicit the expression of much feeling. Counselors were aware of this and were working at developing sensitivity to nonverbal as well as verbal cues. As an example, one counselor told of a boy who kept making funny noises at the beginning of the session. She commented, "I think he's trying to tell us something." Thereupon, the boy took off his shoe and sock and showed where his toe had been bitten by a spider. Others started to talk of their physical hurts, and this led to revelation about what made them cry and how they felt about crying. Group climate developed by the leader resulted in awareness of universality of feelings and cohesiveness by the children.

In another group, a child who appeared sad was encouraged to talk of his grandfather's death. The others were supportive, and considerable expression of the fear of death ensued. Cohesiveness in a group may be a function of the personality of the leader. One counselor promised his group of boys that

---

* A list of techniques were exchanged in the workshop, and a copy was made available to each member.

he would take them for hamburgers at the last session. On the appointed day one of the boys was dejected because his father had refused to sign his trip slip. Within hearing range of the group, the leader called the boy's father. As he talked to the father, an alcoholic who was insisting that the boy had to be punished, the whole group let out a whoop of pleasure when consent was finally given and they knew their friend could attend.

The *technique of behavior modification* was intermittently discussed as another useful procedure. One leader decided to give a star to each child who brought a report from the teacher regarding any changed behavior, and the group reward was to be a luncheon trip. The counselors could accept the effectiveness of a group reward with a homogeneous group, but they were uncertain about how this would apply with a group of heterogeneous maladaptive behavers. Would it then be necessary to determine specific reinforcements for each child?

### Parent groups

School counselors have always felt a need to get parents of problem children into group discussion. Much frustration was expressed that even when a parent group had been started, continuity and regularity of attendance rarely seemed to follow. Two of the counselors decided on an *innovative plan:* If parents would not come to the school, then the *school would go to the parents*.

In one school with a high rate of absenteeism, it was noted that many of the children lived in a particular apartment complex with one-parent families. With the cooperation of the apartment owner and manager, mothers were invited to attend a group meeting. These mothers had always been apprehensive of any school-related request because they were generally contacted only when a child was in trouble. Only two women appeared at the first meeting, but ten women with babies and preschoolers attended the second session. They said they had come because they now understood the reason for the meetings. The manager acted as interpreter, since many of the women spoke only Spanish. It was quickly evident that these mothers were deeply concerned about their children, particularly in regard to inadequate play areas and lack of plans for summer activity. Discussion moved into areas of child management, school achievement, and poor attendance.

As the women felt more and more secure, they were able to talk of their feelings about limitations in providing for their children and the way this might contribute to their children's problems. Honest gratification was expressed that their children were so important that the counselors would come to help the mothers. This was a vivid example of the movement of school services into the community.

### Evaluation of the children's groups

Because most of the counselors had not led groups before and were aware of their many insecurities in regard to starting and maintaining groups, they did not want to burden themselves at that time with systematic evaluations. In the groups reported here, no measuring device was used, nor was any measure made at termination.

The effect of the group counseling intervention was one of impression by the counselor, the teacher, the parent, and the child. Most of the children appeared to regard the experience as pleasurable and wanted to come to the "club" next year. Others asked to have their friends come in. One leader taped the termination meeting. Comments were: "I don't talk so much in class." "I can listen to the teacher." "When I get mad at a guy, I stop and think what is the best thing to do." Teachers also reported positive changes in some of the children.

However, it is important to evaluate effectiveness of group counseling by more than impression.* Specific measures might tell us if a group had sufficient impact on a child's life to modify maladaptive behavior. If this modality is to be used more extensively and consultants are to be provided by public agencies, then accountability to the agencies must be provided.

### Evaluation of the consultation group

Following the last session, participants in the consultation group were asked by the area supervisors* to fill out an evaluation survey. Their responses are shown in the table. From the questionnaire and from comments made at the last meeting, it appeared that the *support derived from the consultant and from colleagues was paramount.* To be able to share insecurities, resistances, techniques, and experiences in the group process itself was of invaluable help. Participants felt that self-exposure and its acceptance produced growth in individuals. All agreed that the interchange of techniques and their workability at various age levels increased the fund of

---

* See Chapter 29.
* The writer expresses thanks to the two area supervisors, Beatrice Broomell and David Duke, for their suggestions and cooperation during the course of the workshop.

## TABLE EVALUATING THE CONSULTATION GROUP

| | Yes | No | No Answer |
|---|---|---|---|
| 1. Did you learn more about group counseling and group process than you knew before? | 9 | 1 | — |
| 2. Was the greater emphasis on current problems rather than basic group process fundamentals at times? (Members felt this question was ambiguous.) | 7 | 3 | — |
| 3. Did facilitator demonstrate skills needed in working with groups? | 7 | 1 | 2 |
| 4. Did facilitator have realistic understanding of schools and how they function? | 7 | 2 | 1 |
| 5. Did sessions help you decide whether you did or did not want to pursue further training in group counseling? | 7 | 3 | — |
| 6. Was there increased awareness of problems encountered in group process by participants in this program? | 9 | 1 | — |
| 7. Was consultation group helpful to you in coping with problems you had with your children's group? | 8 | 1 | 1 |
| 8. Were materials/bibliography helpful? | 8 | 1 | 1 |
| Were they sufficient? | 3 | 6 | 1 |
| 9. Do you hope to continue/start group counseling in any of your schools next year? | 9 | — | 1 |
| 10. Would you recommend this program with the same consultant for other PSA interested in learning more about group counseling? | 8 | 1 | 1 |

11. Additional comments:

As one with considerable experience in working with groups, I had formerly been very much alone. It was valuable sharing experiences, techniques, and resistance.

I would have liked more direction and interpretation by consultant rather than take-over by members.

Need more input from consultant concerning techniques.

Consultant had realistic understanding and was very frank about areas she did not know.

knowledge of each one present. Some indicated that they would welcome more didactic material as well as more direction and interpretation on the part of the consultant instead of having so much time taken over by the counselors. Although they focused on their limited time for reading, they expressed need for more reprints and bibliography.

*Summary*

This chapter has described a consultative workshop which met over a period of several months for 21 sessions. Considerable focus was on the feelings of the counselors as they dealt with all aspects of groups they were leading or preparing to lead. This was in relation to school personnel, selection, and composition of the groups, and techniques and procedures within the group process itself once it was in operation. Experiences, information, and techniques were shared and exchanged by the participants and the consultant.

Discussions indicated a need for school personnel to have further orientation of goals and purposes of group counseling with children. Also, it was evident that counselors need to feel more secure when interacting with school personnel.

## BIBLIOGRAPHY

GARDNER, R. (1972). *Boys' and Girls' Book of Divorce.* New York: Science House, Inc.
ROGERS, C. (1961). *On Becoming a Person.* New York: Houghton, Mifflin.

# PART III: C. CONSULTATIVE ASSISTANCE (WITHOUT COLLABORATION)

## EDITOR'S NOTE

*The preceding chapter raises the dilemma of optimum training methods for helping counselors to overcome anxieties about beginning group counseling. The choice may seem to lie between the more passive see-the-expert-conduct-the-group supervision as described in the following chapter, or the more active collaborate-with-the-expert-in-the-group, as described in previous chapters. Many educators request demonstration projects, but unless it was the particular design used here which was at fault, it would not seem as productive to provide demonstration projects other than to satisfy curiosity.*

CHAPTER 31

# The Use of Demonstration Student Groups in Teaching Group Counseling

Steven M. Jacobs, Ph.D., and
Maurice Deigh, Ph.D.

BEFORE MENTAL HEALTH PROFESSIONALS from outside the schools may present information to school personnel, it usually is necessary to obtain the permission of the superintendent, the principals, and the heads of departments.* After obtaining top-level sanction, the professionals must bring about the interest and participation of the personnel they hope to reach, i.e., the consultees. In the group-counseling training project to be described here, consultees were the counselors and pupil personnel workers of four high schools in a Southern California school district.

The district's superintendent and the principals had given authorization to the consulting agency** for other projects in the past. Their active involvement in this particular project, however, was not solicited.

The principal focus of this project was to test the teaching value of demonstrating live group counseling sessions. The importance of explicit administrative support for expansion of group counseling services unfortunately was not fully realized.

---

\* See Chapter 3.
\*\* A regional office of the Los Angeles County Department of Health Services (Mental Health).

*Obtaining consensus of counselors and pupil personnel workers*

Three people were involved in early negotiations: the consultation coordinator of the South Bay Mental Health Service; the chief counselor of the district; and a counselor who was also the president of the district's school counselors' association. These three agreed that an in-service training program would be helpful to the district's counselors. Two important questions had to be decided in these early discussions: first, a choice had to be made between two desired subjects—crisis intervention techniques or group counseling techniques; second, a decision had to be made about the method for teaching the chosen subject.

To help arrive at recommendations which would be most agreeable to the counselors, several members of the South Bay Mental Health Service met for consultation sessions with the counselors.* At one of the sessions, it was decided that other pupil personnel workers would be invited to join the program and that a poll would be taken to learn whether crisis intervention techniques or group counseling techniques would be the preferred subject. The poll showed group counseling as the preferred subject. It may seem overly cautious to arrive at a consensus so painstakingly, but it was believed that thorough determination of consensus would result in later optimum learning and participation.

No later polls were taken, but similar procedures brought about the decision to use, as the chief training method, demonstration of a series of group counseling sessions. High school students would be members of the group and the demonstration sessions would be conducted by a professional skilled in group counseling techniques.

A psychologist (Jacobs) experienced in consultation to school personnel as well as in group counseling techniques was recruited. He joined the next meetings of counselors and consultants, and the following decisions were made:

(1) Each demonstration group counseling session would be followed by a discussion period which would include the consultant and the trainees. Students would not be present.

(2) The whole training project would be videotaped, including the demonstration sessions and the discussion periods. Selected portions of the tapes would be used in future consultation meetings for counselors who would be

---

* The staff members undertaking the consultation were: Steven Charles, M.D., Harold Faber, M.D., Dee Flacy, M.S.W., Alex Goda, M.S.W., and Sharon Pearlstein, M.S.W.

doing group counseling. The tapes would provide examples of how specific group counseling situations were handled.

(3) Students to be used in the group counseling demonstrations would be volunteers selected from two elective psychology courses composed of junior and senior high school students. Because the demonstration sessions were to be videotaped and observers were to be present, students who were members of other available counseling groups would not be selected.

## Obtaining students for groups

With the teacher's permission, the first author met with each psychology class at its scheduled time. After a brief introduction by the school counselor, he gave the class the following information: ten student volunteers were needed to participate in six group counseling sessions, which would take place after school in the audiovisual studio; the purpose would be to train school counselors in group counseling techniques by the use of live demonstrations; counselors would be in the room observing the sessions; the sessions would be videotaped, and the tapes would be used exclusively for the training of professionals; the subjects to be discussed during the sessions would be left up to the students and the leader to decide; students would be required to make a commitment to participate in all six sessions and to have their parents sign a consent form; an equal number of males and females would be chosen; those students who returned their parent consent slips first would become members of the group.

Few questions were asked by students in the first class, but students in the second class asked questions for about 15 minutes. Their questions dealt with the nature of counseling, with the specific project, and with the difference between psychologists and psychiatrists. In order to help the students become acquainted with the person who was to lead the sessions and to increase their trust and willingness to volunteer, all questions were answered as completely and directly as possible.

Many more students volunteered than could be included in one counseling group. Ten were chosen. The fewest number of students present at each of the six demonstration counseling sessions was five. At two sessions all ten were present. The number of counselors observing the sessions ranged from a high of about 20 to a low of 5.

The consultant had had no previous experience with videotaping. At times the talk among the cameramen tended to distract the counselors. In the main, however, the job done by the technical crew was excellent. The use of two cameras allowed the group to sit in a circle and still have every individual's face clearly in view.

*Content of the sessions*

Because the students had not requested counseling for specific needs or problems, no particular problem areas determined the content focus. The students were encouraged to choose the areas or topics to be discussed, but this freedom to choose topics was not clearly or sufficiently explained. At the end of the sessions, a few students said that they had thought a specific topic was to be selected for each session and that the topic was to be adhered to rather closely. This was not the intent of the consultant.

For the *first session*, the students had some difficulty deciding what they wished to talk about. To help them begin, the leader suggested the relevant topic of the transition from dependence to independence, with home and school used as examples. The students readily picked up the topic and discussed it in terms of its relationship to home and parents. At the end of the session, one student in particular expressed a desire to change the topic. The leader supported and encouraged this desire.

At the *second session*, the students displayed some initial hesitation. They had picked a topic between sessions, but it was one which embarrassed and frightened them to mention or deal with. Finally, one of the members stated that the group's desire was to talk about premarital sexual relations. All of the students approved the topic, and a freewheeling discussion followed, which revealed a variety of attitudes, values, roles, and feelings. No limits were set by the leader; his role was that of facilitator. At times he asked questions to clarify or elicit the students' feelings, attitudes, and values. He made a conscious effort not to express his own attitudes or values or impose them on the students.

For the *third session*, the group again had some difficulty getting started. The students began to discuss school rules and society's rules in general. The consultant played the role of devil's advocate by questioning the reasons the students gave for having or not having a rule and by asking what effect the rule had on certain portions of society. The leader put his questioning rather strongly, not in terms of there being the existence of absolutes in regard to rules, but to force the students to consider the consequences of the presence or absence of certain rules. In fact, one student commented that the leader always had a "comeback."

The *fourth session* took place after a two-week school holiday. Again, the session started rather slowly. The leader did nothing to help the students begin. After some periods of silence, the students finally began to talk about strictness at school and the pros and cons of having rules that were more or less strict. Discussion then moved into the area of occupations, school preparation for occupations, and the general purposes and values of education. The students were more interactive with each other during this session than they had been in other sessions. They talked directly to each other, rather than talking to each other through the consultant.

The *fifth session* was probably the slowest of all. There were many silences, but the students seemed to weather them all satisfactorily. Again, the discussion was centered primarily around the members' goals, and the students seemed to be very supportive of each other.

The *sixth and last session* dealt with terminating. Some discussion took place about what the students had derived from the group meetings. Toward the end of the session, the counselors who were observing were included in the general discussion.

### Teaching value for counselors

These group counseling sessions had been designed primarily for counselors. They had been set up as a demonstration to stimulate the discussions between consultant and counselors which followed. A problem in using this training method was discovered: more time is taken up in demonstrating than in talking afterwards with counselors. The demonstrations did, however, reveal dramatically to the counselors that during counseling by an expert there can be difficulties getting started, periods of silence, and—most important of all—that not every moment of the session is of dynamic importance. Before the demonstrations, many of the counselors had thought that every moment of a session should be filled with exciting solutions to problems. One counselor succinctly expressed his change of mind when he said, "I see I'm not so bad."

In the sessions dealing with premarital sex, the counselors were able to see that this subject could be dealt with openly, without the group leader moralizing or inserting his own values. Some of the counselors were able to verbalize that they would not feel comfortable discussing this subject with a group of students.

An area of concern for the counselors, which was expressed repeatedly by their questions and discussion, was their need to justify the use of time— their own and the students'—for group counseling. Anxiety was caused both in leaders and members by silent periods. Counselors were concerned that periods of silence and time taken to become involved in active discussion was not being used more productively.

Recent legislation in California established evaluation and accountability as a requirement for all credentialed personnel. This probably contributed somewhat, but not entirely, to the counselors' anxiety about the need to justify group counseling and demonstrate definitive results.

The issue of the use of time came up repeatedly and was always discussed at some length. Goals and subgoals were gradually brought forth for discussion and used to demonstrate the value and worth of group counseling. These goals applied even to the demonstration group, where initially there had been no identifiable goals.

The counselors were able to recognize that when the leader did not direct the session by suggesting an area for discussion, but allowed silent periods to be handled by the members, the students became more interactive and supportive of each other. *The group was not lost by periods of silence.* Although the counselors asked the leader how he felt about these silences, they said that they had been able to observe a genuine feeling of calm and patience throughout the silent stretches.

The *leader made a point of revealing* to the counselors the feelings and introspections he had had during the counseling sessions themselves. This served to give the counselors permission to have their own feelings while doing counseling and to open them to greater self-awareness. Several times the counselors suggested gimmicks or manipulations to hurry up the counseling process.

Other questions raised by counselors involved ways of choosing students for a counseling group, of closing the session, and of ending the group. It was evident that termination needed further discussion. One counselor wondered what to do when he felt inadequate. He cited as an example a student who expressed the feeling, "Is life worth living?" Other counselors wondered what ought to be done when students mention certain teachers by name in a negative, complaining, fault-finding way. Should a group be required to keep in confidence the matters and people discussed in the group? All of these points were discussed at some length, with considerable interaction among the counselors themselves.

*Results*

The effect of conducting these demonstration group counseling sessions was clearly evident in the requests of some students for the group to continue. One suggested that group counseling might pull some potential drop-outs back into attendance at school.*

## Disappointment

At the start of the project, it had appeared as if all the counselor partici-pants were fully involved. The counselors and pupil personnel workers had attended meetings and had taken part in making decisions and planning their implementation. During the stage in which negotiations were made, several features had seemed conducive to the development of more group counseling: (1) "total push" consultation efforts; (2) the counselors' strong desire to observe demonstrations of what an "expert" accomplishes in group counseling; (3) the high degree of interaction among the counselors them-selves and with the consultant during the discussion meetings; (4) avail-ability of taped material for additional assistance and edification. Despite these favorable signs, it became apparent that the counselors were not being motivated to do more group counseling.

Although the demonstrations were followed by active discussions of many issues which were pertinent and seemingly useful to counselors, the project did not seem to promote more group counseling in the district that particular year. Consultation sessions after the demonstrations ended were sparsely attended and after several weeks were all but completely discontinued. The productive outcome of some consultation experiences may occur months or years after the experience. It's possible that the fruits of this experience will be more and better counseling groups in the future.

## Speculation

The major goal of the demonstration project had been to encourage the counseling staff to conduct more counseling groups. Why this goal was not achieved is open to some speculation.

As described, considerable negotiation had taken place in regard to subject matter and form of the consultation. A poll had been taken. The poll had been, however, a choice between two alternatives: crisis intervention or group counseling techniques. The results of the poll may have indicated a choice between two negatives, rather than a desire or commitment to partici-pate in group counseling.

An extremely important factor may have been the matter of neglecting to include the counselors' immediate superiors in the negotiations. The dis-

---

* See Chapter 19.

trict superintendent had given tacit approval to the project, but the counselors' *school principals and vice-principals were not significantly involved.* *
Therefore, the principals gave no indication to the counselors that group counseling had some importance in their job role. Comments by counselors regarding accountability indicated concern that their immediate superiors on the school grounds would not place group counseling high on the priority list of counselor activity.

In retrospect, the school principals should have been contacted by the consultants at an early point in the negotiations. The consultants should have obtained the principals' direct approval and desire to have group counseling in their schools and their understanding that significant time would be spent in this activity.

Another factor may have contributed to the fact that the number of counseling groups did not increase. School counselors are accustomed to dealing with student problems on a one-to-one basis. A relationship with an individual is less threatening to many counselors than a relationship with a group, because it can be more easily controlled. All school counselors had been classroom teachers. Some even chose counseling as a way to leave behind the anxieties of the group situation in the classroom. These individuals certainly might not feel comfortable in doing group counseling. This can be a much more threatening situation to some than the classroom situation. Participation in the training program was voluntary. Participation in group counseling also should be voluntary.

However, some individuals in schools do feel comfortable in group situations. As well as some counselors, there are some teachers. They are accustomed to dealing with students in groups, and their volunteer participation in counseling programs might be encouraged. With supervision and training, it is probable that many teachers can become effective leaders of counseling groups.**

* See Chapter 3.
** See Chapter 26.

CHAPTER 32

# Assisting Teachers in Group Counseling with Drug-Abusing Students

Dorothy Flacy, M.S.W.
Alex Goda, M.S.W., and
Robert Schwartz, M.D.

THE SOUTH BAY MENTAL HEALTH SERVICE responded to a request from the Director of Narcotics Education Resources to give consultation and assistance in the training of teachers for group counseling of young drug abusers in a district of five large high schools.

The first meeting of *35 teachers who had volunteered* to participate in the program was held in October, and from this meeting three training groups were formed. Most of the teachers had volunteered out of genuine concern for students and a need to do something about the drug problem, with the understanding that they would not receive extra compensation for their work.

Initially, considerable *apprehension and feelings of inadequacy* were expressed by the teachers. Many had expected to be given a course and presented with effective techniques by the experts. A part of the consultants' task involved preserving the enthusiasm of the participants while avoiding pat answers. The need to do something was approached by redirecting the focus toward acceptance of the probability that no student was going to give up drugs solely because of the teachers' efforts, and the teachers should not impose this responsibility on themselves. Rather than expecting to solve the psychological problems of the students, they could offer themselves as listeners, sounding boards, and perhaps models, creating a climate for new experience to take place within individuals so that alternative behavior could become possible.

At first the *teachers worried about role confusion,* fearing the students would be hostile toward them as authorities. Encouraged to examine closely their own values and attitudes about drugs, unlawful behavior, authority, and obscene language, they recognized with some humor and relief that much of their anxiety related to their own ambivalence. As a result, they reported feeling more comfortable in handling provocations from group members.

The suggestion that the *teachers work in pairs* as co-leaders was accepted by the group. While it meant fewer groups, the teachers would benefit from mutual support, exchange, and feedback, experience less pressure, and be better equipped to deal with negative responses. Male-female teams were assigned to work together. It was understood that if leaders found themselves incompatible, they were free to acknowledge this and make changes.

The question was raised early as to *whether teachers should lead groups on their own campus* or go to another school. Some were afraid that sharing of confidences by students in group would affect classroom or campus contacts. They were further concerned about their relationships with colleagues, since some suspicion and antagonism toward the program had been voiced. The teachers decided to hold groups on their own campuses, choosing to risk handling whatever situations might arise rather than involve themselves in the personal inconvenience of going away from their own campuses. This decision allowed adding another dimension to their experience, i.e., the observation of how the group members related to them in settings outside the group. In later consultations some leaders reported on a variety of these exchanges, stating that the quality of communication was somehow different from the usual student-teacher exchange. Though difficult to define, they implied there was a lessening of tension—something akin to goodwill—a relaxing of barriers yet no loss of respect or position.

The three training groups met weekly until after the holiday vacation. By then, the attrition caused by heavy schedules and personal reasons *had cut the group from 35 to 18.* The training groups merged into one unit and continued to meet weekly for an hour-and-a-half until the end of the school year.

As the student groups got underway, the teachers brought *specific situations to the consultation* for discussion. Some of these had to do with hostility of group members toward leaders and fellow group members, and leaders toward members (this last possibility was introduced by the consultants); resentment stemming from mandatory attendance; long silences; the manipulative group member; confrontation; a curiosity about the leader;

how to avoid endless rapping about drugs; reacting to four-letter words; talking about uncomfortable things; and dealing with the student who comes to the group "high."

It was noted that with experience the teachers began to *recognize when their own emotional involvement was interfering* with group process. They were increasingly able to handle situations within their group or among themselves, relying less on referral and consultation. They often expressed amazement, as these students revealed themselves, at the staggering amount of family chaos and the kinds of home situations in which these young people had to exist. Most leaders showed that they were becoming more sensitive and empathic toward the students. They were also less preoccupied with the drug taking than with helping the students handle their realities, enlarging their view of possibilities, and encouraging them to stand on their own feet and use the support of the social network around them.

At the end of the year an *evaluation meeting* was held for all who had participated in the planning and execution of the program. Group leaders were candid in sharing both positive and negative aspects. They spoke of having their morale boosted when other teachers began to comment to them on some change of behavior they had observed in a student from a group, and most of them expressed willingness to continue with groups the following year. The majority said that working with a stranger as co-leader had resulted in cooperation, mutual respect, and friendship for one another. Only two admitted that personality differences had interfered with their effectiveness with the students, and they acknowledged they had not taken the responsibility for asking to change partners.

*In summary,* this consultation began as in-service training and education. The consultants made no attempt to impart a systematic body of knowledge about techniques or to offer specific methods which they felt might only be imitated. The effort was made to promote the self-awareness of the teacher and counselor group leaders without infringing on their privacy; to let them know that it is normal for new leaders to feel inadequate, and that this does not mean they are inadequate; and that common sense and past experience can often serve them well when they feel a lack in skill, knowledge, or self-confidence.

## PART III: D. OTHER USEFUL GROUPS IN JUNIOR AND SENIOR HIGH SCHOOLS

## EDITOR'S NOTE

*"Other useful groups" refers to groups other than the more formalized group counseling procedures described in the previous chapters of this volume. Small group process is a powerful tool for affecting individual minds and practices, as well as for affecting events in a larger group or system.*

*Small groups can have special value in facilitating smoother routine operations or dealing with crises, and improving intergroup relationships. Any conference which includes more than two persons can be considered a small group process used to influence individual or school-wide issues.*

### In junior high schools

*The junior high school period (grades 7-8 or 7-9) is a difficult time for most teen-agers. Small group assistance programs, counseling or otherwise, are not offered as frequently in these schools as in the senior high school. Kaplan (Chapter 29) indicates in her study that junior high school group members seemed to improve less than those in elementary school or senior high school (at least by the criteria used in her study). This may be related to the more turbulent emotions involved, as well as the institutional difficulties of fitting these youngsters into traditional classroom activities and settings. It is understandable if educators hesitate to meet these turbulent young people in counseling or other small groups. Yet, the need is more strategic and acute at this stage (see Chapter 42).*

*The next three chapters describe three very different kinds of small group experiences in junior high schools. Berkovitz and Boffa (Chapter 33) describe a two-hour communication seminar designed to help give eighth and ninth grade students an opportunity to participate in management of their school by registering complaints and suggesting changes. The fact that many students felt it to be an impotent exercise adds to the concern that our schools at times do not always inculcate hope or encourage innovative change.*

262

*In Chapter 34, Vanderpol and Suescum provide a neutral observation of teen-age fantasy and behavior in "discussion groups." The goal was to help teach educators about adolescent psychology. The feelings described lie thinly hidden under the facade of orderly classroom behavior.*

*Chapter 35, by Rueveni, is an example of group counseling as performed by an outside mental health professional without the goal of teaching methods to school personnel. The term "sensitivity training" unfortunately connotes different features in different locales. In California, for example, Rueveni's techniques would be called "gestalt" or "encounter." Whatever term is used, the techniques are in the category of activating procedures, contrasted to allowing interactions to emerge as in the other two chapters. The earlier chapter (16) by Bates also describes several possible types of confrontation. Caution and supervision are required in the use of such procedures. Rueveni's group did see a potentially dangerous physical conflict during one of these procedures.*

*It may be tempting to use such activating procedures when the leader feels anxious and needs to establish a feeling of control or direction, especially when young teen-agers appear restless, angry, or bored. Vanderpol and Suescum tolerated such anger in a comparatively unstructured situation.*

*Activating procedures or simulated games are potentially useful, but there is danger of loosening controls on explosive emotions. The adults who are exhilarated by such interactions with fellow adults need to keep in mind their previous younger years of acquiring controls and protection for tender or strong feelings. Adults can often benefit and regain equilibrium after such exposure. Most teen-agers, especially younger ones, are still learning effective personal organization and self-discipline. They often have difficulties recontaining the difficult-to-control, highly irrational, and poorly reasoned impulses.*

*On the other hand, a less intensely emotional experience, such as the communication seminar (Berkovitz and Boffa), avoids the danger. It was task oriented and conducted in a group of usual class size, though without class agenda. The structure was not intended to tap and expose intrapsychic issues, although many probably did surface. These were redirected to the agenda of the seminar. But such an exercise was less involving to many.*

*It is the need to expose and understand these strong adolescent energies which makes small group experience so relevant and useful at this age.*

*The chance for a brief, less-structured experience makes for more vivid and effective learning about one's emotions. Confident guidance and safeguards are necessary.*

CHAPTER 33

# A Communication Seminar in a Junior High School

Irving H. Berkovitz, M.D., and
Michelle E. Boffa, Ph.D.

THE JUNIOR HIGH OR INTERMEDIATE SCHOOL EXPERIENCE (grades 7-9) occurs at a crucial period in the growth of the 12- to 14-year-old. This period of development includes the early stages in the establishment of a firm and realistic identity, socially, familially, individually, and sexually. It also involves the frequently turbulent and uncertain emancipation from the previously secure parental relationship. Most junior high or intermediate schools do not provide sufficient support, guidance, and understanding to these developing and confused boys and girls.

In combination with other growth pressures directing their energies, entering junior high students must make a transition from the self-contained classroom of the elementary school to a more independent and complicated five- or six-period day. The supportive parent-surrogate sixth grade teacher or teacher team is absent. The campus is larger. Such challenges as cafeteria lines and lockers must be negotiated. Larger and more mature young people prevail, and fear of, or actual experience with, bullying, aggressive boys and girls occurs. While most young people survive and grow from this challenging experience, many others are hurt, educationally and emotionally.

Some school districts have attempted structural modifications to meet these maturational complications. In one community, a 7th grade school organized within the junior high provided group closeness as a source of security. Putting grades 7 and 8 in a separate building located on the grounds of the previously attended elementary school provides a more gradual transition to some. Some districts use an intermediate school of grades 5 through 8, in order to minimize the abruptly sharp transition for 6th graders. Change is a necessary and unavoidable challenge in life at all ages. However, an experience of gradual and supported change earlier in life often facilitates acceptance of later changes and aids in personal growth.

A significant step in growth and integration of impulses occurs when words and feelings can be balanced in an effective, expressive blend. Certainly the school experience itself provides the opportunity for this development. The large-population classroom manages to inculcate this ability for some but often for only a fraction of the group. Small group counseling offers help to a small portion of students who did not successfully or happily negotiate this growth task in the larger classroom group. Classroom-affective discussions are another means of encouraging this ability as opposed to the lecture or the content-oriented recitation format. However, the teacher at the junior high level may have difficulty in assisting students to express their feelings in a meaningful way. Students at this stage are strikingly partly adult and partly child and the subject-oriented teacher may have trouble shifting the focus from cognitive learning to regulation of immature impulses, both of which can occur closely side by side at this age level.

With these thoughts in mind, the administration in one junior high school acted upon a suggestion made by the school Community Advisory Council.* Its members believed there could be value in providing an opportunity for students to express their feelings, opinions, and suggestions about the junior high experience. The administration** planned a communication seminar, to be conducted in groups of usual class size, but without class agenda. In order to avoid disruption of the entire school program, the seminar was offered at first to only one-third of the students. Ninth graders were first choice, since they were considered most mature and perhaps best able to offer useful suggestions for improvements in the school program. Their two-and-a-half-years in the school seemed to put them in a better position to know the strengths and weaknesses of the school program.

A year later, the experience was provided for the eighth graders. It was

---

* This group consists of 12 parents, 6 teachers, and the principal, who meet monthly to discuss affairs of the school [which are of concern] and to advise the principal. Parents and teachers are elected yearly. Some are also members and officers of the P.T.A. While the P.T.A. and C.A.C. may be similar, many functions differ.

** The principal, Mr. Robert Hawkins and, for one semester, Mr. Douglas Bemish, acting principal, approved the project and facilitated necessary cooperation of the faculty and scheduling of the students.

hoped that they would retain the values from the seminar in the school for the following year and also that it would be possible to evaluate the educational and personal benefits of the seminar over a year's time. Seventh graders appeared to be too new in the school, had not become adjusted to the new surroundings, and could not yet offer useful, well-informed opinions about school problems.

The communication seminar was designed to occupy two class periods between 9 and 11:30 a.m. The ninth grade class of over 600 students was divided into groups of 30-40 students each, avoiding accustomed homeroom associations. Volunteer group leaders* were mental health professionals: psychiatrists, psychologists, social workers, public health nurses, and lay persons experienced in group discussion techniques.

Leaders were instructed to facilitate discussion among the students, but *not* to suggest attitudes or to moralize. A teacher, preferably one not known to the students, sat in the back of the room to maintain order if necessary. Usually, these teachers did not speak during the discussion. However, in the eighth grade seminar some teachers felt so strongly about matters under discussion that they felt compelled to express their opinions. Some teachers took notes in order to report on the experience more accurately. This teacher participation may have had some effect on the discussion. Student recorders were designated in advance for each group and were instructed to take the fullest possible record of the main topics of discussion including any suggestions for change. These written accounts were then compiled. Some of the subject matter cited here was obtained from them.

## Content

The meetings consisted of open discussion of the students' concerns about their school experience and suggestions for change. Topics ranged from regulations for gym dress to broad issues of interpersonal relations within the school. Considerable concern was expressed about the physical environment of the school, including a cleaner campus, vandalism, and improved grounds. Other concerns were voiced about food, clothing, and gym shower requirements, revealing the importance of bodily concerns and satisfaction to these adolescent youngsters.

Other topics dealt with *teacher and administrator behavior* and *school regulations*. Here the major concerns were with fairness in dealing with the

---

* In the ninth grade seminar, Mr. Roy Azarnoff was co-recruiter and co-planner.

students in relation to discipline, grading, freedom from behavior-regulating restrictions (e.g., rules against holding hands), and a desire for a better relationship with the adults in the school. A wish was evidenced for relationships of mutual respect and equality of treatment.

A closer examination of the content of the two seminar meetings revealed some interesting *differences between the two grade levels.* Whereas the general concerns and problems raised by the two student groups were similar, the emphases and perspectives differed in some areas.

In their concern about student-teacher relations, some eighth graders were prone to focus on specific behavior of teachers: "Teachers should not read notes that have been passed." While both age groups expressed strong desires for autonomy, the ninth graders did so in the context of greater understanding of teacher difficulties and insight into both student and teacher motivations. In general, the younger students were more concerned with specific regulations administered by teachers whom they perceived as infringing on their rights, while the ninth graders expressed greater concern with interpersonal relations and were more ready or able to offer suggestions.

A similar difference between the age levels was noted in the discussions of *student-administrator relations.* Again, it seemed the younger students expressed a more passive outlook, while the ninth graders indicated a desire for more responsibility and were able to produce a variety of specific suggestions for improving communication. In addition, they revealed a capacity to ask for and presumably accept more help from faculty and staff.

Some *grade level differences* were apparent in the students' discussion of the educational process, including concerns about classes, curriculum, and grades. Eighth graders were dissatisfied with specific requirements, noticeably time and attendance regulations, whereas the older group showed interest in improving the learning process by suggesting innovative teaching approaches, many of which involved increased student effort and involvement such as seminars and current events discussions. Both groups expressed dissatisfaction with the grading system and suggested a variety of alternatives. In this area of concern the two age levels resembled each other considerably.

Two areas of concern received attention from both groups, but interest was more intense among the younger students. Problems revolving around food, its quality and distribution, and the freedom to leave the campus at noontime were apparently a larger issue for the eighth graders. In this matter the younger students produced a variety of suggestions which indicated some understanding of the complexity of the problems and an acceptance of the need for some external control by the school.

It would seem that in *dealing with specific issues of* a fairly concrete nature, the eighth graders were able to deal with them somewhat constructively and to offer some solutions. On the other hand, the older students could handle situations involving interpersonal relations, particularly those with authority figures such as teachers and administrators in issues of personal autonomy versus external control, with a more mature perspective. In addition, the older students seemed to be more aware of the structure of the school, the complexities of interpersonal relationships, and the relationships and responsibilities of the school administration to other members of the community, such as the parents. These differences may be attributable to the increased maturity of the ninth graders and their greater experience with the larger and more complex junior high school organization. It may be that the additional year of participation has given these students a broader perspective and permitted them to be more creative and comprehensive in their view of the school and its problems.

These differences suggest that grade levels should be taken into account in planning, implementing, and evaluating similar types of group experiences at the junior high school level. For example, it *might be helpful for eighth and ninth graders to meet together,* so that some of the younger students could gain in their viewpoints. Sensitizing teachers and administrators to the possible presence of these differences might assist them in understanding more fully some of the younger students' concerns and in planning orientation programs more effectively. Both groups of students agreed on the need for increased information and communication regarding state laws, board of education regulations, and school rules, and on improved dialogue between teachers, administrators, and students. These junior high school students were eager to become informed members of the school, participants in the learning process who are consulted and whose opinions are respected.

Both groups expressed the desire for *better relations* and communication with teachers and administrators. Students voiced their wishes to be respected, listened to, and treated as important and contributing members of the school. A major theme in these discussions was the request for increased opportunities for students and teachers to come together in expressing their views and discussing their mutual concerns. It is perhaps the sincerity and depth of this concern as voiced by these students which speaks most strongly for the value of seminars such as these.

*Follow-up meetings*

In the planning for the first seminar all groups involved—parents, teachers, and students—thought the communication seminar concept was a good one but that a follow-up should be made to obtain some resolution about the ideas that had been expressed. Therefore, a forum was planned and held six weeks later during lunch in the gym. The meeting was student initiated, student organized, and student conducted. The express purpose was to open an additional line of communication between students and teachers and to offer a platform for the expression and discussion of both positive and negative ideas and suggestions about student-teacher relations. Publicity regarding the forum was given through bulletin notices, public address announcements, homeroom talks, and posters. Approximately 50 students and 8 teachers attended. The announced topic of the forum was student-teacher relationships but other topics from the original seminar were covered as well. Discussion was free and open, and subsequent weekly forums were planned.

Forums were held weekly for the next month. The first two of these were attended by 30-40 students and several teachers. The last two were attended by a smaller number of students and teachers. Announcements of the forums always stated that only a limited number of students could be admitted, because large numbers preclude communication and expression of feelings and ideas. Only a small number of student council members attended, so that a greater cross section of the student body could participate. All teachers were given a general invitation, and three teachers were invited to participate specifically as a teacher panel for each meeting. The format of the meetings included opening remarks from the teacher panel followed by free discussion by students and teachers. Those in attendance sat informally on floor mats. Most people brought their lunches.

Discussion in the forums focused on a variety of issues. Student-teacher relationships were of major interest and were examined in detail in at least two meetings. The needs of both faculty and students for better learning/teaching conditions were suggested by the range of concerns, from increasing the physical space of the school to improving interpersonal relationships and communication in the classroom. One meeting was devoted to discussion of changes in grading procedures and a later forum included other suggestions, such as ways in which students might be helped in effecting changes in the school and approaches to improving the communication procedures used to convey information to the student body.

Among the less desirable of the outcomes of the first seminar (ninth grade) was the annoyed reaction of a few of the teachers regarding the personal nature of some of the comments made about the teaching staff during the seminar. Possibly as a result of this, enthusiasm in the school generally was less for the eighth grade seminar and an attempt was made to exercise greater control over it. This may account in part for the lack of student response when the principal, as a follow-up to the seminar, held a meeting with a small group of interested eighth grade students to try to work out a set of rules for school behavior which would then be compiled and distributed to the student body. These meetings did not continue with the same enthusiasm as the year before. The following year articles about the rights and responsibilities of students did appear in the school newspaper.

The lack of interest in follow-up in the eighth grade may also be due in part to age differences. It may be that the ninth graders were more capable of initiating and sustaining continued involvement with the task of communication and that full student-faculty-administration participation in the follow-up stage is especially important.

*Evaluation*

Within the 7 to 10 days following each seminar, questionnaires were filled out by all participating students, some teachers, and some of the leaders. In the ninth grade year some parents also filled out the questionnaires. The following figures were obtained:

1. Communication Seminar (was) (was not) a good idea.

| | Was | Was not | Number Responding |
|---|---|---|---|
| **STUDENTS** | | | |
| Eighth grade (1973) | 89% | 11% | 450 |
| Ninth grade (1972) | 94% | 6% | 636 |
| **TEACHERS** | | | |
| Eighth grade (1973) | 85% | 15% | 13 |
| Ninth grade (1972) | 50% | 50% | 6 |
| **PARENTS** | | | |
| Ninth grade (1972) | 86% | 14% | 14 |

2. Ideas about seminar (were) (were not) suggested to our group by discussion leader.

| | Were | Were not | Number Responding |
|---|---|---|---|
| **STUDENTS** | | | |
| Eighth grade (1973) | 56% | 44% | 445 |
| Ninth grade (1972) | 60% | 40% | (not recorded) |
| **TEACHERS** | 61% | 39% | 13 |

3. Discussion leader (did) (did not) encourage most of the group to speak.

|  | Did | Did not | Number Responding |
|---|---|---|---|
| **STUDENTS** | | | |
| Eighth grade (1973) | 83% | 17% | 459 |
| Ninth grade (1972) | 78% | 22% | (not recorded) |
| **TEACHERS** | | | |
| Eighth grade | 93% | 7% | 13 |

4. If future communication seminars are held, attendance should be (optional), (recommended), (required).

|  | Opt. | Rec. | Req. | Number Responding |
|---|---|---|---|---|
| **STUDENTS** | | | | |
| Eighth grade (1973) | 47% | 33% | 20% | 447 |
| Ninth grade (1972) | 18% | 49% | 33% | (not recorded) |
| **TEACHERS** | | | | |
| Eighth grade | 9% | 16% | 75% | 12 |

5. If future communication seminars are held, they should include the following grades: (7), (8), (9), (all).

|  | 7th | 8th | 9th | All | Number Responding |
|---|---|---|---|---|---|
| **STUDENTS** | | | | | |
| Eighth grade (1973) | 9% | 34% | 11% | 46% | |
| Ninth grade (1972) | 1% | 22% | 46% | 31% | |
| **TEACHERS** | | | | | |
| Eighth grade (1973) | 12% | 31% | 12% | 45% | 16 |

6. If future communication seminars were held during lunch period, I (would) (would not) attend.

|  | Would | Would not | Number Responding |
|---|---|---|---|
| **STUDENTS** | | | |
| Eighth grade (1973) | 26% | 74% | 441 |
| Ninth grade (1972) | 47% | 53% | (not recorded) |
| **TEACHERS** | 45% | 55% | 11 |

It is striking that 89% of eighth graders, 94% of ninth graders, and 85% of teachers in the eighth grade groups felt that the seminar was a "good idea." However, despite this overwhelmingly positive response to the seminar itself, only one-fifth to one-third of the students felt that the seminars should be required. In contrast, 75% of the teachers responding felt that these meetings should be compulsory. This could suggest that students of this age do not like the imposition of adult views, even if they agree.

It is puzzling that such a large percentage of students and teachers felt that ideas about the seminar were suggested by the group leaders. Without tape recordings of the meeting it is difficult to know exactly what might have been "suggested." It is possible that when group leaders summarized the theme or leading idea of a group discussion, this was seen as the suggestion of an idea. The set of responses to question (3) indicated overwhelmingly in both groups that the discussion leaders encouraged most of the group to speak. This would seem to contradict the previous set of answers in that it would indicate the leaders were truly interested in the opinions of the students.

Responses to question (6) indicated that a large percentage would prefer some time other than lunch. These responses would certainly suggest that in future seminars a first meeting should be required. Furthermore, this first meeting should occur during regular school hours rather than during lunch time or after school in order to obtain full attendance.

Interestingly, both eighth and ninth graders expressed opinions that the communication seminar should not be open to seventh graders but, by a small percentage, wished to reserve it for their own grade. However, a considerable number (31% and 46%) would like to include all students.

Of the 450 eighth grade students who filled out questionnaires, 138 made additional comments about the seminar. Thirty-six (26%) felt that the seminar was "hopeless" and a waste of time, that school people would not listen, and no suggestions would be honored. Thirty-six (26%) felt that the seminar should be longer; that two hours was not enough time for full discussion of the issues. Some of these 36 also felt that seminars should be held more frequently. Four (3%) thought the seminar took too long. Twenty-nine (21%) took the time to comment that they found the seminar "interesting and valuable." Fourteen (10%) expressed various criticisms without being totally negative. Nineteen (14%) offered suggestions for changing the structure and format. Unfortunately, similar comments from ninth graders were not collected.

*Follow-up one year later*

Questionnaires were distributed to the ninth grade students, requesting their reactions to the seminar. in which they had participated as eighth graders. Approximately 251 (47%) students responded to the follow-up, which consisted of seven closed questions and four open-ended inquiries. Procedural difficulties, not negative feelings, accounted for the low response.

Of these 251 responses, 187 (75%) indicated strong approval of the communication seminar.* Only 39 (15%) thought it was not a "good idea" while the remainder had no comment. However, in answering the question, "Was it a good or bad experience?" 139 (53%) of the students replied "good," with 39 (15%) giving the negative response. Seventy-seven (32%) were uncertain or noncommital in their responses to this item on the questionnaire. Thus it seems that after the passage of a year's time, these junior high students felt most positive about the *concept* of a communications seminar but less strongly about the actual experience.

A possible explanation of this disparity in evaluation may be found in an examination of the comments given in response to the open-ended questions. When asked, "What do you remember most?" about the seminar, 23 (9%) spontaneously mentioned their feelings that no one would respond to their suggestions. In response to the question, "Are there statements you would wish to say now that you did not then?" only 33 students replied. Five of these expressed dismay at the lack of any action or improvement following the seminar.

Most interesting, however, is the students' reactions to the question: "Any other statements?" Of the 43 students who took the time to reply to this quesion, 18 spoke in the same vein, expressing their disappointment and anger with the absence of any change. Whether the comment was quietly plaintive as in "our suggestions were not heard" or more brusquely frank—"Yea, stop asking so many questions and do something"—a number of these ninth grade students apparently had become aware that the year since the communication seminar had brought few visible changes in their school. When evaluating the seminar shortly after its occurrence the year before, 36 of the students had expressed rather unequivocally that "nothing would be done" while several more had suggested feelings of hopelessness and anger. A year later, almost the same number expressed this discontent. This 10% seems small for the expected number of apathetic students. Others may have been too apathetic to have recorded a response.

---

* Question: Do you think a communication seminar is a good idea?

It would appear that as junior high school students mature, they continue to seek out and welcome experiences which permit and encourage the coherent and safe expression of feelings but that as they undergo such experiences, they become more aware of the need for appropriate activities which will express and channel their concerns.

*Conclusions*

The potential value of a communication seminar, which encouraged the open, uncensored expression from eighth and ninth grade students about the quality of their education, was very striking. The need for administrative and teacher willingness to accept opinions or criticisms, whether they be mature or immature, seemed essential. Such an expression of opinion offered a valuable sampling of the feelings of the consumer about the educational process being delivered. To ensure optimum student participation, it is important to avoid any unconscious negative attitudes when the seminar is presented to the students. The degree of organization, the provision of student recorders, and the participation of teachers who may be in the room during the discussion are details which reflect to students the values or lack of values intended. The subsequent collation of recorder reports required some manpower and may need to be a part of some classroom task requiring the help of several interested teachers or other personnel, including volunteer parents.

It would be desirable, if follow-up committees are a part of the organization, to include students, teachers, and parents. In some ways this kind of opinion sampling might be considered a report card for the faculty and administration. Not all faculty and administration may be willing to be graded in this way. However, if receptivity is optimal, it would seem that valuable opinions are available.

One question which might arise is the value of this experience for the students in any particular school, in comparison with the values of a large after-school club program, increased group counseling, or optional lunchtime discussion groups. It was apparent from the questionnaire filled in by the students at this school that lunchtime discussion groups would be attended by only a few. Even though 25% or so of the students resented the communication seminar as being too long or taking time away from desired course study, it may be that the involuntary participation of the first meeting would be necessary in order to overcome the nondiscriminate rejection which many of the students would practice.

All in all, it would seem that this type of communication seminar or some variation of it might be considered as a valuable regularized part of the educational program in junior and possibly also senior high schools. It could well become an educational experience indicating respect for student attitudes, as well as obtaining valuable feedback for creating a relevant and responsive educational program.

CHAPTER 34

# Discussion Groups: Research into Normal Adolescent Behavior in a Junior High School

Maurice Vanderpol, M.D., and
Alfredo T. Suescum, M.D.

*Introduction*

ALTHOUGH BOTH PSYCHIATRY AND EDUCATION have their own traditions, expertise, and purpose, a common direction needs to be found. The bridge is built upon a basic tenet: *primary prevention in psychiatry safeguards healthy development, which in turn underlies sound education.* Educators stimulate and work with the growth process; psychiatrists or mental health workers prevent possible blocking of that development or advocate remedies or solutions if blocking has occurred. Educators cannot artificially separate intellectual, cognitive learning from the other processes of psychological learning and development. If they do, they reduce the learning experience to an exclusively compulsive rote integration of facts.

We could say that it is the purpose of our school study to define more clearly *how students relate to the school setting as they master the developmental tasks.* We need to know how these tasks are manifested and identified and how we can work with educators to make the schools relevant to the development of the child. Hopefully, we might work toward creating a school environment which will have optimal influence in preserving the psychological openness, allowing each child to find individual compromise solutions for the various developmental tasks that will result in optimal growth.

276

## Method

One of the difficult aspects of doing research involving young people is to get a picture reflecting to some depth what their inner life is like. Their expression of candidness and openness depends largely on the positive relationship one has built in a very careful way. Our model for the psychiatrist's relationship in the schools is similar to the *therapeutic alliance, a term used to describe the cooperative effort between the therapist and a patient.* The better the alliance, the higher the reliability factor of the material produced. This *type of alliance* is not something to be created in a few days or weeks. It needs to be built up gradually and carefully between psychiatrists, teachers, and children until all members fully contribute of their own expertise, knowledge, or personal experience. This makes it possible to gain insights of considerable depth and richness.

We have found that in order to build up an optimal alliance: (1) one has to be present in an informal way; (2) one is not necessarily active but shows active interest in what is going on; (3) one focuses on appropriate questions either by asking them of other members of the group or by answering appropriate questions ("No, we are not here because you are crazy"); and (4) one must clarify how cooperation might be increasingly possible and effective. In our approach with the students, *we defined the task as learning a lot more about what youngsters think in order to make schools better places for learning.* The best source for the answers to these questions is the youngsters themselves. This approach made them an active part of the research team. By doing these studies with children at different age levels simultaneously, we approximated the equivalent of a longitudinal study. We saw developmental issues evolve with the highlighting of such features as life styles, ability to abstract, specific age-appropriate preoccupations, affective components, and the influence of physical factors.

Practically speaking, we were seen in the schools as mental health professionals who were interested in people and how they functioned together. We were outside the formal structure of the school and had to develop our working relationship accordingly. We were available to anyone who felt the need to ask us to listen or get involved in some aspect of school life. We always tried to define the purpose of the task at hand and the roles expected to be played by each participant, whoever he or she might be. *Some groups were co-led with educators,* but the teaching and training of these educators was directed towards imparting better knowledge of adolescent psychology as well as styles of group leadership.

*The groups*

Our activities in the schools took many forms, organized by us or elicited by teachers, administrators, or students. In this chapter we want to restrict ourselves to our experiences with the *discussion groups* in a suburban junior high school. The groups consisted of 6 to 12 students, either of one sex or mixed. Forty-five-minute meetings were held on a once-a-week basis for 5 to 10 months. The membership was entirely voluntary. No students were referred by teachers or the guidance department. As one would expect at this age, many students decided to register in the group with one or more friends and rarely on an individual basis. The group usually included some students who had difficulties in the school. This suggested that they saw this experience as outside the school culture because of its openness and lack of judgmental attitudes.

The groups were not structured, and no explicit tasks were defined. The basic contract identified the purpose as one of "discussion," and therefore necessarily provided that respect would be shown for the verbal expressions of group members. No restrictions were imposed on content of discussion; content was confidential unless specific exceptions were agreed upon by the group. Candy or other food was sometimes used to make a situation more congenial. The group leader was identified as a psychiatrist or psychologist, and the students usually called him a "shrink." This term suggested curiosity and interest in looking at odd feelings and thoughts. The parents were notified that a psychiatrist was running a voluntary discussion group and that their child had indicated an interest in being a member. If the parents required more information, they might be in touch with the principal or the psychiatrist. The group meetings took place indoors or outdoors at a private location. Occasionally, guests were allowed to take part in the discussion. Usually, these were other students of the school.

To demonstrate the informal way we went about gathering the information, we will highlight some process and illustrate the content of some of the various groups. We had rejected a more formal approach, because we felt that we would lose important data at this stage of our research, if we had chosen a more directed or restricted course. The richness of the material can best be picked up while in the group. After each group session careful notes were made. These were *analyzed and discussed with educators and mental health professionals*, without violating confidentiality.

*A boys' group*

The first description is of a typical, lively, *seventh grade boys'* group with approximately 12 members. The psychiatrist suggested to them that there would be no predetermined topics, but freedom and the expectation (group task) that they could talk about anything they liked. This type of task seemed at first hard for them to accept, especially in the presence of an adult. Some boys handled their uneasiness by compulsive talking on irrelevant topics. Others—and we think this more characteristics of boys—reacted with motility, compulsive moving around, and getting into things in the room. In order to come to a more coordinated group effort, which happened toward the end of this particular session of group meetings, *they had to settle various issues of trust, activity-passivity, and peer approval.* For example, when the psychiatrist brought in potato chips and doughnuts at the first meeting, they immediately felt it necessary to rotate the responsibility for this among the members. One had the strong impression *that they defended against passivity,* and that the reaction was strong and immediate. On the other hand, equally characteristic was the fact that they did not react consistently but continued to accept the food that the leader supplied.

The *next big problem* they wanted to settle was the group leader's respect for material discussed. This concern was first directed at inanimate objects or at people not present in the room; their first concerted effort was the wish to put a firecracker in the public address speaker in the room to be sure no one outside could hear what they were talking about. They particularly fancied the principal was listening to every word; they feared this, but also wanted to be listened to. They watched the adult leader for feedback as to his interest and approval. They shifted to themselves by expressing great apprehension that events in the group would get out of hand, and they described in detail the incident of the previous school year when a homemade bomb was placed in the boys' room and exploded. They expressed serious disapproval of a few severely delinquent students in the school, mentioning them by name.

In subsequent sessions they were loud—eating, fighting, and testing the psychiatrist out as to whether he would set limits. They talked of appearing tough, big, small, bullying, strong, or weak. The student who was most advanced academically had been quite silent, while many of the others who were not as advanced as he were very verbal. (An observation shared by many teachers is that frequently the A students are less apt to enter freely into an open, unstructured discussion than those with lower grades.)

When the leader did not move in strongly to tone things down, anxiety rose among the students. One of them introduced the character of Captain Klutz, whose name suggested the man's unsatisfactory character. He was someone who was supposed to be a captain but was there to be an object of fun. The last test consisted of a repeated, off-hand proposition to talk about sex and to bring girls into the group. They also wanted to select a chairman. They were about to select one of the boys to chair the meetings when someone reminded them that, after all, the psychiatrist had started the group, and he was to be the leader. In other words, they clearly assigned the role to him and asked him to perform it.* It was as if they understood their anxieties and the need for protection against their own impulses. They saw the possibility of the group process leading to anarchy, loss of control, delinquency, and other unacceptable actions.

Related to dealing with these group issues, some of the more serious discussions took place around sensitivity about families and the different ways these operated. The boys voiced feelings of "never being big enough"; they observed that after thinking of themselves as big in sixth grade, they moved to the junior high school and were small again. This process repeated itself into high school, into college, and maybe several times after college in real life. As mentioned before, they were very concerned with "unacceptable" impulses. In brief ways they referred to sex, smoking, smoking marijuana, and drinking.

During the *tenth meeting,* the psychiatrist announced that the group would terminate after a few more meetings. The boys dealt with this in a rather elaborate way. They became convinced that the reason the adult leader had the interest to start such a group was to see "how stupid" they were. Another time, one boy started hitting the psychiatrist "in fun."

In the *next-to-the-last meeting* they decided to have a round robin of dirty jokes. This made it more apparent that they once again wanted to reassure themselves that they could be with an adult and indulge in expressing sexual fantasies without being severely punished. Many of the jokes were rather typical, sexual jokes, but one was rather interesting and possibly characteristic of this age. The story was about a huge woman who was going to have intercourse with a man but prior to this had put a belt around her waist very tightly, so that she was bound in. When the man entered her, she suddenly released the belt and sucked the man in, *in toto.* This joke was greeted with great hilarity, and it highlighted many expressed fears of women. Every time a joke was told, the boys looked at the adult closely to catch his reaction.

Elaborate plans were made for a party for the *last meeting.* Food was

---

* Editor's note: Some of these events might be seen as indicating age-appropriate anger at an unstructured group situation, fear of loss of control, and spontaneously self-instituted controls, with the recognition of a need for adult assistance.

brought in by the mothers. The food and drink were gorged. Then everyone sat around deliberating what was going to happen to close the last group meeting. They decided to tell dirty jokes, and an exact repetition of all the jokes of the previous time ensued. Handling of loss and separation was done by different boys in their own different ways. One boy eulogized the psychiatrist as if he had died. Some of the more kinetic boys started acting up. One boy, who was going to move out of the community shortly, acted this out by isolating himself in a tent-like structure in the room.

*A girls' group*

We began meeting with a group of 10 seventh grade girls, and were interested in the quality of differences from the boys' group. The basic preoccupations were, in important ways, entirely different. In comparison to the boys, there was less motility, moving around, or acting out. Their relationship to the psychiatrist as group leader was entirely different.* They were much more concerned about what the psychiatrist thought of them, not in the sense of approval, but rather in the sense of whether they were good enough or whether something was wrong or deficient about them. They verbalized their concerns more easily than did the boys, and showed little evidence of competition as to who would be in charge. Physical or intellectual power and strength were not relevant. It was much more a matter of who knew more everyday shocking information and who was freer to express feelings and thoughts.

This agreed with our findings that social maturity is a greater determinant of the girl's position than physical or intellectual maturity. They had very little trouble accepting the way the group was set up, that is, its being unstructured with no specific topic of discussion. They seemed to have little difficulty with some changes in group membership. They had their own topics of discussion, which seemed to arise very naturally. One thing they had in common with the boys was the expression of fear of the opposite sex. The boys had described how strong women were and illustrated it particularly by the aforementioned joke. The girls felt that the boys were stronger. They revealed a certain amount of fear of boys and their strength, particularly expressed in the idea that therefore something must be wrong with the girls themselves.

A great deal of concern was expressed about what the psychiatrist or the

---

* Editor's Note: The concerns of these sessions would likely have been very different with female leadership.

principal might ask of them. Characteristically, one of the most outspoken girls, whose name was Lillian, wanted to be called "Bruce." These girls had a great deal of preoccupation with their bodies and whether something might be wrong with them. This seemed to center around the sexual function and anatomy. The girl "Bruce" mentioned with pride that a boy had called her a "hole." Puzzled by this, the girls asked her for an explanation. She said that "hole," although written "h-o-l-e," can be written "w-h-o-l-e." To her this meant that there was something complete about her. She felt this was what the boy meant, and it made her very proud. They had to keep many private thoughts secret, producing guilt. They felt their *reputations might be ruined* if they talked about these thoughts.

Several girls stressed that their mothers wanted very much to find out what was being discussed in the group, but that this was a secret and they would never breathe a word. Nevertheless, they seemed interested in letting mother know some of the things they were talking or thinking about while in the group, though they were not necessarily verbalizing them. One other topic of conversation, accompanied by great glee and excitement, had to do with the fights their parents had in the bedroom. These perceptions were obviously sexually linked and probably appealed to many violent, primal-scene fantasies girls have at this age, revived from earlier years.

Another interesting event occurred at one session when, for a solid 45 minutes, they "dumped" severely and unabatedly on one female teacher, whom they all hated with a passion. Never had we witnessed such intense dislike and hatred for a teacher without anyone saying a few nice words to compensate. What could be the reason for this display? She was described as very punitive to any girl or boy who showed any sexual interest. At the same time, she would act very seductively, for example, displaying her legs when a male teacher came into the room. The children became confused, frightened, and very upset, because she stimulated their sexual fantasies and at the same time exaggerated the "badness."

### A mixed group

A mixed seventh grade boy-and-girl group of 12 members illustrated even more dramatically the involvement of strong dynamics. The unconscious coping was indicated through topographical arrangements in the room and self-selection of seats. The girls sat together, and the boys sat together. Frequently, the boys would shut out the girls by sitting closer to the leader. One boy who showed confusion about his sexual identity in certain ways formed the link between the boys' and girls' groups. Because of frequent disruption, the leader made a slight change in the seating arrangement. This created panic in the child who was moved and great disruption in the group as a whole. The move aroused strong feelings of anxiety because the security of the established seating arrangement had been disturbed.

Many times the girls brought up topics that they thought would be interesting to discuss. The boys, partly in competition and partly because they were uncomfortable with the topics, united defensively against the girls and out-shouted them, so that there was no chance to work on the proposed topic. The various children were in more or less advanced stages of adolescent development. One more mature girl seductively invited the adult leader to enter the group discussion. Two girls, less easy about the adult's role, actually excluded him, as did two boys who were ill at ease. It was apparent that because the maturational factors varied in this particular group, more had to be done before the group could function in any cohesive way. The ground work *necessary* for cohesiveness can usually be handled very well by one or more of the students. They can do a very effective job of bringing the group together by calmly verbalizing some of the difficult feelings and concerns and by handling these together with the group leader.

These groups give the observer a unique and unusual opportunity to observe some of the indigenous teen-age games and topics of conversation. For example, during the fifth session of a seventh and eighth grade mixed group, they talked for half an hour about their opinion that movie ratings should be based on violent rather than sexual content. To the leader's surprise, this discussion provided the opening gambit for discussion of a 19-year-old's suicide, which had occurred three days previously. This was an act of violence of more immediate concern than any movie.

At the *last session* of this group they demonstrated *a game called "chicken."* In this game a boy stared at a certain girl's breast area until she became very uncomfortable and started giggling and jiggling. In reverse, a girl would look at a boy's crotch until he became completely uncomfortable and embarrassed. These were visual sexual interest games that did not involve any touching or more advanced sexual acting out. They are considered parlor games and are done by average boys and girls of this age. They are, to be sure, performed with a great amount of hilarity, tension, and excitement. On the other hand, it greatly amazed us how these young people at times were able to verbalize deeper feelings about themselves and each other in a tactful, sensitive, and intuitively correct way that would put many adults to shame.

*Discussion*

Within the general framework of a working alliance between psychiatrists and educators we describe one particular aspect illustrating the thinking and reaction patterns of seventh and eighth graders in discussion groups. When the psychiatrists started groups, it served to study those spontaneous group and individual patterns in a setting free from curriculum and other adult-imposed restrictions. We began to use these groups by *co-leading them with educators* to demonstrate psychological activities present but not as obvious in the traditional classroom setting. The richness helped the teachers and the mental health professionals to understand more about hitherto unexplained phenomena evident in the traditional classroom.

It was striking from the descriptions of the groups how much vital material and how many basic issues were thought of and felt by these students. At this age the students felt a certain loneliness and need to talk, but they hid this need lest they meet rejection. There is the suggestion that if the institution offers a setting such as a relatively safe group discussion, many students will eagerly accept the opportunity. Components of the developmental tasks of early adolescence become evident: coping with sexual and aggressive impulses, intense affects, and external authority and representatives of primal figures (parents). These coping mechanisms, some of them basic and primitive, are often unacceptable in the classroom—for example, the use of nonspecific moving about (motility) to relieve tension, especially by boys. Disturbing as this may be in a traditional classroom, this type of motility can be seen as an attempt at initiative by the student which is relevant to the development of skills in interpersonal relationships.

The anecdotal material impressed us with the primitive and concrete quality of intense feelings. The girls were preoccupied with body integrity, body injury, and bleeding—the body being "hole" versus "whole." The boys were interested in the example of the woman swallowing the man vaginally. Abstract-logical and symbolic thinking seemed to be developing and gave the ego more ways to channel feelings and fantasies. Not until older adolescence does the process of bleeding become more realistically associated with menstruation, for example. Categorical or philosophical preoccupations such as truth and justice are also of later date. In younger adolescents, interpersonal relationships are more often transacted through body language.

In one seventh grade group a change could be seen in use of coping mechanisms dealing with various emotional tasks, between early and late in the school year. The anxiety tolerance improved, as did the ability to verbalize and use confrontation, while motility and action decreased. Fantasies were richer, and concreteness was less evident. One could also notice a change from a need to meet many new people, students, and teachers, to a more discriminating pattern with fewer people and closer relationships. It was as if initially there had been a greater need to connect the new inner experiences to many external objects and situations. The new class and teaching arrangements may have been of importance here; i.e., the change from the elementary school one class-one teacher situation to the junior high school many different classes-different teachers situation. Many schools, however, unknowingly make it very difficult for the students to go beyond the multiple relationships because of the distance or unavailability of one particular teacher to a student.

Although these discussion groups were not intended to be therapeutic in any sense, they offered interesting opportunities for some uncovering of psychopathology and help in coping with it. One boy was quite depressed when a change in his family structure occurred over which he had no control. A seventh grade girl, who was severely overweight and a loner, was able to make contact with other members of the group and express some of her difficult feelings about her weight problem, her isolation, and her mother's overprotectiveness.

The groups also gave us an opportunity to observe the students' reaction to serious and disturbing events. They talked about these in group sessions, but less so outside the group and rarely in the classroom. Cases in point concerned a 19-year-old boy's suicide, an 18-year-old's death from heroin, and other such tragic events. The instance of the universally disliked teacher showed how the young people easily projected their own confused age-appropriate feelings to adults, almost to observe the way the adults would handle these issues. The average healthy adult by behavior or response will clarify the issues involved and in a certain way either give the growing adolescents a model or help them to have a corrective emotional experience. If the adult does not clearly refute these projections, the young person can be left in an anxious, helpless confusion, potentially damaging to growth.

By observing the dynamics of this process in our discussion groups, the psychiatrist as adult-model helped the youngsters work through the projected feelings in order to achieve a partial resolution of these infantile fantasies. For the boys, he was at first the forbidding, punitive father they admired and hated, as well as the weak, permissive father they wanted to destroy. For the girls, he was not only the man whose support they needed to prove their worthwhileness and to keep it a secret from mother, but also the sadistic violator who saw a girl as a "hole" with a body around it. The fact of having secrets from mother seemed more important than what the secrets were about. These fantasies are not pathological but are aspects of normal growth, to which psychiatrist and teacher alike can respond. The girl, Lillian, alias "Bruce," who played such a dominant role and was such an admired figure in this group, was not remembered at all by other group members in a two-year follow-up. This indicated the transient importance and subsequent repression of some of the difficult impulses.

## Educational applications

All these studies done in the school by two disciplines created an *atmosphere of mutual insights and cross-fertilization.* Many relevant exchanges of knowledge occurred. For example, the losses and separations that occur so frequently in school life were discussed as to relating them with English poetry and prose which describes the process of grief and mourning. The psychiatrist can help the teacher by providing other insights and some basic psychodynamics of the loss experience.* In turn, the educator can then be more knowledgeable in helping children express these feelings, as painful as they may be. Accepting and working out feelings about loss is an important part of life, for child and adult.

Another outstanding feature of importance to the management of junior high school students is the *need they show for a high level of tension and excitement,* which many can sustain for long periods of time. For the faculty to force this level down is often futile and counterproductive. To supply feasible ways of working out the tension and excitement could be very helpful to everyone concerned. It can be good to realize that early adolescence is an exciting period of life in ways which may seem strange or even contrived in the eyes of people of other ages.

These useful findings were but two of the several which arose from this fascinating journey into the junior high school culture via unstructured discussion groups.

## BIBLIOGRAPHY

BUXBAUM, E. (1945). Transference and group formation in children and adolescents. *Psychoanalytic Study of the Child,* Vol. I, pp. 351-366. New York: International Universities Press.

---

* See Chapter 39.

ERIKSON, E. H. (1959). Identity and the life cycle. *Psychol. Issues*, 1:1.

FRIEDMAN, L. (1969). The therapeutic alliance. *Int. J. Psychoanal.*, 50, 139-155.

HARTMANN, H. (1958). *Ego Psychology and the Problem of Adaptation.* New York: International Universities Press.

INHELDER, B. and PIAGET, J. (1958). *The Growth of Logical Thinking from Childhood to Adolescence.* New York: Basic Books.

JONES, M. C. and BAYLEY, N. (1950). Physical maturing among boys as related to behavior. *J. of Ed. Psychol.*, 41.

KAHNE, M. J. (1969). Psychiatrist observer in the classroom. *Med. Trial Technique Quarterly*, June, p. 81.

OFFER, D. (1969). *The Psychological World of the Teen-ager.* New York: Basic Books.

OFFER, D. and OFFER, J. (1969). A follow-up study of normal adolescence. *Seminars in Psychiatry*, 1, 46-56.

SCHIFF, S. K. and KELLAM, S. G. (1967). Community-wide mental health program of prevention and early treatment in first grade, in *Poverty and Mental Health*, Research Report of American Psychiatric Association, No. 21.

SNYDER, B. (1967). *Report on Massachusetts Institute of Technology Students' Adaptation Study.* Cambridge: Education Research Center, M.I.T.

SNYDER, B. (1971). *The Hidden Curriculum.* New York: Alfred Knopf.

STICKNEY, S. B. (1968). Schools are our community mental health center. *Am. J. of Psychiat.*, 124, 101-108.

WINNICOTT, D. W. (1965). *The Maturational Processes and the Facilitating Environment.* New York: International Universities Press.

WOLFF, P. H. (1960). The developmental psychologies of Jean Piaget and psychoanalysis. *Psychol. Issues*, 2:1.

CHAPTER 35

# Using Sensitivity Training with Junior High School Students

Uri Rueveni, Ph.D.

TODAY MANY SCHOOLS are seeking new ways to modify the classroom behavior of disruptive students. One such effort, to be described here, has involved the use of sensitivity training by the formation of a "T-group" of *15 aggressive junior high school students* whose behavior has been characterized by destructiveness, truancy, and fighting. The experiment took place during the last five months of the 1969-70 school term in an inner city junior high school in Philadelphia, attended primarily by Blacks and Puerto Ricans. Its success led to the formation of a similar group this school year.

The program was developed in response to a request from the junior high school's unity team, a decision-making body composed of counselors, teachers, the vice principal, and parents. Located in a heavily populated Black neighborhood, the school has about 1,500 students, 95 percent of whom are Black and the remainder Puerto Rican. The unity team approached the author early in the 1969-70 school year, seeking a consultant to organize and conduct an in-school program for students who were manifesting behavioral problems.

As a school consultant, I—a white male psychologist—agreed to work with the unity team in devising a program. After several meetings we decided to establish a sensitivity training group for students with whom teachers had been unable to cope. A counselor at the school—a Black woman—was named co-leader.

From the beginning we attempted to make the program known to the

---

Reprinted with permission from *Children*, 18, 69-72, March-April, 1971.

entire school faculty. In addition to describing the proposed program and its purpose at a faculty meeting, we sent a letter about it to each teacher.

The teachers were asked to submit names of students who would be likely candidates for such a program. Thirty names were submitted. The co-leader and another school counselor contacted each of the students whose names were suggested. After a discussion of the purpose and goals of the group, the students were asked if they wished to join the group, and it was made clear that participation would be a voluntary choice on their part. Twenty students accepted, but five dropped out during the first two weeks.

The continuing group included *10 Black and 5 Puerto Rican students from 13 to 15 years of age—8 boys and 7 girls*. It met for two hours once a week for five months, closing only at the end of the school year.

## Rationale and objectives

Sensitivity training may be defined as learning to develop an increased awareness of the nature of one's own feelings and behavior based on experience in a group situation. The basic data for such learning are generated by the group members themselves, from their past experiences, and from their current interaction with other members of the group.

Sensitivity training methods have been used therapeutically in a variety of settings—for example, residential institutions, psychiatric clinics, and hospitals. In a recent study, Pollack (1969) used sensitivity training as an approach to group therapy with 8- to 10-year-old students; he found that teachers and counselors reported noticeable improvement in the behavior of such students. My own work with adult schizophrenic patients has suggested that the techniques of sensitivity training enhance conditions that foster group support and trust for a troubled person and his or her family.

The program in the Philadelphia junior high school was initiated primarily to find out whether 13-, 14-, and 15-year-old students who acted out their problems through disruptive behavior would be able to create some common bonds, share mutual concerns, begin to understand the nature of their own behavior, and explore their relationships with other students, their teachers, and parents. We were not so much interested in analyzing all the children's behavioral problems as in developing their ability to communicate and to manage their feelings in the here and now.

Our objectives were to help the students increase (1) their *social sensitivity* (perceptions of and feelings about the personalities and emotions of other children, teachers, school personnel), and (2) their *behavioral flexi-*

*bility* (ability to act appropriately in situations of an interpersonal nature that they encounter daily in and out of school). We believed that through the group process of interaction and sharing of experiences, the students would learn to modify some of their earlier behavior patterns and seek new approaches or alternatives in situations that require interpersonal skills.

## Procedures

During the sessions we used a variety of group techniques and exercises to enhance the group process and realize our objectives.* The following are some of the exercises that we introduced:

1. *The grab bag.* A paper bag filled with slips of paper is passed around the group. Each slip contains a familiar word, such as school, teachers, counselor, anger, fight, hate, and cool. Each group member picks one slip of paper, reads the word on it, and describes his or her feelings about the word to the rest of the group.

This game-like exercise was beneficial because it encouraged many of the teen-agers for the first time to express in words their feelings about their own behavior and their concerns with the school setting. We had selected words that we thought would evoke the emotions of these students. Initially, the student responses were negative. Their reactions to the word "school" were "boring," "I don't like it"; to the word "counselor," "we can never see her," "too busy"; to the word "fight," "I like it"; to the word "teachers," "they don't understand." At this time we leaders merely listened, recognizing the students' feelings of disappointment and frustration, but refusing to take sides or lecture. We encouraged the students to express deeper feelings about these words. As the program progressed, the students changed thir concepts significantly. Teachers became more "friendly." School became "a good place to know friends" or a place where "we can really learn if teachers will listen to us." Several students made a more positive association with the word "fight": "We don't have to fight."

2. *Strength bombardment.* The teen-agers take turns being "it" and sitting in the center of the circle. All the group members in turn describe what they like about the ones who are "it," and express all of the positive feelings they have toward them.

This exercise evoked much feeling in the group. At each meeting almost all of the group members wanted to be "it." The teen-agers were visibly delighted when they received positive feedback. When teen-agers who were

---

* Editor's note: See Chapter 15.

"it" heard a strength identified that they did not expect to hear, they usually reacted with surprise, saying, "Who, me?" "You must be kidding," or "I am not like this at all." We encouraged expressions of positive feelings.

3. *Blind walk.* The participants divide into two-member teams, with one member playing the role of leader and the other of blind follower. With eyes closed, the followers rely on the leaders to take their arm and guide them on a walk around the classroom. After five minutes, the members exchange roles.

In this exercise, three teachers and two other counselors who had expressed interest in sensitivity training joined our group. *Each adult was paired with a teen-ager,** and the other teen-agers worked with each other. The leaders were instructed to provide experiences in which the blind partner would substitute the senses of touch, hearing, and smell for sight; followers were instructed to use all their other faculties to perceive what was happening and to determine the mood of those in the room without opening their eyes.

After everyone in the group had played both roles, the members discussed what they had learned. Teachers and counselors said that being dependent on a teen-ager sharpened their awareness of leader-follower relationships with students. Students said they gained a clearer understanding of some of the teachers' problems.

4. *Free time.* During this exercise each group member teams up with another one to plan and engage in a 10-minute activity.

The group members liked this exercise because it enabled them to make noise and be physically active in the classroom without being censored or stopped. The most popular activities included mock fighting or boxing, particularly between the boys; playing the guitar; dictating into the tape recorder; singing "soul" songs; telling jokes; and planning a party.

5. *Expressing negative feelings.* A "speaker" selected by members of the group sits in the center of a circle and expresses his or her negative feelings toward teachers, principals, other members of the school staff, and other students. Then another "speaker" is selected to do the same.

For many group members, this exercise was more difficult than strength bombardment. As we expected, it was harder for the students to deal with their negative than their positive emotions. Initially, we encountered much reluctance to talk about negative feelings, but as the group developed, more students became able to express the hostility they felt toward school and persons in the school environment. When a "speaker" expressed dislike of

---

* Editor's italics.

other students, a prolonged, angry exchange with members of the group often ensued.

We found that although this experience evoked tension, most students could accept the criticism and deal with it constructively. We felt our role was to try to understand the anger and let the student express it verbally, but not physically. We tried to encourage the students to explore further the feelings they had toward other persons and what such feelings meant to themselves and to others.

Although they did not seem to feel guilty when expressing anger toward teachers, many obviously felt guilty when expressing negative feelings toward other students. We were primarily concerned with helping the teenagers who felt guilty toward other students become able to communicate their feelings to the members of the sensitivity training group, who in turn would react with each other on different levels of awareness. As the teenagers learned to share their feelings, members of the sensitivity group developed greater trust in each other.

In one instance, a teen-ager's negative comment about another member of the group provided the stimulus for a physical confrontation. The boy who was "put down" threw a chair at the "speaker," and they began to fight. Both were gasping for breath when we separated them. After an emotional discussion by the entire group, the two students made up. During the remainder of the program they became close friends.

*Student and teacher reactions*

We received many reports from teachers that the students attending the program were enthusiastic about it. Several of the students approached their teachers to tell them what went on in the group. We encouraged the teachers to listen and to help these students transfer their enthusiasm to their own classroom.

We also encouraged some of the students who expressed continuing anger toward authority figures to tell their teachers about it. We found that in those students who did so, a change occurred in their perception of their teachers and school. Students reported that in many instances when they expressed some negative feelings, the teachers seemed to appreciate their frankness. Toward the end of the experiment many of the students asked to participate in future groups. Some of those students were invited to discuss their ideas with the unity team, which was then planning a similar program for the next school year. Some of their comments:

"I like this best of all of my subjects." "It's a cool program." "Boy, it's really great to come in here and do what you feel like doing." "I didn't know school could do this for me."

The majority of the teachers who had students in the program were highly supportive. Some teachers, however, complained that their students' perceptions of them were inaccurate and the criticisms were unfair. We dealt with these teachers individually, inviting them to observe or participate in the sensitivity training exercises to help them understand the nature of the students' interaction.

Near the end of the 1969-70 school year, with the support of the unity team, we initiated a staff development program designed to improve the skills of the entire faculty in solving behavioral problems of students, in dealing with situations involving other interpersonal relationships, and in increasing interstaff communication. This program ran concurrently with the sensitivity training.

## Some observations

Initially we hesitated to embark upon the program because we did not know how it would turn out, and because we anticipated less than enthusiastic support from students and faculty. As the program progressed, our perception became clearer, and we became more confident that sensitivity training can have a meaningful effect on the school. Many teachers told us that changes had occurred in their own attitudes toward the students in our group, whom they now perceived more positively than before the group began.

Incidents of truancy and aggression among the students who participated in sensitivity training were lower last spring than at the beginning of the program. Based on this and other results achieved in the 1969-70 group, my co-leader and other school counselors are conducting another sensitivity training group this year.

I am convinced that sensitivity training has a major potential for use with junior high school students who present behavioral problems during school hours. The group experience helps such students view their own behavior, as well as their teachers' and other students' behavior, in a different light. Many of the teen-agers who participated in our group, for example, have increased their social sensitivity as well as their behavioral flexibility, and are now able to act more appropriately in interpersonal situations with other students and their teachers.

## BIBLIOGRAPHY

GARWOOD, D. S. (1967). The significance and dynamics of sensitivity training programs. *Int. J. Group Psychother.*, 17, 457-472.

HANSON, P. G., ROTHAUS, P., JOHNSON, D. L., and LYLE, F. A. (1966). Autonomous groups in human relations training for psychiatric patients. *J. Appl. Behav. Sci.*, 2, 305-324.

HARRISON, R. (1966). Cognitive change and participation in a sensitivity training laboratory. *J. Consult. Psychol.*, 30, 517-520.

LAKIN, M., and GARSON, R. C. (1966). A therapeutic vehicle in search of a theory of therapy. *J. Appl. Behav. Sci.*, 2, 27-40.

POLLACK, D. (1969). A sensitivity training approach to group therapy with children. Unpublished paper delivered to a PTA meeting at the child guidance center, Los Angeles, California.

RUBIN, I. (1967). The reduction of prejudice through laboratory training. *J. Appl. Behav. Sci.*, 3, 29-50.

RUEVENI, U., and SPECK, R. V. (1969). Using encounter group techniques in the treatment of the social network of the schizophrenic. *Int. J. Group Psychother.*, 19, 405-500.

## PART III: D. OTHER USEFUL GROUPS IN JUNIOR AND SENIOR HIGH SCHOOLS

## EDITOR'S NOTE

*The next four articles about small group experiences in high schools represent for the most part a different focus than the high school groups described in the previous sections. Three of these four articles describe attempts to use small group process to effect a change in the campus milieu, atmosphere, and sociodynamics. This change was desired to deal with increasing group conflict and shifting forces in the student as well as faculty group.*

*The articles in the previous sections demonstrate the usefulness of small group process for helping the student who is not making it in the system of the school. The articles in this section demonstrate the usefulness of small group process in providing communication and sharing of attitudes in a system which is satisfying too few of its component members, and which is approaching the danger of eruption or breakdown.*

*The school which provided the leadership group (Chapter 36) did break down because of a teacher strike. This happening did not necessarily invalidate the usefulness of the small group. Here the small group in the larger system helped individuals better survive the catastrophe. Some small groups may at times possibly help the system avoid the catastrophe as described in Chapter 38 and, to an extent, in Chapter 37. Use of a small group in such cases, e.g., as in Chapter 37, does not necessarily imply a temporizing pacification procedure to avoid more basic necessary changes. If a problem is severe and pervasive enough, it is doubtful that any program of small groups channeling off feelings of anger will prevent appropriate protest and attack on the problem. The small groups may help many students maintain some balance in a difficult situation, while rumblings and push for change occur in the community or legislature, or the school. Some groups, at times, have had significant action components, for example, the classroom groups described by Berlin (1972).*

## BIBLIOGRAPHY

BERLIN, I. N. (1972). The school's role in a participatory democracy. *Am. J. Orthopsych.*, 42:3, 499-507.

CHAPTER 36

# A High School Leadership Group

## Samuel Black, M.D.

THE TYPE OF GROUP TO BE DESCRIBED HERE is based on the premise that if all leaders of the student body were more aware of their position as leaders, the responsibilities of leadership, and their own vulnerability to manipulation, they could discharge the leadership role more effectively. Communication with teachers and administration would be facilitated, and some of the anger generated in teacher-student and administrator-student confrontations might be reduced. If student leaders could learn better to appraise the situation and choose techniques that best fit the person and situation, it was hoped less regression to power-protecting, angry confrontations might occur. Student leader responses so often were largely a combination of intuitive reactions and the manipulations of their followers, but not necessarily appraisal of the situation. With little formal training to fall back upon, the students were more apt to act impulsively and not necessarily in their own best interests. They were not able to clearly define goals for accomplishment. Frustration and anger made them less effective with the administration and teachers in reaching their objectives.

In the spring of 1970, an attempt was made to institute this type of group at a Los Angeles high school. The initial step was to make contact with the school in order to introduce the author and the idea of the group into the school's operating system. The original hope was to begin the group in September as close to the start of school as possible. While the initial preparations were made in August 1969, the first actual group meeting was not held until April 1970.

The school* was in a transitional period. It had formerly served a

---

* This is the same school as described in Chapters 23 and 27.

middle-income population with a large percentage of academically oriented Jewish students. Recent alterations of the population in the school district resulted in a substantial increase in minority students—Blacks, Mexican-Americans, and Orientals. The stresses inherent in this transitional period may have influenced some or all of the experiences that occurred in the establishment of the student group. It certainly influenced the purpose and type of group to be formed. The alteration of the student population had introduced changes in the forces in the student body, as well as in the faculty.

In the past, leadership had been demonstrated by academic and athletic excellence. Student leaders usually received good grades or were active in some extracurricular activity. They represented the expectations of the school's teachers and administrators. Teachers were, for the most part, culturally homogeneous and held common expectations and agreement as to the students' school commitment.

With the changing student population, modifications were made in the teacher population. Some teachers reflected the past makeup of the school, and their aims and expectations were more clearly identified with the previous traditional approach to education and school functioning. They related better to well-behaved adolescents, whose motivation and academic aptitude made them a pleasure to teach. Other teachers tried to be more flexible in the type of student they could handle. They were more willing to innovate in an attempt to meet the varied needs of the new student population. Still other teachers represented a radicalized approach to education. They felt that traditional approaches were unlikely to work and that different approaches were necessary to touch upon the many needs inherent in the new student population.

An example of this latter approach was the teacher who felt that a sense of commitment in the students could be generated by giving the youngsters books of matches and telling them it was their school. The teachers were to leave, and if on the next day the school had not been burned down, it could be inferred that the students were committed to the school. (Several months after this concept had been heard, a student did burn down a significant portion of the school.)

In this atmosphere the formulation of the group began with the *basic concept of helping the group members become more effective leaders.* The students chosen for the group were not necessarily the traditional student body officers, heads of school organizations, or members of sports teams. They were the students who actually asserted leadership regardless of the positions they held in the school. It was felt the elected student body officers acted as leaders to only a small part of the student body and that other student leaders within the school represented or led various groups. These groups included the Black Students Union, the Brown Berets, and groups without official names who made up a group entity within the school. Thus, the group to be formed would include the leaders within the school regardless of grades, office holding, or state of favor with teachers and administrators.

The theory for the group was that a representative group of such student leaders coming together once a week would result in an increased awareness of the responsibilities of leadership. Secondarily, it was felt also that this increased awareness would place them in a better position to perform their roles as leaders.

### Entry into the system

After several meetings with individual members of the administration, including the principal, the school nurse, and the boys' and girls' vice-principals, a meeting was set with a *representative group of 15 teachers*. The intention of this meeting was to offer an opportunity for the teachers to meet me and raise questions as to the purpose of such a group. If there then was a feeling of acceptance of the plan for the group, it was hoped that the process of choosing the students might be initiated. The teachers subjected me to a thorough interrogation. Ultimately, they accepted the concept and began to suggest students for the group. The school nurse acted as my liaison with the school. She coordinated various arrangements, as well as receiving comments from students, teachers, and administration. The lack of direct communication did create some problems, with information not always being correctly received.

It was agreed that teachers should speak to individual students in order to explain the basic idea, to mention the voluntary nature of the project, and to give the students the location and time for the first meeting. The teachers' group had been a cross section of the total teacher population, and each suggested students they considered to be leaders. Many of the teachers served as advisors for such groups as the Brown Berets, Black Students' Union, and student body officers.

The *first group meeting* was not held until the first of April. This was much later in the year than had been hoped. It meant the group would have barely three months to run until termination in June. The length of time necessary to set up the project was longer than had been anticipated, but it would have been difficult to have reduced the time. Hopefully, subsequent groups would be formed and begun with less delay.

Because the teachers had chosen the students and explained the plan and purpose of the group, I had not previously met any of the students. I knew their names and had some information on their activities and the teachers' reactions to them. I think there was some initial awkwardness because of this. I felt afterward that it would have been *preferable to have met with each prospective student individually prior* to the start of group. The initial meeting presented an opportunity for them to meet me and hear from me the purpose of the group. I elaborated on this after initial introductions.

The group appeared quiet and reserved. I could sense that I was being appraised and that their first impressions would be very influential in the subsequent group process. I felt it was necessary to set a few limits and invited the group to raise any questions they might have as to rules. I explained that I would not be lecturing, that no note taking would be necessary, and that there would be no tests or quizzes. The group was to be entirely voluntary, so attendance would not be taken. The students did miss class to attend sessions. A problem was presented on several occasions when students had to miss group meetings in order to attend important classes or tests. While an after-school group would have eliminated this problem, such events as athletic practice and buses would have caused the same difficulty.

When the students asked about smoking cigarettes during group, I felt they were attempting to test me, since the school had a well-known rule against smoking in the classrooms. I reiterated that because of the school rule there could be *no smoking.* They quietly accepted it without further questions on the subject or any attempts at smoking. While no formal discussion on the use of profanity took place, this was covertly dealt with by my allowing the use of any language necessary to express ideas and feelings. Probably the school had a rule against profanity, but I felt comfortable in not putting any limits on their language but not allowing smoking.

The overall most important aspect of the first group meeting was *trust.* I felt we were all sizing each other up to see whether we could trust each other and that several lines of credibility were being examined: (1) the group's confidence in me; (2) my faith in the group; and (3) reliance between individual members. My belief in individual members of the group was distinguishable but separate from my trust of the entire group.

### Disruption of group by outside events (teachers' strike)

At the end of the first meeting, when the students expressed a desire to continue past our allotted time, I explained that it was necessary for the meeting to stop on time but that we would meet again the next week, if they were in agreement. Their response was positive and willing. I left the meeting feeling encouraged and eagerly looking forward to the second weekly meeting. Unfortunately, the Los Angeles U.S.D. teachers went on strike during that week. When I returned for the second meeting, only 3 of the 10 students were there. The school was in turmoil over the strike; many classes were not meeting, and teachers were picketing outside the school. Students were either staying at home entirely or coming to school and leaving early. All group members were contacted after this second meeting by the school nurse. It was decided that the group should meet outside the school, as most of the students would not cross the picket line.

At the *second meeting,* discussion centered on the strike and its significance to the students. The small attendance and concerns over the strike interfered with a continued flow of the first group meeting. The tremendous impact of the teachers' strike was more than the group could handle at this stage. Had 8 to 10 sessions taken place prior to the strike, the effect could have been different. Possibly by then established group process could have absorbed the emotional impact of the strike and enabled the youngsters to define their feelings and roles to a greater extent. Subsequent groups convened across the street from the school on a church lawn. The majority of students attended, but the initial basic question of trust did not get or become established.

Since I had not had time to gain the students' confidence prior to the strike, my reliability was not firmly established, and my position was not integral to the group. As the members' views on the strike varied, they did not trust each other in discussing it. Some meaningful discussion took place in this area, but I felt it did not approach the magnitude that might have been expected. The group moved back inside the school after the strike and continued to meet until the end of the school year. Major themes during this time included an examination by the students of their position within the school, the amount of their power, the extent to which they could use it, and how they could bring about change. The leaders attempted to become more aware in determining what they really wanted as opposed to what their followers wanted and were pushing them to express. This latter concept was very illuminating for the students, and they were excited in exploring it. Many of the students had not really been aware of their role as leaders, and they began to see themselves more clearly in discussions of leadership qualities.

*Accomplishments*

The process of the group after the strike did come closer to the original design of the project. Members were able to comment on each other's behavior and to point out in a non-threatening manner the consequences of such behavior. I was able to take a more passive role in this regard and let the students do more. It seemed evident that they could relate to the area of leadership but would need initial education from the group leader's comments regarding examination of behavior within the group. Previous group experiences did not necessarily prepare these young people for the type of process that examines behavior and feeling in an atmosphere that is not threatening, not judgmental, and not punitive. Since the group members were representative of various segments of the school, their ideas and manner of expression differed. However, the basic group process corresponded to that of a therapeutic group. There were the male-female polarization, the use of jokes and sarcasm to defend against being too serious, and the extensive use of projection. Unfortunately, because of the interruption and the short time period the group was in existence, the group did not seem to be able to think of itself as a group unit.

*The group ends*

In the final session the students expressed their enthusiasm for an experience like the group. Some felt it should be part of a regular class such as psychology. Some thought they wanted more structure to the group, as in a class. Only two of the ten had had a previous group experience. All expressed a feeling that the group was a good place to find out more about one's self. A final meeting with the administration found them satisfied with the group. The idea of someone from outside the school dealing directly with the students caused less concern than when the group was initially discussed.

However, any differences in attitudes could not be clearly demonstrated. Any modification of attitudes or development of insights would more likely be demonstrated in the next academic year and not at termination of the present group. Some type of before and after evaluation would certainly have been helpful. This might have picked up changes in attitude and skills of the students in their roles as leaders.

*Recommendations*

The basic function of a school continues to be education, but this process can be seen in a broad view. Athletics are often brought forth as a means to produce future leaders. Certainly, there is room to offer the known leaders within a school an opportunity to gain awareness of their position and to gain effective techniques for discharging this leadership. The exploration of leadership and its inherent responsibilities can be accomplished in a group setting in which the group leader would facilitate the exploration. The power of the student leaders is a lever which may move the student body in a productive or nonproductive manner. More responsible leaders could move in a more productive manner. This type of group should be tried in a school where a full school year of group meetings can occur, without interference, in order to learn the full potential.

CHAPTER 37

# Fostering Hope and Responsibility in the High School by Student-Teacher-Administrator Discussion Groups

Jeremy A. Sarchet, Ph.D.,
Jack Jines, M.S., and
Gerald Haines, Ed.D.

*Overview*

ALIENATION AND POWERLESSNESS are feelings that are prevalent in our society today. These feelings were found as well in a survey of students, teachers, administrators, and parents at Pioneer High School in 1968. To combat these feelings and replace them with shared hope and responsibility, we introduced a program of dialogue among students, teachers, and administrators.

*Background*

Pioneer High School was opened in 1959 in the wake of rapid suburban population growth in Los Angeles County. Enrollment in 1969 was 2,041, and approximately 35% of the students were of Mexican-American descent. The percentage of Mexican-American students has increased approximately 5% annually in succeeding years. Certificated staff totaled 103.

*Survey*

A school-wide survey in 1968 sought to tap the concerns of all the people with a stake in Pioneer's educational program: students, parents, staff. In

303

discussion and through questionnaires, one underlying message came through again and again: "I really care about the quality of education here; but nobody else does; so it is hopeless to expect that I alone can make the educational process meaningful." A student would tell us that while he clowned around in class, he knew there were more important things to do, but the teacher was only there to collect his paycheck anyway, so why hassle it. A teacher told wistfully of his initial dedication to the enlightenment of his students, but with the attitude of parents merely wanting glorified baby-sitting for their kids, what chance did he have? A parent described his hopes that his youngster have a better education than the parent had been able to get, but felt that the kids were only in school because the law required it, so how could real learning take place? Each felt alone and at the mercy of powerful outside forces which would frustrate his wishes for significant relationships and experiences in school. People saw members of other groups in stereotyped ways as hostile, apathetic, resistant, etc.

The survey had been steered by a small group—the Principal (Jines), the Assistant Principal (Haines) who later became Principal, the consultant (Sarchet), and a few teachers and other administrators. It dawned on this group that the survey uncovered widespread concern that had been dormant because nobody knew it was shared by others. Rather, individuals saw others as selfish and uncaring. The group felt that if people could become more open to each other, they might see they were not alone and would begin to take more personal responsibility for the quality of life at Pioneer.

### Pilot group

To try this out, the consultant conducted a pilot discussion group in the spring of 1969 composed of two or three each of teachers, administrators, and students. Our purposes were to allow people to experience the concerns of others; to gain understanding across the gaps of age, status, and ethnic background; to help members experience the other *person* rather than the stereotype; and to foster hope and personal responsibility for the improvement of school life. The pilot group went well, and it was decided to set up similar groups in the fall.

### Method

Members of the pilot group—both students and members of the educational staff—became leaders of the groups. The leaders met with the consultant every two or three weeks to share experiences and help each other with the difficulties they encountered.

Eight groups were formed, each a cross section of administrators, teachers, counselors, and students. The typical group was made up of one administrator, three teachers and/or counselors, and eight students. Faculty members volunteered and were scheduled during their preparation periods. In order to have a cross section of students in each group and to bring about more rapid contagion of any constructive results, students who were formal or informal leaders—both of "establishment" and "fringe" elements in the school—were invited to join the groups.

Informality and openness were encouraged. The opening topic of discussion was, "What can you and I do to make our life better at this school?" The following guidelines were given to beginning groups:

Any subject may be discussed.

Decisions will be made and actions taken by individuals, who may recruit resources and use appropriate methods available to them already. We do not want another formal structure for making decisions and taking action.

The leader gets the group started but is not responsible for direction or productivity.

Frequency and duration of meetings are up to each group.

No minutes or reports are necessary.

No comment should be made about any identifiable person not present.

The consultant attended the first few meetings of each group. The following are some of the topics discussed while he was present:

Personal responsibility for the quality of school life.

"Cruising" at noon by the students, with frequent community complaints.

School spirit: Is it dependent on winning athletic teams?

What is good teaching? Influence of age, attitude, teaching style on teaching effectiveness.

Poor operation of the school bells and clocks.

Can students do anything to change the school? Or can change be effected only by adults?

Fear of being "chopped" by peers.

Trash on campus.

Inconsistent discipline by school personnel.

School's regulations about students under influence of drugs.

## Observations of group process

Leaders and members were a bit tense in the beginning. Initially, the two groups led by students had more trouble than the six groups led by faculty members. After a few meetings, however, members rated student-led groups as highly as faculty-led groups. Each group had "ups" and "downs." Symptoms of a "down" included trivial or boring discussions, timidity, and lack of involvement.

Groups started with superficial or distant subjects to play it safe; gradually they edged into serious subjects and spoke personally about them. For instance, most groups discussed dress and grooming standards in their first meeting, but little was heard of this later. Faculty members felt comfortable sooner than students; older students before younger students; and "establishment" members before "fringe" members. A few members dropped out of groups. When one group disbanded, several of its members asked to move to other groups. Seniors wanted to improve school for those students who came after them.

Shortly after the consultant stopped attending meetings regularly, several groups seemed to be in serious trouble. Symptoms included absences, silent members, superficial discussions, discussion sagging when a key member missed a meeting, and a member's criticizing others in the group and walking out. The consultant's notes made at that time were, "I am worried. Have I misjudged? Have they enough resources?" It was suggested to the leaders that they try to become more personal in their group meetings and that they have individual follow-up contact with those who were absent or silent. Three weeks after the suggestion was made, the crises seemed to be past; the groups had found ways to be viable on their own.

### Evaluation

Unsigned questionnaires were filled out by all participants after about 10 meetings. Responses by group and the combined responses of all groups in answer to two questions follow.

*In general, I feel the group has been*: (please check one)

|  | *Individual Groups* | | | | | | | *Total Responses* |
|---|---|---|---|---|---|---|---|---|
|  | *IVm* | *VI* | *I* | *IVt* | *III* | *II* | *V* |  |
| Worthwhile | 7 | 6 | 6 | 5 | 5 | 2 |  | 31 |
| Sometimes useful—sometimes not | 1 | 2 | 4 | 4 | 5 | 2 | 5 | 23 |
| Pretty much a waste of time |  |  |  |  |  | 3 | 2 | 5 |
| Destructive |  |  |  |  |  |  |  | 0 |

*I believe that the group has accomplished the following so far*: (more than one check is OK)

| | IVm | VI | I | IVt | III | II | V | Total Responses |
|---|---|---|---|---|---|---|---|---|
| | | | *Individual Groups* | | | | | |
| Greater understanding of people who are different from me | 6 | 8 | 7 | 7 | 6 | 3 | 3 | 40 |
| Increased feeling that I can do something to improve school life | 1 | 5 | 6 | 1 | 6 | 0 | 1 | 20 |
| Increased self-confidence, learning or growth | 3 | 2 | 5 | 0 | 1 | 0 | 0 | 11 |
| Changes in my actions | 0 | 3 | 0 | 2 | 3 | 2 | 0 | 10 |
| Changes in actions of others | 1 | 1 | 1 | 0 | 1 | 0 | 0 | 4 |
| Improved attitude toward people at school | 6 | 6 | 5 | 3 | 5 | 1 | 1 | 27 |
| Improved attitude toward courses, activities, facilities, etc. | 4 | 4 | 6 | 3 | 2 | 0 | 1 | 20 |
| Very little | 0 | 0 | 0 | 0 | 1 | 2 | 4 | 7 |
| Other accomplishments not listed above (please list) | 2 | 2 | 2 | 4 | 4 | 1 | 0 | 15 |

Because the questionnaires were collected only from those present at the meetings, obtaining responses from the few who had dropped out would probably have made the evaluation less favorable. Nevertheless, we were probably justified in making the following interpretations from the data presented and from written comments: most members felt the experience was worthwhile; nobody felt it was destructive; many felt that their understanding of people different from themselves increased and that they became more in touch with the basic motives and strategies common to all human beings; attitudes toward others and toward the school experience improved; feelings of being able to do something to improve school life increased; members no longer feel alone, at the mercy of "the system"; not many see changes in their own or others' actions.

Some of the "other accomplishments" that members listed were:

"Learning to know how teachers feel."
"Restored confidence in Pioneer High."
"Increased analysis by myself of my teaching activities and philosophy. Increased awareness of the general trends among the students as a whole, as well as among the kinds of students I teach."
"Opened many doors to communication—and there is no better feeling than to be able to communicate with others—provides for the well-being of all involved."

"Every person should have a discussion group like this, so that they can get to know teachers and kids and talk with no barriers."

In addition to the questionnaires, the following spontaneous comments and observations helped evaluate the impact of the groups:

The principal felt there was less tension in the school than at any time in its history, and that this was probably attributable in part to the discussion groups.

One teacher suggested that a student who griped about another teacher discuss his dissatisfactions with the "target" teacher. The group worked on the student's fears of such a frank conversation and he later had a good talk with the "target" teacher.

One teacher discovered that his relaxed self in the group was safe and effective. He then tried this out in class.

Some students told teachers how they "turn them off." The teachers began to work on ways of avoiding this.

A senior observed: "I've noticed teachers thinking at a younger level. They don't just go by the book. They deal with you as a person and try to find out about the problem. Not that they're more lenient—they have found another way to think out the problem. What we asked for, we got. Younger teachers are being hired. The whole attitude has a younger look. At other schools you can't see the change; at this one you can. Teachers are like jailers elsewhere."

Another student said, "I have a chance to talk in these groups to a kind of student I'm never in touch with otherwise."

Students said they would rather discuss matters in the group than with their counselors.

A freshman reported, "I told the teachers some kids getting F's are the teacher's responsibility—the class is not interesting. They listened!"

Results like these were widespread, but not universal: One teacher said, "I feel the kids in this group expect something for nothing. They do not want to understand or help themselves—some, not all."

### 1970-74

In subsequent years, discussion groups continued, but their importance and the degree of participation has ebbed and flowed. Many factors, both within the groups and on the campus, have contributed to the changes. During 1969 and the hectic early '70s, when militance was a feature of many campuses, discussion groups allowed straightforward communication and personal contact to take place between staff and students. *The open communication which resulted from the groups was effective in deterring destructive confrontations that might otherwise have occurred.*

It seems that with each passing year internal communications at Pioneer High School have improved. For the discussion groups, however, the improved atmosphere has meant that there is less of a sense of urgency in topics discussed. The open-ended, nonstructured organization of the groups allows for interchange, but often discussion has been felt by students and staff alike to be superficial. As a result, commitment of participants has decreased. The groups that have functioned well have done so as a result of strong leadership personalities and discussion skills that happened to be present in the group.

Survey of the groups has shown that students have continued their positive feelings about group participation longer than have teachers. *Students value the groups as providing them with an opportunity for personal communication* and a place to have an effect on the institution. They can accept the low-key discussions, but the teachers tend to feel a stronger need for demonstrated results.

Several spin-off programs have come from the personal interest generated by the groups. One of these is a teacher-advisor program in which teachers select from their classes 10 students for whom they provide more educational and personal support when needed. More personal involvement of classroom teachers with individual students has resulted.

By utilizing skills in discussion techniques gained by staff members, it has been possible in several instances to bring together students from varied backgrounds for a series of discussions aimed at solving specific problems. For example, *to deal with some of the hostility between neighborhood gangs* in the attendance area, a series of meetings was held which included student leaders from several of the gangs. Two other schools in the district have developed their own versions of this group program.

From our experience with discussion groups over the years, we feel that there are a few important *keys to developing an ongoing program*: (1) The groups need trained leaders who can bring structure to the group and teach the skills of interpersonal communication. (2) The school-day schedule should be adapted to provide time for group meetings which does not conflict with students' regular classes and with teacher preparation time. This is a must if the program is to continue for a period of any length. Time volunteered by teachers is too often subject to other priorities to keep a program running for long. (3) To make it possible to bridge the usual gaps that separate individuals, and to develop meaningful, in-depth discussion, a significant number of meetings must be held. It is necessary at the outset that group members set aside enough time to schedule future meetings.

*Possible Implications for Other Schools*

As with most educational approaches, this one is not a panacea. It did different things for different people at different times. Our findings suggest discussion groups show promise in the following areas:

*Personal support.* Members felt that what they did and what happened to them mattered to somebody else; they were not alone in a cold, impersonal, mechanical system.

*In-service training for faculty.* Serious student input brought about better teacher attitudes and skills, and improved relationships with students.

*Campus leadership.* Teachers and students who were leaders helped each other to overcome the anxiety that leaders often feel and to respond more effectively to the cynicism and discontent of followers.

*Mental health.* A "public health" rather than a "first aid" approach produced benefits. An institution can aggravate emotional sickness, often visible in school as withdrawal, underachievement, or overaggressiveness. A positive, supportive emotional climate can bring out the best in people.

*Youth militancy.* At its best the "student power" movement tried to bring more relevance into education and to make up for previous deprivation of ethnic minorities. In order to achieve these objectives, it attempted to increase the power of the students. Discussion groups helped provide constructive outlets for such motivations.

*Interpersonal effectiveness.* The discussion group approach built bridges of understanding across the gaps that caused people to frustrate each other. It enabled the members to get in touch with more basic motivations and strategies common to all human beings.

Although the above results were far from universal, they seemed to occur often enough to warrant recommendation of further use of such groups.

## CHAPTER 38

# Modified Group Process in the Management of a High School Crisis

Max Sugar, M.D.

CONFLICTS BETWEEN HIGH SCHOOL YOUTH and administration have been related to changes in racial composition or destructiveness in the youth. Various modes of dealing with these confrontations have been described, such as sensitivity training methods (Rueveni, 1971), an open-ended therapeutic group for students (Anshin, 1970), and committees of parents, teachers, and students trying to communicate (Schnell et al., 1970).

This chapter will discuss the use of group process in the successful management of a critical situation in a high school in New Orleans, Louisiana, which had been on the verge of a violent eruption in 1970 and 1971. Transitional developments and their effects on these students will be emphasized.

*The high school*

The high school population was long established as white, male, and predominantly middle class until it became coeducational in 1951 and then biracial in the mid-'60s. Reaction to the latter was one of prejudiced fear, mainly that the intrusion by Blacks with their socioeconomic and educational disadvantages would cause the school's excellent social, academic, and athletic luster to be dimmed.

Published previously in modified version as "Group process in the management of a high school crisis" in *Adolescent Psychiatry*, Vol. III, p. 362-371. New York: Basic Books, 1974.

In 1968-69, the school had many types of difficulties, among which were: polarization in the ascendancy between the races; authority problems; monetary extortion of students by other students; frequent threats to and assaults on teachers and students by students and outsiders coming into the classrooms and washrooms. Many sources for drugs were available inside and outside the school, and many students were "spaced out" during classes. During the academic year students went on strike for three days, led by some militant Black students with outside help. After the strike, classes were resumed, and a community action committee came up with a very bland *non culpa* decision about all the authorities involved and a mild chastisement of the students for having a strike. Later on, the police fired shots at outsiders who invaded the school.

In the academic year 1969-70 events were similar, but without a strike. The situation was developing an increasing tempo of fear, anxiety, and trauma, which led the faculty to plan to build a fence around the school. They compromised with parents by placing unarmed guards at all exits during school hours for the latter half of the year. The remoteness, rigidity, and inaccessibility of the principal made his rumored retirement seem to be the panacea for the school. In the summer of 1970 he retired without any prior announcement to faculty or students.

The officers of the Parent-Teacher Association were extremely apprehensive that major violence would erupt when the new principal took over. He had formerly been a coach at the school. Forebodings were that he would act restrictively and that resultant pressures would increase student difficulties. Additionally, the faculty was uncertain as to how their former peer would function in his new role as their superior.

The problems in the school seemed to be related to the usual adolescent range of difficulties, plus apprehension about the new principal, racial polarization, student-teacher polarization, and lack of a stimulating curriculum, especially for students who were not college bound.

As the school had no psychiatric consultation, the officers of the P.T.A. sought help from private volunteer psychiatrists.

### The forum

After several preparatory meetings, a forum based on a group approach was offered to all students, parents, faculty, and teachers connected with the high school. This was *not to be a therapy* or *an action group, but a dialogue group*. Its aim was to increase communication, sharing, and understanding by discussion.

*Six mental health professionals* served as group leaders. All had some previous experience with group process and therapy and were parents of students at this school. They were the assistant leaders in the forum, with the author as leader. Sessions began with a 15-minute, large group meeting involving all participants. Following this, small groups met in the classrooms for an hour under the guidance and leadership of one or two of the professionals. After this meeting the large group reassembled. A summary, presented by a student or other spokesman for each group, led to further discussion with questions and answers for another 15 to 30 minutes. Then the group leaders were joined by the principal and assistant principal to discuss briefly the developments of the meetings.

Although no confidentiality was offered, it was agreed that no retribution would be forthcoming for statements made in these sessions. Participants could choose which group leader they wanted each evening, so that they did not necessarily meet with the same fellow students, parents, or leader. The purpose of this was to reduce transference involvements to the leaders and to prevent it from becoming a therapy group. The *forum was to be communicative, ventilative, and abreactive, but not probing,* as the sessions were not designed to deal with the intrapsychic conflicts or dynamics of the participants.

A total of *eight forum sessions* convened between September 1970 and March 1971. The early sessions were on a demand basis; the frequency was set by a vote of the group. They were mostly free discussion sessions wherein demanding, oral-sadistic material, such as sarcasm, biting comments, carping, and rage were much in evidence. This was directed particularly at the school principal, the curricula, play time, lunch time, teachers, and counselors. In the second or middle phase, the communications were directed more toward the level of controls, and ambivalence was the high point.

These *developmental changes* were noted over a few sessions. Discussions became less concerned with complaints about the school personnel and courses and more directed to outside events—the police, festivals, sex, getting "busted" for taking or possessing drugs or providing drugs for friends. Discussion also turned to fears about the school carnival and dance. A dialect was heard at times from the Blacks, indicating some assertiveness on their part. This seemed to include elements of defiance and exhibitionism, letting the white man know this, shutting him out, but clarifying when asked. Authority was challenged about the rules concerning bringing in outsiders, despite repeated statements. One demonstration was held in the large group about outsiders not being welcome. Threats and dares were made to the leader of the forum about students' being excluded from leadership functions. This suggested that feelings to the principal were displaced to the forum leader. Attendance declined from the early phase, when it had averaged 100, to 30 to 60 in the middle phase. The principal was given tremendous support and explanations by the forum chairman and other group leaders. Thus he had a moratorium period in which to gain some perspective.

In the later phase, attendance dropped down to an average of 15 persons per meeting. While these were less intense meetings, they were characterized by more open communication, some unity between students, and concern about the students' apathy and boredom. The young people, functioning somewhat more autonomously, began paying some attention to the fact that they were experiencing tension about their separation from the school with their graduation at the end of April. In this phase it was apparent that, besides identifying with interested adults, they also learned from these people who listened and tried to help them deal with issues of importance. Ambivalence about the adult world decreased slightly, and self-responsibility increased somewhat. This was also indicated by the decreased parental and teacher attendance.

There was great accommodation to students' feelings of revenge and anger and to loss of the former principal and acceptance of the new one, as well as a growing acceptance of the different races. The teachers may have had some lessened anxiety about their role vis-à-vis the new principal. The students challenged the group leaders to be honest but expected hypocrisy. When the forum leaders were found to be credible and not omnipotent, the students were helped to gain a modicum of confidence in adults and thereby in themselves.

The marked decrease in attendance coincided with the *decreased need for the forum*. Loss of interest occurred, because there was no longer as much purpose; *the school had been defused*. Thus the forum had seemingly been successful in managing the crisis. *Only 10 ordinary fist fights* had taken place over the school year among the biracial, coed student body of 1,800. This was less than the expected number of fights, based on the previous year's experience, and small indeed considering the interracial and interpersonal problems. Some students who had looked for fights in the previous year were now working hard and doing very well in their classes.

A positive *spin-off* of the forum was the *provision of a model for the students*. During Student Council Week in January 1971, the student council spontaneously divided the students into groups of 20 (segregated by sex) during the daily gym periods and had rap sessions, or a "forum," as they chose to call it, with a student council member as monitor. The discussion in the small groups was presented in summary form to the large group at the end of the meeting and was thus shared by all the groups. This seemed to follow the plan which had been used in the original forum.

Out of these sessions emerged plans for improving the school, dealing with the principal's rules and other school problems. This led to the discussion of pleasant, shared school activities such as planning the school carnival, which was based on improved morale and cohesion. The student council also set up a drug room in the school to give information and to help young people experiencing "bad trips."

Thus, another of the original goals of the forum had been attained: Some of the student council members, who had not been interested enough to attend the original forum meetings, had incorporated the spirit of the forum through identification and imitation. They led their dialogue and discussion by themselves without adults.

### The forum meetings

Some details of the sessions are of interest.

*Session 1.* About *120 parents, teachers, and students attended.* Many realistic complaints were raised, along with questions about the forum, both involving much repetition. The principal clarified some parents' questions and issues. Some parents joined with teachers, but some joined the students in attacks on the faculty. Some students came to the aid of parents embattled with their own offspring. Interruptions were frequent, with reminders of fair play and majority rule.

*Session 2. About 100 were present.* This was held *one week later,* as decided by the participants' vote. The previous gripes continued. Members were reminded that the forum was not just for gripes, but also to correct a problem with communicating, as evidenced by their not listening to peers or others. Both sessions were consumed with marked demandingness and oral sadism. In addition, there were destructive wishes with respect to the older generation and suggestions of students' taking control.

At the school open house a few days later the predominant feeling was one of optimism and enthusiasm. This contrasted with previous years, when teachers left immediately after perfunctorily talking to parents, who similarly walked through the classrooms and departed. Parents, students, and teachers stayed longer than usual and talked with each other over coffee.

*Session 3.* This was held *a week after the second,* with about *60 in attend-*

*ance*. It was opened by the author's reference to the optimism at the school open house, suggesting that some positive change was occurring.

Complaints, demands, and plans for doing things differently were voiced along with restitutive wishes. The seniors complained about (1) deprivation of previous years; (2) not having enough time for lunch, play, or pleasure; and (3) the forum's impotence to provide these.

Complaints were leveled at the good students—student council members—for not being present. Students outnumbered others for the first time, and more Blacks attended than previously. Pupil discussion covering drug and personal experiences were countered by the parents' expressing horror about the dangers. Plans were proposed for positive actions, such as having a powder puff derby, dances, a better school newspaper, and greater forum attendance.

A complaint against a teacher doing her homework during class periods was paralleled and demonstrated unwittingly by one teacher doing paper corrections in the forum session. When this was brought to everyone's attention, she admitted it, but felt she could still attend to the group in spite of reading her papers. The students' self-expressed ambivalence about their own goals and education was not connected with their attacks on teachers as nonstimulating and the curriculum as irrelevant.

Some of the young people's suspicions about the forum leaders surfaced as disbelief that the leaders were professional people. It was argued that they were possibly secret narcotic agents. There seemed to be some decreased rage and projection, with some turning inward and positive planning, balancing destructive wishes.

*Session 4.* This session was held *two weeks later* with about *40 participants*. Three small groups contrasted with six the first night of the forum. Discussion centered on drugs and police, including their pushing youth around. Side conversations occurred but decreased when confrontations took place.

The students were enraged about the adults' use of the term "kids" in reference to them, and they repeatedly pointed this out. The adults denied the belittling inference and continued to slip back to this term. The young people could not accept any aspect of this designation the parents offered, such as protection, affection, responsibility or tenderness.

The Blacks spoke their own dialect for the first time and were difficult to understand, but they explained in English whenever they were requested to clarify. This seemed to be related to the Blacks' hostility, assertiveness, and decreased guardedness.

The homecoming dance seemed to be a focus of racial disunity, as it was being promoted mostly by the Blacks. At the dance the previous year one Black male had been stabbed by another.

*Session 5.* This was held *two weeks later with 32 attending.* An effort was made by one student and a group leader, following the student's lead, to change the forum arrangements. He wished to limit the topics discussed to only one at each session. This was dealt with by referring the proposal to each of the two small groups for discussion.

Later this same student became enraged, provocative, and threatening when he was confronted about having brought an outsider to the forum. This person did not leave as requested, and the issue was managed by bringing it up to the large group for further discussion. Though some others had also brought in relatives not directly involved with the school, the group sided with the forum leader. Discussion was forcefully brought to an end by the principal's reminder that the forum was only for students, their parents, and school faculty, as had been agreed upon initially. The principal sided with the majority of the group leaders in the post-forum discussion and was readily able to grasp the significance of the transference displacement to the forum leader. On leaving, he said to the forum leader, "Perhaps I can get the students mad at me and take the heat off you now."

Now there was obvious resistance side by side with positive effects from the forum and a negative transference shift to the forum leader from the principal. As some students had selected the same group leader for three or four consecutive sessions, it seemed both positive and negative transferences were being furthered, as well as the tendency to therapy. Additional influences in this direction were the close frequency of meetings and the regular attendance of the forum leader.

*Session 6.* This was held *two months later* and was attended by *24 participants.* The long interval was caused by an attempt to dilute intensity but also the practical problems posed by conflicting school events and the Thanksgiving and Christmas holidays. The forum leader did not attend this meeting. It was chaired by another group leader whom he had asked to take over. The meeting focused on curriculum questions and the hypocrisy of faculty as well as other adults. The students also discussed the need for a clean lunch patio, where plants could grow. Later they talked about this to their friends, and the following Saturday about 50 of them cleaned up the patio on their own initiative. They were now actively defusing their environment as they had already defused themselves.

*Session 7.* The seventh session *a month later* was *attended by 12.* The principal was absent, as he was attending an athletic event in another part of the school. Status questions of sophomores relating to seniors and students relating to faculty and other hierarchies led to concerns about changes in status resulting from moving out of high school to college or jobs.

Questions were posed regarding the principal's hypocrisy, e.g., "talking nice when he's scared and talking to only one student at a time"; why the quadrangle was not used after it was cleaned up; why chains were kept on the outside doors; why a school nurse was retained, since she was so difficult to see; why teachers were absent so much; why the public address system didn't work; and why teachers and students were apathetic.

The students seemed to have more unity, and the communication was better, but interfering cross talk still went on. Their concerns were connected with hostility to the principal and other authorities. This may have been related to his absence that night, which had been noted by the young people.

*Session 8. Twelve participants attended* the eighth session *a month later.* The material dealt with the lackluster curriculum and the faculty's not listening to students. The bellicose student of earlier sessions mumbled and seemed confused, but later he recovered his articulation to complain that the forum never did anything. The group tone or mood had changed from defiance and anger to discontent over apathy and boredom among the students.

### Discussion

Although the forum was described as having no power, certain events made it seem that the group leaders did have power: the principal, teachers, and parents attended; they were available and visible for hostile barrages; and decisions in the forum were largely made by the group through majority rule. This may have helped leaders to be accepted by participants, who then *developed a feeling of hopefulness* about some resolution of the difficulties (Lippitt et al., 1958). These feelings were contributing features to the transference reactions (Sugar, 1965, and Bird, 1972).

*Prejudice and social change* were significant issues in the school. The projection of undesirable traits is a frequent explanation of prejudice. Ethnic hostility and prejudice protect against universalistic tendencies and may bolster a weak sense of identity, while facilitating the discharge of hostility. If the hostility is discharged, anxiety may be reduced. But integration threatens prejudice with criticism and guilt feelings about it (Bettelheim and Janowitz, 1964).

*In the forum, participants had an opportunity to express hostility* verbally to the other race, generation, sex, status, and authority groups. But by universalizing and making one person's difficulty a focus of concern for all, even if only temporarily, the result was a unifying effect and a feeling of being part of the larger group of humans. Although prejudices did not disappear, they were reduced.

If a concatenation of traumatic events and too much strain for the available defenses are present, then disturbed behavior or symptoms occur. In this school at that time transitions in leadership and school composition were taking place, along with transitions and usual crises of development in the individual adolescents.

Revengeful wishes for the previous principal may have existed, with these feelings displaced to his successor, coupled with fear of the stranger. This latter fear was probably present as much in the teachers as in the students.

Eissler (1949) noted that riots occurred in a delinquent girls' institution during the transition from a very rigid to a more liberal attitude about discipline. ". . . Whenever equilibrium among the group of adults was labile," the girls reacted with rising tension. This is supported by reports from other sources (Anthony, 1970; Westley and Epstein, 1970; Ochberg and Trickett, 1970; and Schrag, 1971) in reference to identity problems and inadequacy in authority roles.

Rueveni (1971) had a successful sensitivity group for 15 aggressive junior high school students.* Stone and Gilbert (1971) used peer confrontation in a Veterans Administration hospital ward group. Hilgard and associates (1969) used better adjusted peers as therapy resources for adolescents, while Szymanski and Fleming (1971) reported positive results from a therapeutic encounter in prison between juvenile delinquents and adult prisoners.

Our forum had peer confrontation and network therapy aspects (Speck, 1967, and Sugar, 1971). The *principal benefited from a moratorium* during which some of the transference was displaced from him to the forum chairman. During this time the principal was able to regain his equilibrium and function more effectively with students and teachers.

The timing of sessions and dilution of transference involved in the structure of the forum kept it from becoming a therapy group and allowed the school and its members to become autonomous when they were ready and no longer needed the forum.

---

* See Chapter 35.

*Summary*

In order to prevent the possible repetition of violent eruptions such as a school strike, class disruptions, and assaults on teachers or students, a discussion forum was offered to the students, teachers, and parents of a senior high school. In a period of transition, the school was experiencing a change of principal and increasing biracial composition. Group process was utilized in large and small group meetings voluntarily attended by students, their parents, teachers, and faculty for a total of eight forums. A demand meeting schedule was arranged, which varied from weekly sessions at the start to monthly ones near the end of the academic year. No therapy was offered; neither history taking, probing, nor interpretive work was done.

An antagonistic, boiling group of students who were ready to attack the authority represented by the new principal displaced these feelings to the forum leader. Simultaneously, the student body became more cooperative and calmer, while the principal became a more popular figure. Progressively, the militancy abated with improved communication between generations and races. Meetings were less frequent, with decreasing attendance as the principal, teachers, and student body regained their equilibrium.

By the end of the school year interest in the forum had dissipated. The student council and a faculty member organized their own separate rap sessions, and the forum ended. During the year the school had no violence, disruptions, or problems of any greater degree than ordinary fist fights between students.

Appropriate modification of group process, namely, dilution, spacing of sessions, shared leadership in managing transference and avoidance of becoming a therapy group suited the special needs of this situation. Special considerations involved the prejudicial and transitional factors in the high school.

## BIBLIOGRAPHY

ANSHIN, R. N. (1970). "The role of a psychiatric consultant to a public high school in racial transition—challenge and response." Presented at American Orthopsychiatric Association meeting.

ANTHONY, E. J. (1970). The reactions of parents to adolescents and to their behavior. In E. J. Anthony and T. Benedek (Eds.), *Parenthood, Its Psychology and Psychopathology.* Boston: Little, Brown & Co. Pp. 307-324.

BETTELHEIM, B. and JANOWITZ, M. (1964). *Social Change and Prejudice.* Glencoe, Ill.: Free Press.

BIRD, B. (1972). Notes on transferences: Universal phenomenon and hardest part of analysis. *J. Am. Psychoanal. Assn.,* 20, 267-301.

EISSLER, R. S. (1949). Riots. *Psychoanalytic Study of the Child*, Vol. IV, pp. 449-460. New York: International Universities Press.

HILGARD, J. R., STAIGHT, D. C., and MOORE, U. W. (1969). Better adjusted peers as resources in group therapy with adolescents. *J. of Psychol.*, 73, 75-100.

LIPPITT, R., POLANSKY, N., REDL, F., and ROSEN, S. (1958). The dynamics of power: A field study of social influence in groups of children. In E. E. Macoby, T. M. Newcomb, and E. L. Hartley (Eds.), *Readings in Social Psychology*. New York: Holt, Rinehart, and Winston. Pp. 251-264.

OCHBERG, F. M. and TRICKETT, E. (1970). Administrative responses to racial conflict in a high school. *Commun. Ment. Health J.*, 6, 470-482.

RUEVENI, U. (1971). Using sensitivity training with junior high school students. *Children*, 18, 69-72.

SCHNELL, R. D., PECKHAM, A., and MILFORD, R. (1970). Problem-solving structure for a local high school in the Rio Hondo service area (unpublished).

SCHRAG, P. (1971). The Ellsberg affair. *Sat. Rev. of Lit.*, 54, November 13, 34-39.

SPECK, R. (1967). Psychotherapy of the social network of a schizophrenic family. *Family Process*, 6, 208-214.

STONE, W. V. and GILBERT, R. (1971). Peer confrontation—What, why, and whether. Presented at American Psychiatric Assn. meeting.

SUGAR, M. (1965). Relationship processes in the use of drugs. *Southern Med. J.*, 58, 314-318.

SUGAR, M. (1971). Network psychotherapy of an adolescent. *Adolescent Psychiatry*, 1, 464-478.

SZYMANSKI, L. and FLEMING, A. (1971). Juvenile delinquent and an adult prisoner: A therapeutic encounter? *J. of Am. Acad. Child Psychiatry*, 10, 308-320.

WESTLEY, W. A. and EPSTEIN, N. B. (1970). *The Silent Majority*. San Francisco: Jossey Bass.

WINNICOTT, D. W. (1962). Adolescence. *New Era in Home and School*, 43, 1-7.

# PART III: D. OTHER USEFUL GROUPS IN JUNIOR AND SENIOR HIGH SCHOOLS

## EDITOR'S NOTE

*In the next chapter, the particular intensity of anxiety and loss reactions described in the group of adolescents in this London secondary school may be special to the position of some teen-agers in English urban society. The cultural emphasis on vocational and academic tracking prevalent for so many years, and changing only recently, may imbue that age of decision with a heavier degree of anxiety and fatefulness than the equivalent period for American youth.*

*Certainly all youth feel anxiety and loss at leaving school, especially if there has been a satisfying and sustaining, even if not successful, experience. However, it seems that discussion groups in most American high schools have not highlighted a strong degree of such anxiety. Any group is different and special compared to any other group, especially ones in different countries. Kaplan (Chapter 29) described the high school group in her project as dealing with a variety of personal, family, and school problems. Feelings about leaving school undoubtedly were significant, but were not described as a prime conflict, as they are by Scharff in the next chapter. The significance of work in England, the sheltering quality of the schools, and the special contribution of the particular minority cultural characteristics of the London adolescents involved may all have been factors contributing to the special quality of this experience. Perhaps such feelings need more awareness in groups of graduating senior high school students.*

*Another unique aspect of Scharff's chapter is the detailed discussion of one member's dream. Most counseling groups will not deal with dreams, except when a particular nightmare forces one of the counselees to bring this in. If the counselor is experienced with use of dreams in a group context, the gain and interest to all members can be striking. Adolescents often have very clear and crucial dreams. However, consideration of dreams can be time consuming, distracting, and unproductive, if the leader is unfamiliar with arriving at the here-and-now relevance, as described by Scharff.*

CHAPTER 39

# The Transition from School to Work: Groups in London High Schools

## David E. Scharff, M.D.

THIS CHAPTER* presents a selection from work done with several student groups in London high schools in the 1973-74 academic year. In each case, we were interested in the vicissitudes of the transition from school to work for those adolescents who left school at age 16. They had less time to reach mature decisions about how to satisfy inner needs than the more academic child, who can "buy time" by continuing in education and sorting out strategies for meeting inner needs. Several themes emerged which related adolescent developmental issues to the responses of schools.

The *school as an organization* and the teachers in it could act either to facilitate the transition, or to isolate the adolescent, out of a need to defend themselves. Our work atempted to develop methods and principles of intervention which could aid in better preparing the adolescent to develop strategies of approach to work and to life planning, to meet inner needs as well as pressures of reality. Although our project focused on the student's perception of the difficulties in the transition, our aim was also to help the school become more effective in aiding the process and facilitating aspects of adolescent growth.

* This material is abstracted from a chapter of a forthcoming book, *Between Two Worlds: Aspects of the Transition from School to Work* by David E. Scharff and J. M. M. Hill, Careers Consultants Publishers, London. This book describes two studies carried out by the Tavistock Institute of Human Relations (London, England) as part of a Social Research Programme financed by the Baxi Trust from the P. S. Baxindale Settlement. I am indebted to J. M. M. Hill and Marion Davis for their assistance and contributions throughout the study.

Our work took place in three London comprehensive schools (approximately the equivalent of the American public high school), each with students of a wide range of ability and backgrounds, including a wide range of minority groups. We restricted the composition of our groups only in that we did not take students who were clearly bound for university. Once we selected a group, we met regularly over a three- to eight-month period to explore issues in depth, including planning of life and work strategies. It was important that we also worked closely with school staff to understand their view of the students' dilemma. By working with both staff and students, we felt we came to appreciate the students' position of often feeling in the middle between the pulls and requirements of school, job, and family. An important goal was to facilitate what staff could do to help them.

### The mutuality of loss and mourning

Students expressed feelings of loss as they faced the prospect of leaving school, but it was not only they who spoke of loss. The teachers also experienced the pain in losing a child during the growth process. This was one major theme which emerged in the groups. The *adolescents were losing a second home* at a time when their bodies were newly full-grown. They were unsure of themselves, and they faced a threatening, unknown world. At such times, children are used to looking for support from guiding and loving adults. But in this case, the support of teachers was lost with loss of the school. We know from discussions on loss and grieving (Bowlby, 1969, 1973) that ambivalently held relationships are the hardest ones to mourn. Angry reactions, detachment from the ambivalently held object, and denial of the meaning of the loss are frequent in such cases. If we look at the group of students who have not been very successful in school, we can expect a large number of such reactions to ambivalent losses. We did find them in the guise of adolescent rebelliousness, apathy, withdrawal, and delinquent detachment from adult values. If one thought of these as deviant forms of grief reactions, the relationship to loss and mourning was apparent. If one did not, they were difficult to comprehend.

Then there was the *adult's side of the loss and mourning partnership.* The school and teachers experienced a yearly loss of school-leaving adolescents. It was easier for the teachers to deal with the nostalgic loss of those continuing on into successful careers in further education. But one might expect teachers would have more difficulty coping with the loss of the ambivalently held students. They have not been a success in the teachers' terms. In this regard, one should note that teachers, by choice of profession, have themselves valued academic work. These students either do not value it or are not successful at it. Another complicating factor is that most teachers have never really left school. Thus, these students are doing something their teachers have never done.

We may then expect that it could be more difficult for teachers to mourn the loss of this category of adolescent. The result was often the mutual withdrawal and distancing of adolescent and teacher from each other. Many teachers confirmed that they withdrew from students in the last weeks before school leaving. One teacher said, "I'm glad they come in less now. I can get my work done." A second said, "We're least available when some need us most—in the summer after they leave." At the moment the adolescents were losing a familiar world and entering a strange, new, and threatening (even if also beckoning) one, they were alone. They had to make a solo voyage between the two worlds of school and work.

## *The uses of the group in facilitating the transition from school to work*

Whether the group format involves group discussion, role playing or other group techniques, it can provide a place to anticipate, rehearse, and become familiar with elements of the new and unknown world. Such a group can be a place to "play" at alternative strategies, to try various approaches to getting and working at jobs in any way to fulfill life wishes. Overt and covert anxieties about the transition from school to work can be explored and strategies of approach to occupational and life-planning developed. All themes relevant to this general theme can be considered, e.g., the relationship of the adolescent to social authorities like police, as well as issues of family, marriage, and leisure. The material which follows is from a group in one of the three schools entered. The group, and especially one member, are influenced by an ideological split within the school.

## *The school*

This group of "nonacademic" adolescents in the sixth year of this secondary school described feelings and difficulties which closely resembled those of the other groups we had encountered. They seemed a more articulate and mature group than most other groups we met and could explore issues which, in other settings, we had to elicit painfully and painstakingly. But the issues were the same as for those other groups. Mr. M., the school's second master, was in charge of the sixth form. He had established a program in community studies which encouraged development of the students' individual interests by discussion groups and forays into the community. But he also readily examined the shortcomings of his program. He repeatedly questioned the rationale for the overall school experience of the adolescents whom we met. For example, he states:

> As an ex-grammar school, the curriculum still fits more readily with the more academic students and is not well tailored to the needs of your group. We really don't want to know what to do for these children who are not going into academic careers.

### The group in the school

Our group came from the less academic group of the lower sixth form (16-17 years old). The group was originally selected randomly for us by Mr. M. to replace one morning's community studies activity. This group of eight included four members of Indian and Pakistani derivation and one West Indian. Of the Caucasians, Paolo (mentioned prominently below) came from a family which had immigrated from Italy just before his birth. This group did not reflect the overall ethnic composition of the school.

Mr. M. stated:

> The children you are working with are the ones who were not able to start a project of their own in the general studies; it may have something to do with racial issues. The Indian and Pakistani children have a respect for formal education and its significance. They are often forced into this pattern by their parents. They have a blissful ignorance of what is going to happen to them and may tend to stay in school for protection longer than others. Or they may stay on for the prestige and valuing of education itself without any particular goals. When they go outside into the community, I think they often feel more vulnerable. They may be coping with this by looking unmotivated and taking a back seat.
>
> We have a lot of pressure from parents to continue with the traditional curriculum. One father wanted his child to learn Latin because he had as a child—even though this child was barely literate. Others want their children to take exams without any particular reason, with a feeling that exams are a good thing. We feel that there is a lot of pressure from parents not to change our curriculum.

A split existed in the faculty between those who believed that less emphasis on hard work and discipline was a dissipation of traditional values, and those, represented in part by Mr. M., who felt that new skills and approaches were required. This split was underscored in our discussion with other members of staff who felt that what was missing was not primarily more sensitivity to adolescent needs, but a respect by students and junior staff for traditional values, discipline, and work.

## The group

We were struck immediately with the ability of the members of this group to articulate their concerns, to reflect, debate, and grow. The easy use of verbal material came as a striking contrast to the less articulate fifth form groups with whom we had previously been meeting. The group made particularly rich use of their experience, including illuminating dream material of one of its members. But first, let us consider some of the major issues confronted by them during the *five-month span* of our meetings.

## "Leaving school is like being born."

Midway through our first meeting with this group, one boy, Benjamin, said, "Leaving school is like being born; it's like being pushed out of your mother's womb, and when you're out, you're useless. It seems your whole life is getting and taking exams—and that they all lead to nothing." Another boy, Tom, compared school to a prison: "Even though it's like a prison, I'm scared to leave because I don't have anything fixed up outside. I'm afraid if I leave without anything fixed up that's good, it will be like going to pieces. It would be nice to be pushed out into something you enjoy and want to do."

The view emerged quickly of the school as a poor parent, one who does not prepare her children for growing up into the world outside the womb. In contrast to one senior teacher's view that nonacademic adolescents were happy to leave, we had this group, somewhat more academic, to be sure, saying that they could see no sustenance beyond school. That feeling persisted throughout our work with the group, and our focus came to lie in modifying the feeling of dread about the unknowns which lay ahead—unknowns stemming both from the wider world and from within themselves.

## It's frightening because you have no one to turn to

Mr. M.'s feeling that school was a protected place for several of our group members was confirmed by contrasting the isolation they anticipated in facing the world after school. There seemed to be no knowledgeable, sympathetic person to turn to as the adolescent began to grow up. The process of leaving school and beginning a career was seen as having to perform alone. It was here that the inability of the counseling or "pastoral care" system* to be more available seemed particularly evident. Parents were also felt to be frightened and not helpful at this point. The group members agreed that a sister or older friend might be most helpful and less frightened. Consequently, the adolescents felt most isolated at a time they had expected to be able to look to wiser adults for help with major decisions.

> Bhunu, an Indian girl, said, "My parents are more worried than I am, and I don't want to worry them, so we don't talk about what I'm going to do. My mother married early and can't communicate with me because she thinks I should be sitting and revising (studying) all the time and should never go out. She kept on at college while she was having children and worked hard at it. She liked it when I wanted to be a nurse, but now that I'm changing my mind, she's upset." A West Indian girl, Sonya, said, "Parents know less than you do about what jobs are available, because it's all changed since their time."

Although parents do not appear to know how to help, they did seem to know what they wanted for the child. The gap between the parents' expectations and the adolescents' intentions led group members to feel that one might "let them down" during a "descent into adulthood." One of the childlike advantages had been the ability to fulfill parental fantasy about what one would become. Now, our group expressed the feeling that one of the liabilities of growing up was that parents grew more anxious as the children were seen not becoming what parents had hoped.

Teachers were also seen as not able to help. Often this complaint came out around the feeling that inadequate course offerings and poor counseling about subject alternatives seemed to threaten career choices after school. There were complaints about high staff turnover, "so that no one gets to know what you can do in math." The school was seen as a place which often functioned without adult personalities and which treated the student as a cipher. The most intense contact with teachers for some students came in disciplinary action. In one case (that of Paolo, who is discussed later) the student seemed to have provoked the disciplinary action in order to get attention immediately before exam period, when his anxiety was extreme.

---

* "Pastoral" and "tutorial" are used interchangeably as expressions for the function of a teacher attending, as his principal duty, to aspects of personal growth needs. Actually, the caring came mainly in crises.

The picture emerged of school, parent, and child all losing the idealized view of each other simultaneously. The parents and children were losing the ability to carry idealized fantasies for each other, and the school could no longer live up to the fantasy the children and their parents had shared: that the school would provide when the chips were down. When child and parent realize that they each have human failings, the child loses the notion of the all-powerful parent, and the parent loses the notion of the child who will fulfill all the dreams and expectations. Both often turn to the school as the place to fulfill more realistic dreams of worldly success, but they find the disappointments are here as well.

Under these multiple pressures, individual adolescents felt increasingly isolated, even from peers. For instance, the group members discovered that mostly they did not talk with each other about their anxiety as exams approached, out of a fear they would further frighten themselves and each other by sharing worries.

### The fate of earlier ambitions

Some of the reluctance to pinpoint specific goals at school leaving seemed to relate to earlier disappointments. One boy, Idris, said, "You drop an idea when you find it is too hard and the qualifications required are beyond what you can do." Sonya said she wanted to be a doctor but decided not to, when shown a film of people cutting up mice. Tom said, "You don't set your eyes on something that is impossible. I wouldn't even try to think of something that is out of reach." Paolo joined in, saying, "I wanted to be an architect but was always told by teachers, 'You're a year too late to be an architect. You can't get into the courses you need now. You would waste a year.' "

In seeing the increasing reality needs for their ambitions, each of them felt a sense of loss at having to cope with both fantasy and reality. In our group the members often covered their suspicion that their personal resources were inadequate by narrowing the number of options to be considered and by surrendering to depression. It was as though the options had been stolen from them by their growing up, and nothing given in return in the way of increased adult options and ability to cope. Paolo could see only narrowing of alternatives, so that now he clung to the wish to become a draftsman as a kind of lesser architectural career. Benjamin felt he had had to forsake the system and go outside it for a spur to his interest, in becoming a maker of musical instruments. Idris felt he might not do well enough to become an

engineer but had nothing else to elect. Yet, it was hard to begin a search
for other occupations.

### The development of a strategy

The entire course of the group focused on the development of a strategy
of approach to ocupational choice, melding the effects of one's own anxiety
with the constraints and the opportunities in reality. But one session was a
particularly graphic demonstration of the way in which planning any
strategy involved a weighing of the defensive aspects against the creative
and constructive aspects.

In this session, we took up the question of what group members would
do if they failed an exam en route to pursuing a career, for instance, in attempting to become a doctor. Paolo said he would have to choose an
entirely different life if he failed an exam en route. The difficulty became
more graphic when we decided to describe the route of two friends who had
the same ambition, but one of whom had difficulty pursuing it. By diagram-
ming the life course of each, we located the nodal decision points, the kind
of performance required in different phases, and the consequences of success
or failure. In so doing, we were able to imagine, describe, and investigate the
kinds of anxiety and the personal constraints for each of the paths, and to
compare differing personal reactions among group members.

### The pull to regression when anxiety was high

Anxiety about impending exams, school leaving, and planning for a job
became greater as the year progressed. Some adolescents withdrew to a new
isolation. Others became more ambivalent and undecided about plans for
the following year. One boy said, "I'm staying on because I'm too lazy to
leave." We knew he was not particularly lazy, but he did become increasingly
confused. They discussed the temptation of old, discarded ambitions, although no one opted for them.

With the threat of the loss of school and the feeling of impending helplessness, crippling anxiety became more manifest. The anxiety began to
yield at the end of the year with the acknowledgment of sadness and a
feeling of loss. I doubt that they could have recognized the significance of
the feeling of loss without the kind of experience we shared, but with it
they were able to look at the defensive aspects of shutting out sadness. In
our last session Gopal said:

A friend comes up and talks to me, and I begin to feel sad and out of place because I'm leaving. I was happy at home this morning, but when I get here, I'm sad.

## Paolo's dream

One of the group members, Paolo, failed dramatically to complete his plans for successful school leaving. Because he had frequently stressed the importance of doing so, it was a particularly poignant failure. Because he had shared a good deal of himself with us, we were in a position to learn from his experience. Paolo is presented as a vivid illumination of the role of anxiety, loss, and mourning during the psychosocial transition from school to work. Our intervention was not enough to help Paolo overcome his anxiety, but it was clear that he had cut himself off from others at the school who were available and might have been able to help him. His anxiety mounted unnoticed at a time when he was *threatened not only with the loss of school but also with the loss of his entire family*.

Paolo's material is presented in detail for three reasons: first, it illustrates clearly the role of loss and fear of loss in the transition from school to work; second, it provides us with an opportunity to look at the way in which one person's contribution to the group—in this case, a sharing of dream material—can be used by group members for their general benefit; third, examining Paolo's difficulties in some detail will give us a new way to examine an important aspect of staff disagreement, and attempt to increase our understanding of the practical meaning to students of this kind of split among staff.

A tutor had summed up a view of Paolo two years earlier in saying, "This is a good report of a solid and reliable worker." There was a brief mention that his mother had died four years before we met him and that a family agency had been involved with his family for about six months following that. He was said to have coped well, with his father's support, and to have continued to work hard throughout the period immediately following his mother's death. In general, he worked harder in subjects he liked and did well in them, but occasionally made a poor effort in subjects less related to his interests in architecture.

About three weeks before our group ended, there was a lull in discussion. After a discussion of the way dreams and daydreams fill gaps, Paolo paused and then said he had recently had a dream.

I have my art exam in 10 days' time and don't think about it, but I had a dream about my art exam. I saw myself drawing these pictures and had several small pictures of ideas on one picture—showed them to Mr. Z., the head of art. He said, "You can't do that for the exam." Then I drew a picture of a crucifix, looking down from above in the center (here Paolo sketched the picture for us). A man was on the crucifix, and the picture rotated so that I could see his face, which was very blurred. It wasn't at all clear who it was. There were two other pictures, one above and one below the crucifix. One was of a car and a house; it was in color, all red and misty. In front of the crucifix was a pale brown and pink, and back of it was a dark cloud, and there was nothing there. I wanted to do that picture. Mr. Z. keeps telling us to make a selection for the picture we're going to do for our exam, to choose the best idea we have and then improve on it. I told him I wanted to do that one, but he didn't quite get the idea of it.

When I asked Paolo who it was on the cross, he said he didn't know, but it might be him when he was taking the exam. He described the picture as rather pink with rosy clouds before it and said neither the face nor the genitals of the man could be seen, because he had a loin cloth on.

There wasn't any face on it. I thought it might be me up there. I'm going to be dead if I fail my exams. The picture of the car is a symbol of a job and of passing the exams. The whole area is cloudy, but I couldn't see any other people whose face it could have been. My art teacher, and the head of art, were there when I said I wanted to do this picture. To begin with, the teacher wouldn't let me do it, and then he said I could. I think it's a "get down to work" dream. That night I was meant to be revising (studying) for the test. I went to see my girl friend, who was out, so I came back, but I had trouble working.

The material was used by the whole group to explore the shared themes of anxiety, loss, and mourning in a learning sense. No deliberate attempt to be therapeutic was made or intended. I asked about his going to see his girl friend. He said:

I hadn't been thinking about my art exam. I'd just been out, and it was late, and I had been thinking about my girl friend. I was thinking, "silly female." I went to her house, and she wasn't in. I was thinking she was at a party, maybe babysitting, making up things where she might be. Perhaps she went with her mother to the cinema.

I wondered if he had been searching for his girl friend as someone who could give him comfort when he was feeling anxious about revising and when he was feeling that he was in a dangerous position. I said to the group that "sometimes when people are anxious about exams they like someone to make them feel more comfortable, and girl friends might be a pretty good bet for that. If it were really Paolo on the cross, it sounded as though he was pretty alone." He added:

> Well, I wouldn't have been able to revise if I had been with her, so we planned not to be together that evening. I got home and sat down to study and then decided I wanted to see her, so I went six or seven miles by bus. I could have called her, but I didn't want to. When I got there, she was out. I felt even more alone, so I came home and went to bed thinking about her; that's when I had the dream. I don't know why I didn't telephone her! I could have.

Gopal then said, "My girl friend called me up earlier in the evening. I said I'd like to go over and see her, but she wouldn't let me. I got the feeling that something would happen to her." Bhunu said she thought it was the usual practice for the art teacher to allow people to do pictures they wanted to paint, and Paolo replied that, "In the dream, I asked because I wanted to be sure I was doing the right thing." Bhunu said, "I think it has something to do with his girl friend. He's left alone, and then he has to decide to ask the question." Gopal agreed that talking about this dream stirred something up. Others were also active in thinking about Paolo's dream.

At this point I said I thought that the anxiety in the dream was about "getting crucified" if one failed one's exams. That was a situation that all of them seemed to be in. Paolo's earlier denial of anxiety left him in the more vulnerable position of having to look for comfort without knowing quite why, and therefore seeking solace in ways that kept him from meeting his anxiety with appropriate steps. For instance, he could have revised part of the time and then arranged to meet his girl friend. The issue was shared by all members of the group, who were learning from their own involvement in looking at Paolo's dream and his vivid picture of the consequences of exam failure. Paolo was then able to see that he thought:

> The cloud in the back of the man was very threatening—dangerous and dark . . I can't say anything about it. But it is what will happen if I fail.

I said in a few words that anxiety could be used as a positive spur toward work rather than as an overwhelming inhibition. After all, "People don't have to put off revision longer than they should, and it might answer your anxiety to buckle down to work."

The next week Paolo arrived in the middle of the group session, reporting that he had been to see the senior house master even though he had not been called to see him. He had accompanied his girl friend, who had been called in for something else, and had proceeded to get himself in trouble. He said it was time to tell the house master off. The predictable result was that he was censured severely. The previous week he had only dreamed about "being crucified." This week he had effectively gotten himself crucified. I wondered out loud if this wasn't still a function of his continuing anxiety. He confirmed this by saying that his open physical relationship with his girl friend in school was constantly getting him into trouble with some of the more traditional masters. We were able to wonder together whether Paolo wasn't in the process of getting into trouble for the first time in his school career as a solution to his anxiety about leaving it. Paolo said, "I decided to go and see him because he can't throw me out of school. So I can have a go at him and say what I've always wanted to say." It still looked as though Paolo's acting out was not too severe to be managed.

The last week of our regular meetings Paolo showed a good deal of denial, saying:

> I don't think leaving bothers people. People have left me. My mother left four years ago (when she died), then my little sister left; now my big sister and father have left. Being left is nothing new to me. It's what happens every day. You get used to it. School just seems to fade away in the background. I don't feel anything great about leaving school. I'll just go home the same as usual, and that's that.

This was just before exams. He was also able to report on having finished the art exam involved in the dream the previous week.

> I did the dream as a nightmare and painted an open cavern, a tombstone, and a broken cross. The man was asleep on a bed. All the things in the bedroom were with him. It came out quite well. I used dull grays and greens, pale brown, and only a little pink. The bed was pink. I thought I'd use dull colors for a nightmare to make out that he was alone.

I pointed out that he had left out much of the previous use of pink, which might have been more optimistic. He retained that only for the bed. Someone else pointed out that he was having a bad dream, but on a comfortable bed. We did not pursue the art exam, and Paolo seemed satisfied with it.

Alarmingly, we heard from Mr. M. that on the evening before his first set of written exams Paolo had been sitting revising in his bedroom and had thought he had seen a face outside the window. In alarm he hit out at the face in the window, breaking the window and injuring his right hand so badly that he could not write. As a result he was unable to take any of his exams. It was clear both to Mr. M. and to us that Paolo had been overwhelmed while studying for exams. He had not been able to contain the anxiety that had been evidenced in our sessions. In his denial, the staunch but brittle containment of his anxiety had broken down, and the worst of his nightmares had been realized. Fortunately, he was able to take the same job he would have taken if he had taken exams. He planned to take the exams the following year.

Paolo's experience was one we saw developing right under our noses, but we were unable either to predict or to contain the outcome. For him a brief intervention was inadequate to avert a crisis that had been developing over a number of years. Paolo's denial, his search for superficial solutions, and his refusal to face the underlying issues made up a long-standing pattern which had gone unnoticed. His contact with tutorial staff was significant only when he finally went essentially in order to be punished.

Paolo's experience underscored that there will always be some adolescents for whom nothing offered by the school will be enough to prevent a crisis. He was severely threatened by a number of serious concurrent losses. His mother had died four years earlier, and his family was moving out of the country just as he was leaving school. The superficial "Maginot Line," erected defensively against "invaders" from all directions, failed finally when the unexpected invader from his fantasy appeared in the window. The description of the face in the window seemed clearly to Mr. M. and to us to be an imaginary, almost hallucinatory projection, an anxious messenger from his inner world.

There is nothing in the available records to indicate that Paolo had an unstable or anxiety-laden young childhood. Indeed, his development and presentation had been that of a rather stable, solid citizen. A bit of bravado and mild superficiality formed a shell surrounding a ferment of anxiety. His facade was only a cover masking a tumultuous interior. The interior was unavailable to his own process of inspection. In the group, we seemed to be making some inroads.

The mode of coping with the crisis presumably established at that earlier loss (of his mother) was to "get by" with a good show, without any outward sign of weakness or emotion. This detachment was a poor defense against the overwhelming anxiety stimulated during exams. The complex, intense focus of issues from several sources surfaced dramatically as exams began. In Paolo's own terms, the black, unknown, nightmarish fate he feared if he failed his exams had descended.

Paolo can be seen within the theoretical framework of someone who has handled his losses and his mourning by becoming detached from the lost figure while clinging urgently to those who remain (Bowlby, 1973). Overtly, he got along well with peers, but from the material volunteered in the groups and given in his projective psychological tests, we know that he clung to important figures who he felt always threatened to abandon him. The pattern was reminiscent of children who clung anxiously to mothers whose continued presence was felt to be uncertain. One of the responses to loss in early childhood is the development of a kind of detachment with pseudo-independence, which makes the further growth of personal relationships difficult. This pattern leads to a personality characterized by superficiality of relationships, which serve to avoid the danger of being abandoned by someone with whom one develops a deeper relationship.

Paolo fit this pattern of someone who was afraid he would be unable to find a supporting mothering person. In projective tests, his stories were full of characters seeking love, unable to get it, being fired from jobs, being unable to support the ones they loved, and feeling abandoned. Paolo's pseudo-independent singlemindedness emerged as a fragile attempt to cover his loneliness, grief, fragility, and fear of abandonment. There was no one in school to turn to for guidance through the final educational experience of examinations. In this context a haunting internal figure came to pay a visit.

From Paolo's own report, what happened to him from this point on was, to use a favorite word from the school reports, "a bit dicey." He had now passed out of the tutorial system of the school, and whether he took his exams in the future would depend almost entirely on whether he could muster the ego strength to face his anxiety yet a second time. From covering his wish for attachment with a pseudo-independent detachment and a pseudo-self-reliant stance, Paolo had entered the unknown world of his own nightmare. Paolo's own comment about this event was, "I guess I'll have to stay on until January and take my exams then." Fortunately, it turned out that his employer was willing to give him provisional employment, so that he did not have to stay on in defeat. A benign employer could help him overcome this major setback.

## Work with group materials and dream images

Paolo's dream was not the only example of intensely personal dream material which emerged in the group context. In each case, the material was used by the group as a whole to explore the shared themes of anxiety, loss, and mourning in a *learning* sense. No attempt to be therapeutic was made or intended. We did not work in order for the group to understand Paolo, but took his statements as ones to be considered by the group as a whole as relevant in some ways to each participant: What could we learn about anxiety about exams? about running from a task? and about "signal anxiety"— that feeling from within—trying to tell us that something needed doing?

These considerations allowed the group time and room so that each individual could explore his or her own way of meeting these issues. It could be seen that the feelings and difficulties were mainly ones all the members had to deal with, and that there were many styles of coming to terms with them. The assets and liabilities of several styles were explored, acknowledging that individuals had a right to change that style if they chose. This was the process of working on "strategies" within the group. Paolo's dream material was grist for this mill which, hopefully, benefitted him and his peers. Other material which served the same purpose included questions about course planning, ideas about kinds of work, fantasies about "bosses" in the world of work, and practically anything the group had on its agenda for a given day. In the dream material, the difficult feelings were graphically and vividly illustrated in a way which not only reverberated with anxieties of others in the group, but also caught their imaginations. Instead of working back to the origins of the images for Paolo, the material was used as a vehicle in "problem-solving" around the commonality of the anxieties represented.

## Paolo and the school

An example of the potential for relating staff and student issues also came from Paolo's experience. In the beginning of this chapter, I drew the contrast between two staff attitudes: one group wished for increased flexibility and attention to student development through increased tutorial programming; the other group advocated a firmer approach to work tasks and goals. An interesting aspect of the student group was its sharing of both attitudes, and the difficulty of resolving the two sides of the school's split. The adolescents felt the school lent them less support than they needed in achieving goals for specific skills and that it provided too little of the more personal aspects of support. This dissatisfaction echoed the feelings of some of the staff, some of whom felt that neither task was adequately served. Mr. M. had felt that the pastoral tasks were given too low a functional priority, while a group of senior tutors felt that inadequate attention was paid to traditional learning.

In a sense, the adolescents' debate in this school about the uses of education echoed the staff division: Was education an end in itself, or was it a means to an end? And if the question was asked in this polarized way, was the adolescent the one to live out the debate, feeling torn himself in the process? Paolo, living half the argument by treating his education solely as a means to the end of supporting a family to satisfy his longings, was confronted finally by his dread and isolation. Agreeing with the implications of one of the positions in the school (that education is a means to financial support), he was let down by his own inability to use the tutorial system for support and by the school's inability to provide adequate support to him in the crisis deriving both from his personal situation and from the process of school leaving.

My purpose here is not to decry the school's lack of support. Indeed, as it happened, Paolo had more recourse than could reasonably be expected of any counseling system. It is rather to present his dilemma as representative, because of its extreme nature, of the irresolute student whose inner conflict echoed the polarization of attitudes within the school. When the school cannot mediate such differences, the students are thrown back on their own failing resources.

### Work with school staff

The example of Paolo highlights what needs—though difficult—can be met by the student group. Such a group can serve many purposes; the primary one of facilitating the transition from school to work is aided by the secondary ones of understanding the adolescent, family, and school processes involved. An additional and essential purpose to be served by such a group is the obtaining of material to be communicated to school staff, so that the tutorial and counseling functions within a school can be improved. I am not advocating breaking confidentiality by sharing *details* of student participation with faculty, but the general concerns and developmental needs which are highlighted in a school *can* be shared as a beginning in the process of increasing each teacher's ability to facilitate adolescents' development as they leave school.

Within our project, we met regularly with teachers and other staff to exchange ideas. We began by meeting with a Deputy Head of each school, and then expanded our efforts to meet with senior tutorial and counseling staff in two of the schools. In some cases we were able to help develop strategies of helping individual students, but the more important function was to help the schools move towards more effective methods of dealing with the personal and developmental needs of nonacademic adolescents. These needs were shared by academic adolescents as well. In sharing the issues which confronted teachers daily, and comparing them to our own experiences, we were able to develop a plan to train interested staff to deal more effectively with adolescents, to use an increased understanding of developmental issues, and to look at difficulties within the school itself as relevant to the work of helping individual students. In one school, we joined staff in initiating a curriculum revision project aimed at making curriculum fundamentally more relevant to the nonacademic student. We have found that within such staff groups, issues often surfaced which illustrated the adolescent experience, so that these groups can be the beginning of the training experience the staff wanted and needed.

## BIBLIOGRAPHY

Bowlby, J. (1969). *Attachment and Loss*, Vol. I. London: The Hogarth Press.
Bowlby, J. (1973). *Attachment and Loss*, Vol. II. London: The Hogarth Press.

# Part IV

## GROUPS TO HELP PARENTS AND STUDENTS

## PART IV: GROUPS TO HELP PARENTS AND STUDENTS

### EDITOR'S NOTE

*While this volume deals primarily with groups containing young people and one or two guiding adults, there have been occasions where the provision of groups for parents, and even parents side by side with young people, has been found effective. Many educators, including counselors, have had variable experiences with parents singly or in pairs. Unfortunately, training in this interaction has not been a part of most educators' experience, sacrificed to the priority of the child and classroom.*

*The first chapter (40), discusses some categories of parent behavior—associated with drug-abusing young people, but relevant as well for parents of many other young people. This description may increase the readiness for later meeting parents in groups, with or without young people. Other chapters describe interesting variations in mixing and providing confrontations for young people with their own parents, or the parents of peers. Chapter 41 describes an experience in a small private therapeutic school. This may be applicable to some public continuation schools or opportunity schools.*

## CHAPTER 40

# Counseling with Parents of Adolescent Drug Abusers

### Paul W. Pretzel, Th.D.

A MAJOR TASK OF COUNSELORS is to recognize when students are in a state of crisis and then to take initiative on their behalf. This initiative often includes contacting and working with parents, which is an unfamiliar area for some counselors.

Apprehensions frequently arise in the minds of the counselors as they think about contacting parents, since they are aware that they may encounter a variety of realistic problems. However, the apprehensions and the actual difficulties often do not correlate well. The fears that the counselors may be experiencing have little to do with the actual difficulties that might occur when contacting parents. The source of their fear is usually their own understandable anxieties rather than the reality situation.

*Counselor concerns*

Counselors, like everyone else, tend to bring their own anxieties into a situation. For them, when thinking about contacting parents, these may be expressed in some of the following ways:

1. *Concern that they will get into legal trouble.* "I'm going to get sued for meddling, or for taking too much initiative, or for interfering."

2. *Concern about trouble with their job.* "My supervisor, who is very conservative in this kind of thing, won't like it." Counselors even sometimes

---

Reprinted with permission from the *Research and Pupil Personnel Services Newsletter*, Office of Los Angeles County Superintendent of Schools, 10, 3-6, 1972.

say, "If I put myself out in this way, they (the students and sometimes the parents) are going to get me." In some ultraconservative school districts there is enough reality in that fear to give support to it, but the number of teachers and counselors who actually get into trouble, either legally or with their job, for extending a concerned, helping hand in time of crisis, is extremely rare.

3. *Fear that they will risk losing rapport with the students.* They are apprehensive that students may feel they have been betrayed, and not only will this spoil the relationship with those students, but word will get around and the counselors' opportunity for rapport with other students will be jeopardized. This is usually an inappropriate, even though common fear.

When students are in trouble to the point where counselors are appropriately feeling that other resources should be mobilized, the counselors must act. Even though the students are resisting it, and even if they are angry, the anger tends to be temporary. Unfortunately, what frequently happens is that counselors anticipate that the students will be angry and rejecting, and so they do not make themselves available. The students pick up this withdrawal on the counselors' part and respond by staying away. This confirms the counselors' fears: "See, I knew I was going to blow it." It is a case of self-fulfilling prophecy.

4. *Resistance to getting overinvolved* and becoming caught in a situation that demands more of them than they can comfortably give. This, of all the concerns, is the most complex and is probably the most realistic. Some of these situations *are* consuming and do require time as well as energy that could be spent for other things, but once in the situation with a student, it is hard to get out.

Another fear related to getting overinvolved is the fear of getting in over one's depth. The comment sometimes comes: "After all, I'm not trained for this; I'm not trained to handle suicidal kids or hard-core drug addiction or marital problems in the family; this is not my area." Often, responding to the distress cries of adolescents leads counselors into situations that are sticky and deep, but most situations can be handled well if one takes advantage of consultant help that is available from fellow workers or from community agencies.

*Handling anxiety*

When counselors feel these concerns rising, their task is to handle their anxiety in the most creative way. They should first get the fear or anxiety as clearly focused in their minds as they can: "Specifically, what is it that

I'm upset or worried or nervous about?" Once this is in focus, the next step is reality testing. "How realistic is this fear? Are they really going to sue me?" Statistically, this happens so rarely it is almost negligible. "Are they really going to gang up on me? No, they are not really going to do that, especially if I do the intervention prudently, letting my colleagues know what is happening and getting their consultation as I go along." This simple procedure usually brings counselor anxiety into workable limits. Once the anxiety is under control, counselors are ready to face the realistic difficulties in working with parents.

At this point, let us presuppose a drug crisis situation. A counselor has had reason to become seriously concerned about one of the adolescents under his area of responsibility. The student has a stable history, has always achieved well, and has stayed out of trouble. All of a sudden there is abundant evidence that he is using drugs and using them hard. He's not maintaining very well in class, his performance is suffering, and his social relationships are shifting. The counselor talks to the adolescent and gets an answer like, "Mind your own business. I'll work things out by myself." He says things that hold the counselor off, get him angry and concerned (if he is not too angry to be concerned), and he realizes that this is a situation which the adolescent cannot realistically be permitted to handle by himself, and some coordination is needed between him and the parents.

He decides to take the initiative of contacting the parents in order to let them know what is happening. This is not with the intent of blowing the whistle, but rather of getting some affirmative action going for the adolescent.

### Parent categories

These are derived from a selection of 30 adolescents I have worked with in private practice, who have come to me after first being identified in a school situation and usually by a counselor taking the kind of initiative described above. I have listed some characteristics of the parents of these students, grouping these into five categories of parent response. The categories make no pretense of being exhaustive, but they represent a fair proportion of the situations with which counselors most often come in contact.

1. *Moralistic Anger.* Characteristically, these parents tend to be super-straight, super-stable, hard working, rational, moralistic people. They are the kind who feel threatened when things do not fit into neat categories of morality as they know it, and their reaction is one of anger. Examples of this type of parent might be the chief of police in a suburban town, or a C.P.A. who delights in getting balance sheets balanced and who loves things

to be orderly, or a physician who came out of a deprived childhood, worked hard to get through school and did it mainly by repressing everything except a driving goal to keep straight and get ahead. These people are not hypocritical; their own lives are run according to standards which have been carefully thought out, and they contribtue significantly to the community.

The response that counselors are likely to get upon first contact with such a parent is one of indiscriminate anger. The anger might be at the counselor for breaking the schedule of the day and calling him, or anger at the child for causing the call in the first place. It might also be anger at the counselor for seeing something the parent does not believe is happening, or, more likely, he knows is happening but has not wanted to admit to himself. If the next attitude is likely to be, "Don't involve me. I know what Johnny is doing. We have talked about it, and he knows he has a choice. He can either give up the stuff and stay happy at home, or he can go that route and we're done with him." Too frequently, the latter is precisely what happens.

The natures of adolescents become evident in their reactions to this kind of moralistic, angry parent. Some are withdrawers who use the drugs as a kind of cover. Some are clever, passive-aggressive adolescents who know how to incite anger and frustration in authority figures by passively frustrating every goal that may be held up for them. It gets to be a game for these, and drugs are the important weapon. Sometimes such an adolescent will even implore the counselor, "Whatever you do, don't tell my parents," and one does not have to be unusually astute to feel beneath that: "Please tell my parents because it'll blow their minds, and I'll be one up."

Useful techniques are available to counselors when they encounter such a parent. Principally, they will want to avoid a direct argument, because often this kind of parent will permit the tactful counselor to go around him. By using a little reflective listening to let the parent know he is heard and his point of view is understood, the counselor can then, without contradicting it by being tangential to it, say something like, "I know how that is. They can really get to you, can't they? You lay out the right way, and then they take another way, and it's horribly frustrating. We often have such different goals and aspirations for them. At least you're giving a good example." Then the counselor can go on to offer help, "One of the things we have found helpful with adolescents involved in drugs is rap groups. There are several here at school, and I wonder if you would mind if we included Johnny in one."

The most common response from the angry, moralistic parent to this approach is, "O.K., although as far as I'm concerned that isn't the answer. You've just got to be tough with the kid, but if you want to try something else, you can." The point is not to challenge or to press, but to recognize his point of reference, and then come up with something you have in mind that you think will help.

Sometimes talking to the other parent can be helpful. Where the father is moralistic and angry, sometimes the mother is not. She is just put down and frightened. More understanding can be developed with her and more support obtained for appropriate help.

2. *Dependent Overwhelmed.* The dependent, overwhelmed parent is usually the mother, and she responds to the counselor's call by saying, "I know, I've been having sleepless nights. I've had anxiety attacks, and my friends are all wondering what's wrong." She continues by relating a long story about herself, and the counselor realizes that here is an overwhelmed person, one who is frequently either divorced or widowed, who is herself often a product of a broken home and who needs whatever the counselor or anyone else has to offer. These people are depressed, and they are frantic. If one continues to listen sympathetically, one soon gets drawn in on the whole story of how hard it is for her, and the child gets forgotten, which is, of course, exactly what is going on at home. The mother's needs are so overwhelming, the child's are forgotten. Such parents will take from the counselor whatever is offered. They love to be told what to do, and one can set a whole schedule for them. They'll accept it and then probably will not do it, but they love to be told anyway.

The adolescents react to this kind of needfulness of the parent by running wild. They are usually angry, unstructured, and uncontrollable and are doing wild things with dope or anything else that occurs to them. At this point counselors feel let down and angry because what they hoped would be a good resource in the parent turns out to be another liability.

The helpful response in this case is to respond to the parent's feelings of need with statements such as, "I can well understand that it's very hard for you and that Junior is very difficult. Have you thought about getting some help for yourself? There are many good public agencies, or private treatment if you can afford it, and we can help you find a resource that will supply some of the help you need." Often parents are not aware of community resources, and the counselor can be very helpful by having a referral list at hand. It may be necessary to postpone the adolescents' needs for a while longer until the parents can get their emotional feet on the ground.

3. *Denial.* This category of parent simply denies existence of a problem! "It's just not happening, that's all! No, Susie would not do that."

One case illustration of this comes from a Help Line, on which calls were coming from a teen-age girl who would tell wild, bizarre stories. The stories often included brutality, and sometimes they would be sad and heartrending, but whatever they were, they were always dramatic. The calls finally were traced to the girl's home, but the parents, when confronted, simply said it was impossible. They had a family of five children and calmly said, "Our kids just wouldn't do that."

When a social worker from the local mental health association visited the home, she felt sure she knew who had made the calls when she walked into the room where the family was gathered. One girl just sat in the corner looking terribly depressed and obviously not integrated with the rest of the family. Eventually, the girl admitted to the social worker that she had made the calls, and when this was relayed to the parents, they were finally able to accept the fact and proceeded to get help.

Meeting this kind of denial from parents can be a serious problem. To attack it straight on is usually to make it more rigid. The denial is there because it is a defense. The parents are making an attempt to defend themselves from the anxiety of having a child who has a problem. Such defenses should be respected because they are needed. Usually, the counselor should back away from the confrontation by such a statement as, "Well, you and I are perceiving this quite differently. Would you mind if I continued to see Susie for a while?"

Sometimes the parents' answer will be negative, but frequently the thought has in this way become planted in their minds, and once the anxiety of the confrontation is lessened, they are able to reconsider. They may then start to make more realistic, quiet kinds of observations or inquiries. In several cases, parents have been able to take the initiative and call the counselor back with such an explanation as, "You know, I just didn't believe it, but I started thinking after we talked, and I'm worried about this problem." Once it gets through that the counselor really has not called to accuse, the parents may be able to soften their defenses and talk.

4. *No Response.* This often happens in a split family in which both of the parents are so caught up in their own problems the children have fallen through the cracks. No one at home is willing to take responsibility for the child. Either the counselors are not able to contact the parents or they get the feeling that the parents really do not care, that they have given up and are concerned about something else now. Usually, they are either concerned

with how much they hate a former mate or how much they like current friends. But little pretense is made of taking personal responsibility for the adolescents involved. The children, feeling this, are internally out of control and are terribly confused, although they work hard at presenting a facade of being quite clear about what they think. They act toward themselves the way their parents act toward them, uncaringly. They put themselves in ridiculously dangerous situations without even having the fun of being in them. Counselors worry about these students' overdosing, about their being on the freeway, or about their simply wandering off into a different city, never to be heard from again.

The need, of course, is for some kind of concerned structure, but that is much easier to state than to produce. Sometimes legal action is available. Sometimes other family resources, such as aunts, uncles, or friends will take over the parental role for a while. Frequently, however, no such resources are available, and the school is left with a terribly immature, confused, acting-out, irresponsible, troublemaking, scared adolescent with no family contact. To make things even worse in this kind of experience, it is very difficult to get a relationship going even with such students. The rapport just does not develop; but remember, they need you, so give them what you can.

5. *Helpful.* This category includes parents who are concerned, although threatened and upset, and want to help. Then there is no problem. Counselors can refer them, if that seems appropriate, or work with them themselves for a while.

CHAPTER 41

# The Parent-Student Encounter Group as an Important Treatment Modality at a Therapeutic School

Roman Anshin, M.D.,
Roger Mandel, LL.B.,
Zanwil Sperber, Ph.D., and
Ellie Schnitzer, A.C.S.W.

IN RECENT YEARS, there has been increasing emphasis on the encounter group as an instrument for providing therapeutic change, promoting communication, and increasing the potential creativity of "normal" individuals. Various definitions of encounter groups have been given. As used here, the encounter group consists of mixed groups of parents and teen-agers involved in a single or short number of sessions. The purpose of this chapter is to provide some anecdotal material derived from several experiences with an encounter group involving parents and teen-agers, and to more fully define the potentialities of such an instrument in the setting of a therapeutic school.

### Background

. . . Prior to the onset of this group meeting, several youngsters from a local organization (D.A.W.N.—Developing Awareness Without Narcotics) consisting of youngsters who had formerly been involved with drugs and were now interested in proselytizing youngsters against drugs, discussed their experiences in front of all the parents, teen-agers, and group leaders.

The first group meeting at The Walton School took place in the spring of 1968. At this time, approximately 40 parents and youngsters were present.

350

The meeting started with a short warm-up session, in which teen-agers from D.A.W.N. discussed their experiences. Four separate group sessions were then held, each running two hours. Teen-agers were, by plan, placed in separate groups from their own parents, with about 10 to 12 individuals per group. One or two D.A.W.N. members were also in each group. The leaders of the groups were respectively a psychiatrist, a social worker, and two clinical psychologists.

In the fall of 1969, a one-day encounter session was held with approximately the same number of people attending, D.A.W.N. teen-agers again participating, and with similar group leadership. Parents and adolescents were enthusiastic after the encounter sessions as to the increased awareness they had of the other generation's point of view, and the greater appreciation of individual differences among other-generation members. Further encounter sessions were asked for by parents and adolescents. Therefore, a four-session parent-adolescent group workshop was held in the spring of 1969.

Approximately 30 parents and 20 teen-agers were enrolled in this group workshop, with each of the four individual groups in the workshop consisting of eight parents and four to five teen-agers. Group leadership consisted of two social workers and two clinical psychologists. No members of D.A.W.N. were in the groups. School staff members were in each group, as had occurred in the last encounter conference.

### Description of material from four encounter group sessions

While the following material is gathered from the report of one group leader (Ellie Schnitzer, A.C.S.W.), it was found that in general the material from the other groups was similar in content to that presented here.

### First session

Parents participated more than the students in the session, bringing out two themes: (1) anger at their youngsters because of youngsters' rebelliousness along with what they saw as the young people's lack of appreciation for their own efforts, love, and financial support; (2) ambivalence and confusion over setting of limits along with fear of losing their children's approval and love. Parental decisions were revealed as often inconsistent and impulsive.

### Second session

The students were more active participants in this meeting, expressing a wish for more meaningful communication. However, they felt resentment and disappointment in their parents along with fears of being criticized. Several students mentioned a change in their view of their parents, seeing them as people with feelings and needs of their own and not just as sources of gratification or denial. Parents were sympathetic and tended to be helpful, encouraging students to be more responsible. Some role playing was attempted in several groups in a very limited way. This seemed particularly helpful because of the time limits of the meetings.

### Third session

Participation was balanced between parents and students. Some role playing was attempted with groups bringing up problems and trying to help each other. On several occasions, students corrected parents' evaluations of their relationships with children by reporting other children's statements about their relationships. Specific situations provided opportunity for exploring motivation on the parents' part, along with clarifying how their "double bind" messages caused conflictual communications toward children. It should be noted that parental guilt may have elicited this particular type of material.

### Fourth session

Direct confrontation took place between a father and son when the boy, who had asked to meet in the same group with his parents, joined the group. Much more freedom was asserted in exposing anger than in previous sessions, and a husband and wife disagreed with each other. At the end of this session the participants expressed interest in continuing group meetings.

### Evaluation

Group members seemed to make some gains in terms of feeling comfort and freedom to express both positive and negative feelings. Some beginning breakdown of the gap between parents and children was evidenced. The presence of clinical staff members was helpful for both leaders and groups.

### Discussion

Some authors, such as Rogers (1967) and Gendzel and Porat (1967), have written extensively on the process of the basic encounter group. Rogers, who perhaps may be accused by some of being unrealistically optimistic and charismatic in his feeling about the encounter group, has recently described a number of the processes that occur in the basic encounter group or workshop. In his descriptions of T-groups or lengthy encounter sessions, a number of phenomena are listed, a sampling of which can be said to have occurred in our rather short encounter sessions. Expression of personally meaningful material and of negative feelings, descriptions of past feelings, expression and exploration of immediate interpersonal feelings, the beginning of some development of a healing capacity in the group, and some correction of the facade can be said to have occurred in our four-session workshop, and perhaps on a lesser basis in our one-session group. All the aspects of feedback, change in attitudes, and paratactic distortions that have occurred in group, along with the facilitation of improved verbal communication, are extremely important.

Two weeks subsequent to the end of the last meeting, questionnaires were distributed to adult and adolescent participants in the workshop. Seven parents and three students completed this questionnaire. Parents were almost unanimous in noting improved communication in their families, and they noted greater awareness of the differences between adults and young people. Adolescents were more critical in their comments. One teen-ager suggested a marathon weekend. Questionnaires after previous one-day sessions had yielded similar responses.

The staff and consultants in specialized schools are increasingly called upon to work with both students and families in ways that will facilitate the communication process to provide some sense and meaning for youngsters. This particular school, like other therapeutic schools, accommodated many middle-class and upper-middle-class youngsters in a large city. The majority of young people attending the school had not only learning problems, but also serious emotional difficulties and interpersonal problems in their family lives. Many were in psychotherapy, with or without concomitant family therapy.

It is important to provide a school for these youngsters as a nidus around which they can develop some sense of worth and value. They need to learn the importance of self-observation, the appropriate expression and perception of feelings, and the attainment of greater respect for themselves and others as individuals. We thought that in this particular milieu the encounter group provided a breakdown of stereotypes. This was especially likely since the groups did not have to deal with the intense family conflicts that would have occurred if the groups had included entire family triads. Inclusion of family triads might have fostered much more overt negativism, stereotyping, and closed-mindedness. Yet this may not occur in multiple family therapy* when led by highly trained professionals. These group meetings are not intended to replace psychotherapy, but they are useful as a supplement to psychotherapy with both parents and adolescents. Both help the therapeutic school to have a positive and growth-emphasizing influence in their lives.

## BIBLIOGRAPHY

GENDZEL, I. B. and PORAT, F. (1967). "Application of nonverbal techniques in marathon group therapy." Presented at the 1967 meeting of the California State Marriage Counseling Association, Los Angeles, California.
ROGERS, C. R. (1967). The process of the basic encounter group. In J. F. T. Bugenthal (Ed.), *Challenges of Humanistic Psychology.* New York: McGraw Hill.

* See Chapter 42.

CHAPTER 42

# Adolescents in Multiple-Family Group Therapy in a School Setting

Viviane G. Durell, Ph.D.

JUNIOR HIGH SCHOOL presents the young adolescent with a new and often difficult adjustment problem. Many who have managed satisfactorily in elementary school are unable to develop the greater degree of autonomy required of them. In spite of the efforts of the school staff, some students begin a downhill course that continues into high school and results in severe disruption of their secondary school eeducation.

Some sit in class withdrawn and preoccupied. Others become behavior problems, are suspended, fall further and further behind in their work, and get involved in a cycle of increasing misbehavior and academic failure. This may lead to delinquency, court action, and, ultimately, to training school. By the time such students have reached high school, their adjustment pattern may have solidified and useful intervention may have become difficult. Intervention while in junior high school seems to offer the possibility of help before the pupil has progressed to hopelessness.

In the spring of 1963, it was decided to investigate the possibility of assisting junior high school pupils with short-term multiple-family group therapy. In work up to that time, the importance of meeting with both parents of the referred student in an effort to achieve a shared family view of the problem and the path to its solution had become apparent. Though the literature contained very little on multiple-family group therapy in schools (Shaw and Wursten, 1965), trial utilization of this technique in several clinical settings (Durell et al., 1965; Lewis and Glasser, 1965;

Reprinted with permission from *International Journal of Group Psychotherapy*, 19:44-52, 1969.

Levin, 1966; Davies et al., 1966) suggested that it combined the advantages of conjoint family therapy (Jackson and Weakland, 1961) with the advantages of group therapy in that a perspective could be gained on intrafamilial problems through observation of other families and through interaction with other family members.

Since current philosophy in the school system did not provide sanction for a long-term therapeutic approach, it was decided to limit the effort to a short-term approach and to restrict the goals accordingly. We defined our purpose as assisting the families in the development of a shared view of the students' difficulties and in the evaluation of a collaborative plan of action. This sort of goal seemed appropriate to "counseling," and that term, rather than "therapy," was used to describe the multiple-family group approach.

### Establishment of the first group

The chief counselor of the selected junior high school, in consultation with the other counselors, compiled a list of 18 problem pupils for whom additional help seemed imperative if they were to derive any benefit from their subsequent education. Most of them had been having marked academic difficulty, and many were disciplinary problems as well; several were known to the courts. In general, the families were considered uncooperative. We decided to select only boys of at least average intelligence. The group consisted of four families and was limited to 11 sessions of one-and-a-half hours each. The chief counselor provided a liaison between the school and the group, a psychologist was the group leader, and the assistant to the supervisor of guidance functioned as an observer and discussed the meetings with the leader in a joint effort to clarify the process. In addition, the latter participated in the meetings as a resource person, an expert on the school system, explaining matters of education, administration, and policy as they became relevant to the group discussion.

The chief counselor contacted each family by telephone and requested their participation in a group being formed. He emphasized the gravity of the boy's problems and the recognition by the school administration that the situation was deteriorating and the boy's education was suffering severely. It was stressed that the group was a trial approach which, it was hoped, might offer an opportunity for help at a crucial stage in their son's development. The counselor urged each family to attend the first meeting, at which time the details would be discussed, and they could decide whether they wished to continue. The first four families contacted agreed to come to the first group meeting, and these same families continued for the entire 11 sessions.

## Description of participants

*The first family:* Andre was a 14-year-old eighth grader of average intelligence. He had failed many courses, and his behavior was defiant and insubordinate. He had been suspended from the school many times. His mother appeared depressed and overburdened with family problems. His father spent little time at home because of long hours at work. As in most of these families, communication between the parents was poor.

*The second family:* Sam was a 13-year-old eighth grader whose intelligence was barely in the average range and who had been underachieving since the fourth grade. He was passive and lethargic in class. His mother had expressed strong dissatisfaction with the school to the central office of the board of education. She appeared overconcerned and aggressive, whereas the father appeared passive.

*The third family:* George was a 15-year-old who was repeating the eighth grade despite his superior intelligence. Poor academic performance, defiance, and truancy were his mode. He was known to the courts and had been placed on probation. His mother was tense and controlling. His father was easygoing and passive and was known to have a problem with alcohol. He was rarely home because he held two jobs.

*The fourth family:* Henry was a 15-year-old ninth grader with average intelligence who had repeated the eighth grade. He was frequently truant or absent with the excuse of illness. He was known to the courts for repeatedly running away. His mother felt overburdened and ambivalent about her responsibilities. Nevertheless, she frequently made excuses to protect her son or her husband. The latter did not attend the initial meetings because they allegedly conflicted with his work. Subsequently, it was learned that he had not been motivated to attend because he despaired of being useful. He was seen with his wife and son in several special family conferences, and his attitude gradually changed.

## The group leader's role

At the outset, the group leader had only a general idea of her role, deciding no more than that she would remain alert to do what she could to facilitate the attainment of the goals originally defined. The role soon developed into an unusually active one. This was evidenced not only in the group meetings themselves but by the fact that over twice as much time was spent in meetings on the periphery of the group as in the group meetings themselves. These outside meetings, which usually included the group's resource person, were always aimed at restoring the internal milieu of the group to a homeostasis optimal for the continuation of its task. Sometimes forces operating within the group or within one of the families necessitated these special meetings. At other times, the behavior of one of the boys within the school created a problem. Outside meetings were held with individual families, with individual pupils, and with the group of four pupils. Meetings were also held with individual teachers or a group of teachers involved with the boys, and sometimes one of the boys himself was present. Most important, however, were the meetings with the school administration (principal or assistant principal) and with the chief counselor. The latter played a crucial role in relating the activities within the group to the school and vice versa. He undertook the counseling of the four boys and coordinated communication with the teachers. Though present at only the first and last group meetings, he met with the group leader and resource person before and after each group meeting to report and to be informed. As a result of his involvement, the boys voluntarily sought him out to speak with him on a number of occasions.

It is interesting to consider how the active and complex role of the group leader evolved. Initially, it had been stated to the families that the group leader would not interfere with the school's administrative authority. By the third meeting, however, events led to a modification of this position. Henry had been suspended the day prior to the third meeting, and neither he nor his parents attended the session. The leader told the group that she would attempt to establish an understanding with the school administration to treat any disciplinary infraction potentially requiring suspension as a crisis. She then requested that the chief counselor contact her immediately in such a crisis before a disciplinary decision was made, so that the matter could be discussed. When it was deemed advisable, the family would be asked to attend a conference immediately. The school would retain its ultimate disciplinary authority, but there would be an opportunity for communication prior to the disciplinary action. The misbehavior of the pupil was conceptualized as unilateral and maladaptive problem-solving behavior, in direct opposition to the expressed goal of the group, which was to achieve a shared conceptual base within each family from which to plan mutually-agreed-upon, effective problem-solving behavior. It was theorized that if the school administration simply responded to misbehavior with unilateral action of its own, feelings would become so intense that the atmosphere of evolving collaboration would be seriously jeopardized. On the other hand, if the crisis was utilized to clarify the problem from each individual's viewpoint, then collaborative efforts to define and solve the problems would be strengthened.

The suspension of Henry was the first crisis and provides a good example of how this policy was implemented. His mother had repeatedly expressed her ambivalence about attending the group during the first two meetings. In a separate meeting with the chief counselor just before the misbehavior that led to his suspension, Henry had said that his mother had told him that she no longer planned to attend the group meetings. She had essentially threatened unilateral action: withdrawal from the group. Immediately after the third session, the chief counselor telephoned Henry's mother informing her of the new arrangement regarding crisis meetings and the importance of her continued participation. He then reported back to the group leader that Henry's mother remained ambivalent. An immediate family conference, including Henry's father, was then held in an effort to encourage the mother's attendance. The family expressed ambivalence during the conference until the group leader stated that whether or not the parents came, she believed that Henry should continue attending the group meetings. The father then stated that the mother should even run the risk of losing her job so that she could attend with Henry. Following this meeting, Henry's mother attended regularly. The meetings around this crisis served to facilitate communication within the family, diminish ambivalence, and increase the commitment of the parents.

After this policy toward disciplinary infractions was formed, there was occasional testing behavior, particularly by George and Henry. On the whole, however, there was a marked diminution in misbehavior, and the teachers commented in a conference following the fifth meeting that the boys showed marked improvement in both behavior and academic performance.

*Evolution of the group*

In the early meetings, the parents were prone to place blame upon the school system and the lack of adequate discipline. They expressed ambivalence about the group, doubted that it could do any good, and questioned the qualifications of the group leader. They particularly expressed concern about the usefulness of participating in a group with their sons. By the third and fourth meetings, an atmosphere of mutual trust and increased communication had developed. Wives commented that they had never talked so much with their husbands and that these meetings were forcing them to think. Without engendering defensive responses on the part of their parents, the boys could begin to clarify how their parents' attitudes and responses were contributing to their difficulties. The parents began to recognize how experiences with their own parents had resulted in attitudes which pre-conditioned their responses to their sons, often in ways which were not useful. By the fifth meeting, the focus had shifted almost entirely to the family relationships, which all considered strongly contributory to their sons' difficulties.

There was evidence of much hostility between the parents, sometimes open and sometimes covert. There was a striking similarity between all four families: the mothers had assumed responsibility for decisions about the boys, while the fathers had withdrawn and were playing largely passive roles in connection with their sons. Though this equilibrium had offered a partial solution to the marital conflict, it was increasingly recognized how this had deprived the boys of necessary interaction with their fathers. The remaining group sessions were not employed to explore further difficulties in the parental relationships, since most of the participants felt that this was not an appropriate setting in which to do so. The recognition of the existence of these difficulties, however, and the increased sense of shared responsibility created an atmosphere of mutuality in which the school problems could be discussed more successfully. In several instances, it became possible for fathers to move into closer relationships with their sons and to assist them with problems which had been previously disregarded. This evolution in Henry's family was, interestingly enough, the direct aftermath of another disciplinary crisis. It will be remembered that Henry's earlier misbehavior, which had led to the development of the crisis policy, had also led to increased commitment by his parents in the sense that his mother afterward attended the group regularly. His father had not agreed to attend but had stated that his wife should, even if it jeopardized her job. As the group approached termination, Henry promised in the meetings that he would try harder to manage things with the level of support he was obtaining. His behavior, however, became more openly defiant, particularly in his algebra class. In the series of special meetings that followed, it became increasingly clear that he was feeling abandoned, and his mother again felt overburdened. It was possible to negotiate increased support and participation from his father and from his teacher and counselor as well, and his subsequent school behavior improved dramatically.

There were marked objective changes in each boy's school performance, and their behavior improved considerably; they seemed happier and more cooperative, and their level of academic achievement rose. The immediate improvement was not completely sustained, however, and the boys regressed somewhat following the cessation of the group meetings. Fortunately, the regression was not complete, and all of the boys did better than would have been anticipated from their performance prior to the group sessions. On several occasions during the succeeding months, the boys requested meetings with us, and these conferences proved quite useful. Perhaps, had the group been continued for a longer period, the gains could have been consolidated and the subsequent regressions prevented.*

*Discussion and conclusions*

By both subjective and objective criteria, the limited goals that had been defined for the group meetings were at least partially attained. In the 11th meeting, which was devoted to a review and evaluation of the results, the family members spoke of what had been achieved. They talked of an increased ability to solve problems step by step, increased communication between parents, increased insight, more realistic expectations of their sons, an increased sense of belonging to the community, and an increased understanding of the school's role and the teacher's task. Two families obtained further psychotherapy. The boys spoke of recognizing that they were not all bad and that they were in fact trying to live up to their parents' expectations when this seemed at all possible. Moreover, the boys' academic performance and behavior had substantially improved. Though this was not a controlled study, experience with pupils with similar school problems suggests that there would have been a deterioration of adaptation. It would appear, therefore, that the group experience made a substantial difference to the boys and their families.

When the original plans for the group were formulated, a number of members of the school staff expressed considerable doubt about the feasibility of such a group. They did not believe that parents and sons would be willing to communicate freely with each other in a group session, and they doubted that the uncooperative parents would even be willing to attend. Our experience demonstrated that this concern was not valid. Each of the four families approached participated. They themselves expressed similar anxieties during the first few meetings, but these were forgotten as the group progressed. In establishing later groups of this type, particularly if

---

* Editor's note: See Chapter 29 for differential effects of duration of group.

the family had undergone previous psychiatric evaluation and treatment with apparently unfavorable results, we found it useful to meet with each family separately before starting the group in order to overcome their initial reluctance. It must be reiterated, however, that the obstacles to open communication were far less than might have been anticipated.

The relationship of the group and the group leader to the school milieu deserves particular emphasis. It must be apparent how different was the group leader's role from that of the traditional group therapist who does not generally interact with the other social systems to which the group members belong. It has become increasingly clear that effective work with problem pupils within the school system, individually or in groups, necessitates intensive work with school personnel, since the pupils, when first seen for counseling, are already involved in negative interactions with the school staff. At crucial stages in the development of the therapeutic process, the pupils reactivate their conflicts with the school. Unless the school staff's reaction communicates a genuine interest in facilitating efforts at effective problem solving, the obstacles to progress are immense.*

The fact that the multiple-family group was established within a school framework may have increased the tendency of the boys to "make noise" in school, knowing that it would be heard in the family group. Perhaps some pupils are best treated in groups away from the school in order to avoid this complication. On the other hand, those of us familiar with school problems know of many examples of pupils who obtain much individual or group psychotherapy in outpatient settings without the treatment exerting a substantial influence on their school behavior. If it is the school adaptation that is to be influenced, it might best be done in a group arranged so that the interaction between the group and the school culture can be kept under constant scrutiny. It is toward this end that we have been experimenting with approaches such as the one described in this report and more recently have begun to make efforts to influence the entire school milieu of one junior high school.

## BIBLIOGRAPHY

DAVIES, I. J., ELLENSON, G., and YOUNG, R. (1966). Therapy with a group of families in a psychiatric day center. *Am. J. Orthopsych.*, 36, 134-146.
DURELL, J., ARNSON, A., and KELLAM, S. G. (1965). A community-oriented therapeutic milieu. *Med. Ann. District of Columbia*, 34, 468-474.

---

* Kimbro et al. (1967) have reported on similar multiple-family groups conducted at a mental health center with underachieving and delinquent adolescents.

JACKSON, D. and WEAKLAND, J. (1961). Conjoint family therapy. Some considerations on theory, technique, and results. *Psychiatry*, 24, 30-45.

KIMBRO, E., TASHMAN, H. J., WYLIE, H., and MacLENNAN, B. W. (1967). Multiple family group approach to some problems of adolescence. *Int. J. of Group Psychother.*, 17, 18-24.

LEVIN, E. C. (1966). Therapeutic multiple family groups. *Int. J. of Group Psychother.*, 16, 203-208.

LEWIS, J. C. and GLASSER, N. (1965). Evolution of a treatment approach to families: Group family therapy. *Int. J. of Group Psychother.*, 15, 505-515.

SHAW, M. C. and WURSTEN, R. (1965). Research on group procedures in schools: A review of the literature. *Pers. & Guid. J.*, 44, 27-34.

## CHAPTER 43

# Simultaneous Group Counseling with Underachieving Adolescents and Their Parents

Merville C. Shaw, Ph.D., and
Clarence A. Mahler, Ph.D.

THE PRESENT STUDY was undertaken as an attempt to provide a specific kind of facilitative situation which appeared to be necessary to help ameliorate a specific problem. This was the all too common problem of academic underachievement. It is usually assumed to be a child's problem, as opposed to a parent or teacher problem, and is reflected in poor academic performance in spite of objective evidence suggesting that good academic performance could be expected. The basic purposes of the investigation to be described were to determine whether this approach was practical in the school setting and to assess the subjective reactions of those who participated in the process.

The study was based upon the general assumption that effective interpersonal relationships between the underachievers and their parents had either broken down or had never existed. This assumption grows out of previous findings to the effect that the identification process between underachievers and their parents is not developed to the same extent as is true of achievers and their parents (Shaw and White, 1965). The basic intent, therefore, was to provide a situation in which the psychological distance between the underachievers and their parents could be reduced. Previous

This material is part of a larger report which grew out of a study financed by the California State Department of Public Health: Shaw, Merville C. *The Interrelationship of Selected Personality Factors in High Ability Underachieving School Children*, Final Report, Project 58-M-1, California State Department of Public Health, 1961.

attempts at remediation have ignored this particular aspect of underachievement and have generally concentrated on some kind of remedial situation in which reliance was placed on exhortation of the child to do better or on some form of counseling help, either individual or group, with the child only. None of these methods provide a setting in which effective communication between the underachievers and their parents can be developed.

It was hypothesized that provision of a situation in which children must listen to the feelings of their parents and of other parents whose children had similar academic problems and, conversely, a situation in which the parents must listen to their children and also to other children who were academic underachievers might provide the setting and the climate in which more effective parent-child and child-parent communication might take place.

## Selection of the remedial sample

Because of the experimental nature of this program, it was decided to limit both the number of groups participating and the number of sessions involved. Children were defined as underachievers if they had an I.Q. of 115 or higher on their most recent California Test of Mental Maturity (CTMM) and an I.Q. not more than one probable error below 115 on their previous CTMM. In addition, their grade point average (GPA) was 2.8 or less. The number of underachieving children in each group was held to six. This meant that 12 parents were, in most cases, involved in each group. The total number of groups involved was 12, with 8 of these groups being drawn from a 10th grade population, and 4 groups being drawn from a 7th grade population. Two groups were held at each school, so a total of six schools were involved in the project.

## Selection and training of counselors

It was felt necessary to confine remedial efforts to school situations in which trained, competent counselors were available. This of necessity ruled out randomness of choice insofar as schools participating in the study were concerned. However, once the schools were selected, students to participate in the remedial project were selected randomly from those who had been identified as underachievers in an earlier phase of the study. Thus, maximum effort was made to rule out bias in the experimental sample. Of course, it was impossible to rule out the bias introduced by the refusal of some parents to cooperate. When parents refused to cooperate, their children were no longer considered as potential candidates for group work, since one of the requirements·for the participation of a child was that the parents also consent to participate.

Prior to the initiation of actual group counseling procedures, the counselors selected to participate in this phase of the study underwent a series of three group training sessions. A training manual describing the background, purposes, and general assumptions of the remedial project was developed, and a copy given to each counselor participating in the remedial project. It was used as a reference during training, and contained a brief outline of the premises and practices of Adlerian family counseling (Dreikurs et al., 1959). A consultant met with the group counselors for four two-hour training sessions prior to the beginning of the study and three additional times during and at the conclusion of the study. Since few of the counselors involved had previous group counseling experience this amount of time proved to be insufficient.

In the training sessions, counselors were introduced to the principles of Adlerian family counseling and the general purposes of the project. Every attempt was made to clarify issues and answer questions prior to the inception of the actual counseling. No specific attempt was made to control the particular style of counseling with which each counselor was most familiar. The main guides to counselor functioning were the principles developed by Dreikurs and his associates. Following the first actual counseling sessions, all counselors involved again met as a group so that they might raise questions which came up during the first session and get help with any problems which arose during the course of the initial counseling sessions.

*Group procedures*

It was necessary to have counseling sessions in the evening so that the fathers could be included. The total time of each session was one-and-a-half hours. The general plan was that for the first half of each meeting the children would enter into a group counseling situation with parents sitting outside of the group as observers. During the second half of the session roles were reversed and parents entered into a group counseling relationship with the counselor while children acted as observers. Four group counseling meetings were held. For the first two sessions, however, children met in groups without their own parents as observers. The purpose of this arrangement was to permit both children and parents to become used to the idea of expressing their feelings and then, having become acclimated, to enter into the more difficult task of expressing their own feelings with their own parents or children present. Following the cessation of all counseling interviews, all the children and parents were mailed copies of a questionnaire regarding their feelings and attitudes toward their experience in the counseling groups and their changes, if any, in such things as attitudes towards school, grades, etc. The subjective general reactions of the counselors were solicited with regard to the feasibility of the method and their opinion of its potential effectiveness, as opposed to the effectiveness of other techniques they had used. In some cases, counselors held a fifth session with their participants at the request of the groups in order to determine whether gains that parents and children felt had been made actually were maintained. Subjective reports of these meetings were included in the evaluation of results.

The group counseling approach was based upon the assumption that a new program, no matter how well grounded upon sound principles and research, would need to prove itself feasible to a school district before being expanded. Some of the school principals were understandably reluctant about the project being carried out in their schools. This reluctance disappeared during the time the project was being carried out and there was a real deepening of interest in the possibility of continuing the program. In fact, the positive reactions on the part of students, parents, counselors, and school administrators led to an extension of the project for another year. Funds were secured to underwrite a similar group counseling program conducted entirely by school personnel.

*General findings*

1. Group counseling with combined groups of parents and youth of high school age is feasible and offers considerable promise as a means of improving communication between parents and youth.

2. Lecturing at either parents or students fails to help, but setting a climate where both can learn from listening to each other makes the likelihood of learning greater.

3. Well trained public school counselors, with some help in getting started, can do a satisfactory job of group counseling with parents and youth in the same group.

4. Four sessions proved to be an absolute minimum, and the possibility of instituting a longer series of such meetings should be considered. Most parents found they could give the time for four meetings, but indicated that a longer series would have been more difficult to arrange. A series of four meetings followed by a month or two-month lapse of time would be a possible compromise.

5. The value of having students meet for half of the sessions with parents other than their own before meeting in groups with their own parents was strongly reinforced. This seems to be a very important warming-up process for free discussion by children in the presence of their own parents and vice versa.

6. A careful selection of students who are underachieving is necessary. Because of the research nature of this study, a number of students were indicated as underachieving who had, in recent months, brought their grades up very well. A history of underachievement which spans more than the current school year should be a condition of selection.

## Findings relating to parents

1. Nearly all parents were pleased that the school showed an interest in their problems.

2. Parents very much appreciated the opportunity to hear youngsters other than their own and also learned from listening to other parents faced with the same problems.

3. Parents of underachievers are confused and bewildered as to how they might best help their children. Such parents don't know quite what to expect of their child. Restrictions are applied, but in an inconsistent manner. No parents had a consistent pattern of working well with their children on academic progress.

4. Approximately three quarters of the parents who participated reported the sessions to be of value to them.

5. Both parents and youth realized the great value of having both parents and youth in the same group. Only a few children indicated that they preferred no parents present.

6. Parents can learn. For example, one mother wrote, "These sessions presented parental attitudes which were exactly the ones we had just prior to the start of the meetings and were, I feel, the direct cause of our son's underachievement." This would appear to represent at least an increased understanding of the problem.

## Findings relating to students

1. Students feel more uncomfortable talking in front of their own parents than with parents who are not their own. More warm-up by having prior sessions for youth may be indicated to offset this initial reticence to talk in front of one's own parents.

2. A number of students were very pleased to have a mother, father, or both willing to come to such meetings. Such attendance indicated a concern on the part of the parents that some children had not felt before.

3. Students in general felt it a privilege to be considered as equal with adults in discussing problems. The importance of being respected as a worthwhile individual was very evident.

4. Most students are able to talk freely in front of adults and with practice can do so with their parents. A few shy students were very hesitant to express their own feelings and no pressure was put upon any student to do so.

5. Students recognized the real value of helping parents to understand the views of youth by the group participation and also the help it can be to students to see how parents view student's progress.

The feasibility of this particular approach to the problem of underachievement has been demonstrated. All participants, including counselors, students, and parents, responded favorably to their experience. Further, they expressed the belief that it had been valuable to them. It was at no time anticipated that a short series of four group counseling meetings would suffice to deal effectively with the type of problem manifested by these students. Based on current understanding of the phenomenon of underachievement, it would appear that weekly sessions carried on over the period of a semester or a year might be necessary to build the communication between these students and their parents which might ultimately lead to improved school performance as well as to better parent-child relationships. It also is apparent that additional training of counselors in group techniques would be desirable, as would regular supervision by group counseling experts until such time as counselors achieved a higher degree of skill. Introduction of the Carkhuff variables (Carkhuff, 1969) would provide a barometer by which to gauge the effectiveness of the counseling process. The aims of this study were achieved and were positive. A determination of the effectiveness of the method described with the specific problem studied here remains to be done.

## BIBLIOGRAPHY

CARKHUFF, R. R. (1969). *Helping and Human Relations*, Vol. 1. New York: Holt, Rinehart and Winston.

DREIKURS, R., CORSINI, R., LOWE, R., and SONSTEGARD, M. (1959). *Adlerian Family Counseling*. Eugene, Ore.: Univ. of Oregon Press.

SHAW, M. C. (1961). Attitudes and child rearing practices of the parents of bright academic underachievers. Final Report, U.S.P.H.S. Grant M2843.

SHAW, M. C. and WHITE, D. L. (1965). The relationship between child-parent identification and academic underachievement. *J. of Clin. Psychol.*, 21, 10-13.

# Part V

## APPENDIX

# Inviting Group Members, Informing Teachers, Student Evaluation, and Record Keeping in a Junior High School

David Rappoport, M.Ed.

THE FOLLOWING are information sheets used by one counselor to encourage students to enter group counseling, rather than depend only on referrals by teachers, parents, etc. As a result, most of 250 pupils in the two-year program were self-referred.

J. B. JUNIOR HIGH SCHOOL

# ABOUT GROUP COUNSELING

it's for YOU if:

. . . . things "bug" you and you want to do something about them.

. . . . you want to learn more about yourself and your feelings.

. . . . you want to get along better with your friends, parents and teachers.

. . . . you want to become a better person.

. . . . you would like to talk with other kids who have similar interests and problems.

. . . . you would be willing to listen to other kids talk about their problems.

IF..... what you have read describes YOU, then .....

YOU may want to be in GROUP COUNSELING.

Mr. Rappoport will give you more information, if you are interested.

GROUP COUNSELING IS . . . . .

a process which helps you explore your
ideas and your desires to do those
things which you feel you need to do.
. . a way to improve your relations with
others . . . finding out what you can do,
what your feelings are, and how to use
your abilities to your best advantage.

HOW? . . . . .

By talking with a group of your peers
and a trained counselor in a CONFIDENTIAL
setting. They will help you in your
search for answers.

WHEN? . . . . .

Groups meet one period each week. You
are invited to attend a group session.
Group Counseling is a school activity;
however, you will receive an excused
absence. YOU are responsible for
maintaining your work.

HOW LONG DOES IT TAKE? . . . . .

That's hard to say. Some students begin
to feel as if they have answered their
questions in two or three sessions while
others feel they have just begun to
explore their feelings and need more, time.

HOW DO I GET IN GROUP COUNSELING? . . . . .

It is a voluntary program. You may refer
yourself or be referred by your counselor or
teacher. If you are interested in attending
group sessions see Mr. Rappaport in the
Counseling Office.

J     B        JUNIOR HIGH SCHOOL

SPRING 1974

TO:   FACULTY
FR:   D. RAPPOPORT
RE:   GROUP COUNSELING

APPR:                , Principal

Small group counseling is offered to pupils on all grade levels.  Pupils
meet in groups weekly with a trained counselor and share their feelings,
problems, etc. together in an effort to achieve greater success in school.
Participants develop verbal and listening skills in problem solving with
their peers in trust and confidentiality. Groups meet weekly on a rotating
schedule to avoid excessive absences from any one class.  Pupils are
responsible for making up work missed attending group counseling.

Pupils may be referred to group counseling for: lack of self esteem,
loneliness, poor academic achievement, family conflict, racial tension,
poor peer relationships, high school planning, school adjustment,
teacher pupil hostility, lack of self control, behavior difficulty,
excessive pressure to achieve, drug abuse and fearfulness.  Group
counseling is for all pupils at all academic levels.

If you think a pupil would benefit from such a group, please complete the
tear-off below and return to my mail box.  Pupils may refer themselves.
Please pass out group counseling notices and program cards to interested
pupils.  Remind pupils to fill out correct programs so that he/she may be
reached for group placement.

Teachers will be notified in advance of date and period of pupil group
counseling meetings to that accurate classroom attendance may be kept.

Please return counseling notice to the pupil so that he may attend his/her
session on time.

----------------------------------Tear-Off --------------------------------------

NAME OF PUPIL(S)          GRADE_____ PERIOD_____REASON FOR REFERRAL
                                                          (IN BRIEF)

Referring Teacher_____

# STUDENT EVALUATION

The following pilot study was done in seven groups. Eighty-four pupils responded to the statement: "Why I come to group counseling."

|  | Pupils | Approximate Percentage |
|---|---|---|
| 1. I come to group counseling: to get out of class | 7 | 8% |
| 2. I come to group counseling: to help others. | 8 | 10% |
| 3. I come to group counseling: because I need help. | 35 | 41% |
| 4. I come to group counseling: to talk freely. | 29 | 35% |
| 5. I come to group counseling: to listen to others. | 4 | 5% |
| 6. I come to group counseling: because the group needs me. | 1 | 1% |

While most responses were one line in length, some of the responses were fuller. The following are but a few of these, which seemed of special vividness:

I come to group, one reason to get out of class, but most of the time I've got something I want to get off my mind (not that I ever do, maybe once in a while) but I also like listening to other people's problems.

I come to group counseling to get out of class. Also to discuss my feelings about the problems of this school. I feel I have the right!!!

I come to group because I enjoy it and I can talk over my problems and help other people with their problems. Our school is dead and if you take group away, it will be deader.

I came to group because it is what's happening, and like you can't talk your problems over with your teachers and sometimes not even with your parents, and it's nice to talk problems over with the group, and talk about some of these ............ teachers who if you talk it over personally will suspend you.

I come to group because I like to talk. I think I like to observe what is happening a little bit more than I like to contribute to the conversation.

I come to say what I feel, why I feel that way, or to get something out that I can't say about a teacher in class. If I can get to see them in group counseling first, I can tell them the way I feel about them.

I come to group because I like not having the same 6 classes every single day and once a week, it's fun to come to group and talk about anything I want to talk about.

I come to talk and find out how other people feel about me, and other things. It gives me a chance to relax. I like it. I like to listen to other problems, so that if I have them too, or a similar one I can think about what people said to the person in group with that problem.

I come to group counseling to get away from my problems and to try and help others when they need help. I think group counseling is very important to everyone because everyone has some hang up and I know I do. When I need help this is the place to come. Mr. Rappoport, I want you to know you are the *life saver* of the school. Without you to turn to for help, many of the kids at J.B. and me would be lost.

I come to group counseling because I enjoy to listen to people's problems, and to talk about my problems and to get my head together and to see if I can help anybody with their problems. Because I may have had their problems before, I dig on helping.

# RECORD KEEPING

While the formal paper work in most group counseling is held to a minimum, there is often the need for evaluation and follow-up. Especially with the emphasis on accountability, it is appropriate to have some records of results achieved.

Group procedures (as well as individual) are often difficult to evaluate reliably and conclusively. As described in Chapters 2 and 4, Grade Point Average, while handy as a quick criterion, is often not valid. The following forms were used in elementary and secondary school group counseling programs. They are offered only as suggestive models, not as perfect instruments (see Chapter 29).

*When Schools Care*

_____ELEMENTARY SCHOOL

TO:   FACULTY

FROM: PRINCIPAL

### REFERRALS FOR GROUP COUNSELING

TEACHER_____GRADE_____ ROOM #_____

A group counseling program is being organized this school year for the purpose of helping children with emotional or behavior problems. We have indicated below the major problem areas usually encountered. Please list, under each heading pupils who seem to you to have that type of difficulty. If a child seems to fall under several headings, please select the one that is most characteristic.

Please bear in mind that this program is not intended to include children who are very severely disturbed and who may require individual psychotherapy and/or medication. However, please list such referral for possible professional help separately.

Teachers whose pupils are involved in this program will be asked to confer periodically with the group leaders.

Teacher referrals:

1) Appears shy, withdrawn. Avoids contact with other pupils and/or adults.

_____   _____

_____   _____

2) Aggressive behavior. Often fights or bullies classmates and/or defies adult authority.

_____   _____

_____   _____

3) Under-achiever

_____   _____

_____   _____

4) Verbalizes constantly. Compulsive talker.

_____   _____

_____   _____

5) Often appears depressed or unhappy.

_____   _____

_____   _____

6) Behaves in ways that are immature, unpredictable, or inappropriate for his age.

_____     _____

_____     _____

7) Appears to need excessive attention from other children and/or adults.

_____     _____

_____     _____

8) Seems overly dependent for his age on the teacher and/or other adults.

_____     _____

_____     _____

9) Seems unusually tense, nervous, over-anxious.

_____     _____

_____     _____

10) Other (specify)

_____     _____

_____     _____

Children you feel need help of a more intensive or individual kind than group.

NAME                         PROBLEM

_____     _____

_____     _____

Have you had contact with parents of any of the children listed? If so, please describe briefly.

_____

_____

_____

_____

_____

_____

SCHOOL _____ DATE OPENED _____ DATE CLOSED _____

DAY AND TIME _____

EVALUATOR(S) NAME _____ TITLE _____

NAME _____ TITLE _____

| CASE NUMBER | CO-THERAPIST AND TITLE | NAME | | | | | GROUP NAME | REASON FOR REFERRAL | STUDENT CHANGE IN AREA FOR WHICH REFERRED | | | | OTHER PROBLEM AREAS (ATTITUDES, FEELINGS, INTER PERSONAL RELATIONS, OTHER BEHAVIOR) | CHANGE IN THESE AREAS | | | | TIMES IN GROUP | WERE PARENTS SEEN BY EITHER LEADER | | | WAS STUDENT REFERRED FOR FURTHER HELP | TO WHAT AGENCY |
|---|---|---|---|---|---|---|---|---|---|---|---|---|---|---|---|---|---|---|---|---|---|---|
| | | LAST | FIRST | AGE | SEX | ETHNIC | IN | OUT | | | REGRESSION | NO CHANGE | SOME IMPROVEMENT | GREAT IMPROVEMENT | | REGRESSION | NO CHANGE | SOME IMPROVEMENT | GREAT IMPROVEMENT | | YES | NO | NO. OF TIMES | | |

EVALUATION OF STUDENT CHANGE DURING GROUP COUNSELING

Person evaluating (Please check)

___teacher
___counselor
___administrator
___nurse
___psychologist
___PSA worker

NAME OF STUDENT_____

Was in group from_____to_____

Reason for referral/self referral_____

_____

_____

Your evaluation of change in this area since referral

Retrogression  /_____/          Somewhat improved  /_____/

No change  /_____/               Greatly improved  /_____/

Do you feel there are problems in other significant areas (of attitude, behavior, or feeling tone?)_____

Your evaluation of change in these areas

Retrogression  /_____/          Somewhat improved  /_____/

No change  /_____/               Greatly improved  /_____/

Do you feel group was helpful for this student?_____

_____

_____

Did you have any contact with this student's parents during his involvement in group?_____ If so, please indicate substance_____

_____

_____

_____

ADDITIONAL COMMENTS

# POSTSCRIPT

When the reader has reached this point we trust that vistas have been expanded, and many questions provoked as well as answered. There are obviously many forms, shapes, and manners in which caring groups can be provided to young people in secondary schools. Certainly, attitude is as important as structure. Respect for young people, caution, flexibility, follow-through, reliability, and honesty are but a few relevant qualities.

Considering the constant changeability of adolescent culture and customs and the adaptive efforts of educators and mental health professionals to keep pace, many of the group experiences described here may be of only historical interest in the years to come. Yet certain enduring qualities and guidelines do prevail, no matter how extreme the changes in structures or terms may be. We hope that a considered reading of this volume will provide the wisdom, courage, and stimulus to set up more and better, useful, helpful groups in schools—in all periods of time.

*—Editor and Contributors*

# Index

Gendzel, I. B., 352, 354
Gilbert, R., 319, 321
Gilliland, B. E., 30, 36, 193
Girls' groups, 52, 69-73, 95-101, 111-124, 174-176, 177-178, 278-281. *See also* Boys' groups; Composition of groups; Mixed groups.
Gitelson, M., 193
Glanz, E. C., 26, 36
Glass, S. D., 36
Glasser, N., 355, 363
Goal-setting experiences, as mild confrontation technique, 128
Goals of group counseling, 5, 23, 103, 107, 145, 175-176, 204-205, 216, 289-290, 355
Goda, A., 252, 259
Goldman, L., 71, 75, 76
Goodstein, L. D., 28, 36
Grab bag, as sensitivity training technique, 290
Graduate students, as participants in group counseling, 80-81, 185-192
Granada Hills High School, 157, 158
Group counseling. *See also* Communication seminar; Encounter; Rap rooms; Sensitivity training.
  and academic performance, 5, 23, 99, 146-147, 175, 192, 217, 228-231, 235. *See also* Underachievers.
  administrators attitudes toward, 21, 24, 44, 51, 77, 144, 183, 190, 213, 222, 225, 240-241, 258, 266
  administrators as leaders in, 103-109
  advantages of, to community, 204
  advantages of school setting for, 49-55
  in affluent high school, 69-76
  and alienation, 31-32, 202, 303
  and attendance problems, 102-109, 139, 145-148, 157, 186, 246
  attendance procedures in, 78-79
  and behavior problems, 32-33, 99, 102-109, 147, 150-151, 186, 234
  at Beverly Hills High School, 52-54
  at California High School, 139-140
  case descriptions of, 52-54, 81-84, 100-101, 107, 208-211, 325-337, 357-362

Group counseling—*continued*
  for Chicanas, 111-124
  and classroom control, 150-152
  community attitudes toward, 20-21
  competency of leaders in, 17
  composition of groups in, 45, 52-53, 80, 120, 144, 182, 186, 205, 253, 278, 298, 304-305, 365
  confidentiality in, 45, 55, 70, 71, 96, 104, 117-118, 212, 244
  confrontation techniques in, 126-132
  content of discussion in, 12, 13-14, 47, 56-58, 70, 104, 177-181, 189-190, 212, 244-245, 254-255, 266-268, 313
  to "cool" troubled campus, 6
  cost of, vs. results, 237-238
  counselor attitudes toward, 22, 77, 134
  counselor training for, 24, 133-134, 239, 240-249, 251-258, 259-261, 365-366
  at Crenshaw High School, 185-192
  in crisis management, 311-320
  and deaf students, 33-34
  definition of, 11-12, 43
  demonstration groups in teaching, 251-258
  dream material used in, 331-337
  and dropout problem, 111, 189, 198-199
  and drug abuse, 34, 186. *See also* Drug abuse.
  duration of groups in, 14-15, 45-46, 144, 186
  and educable mentally retarded, 34
  in elementary school. *See* Elementary schools.
  and ethnic problems, 111-124, 192, 215-225, 311-321. *See also* Inner-city schools; Minority students; Multiethnic schools.
  evaluation of, 71-73, 176, 191-192, 226-238, 247, 270-274, 306-308, 367-369, 375-376. *See also* Research; Results.
  and family problems, 234
  feelings of leaders in, 242-243
  first steps in attempting, 41-42
  forum process of, 311-320